DISCARD

DANIEL DEFOE

DANIEL DEFOE

Citizen
of the Modern World

By

John Robert Moore

THE UNIVERSITY OF CHICAGO PRESS

Library of Congress Catalog Number: 58-11950

THE UNIVERSITY OF CHICAGO PRESS, CHICAGO 37
Cambridge University Press, London, N.W. 1, England
The University of Toronto Press, Toronto 5, Canada

© *1958 by The University of Chicago. Published 1958*
Composed and printed by THE UNIVERSITY OF CHICAGO
PRESS, *Chicago, Illinois, U.S.A.*

To the Memory
of

GODFREY DAVIES
Keen Adviser
Kind Friend

FOREWORD

The end, I say, of everything is in the beginning, and you must look to the end, or you will never begin right.

Review, VIII, 514 (for 614)

ANATOLE FRANCE told a story of how Pontius Pilate was asked, long afterward, about a Nazarene he had sent to crucifixion. After some hesitation the old Roman gentleman replied serenely, "I cannot call him to mind." In the early eighteenth century a High Churchman and Tory referred to Defoe as "one of those authors (the fellow that was pilloried I have forgot his name)."

We do not have to search far in history to realize that men who are for a time ignored are often those most worthy of remembrance. Leonardo da Vinci is significant when the princes who employed him have long been forgotten. Daniel Defoe—in so many ways a pioneer in literature and journalism and history, one of the germinal minds in political and economic thought, a defender of religious toleration and an opponent of the evils of human slavery, an advocate of most of the effective reforms of the past two and a half centuries—cannot be slighted by anyone who would understand the world in which we live today.

Americans have a high regard for one of their most eminent citizens, who recognized Defoe as a model for his own prose style and an inspiration for his career as publicist and projector. It is of Benjamin Franklin's great predecessor that this book is written.

Even more than through neglect, Defoe has suffered through misrepresentation. He has been blamed for works he did not write and for views he never held. In his more than five hundred books and tracts and periodicals, there is an inner consistency of purpose, together with a sacrifice of personal advantages, which perhaps no prominent journalist or public man could rival today. To understand him we must know what he wrote and why he wrote it.

He has also suffered from misconceptions because so little has been known of his private life. Jests have been accepted as truth, and errors have been made the foundation for serious biographical writing. The notorious Richard Savage professed to explain the virulence of young Benjamin Defoe by saying that he inherited his Billingsgate as the bastard son of Defoe by an oysterwife. All-too-serious men have sought to explain Savage's joke by supposing that Defoe had two sons named Benjamin—one the real Benjamin we know through contemporary records, the other an imaginary person invented to explain Savage's (and Pope's) jest as a supposed biographical fact. Alexander Pope referred to Defoe in the pillory as "earless," although he knew that Defoe was never mutilated; and some readers of *The Dunciad* still believe that this jibe was meant to state a truth. Defoe was once thought to have been married twice, because a carelessly drawn legal document miscalled Mary Defoe by the name of Susannah. Even to-day Daniel Jr. is commonly referred to as Defoe's first son, although the contemporary records indicate clearly that Benjamin was the older brother.

Defoe deserved well of his country, but he was thrice pilloried and several times imprisoned. He was an energetic and at times a successful merchant, yet twice a bankrupt; a citizen debarred from public office by his religion, yet a confidential adviser of the nation's rulers; a loyal Londoner, yet a traveler in many lands; a volunteer soldier and an expert swordsman, yet a projector of plans for the arts of peace; perhaps a lay preacher, yet certainly a government spy. To estimate his character without understanding his motives and his achievements is as unwise as it is unfair. To judge his multitudinous writings by the relatively few bound together as his collected "Works" is like judging Shakespeare by a single play.

Scattered throughout his writings are many stray allusions to his own life, besides four autobiographical fragments. These are of immense value if we realize how frequently they can be checked by external evidence and how accurate they almost invariably prove to be.

When Defoe mentioned his personal affairs, it was usually to illustrate some other point he wished to make or to reply to those who had turned against the memory of King William or who professed on slight knowledge of the facts to explain public concerns. Very rarely, considering the many provocations, he stopped to defend his integrity in order to be free to continue with his work.

But almost always, as journalist and publicist and novelist, he preferred to hide himself in his books—as a clergyman of the Church of England, a Person of Honour, the Right. Hon. the Countess of M——, a streetwalker, a descendant of Sir Francis Drake, a pirate, a stock-broker, one of the people called Quakers, a British officer in the serv-ice of the Czar. No doubt this sometimes helped to promote the sale of his books; but its artistic purpose was to enable him to enter into the role he needed to assume. The author is soon forgotten; but the story or the idea remains in the mind of the reader.

It was Defoe's misfortune to live outside the charmed circle of the satirists of the age of Queen Anne, and *The Dunciad* has left scars more lasting than those of the pillory. More recently even so friendly a writer as G. A. Aitken dismissed Defoe's account of the explosion of the island of St. Vincent as a journalist's hoax, whereas it is demon-strably a careful analysis of earlier and fully accredited reports. But in the end perhaps we may hope to see Defoe's trust vindicated: "There is no argument like that demonstration of fact."

In the chapters which follow, no consistent attempt will be made to trace the minute details of Defoe's personal life, except where these seem significant for understanding him as a citizen of the modern world. The chronological outline is meant to sketch the principal events of his life, as far as these can be known. But a biography of Defoe based on a strictly chronological sequence would be unsatisfac-tory for three reasons. As for Shakespeare, there would be large gaps which could be filled in only by surmise. There would be many other periods in which Defoe is known to have been occupied with a con-fusing variety of interests at exactly the same time. And it is not the minute details of his life which are of real significance today. As for Leonardo da Vinci, it is more important for us to know what **Defoe** achieved and what he thought than how he spent some rainy Thurs-day afternoon in a late November.

Days are given in Old Style, years in New Style. Public men, like Robert Harley, are usually referred to by their more familiar names or titles. The notes are condensed by the use of a key. For any work of Defoe before 1732 the place of publication is London, unless it is otherwise specified. Except where the original text is reproduced as an exact record, I have rarely attempted more than a modern transcrip-tion. However, I have sometimes retained contemporary usages to add color to the narrative, much as one might insert a facsimile of an au-thor's handwriting. Defoe himself leaned toward simplified spelling and the use of abbreviations; I would do no service to his memory by reproducing systematically the bilingual jargon of legal documents or the typographical idiosyncrasies of his many printers.

I owe much to the great writers—from Dr. Johnson to Sir Winston Churchill—who have given recognition to the man who was in so many ways a founder of modern literature. I owe much to the defamers of Defoe—from Charles Gildon to Willa Cather—whose misunderstandings have drawn attention to points which needed clarification. I owe much to thousands of men and women (and some children) with whom I have talked or corresponded about Defoe.

Most of all, I am indebted to the trustees of the Henry E. Huntington Library and Art Gallery for a senior fellowship which enabled me to devote the year 1950–51 solely to this undertaking. To the United States Army (not often remembered as a patron of the humanities) I am deeply grateful for a faculty appointment in the Army University at Shrivenham, which gave me intimate access to several English and Scottish libraries at a time when this would otherwise have been most difficult to obtain. Thanks to the Graduate School of Indiana University, to James A. Work, chairman of the department of English, and to Robert A. Miller and Cecil K. Byrd, director and associate director of the Indiana University libraries, I have enjoyed many privileges.

To the American Philosophical Society I am indebted for a grant-in-aid of my study of the canon of Defoe's writings. In establishing this canon I have worked for some time in close collaboration with the staffs of the following libraries: the British Museum, the Boston Public, the special collections of Indiana University, the William Andrews Clark Memorial, and the Huntington. More recently I have profited by similar co-operation from the staffs of the Bodleian, the Cambridge University Library, the National Library of Scotland, Dr. Williams's Library (London), and the University of London Library. In addition, I have studied in most other libraries in the English-speaking world which seemed likely to afford new material. I have also had aid from the collections of private individuals, especially those of Arch W. Shaw of Winnetka, Illinois, Col. C. H. Wilkinson of Oxford, and Sir Harold Williams of London (who has been most helpful to me in many other ways).

From the Middlesex Guildhall, the library of Windsor Castle, the library of Trinity College (Dublin), the Public Record Office, Somerset House, and the Forster Collection in the Victoria and Albert Museum I have secured photostats of documents. In tracing the prosecution of Defoe in 1703 I have had the assistance of Miss S. R. Dowling of London.

The late Godfrey Davies of the research staff of the Huntington Library and Frederick B. Tolles of Swarthmore College read much of the manuscript. The fine edition of Defoe's *Letters* by George Harris Healey of Cornell University was published too late to be available until my book was nearing completion; but I have drawn on Professor Healey's doctoral dissertation and on his special knowledge of Defoe for many years. The late Juliet Reeve of Friends University sent me copies of two valuable letters. William Matthews of the University of California at Los Angeles gave me the first hint for questioning the common assumption that Daniel Jr. was Defoe's older son. On special points I have had assistance from the late Arthur W. Secord of the University of Illinois and from Lew Girdler of San Jose State College; the late Charles Eaton Burch of Howard University provided much information on Defoe's career in Scotland; R. C. Bald of the University of Chicago and Richmond P. Bond of the University of North Carolina offered significant leads. To R. H. Griffith of the University of Texas I am indebted for a transcript of one of Defoe's insurance policies. To William T. Laprade of Duke University and to the late William T. Morgan of Indiana University I owe much for suggestions regarding the history of the age of Queen Anne. To Edward D. Seeber of Indiana University I owe acknowledgment for information regarding the fictitious *Memoirs of the Count de Rochefort*, which gave Defoe one of his basic ideas for *Colonel Jack*. My former colleague Alexander C. Judson has aided me many times as only a friend can do.

F. Bastian of Trowbridge, Wilts (formerly of Ashtead, Surrey), has been immensely helpful in investigating Defoe's ancestry and personal associations, and he has enabled me to discover much about Defoe's school days in Dorking. F. F. Madan of London has been my untiring collaborator in examining eighteenth-century tracts, especially in tracing out Defoe's share in the Sacheverell controversy. Among the many other friends in Great Britain who have aided me are D. Nichol Smith, L. F. Powell, A. L. Rowse, and the late Rev. Dr. D. C. Simpson, all of Oxford. To James Sutherland of University College, London, I owe the suggestion which led to my identification of the *Commentator* as one of Defoe's periodicals. For assistance on the background of *Robert Drury's Journal* I am indebted to the Rev. James T. Hardyman of Oxford and Madagascar. To Arnold Muirhead and more than a score of other antiquarian booksellers in England and Scotland I owe much for their friendly vigilance. The representation of the ice fair on the Thames is reproduced from a contemporary broadside through the courtesy of the British Museum. Permission to quote a paragraph from *Private View* has been granted by the Society of Authors as the literary representative of the estate of the late Walter de la Mare.

In the Preface to the first authorized collection of his works, Defoe wrote: "I see nothing remains to say of me, or of my book. They that search for faults may find them plenty, and they that will mend them for me shall always have my acknowledgment for the kindness."

And Charles Lamb declared, when the author of the first long biography of Defoe asked for his assistance: "I shall always feel happy in having my name go down any how with De Foe's."

CONTENTS

LIST OF ILLUSTRATIONS

I. LONDON

*I began my travels, where I propose to end them, viz. at
the city of London.*

Tour (Everyman ed.), I, 5

IN THE LATE SUMMER of 1660, perhaps in September, Daniel
Defoe was born in London. Probably we shall never know the exact
date of his birth. His father did not believe in the necessity of infant
baptism, although the birth of Defoe's sisters Mary and Elizabeth,
older than himself, had been recorded at St. Giles, Cripplegate. Defoe
has told us that parish registers were imperfectly kept for children
who were not christened.[1] But the year was certainly 1660; and for a
boy who was to understand the past so well and to look so sharply
toward the future, it was a remarkably good year to be born in. After
the death of the great Protector Oliver Cromwell, the failure of his ineffective son, and the collapse of representative government with the
Rump Parliament, a new world had begun in England. This new
world seemed a very pleasant one, and the theaters had reopened after
eighteen years. The reign of the Saints was over; the reign of the
Merry Monarch had begun.

On May 30 Charles II had come back from his long exile on the
Continent, arriving in London on his birthday, to be welcomed by
maidens dressed all in white. The Act of Indemnity would soon be
passed, pardoning nearly all who had injured the royal cause. There
were rumors of friction between the Presbyterian and Episcopal
wings of the English clergy, but so shrewd an observer as Samuel
Pepys believed that this would come to nothing. One prominent
clergyman was preaching a closing of the rifts made by the late civil
wars and the Commonwealth.[2] Few could have supposed that the attempt to restore the old order in church and state would soon drive
great numbers of Englishmen into dissent from the national church or
that the direct line of the Stuart kings would end with the brother of
Charles.

I

But Daniel Defoe, who would have more to say about all this in later years than most other writers, was unconscious of it now. For some years he would be growing from infancy to manhood—this child who was to become the first modern man born within the medieval walls of Old London.

Defoe's native city had an incalculable influence on his mind. On the title page of *A Scots Poem*, published in Edinburgh in 1707, he might call himself "A Native of the Universe." He did become a citizen of the world, but at heart he remained a Londoner. To him it seemed that "a man that has . . . no residence, no place that has a magnetic influence upon his affections, is in one of the most odd, most uneasy conditions in the world."[3] Long afterward, when he was writing of faraway countries, he turned to London for comparisons. He traveled more widely than any other English author of the age (except men like Dampier, who were more travelers than authors), so that he could speak familiarly of the Scottish Highlands or of the coastal cities of the Mediterranean. But his home was always in or near London. He was born there, he grew up there, he had homes or rooms in different parts of the city and its environs, he engaged in business there, several of his children settled there after marriage. He wrote most of his more than five hundred books and pamphlets there, he read proofs in many of its printing houses, he was imprisoned there and stood in the pillory in its three most crowded places, he worshiped in its dissenting chapels, he lies buried in its earth.

We think of Dr. Samuel Johnson as the great Londoner; but much as he loved it, Johnson knew little of London until he was a grown man. Defoe learned the life of the city as a fearless and inquiring child. He explored the alleys and byways, the glasshouses and markets, which appear in the boyhood of his Colonel Jack. His *Journal of the Plague Year* is not only foremost among books about the horror of sudden death; it is foremost among books about London, and the names of the city wards are the steps on which it mounts to its climax.

The narrow streets led everywhere. When Defoe was an old man, he estimated the circumference of London at about thirty-six miles, but that was after it had leaped beyond the walled city and its privileged districts called "liberties." In his childhood all of London and Westminster lay along the north bank of the Thames in a narrow arc like a capital "C," less than five miles long and a mile or so wide, with the borough of Southwark across the river and with spurs of dwellings along the principal roads into the country.

We do not know in what street Defoe was born; but it was in the parish of St. Giles, Cripplegate, probably in or near Fore Street, where his father certainly lived in 1688.[4] Wherever the boy turned in this greatest of cities, the past and the present looked him in the face, and the future often cast its shadow before him. Not far from his father's home and just south of Fore Street ran the northern length of the medieval city wall which brought the Great Fire of 1666 to a stop. From this wall down to the Thames the city was burned over when Defoe was barely six years old—southwestward to Temple Bar, south-eastward to the Tower. And beyond the ravages of the fire, not so far to the southeast as the Tower, stood the one great bridge over the river, of whose "falling down" children have sung for so many years.

At the west end of Fore Street stood the church of St. Giles, Cripplegate, where the family had worshiped until Defoe was two years old. A little to the north was Ropemaker's Alley, a pleasant residential district in spite of its name, where he was to die in solitude. To the northeast was Artillery Walk (where one sometimes saw the blind old poet John Milton sunning himself); and this walk led northward into Tindall's Burying Ground, later known as Bunhill Fields, the Dissenters' cemetery which was the final resting place of Defoe.

To the south of Fore Street the new cathedral of St. Paul's would soon be rising on the charred ruins of the old one. To the southwest stood an evil-smelling building whose thick stone walls had escaped the Great Fire—the Newgate Prison in which Defoe was one day to be confined.

In the West End were Hyde Park (where one could see the tall, dark King or the ladies and gentlemen of fashion in their coaches, and sometimes soldiers in encampment or on parade) and Tyburn (at the end of the slow journey of the carts dragged from Newgate for the great popular spectacles called hangings). Not so far to the west, and southward along the bend of the river, were the royal palace of Whitehall and the offices of national government (where Defoe was to confer so many times with King William or with the Ministers of Queen Anne and the first two Georges).

Defoe remembered what he had seen or heard of the Great Plague and the Great Fire, and he could describe them vividly as long as he lived.[5] He knew the terror of the days when the Dutch fleet sailed up the river to Chatham and threatened to devastate London. He lived through the coldest of London winters, when the Thames was frozen over so deeply that a market and a carnival were held on the ice. He was there to record the greatest storm which ever swept over the city. He was in London during the frenzy of the Popish Plot, he attended a secret meeting when Titus Oates was present, and he walked through the noisy streets with a short staff attached to his wrist by a leather thong and loaded with lead to serve as a "Protestant flail."[6] He rode with the gentlemen who welcomed the "Glorious Revolution" when William of Orange neared London; he was on hand for the coming in of the Hanoverians. He knew Moll Flanders, and he wrote a newspaper account of her career before it occurred to him to put her into a novel.[7] He helped to present the petitions of dissenting clergymen to King William and Queen Anne and later to George I.

William Cobbett, Defoe's rival as an observer of the countryside, had no love and no understanding of London. To him the city was a diseased excrescence—"a Great Wen"; the fine highways leading to the capital were thoroughfares for wicked politicians or for flashy stockbrokers dashing up to town in their stylish gigs to carry on their nefarious trade. Defoe knew London as a great emporium, the consumer and distributor (and in part the manufacturer as well) of goods without which the nation could not prosper. He knew it also as the center of empire and the temple of learning and of worship.

The conventional travelers of the age sought out the records of remote events and forgotten ways of life. The conventional guidebooks told of vestiges of the medieval church and of the feudal system, of cathedral towns and of the country estates of the nobility. Defoe not only showed a modern interest in the fields and the highways and the navigable rivers, the villages and the market towns; he knew even better the great city which was both political capital and commercial metropolis.

The soundness and the range of his views on economics and government were due to his understanding of what went on at the center of things. He knew the Bank of England as well as the financial needs of the provincial towns, Blackwell's Hall as well as the cottage looms, Whitehall and Kensington Palace and the houses of Parliament as well as the homes of the rural justices, the docks and the foreign shipping as well as the remote country lanes.

Of the major English writers, only Dickens rivaled him in the portrayal of London. But Dickens wrote too often as the star reporter in search of the picturesque or as the embittered man recalling the boyhood degradation of debtors' prison or blacking factory. Only Lamb rivaled him in minute and affectionate observation of London. But

Lamb moved in a narrower sphere, he died eleven years younger, and he lost the best part of thirty-three years within the narrow walls of countinghouses. Defoe was the last of the English writers who remembered the medieval city of Chaucer and Shakespeare which survived until the Great Fire. He was the first to see the new city which grew out of the old.

After the Great Fire had leveled the old city, Defoe heard much of the Phoenix which was to spring from the ashes. He saw the spires of Wren's churches take their places on the horizon. Much of his interest in projects grew out of his acquaintance with London as it rose from the desolation of plague and fire. When the royal palace of Whitehall was burned in 1698, he drew up an elaborate plan for its reconstruction as "a magnificent building," which "would very well suit the grandeur of the British Court": "Here a King of Great Britain would live like himself, and half the world would run over to see and wonder at it." But King William's exchequer was exhausted by the war with France and the revaluation of the coinage, William had no interest in spending a million pounds for a palace he could not live in because of the London fogs, and Defoe was obliged to bury his beloved project in six pages of his *Tour* and to "return to the description of things which really exist, and are not imaginary."[8]

The ideal plans of Defoe's elders, put forward so hopefully after the Fire, were ignored or lost in practical difficulties. The "famous city builder, Mr. Fitch," when he was blamed for the shoddiness of his houses, answered sourly that "the city was hastily built and slowly paid for."[9]

Defoe saw the slums and the vice, the squalor and the brutality, the dirt and the diseases of the city as clearly as anyone has ever done; but he saw the rare beauty as well. If he had ever attempted a sonnet on London, he would not (like his fellow cockney John Keats) have expressed the relief which open fields give "To one who has been long in city pent," but more nearly the feeling of a poet who came up from the Lakes:

> the very houses seem asleep;
> And all that mighty heart is lying still!

His account of the neighboring countryside becomes eloquent when he thinks of the beauty of the homes on the river above London: "The banks of the Seine are not thus adorn'd from Paris to Rouen, or from Paris to the Loing above the city: The Danube can show nothing like it, above or below Vienna, or the Po above or be-low Turin." When he catches an open view from the Surrey side, his prose rises almost into song: "looking north, behold, to crown all, a fair prospect of the whole city of London it self; the most glorious sight without exception that the whole world at present can show, or perhaps ever could show since the sacking of Rome in the European, and the burning of the Temple of Jerusalem in the Asian part of the world."[10]

In the judgment of Dr. Johnson, "when a man is tired of London, he is tired of life." Defoe never tired of life—or of London.

II. THE FOES

Queen Elizabeth entertained 200,000 foreigners, and where are they? They are all run to seed; they were sown foreigners, and they came up True-born Englishmen.

Review, V, 575

TWO AND A HALF CENTURIES ago England was the richest nation in the world, and its citizens enjoyed an unusual degree of religious and political freedom. Their prosperity was due primarily to the manufacture and exportation of woolen goods. As early as the Middle Ages there had been wealth wherever sheep were raised for their wool; even today the stone walls and slate roofs in the Cotswold villages bear witness to this era of prosperity. The English woolen manufacture had been developed long before its traditional beginning in the sixteenth century; but the craft was greatly improved when religious persecution under Philip II of Spain drove Flemish artisans across the Channel.[1] Defoe grew up in the proud knowledge that his paternal ancestors had helped to establish English supremacy in the wool trade.

He might toy with the idea that he was perhaps kin to the ancient Norman family of De Beau-foe. But he knew that his father was descended from the Flemings, who (with the Dutch) "are allowed to be the most industrious people in the world." When he spoke of the time of Queen Elizabeth, he could quote the printed histories—but he could also recall what, he said, "my great grandmother (who lived in those days) has informed our family."[2]

It has been supposed that he showed snobbishness in prefixing "De" to the plebian name of Foe in middle life. Defoe himself jested about the inconvenience of the name Foe for a man so often engaged in public controversy. But the obvious truth is that he never did change his name. The original spelling was something like Defawe, and that had been anglicized to Foe by his ancestors only a few generations before:

It was not so easy a matter for foreigners to be naturalized among the English in those times, as it is now, which made those that found means to settle here, and turn their hands to the manufacture, take what care they could to conceal themselves, and so to change their surnames, or at least to shorten and abridge them into differing sounds, that they might be made to speak English as much as possible, that is to say, to sound like English. For example, *Jean de Somieres* would be called *John Sommers; Guillaume de Tournay, William Turner; Estienne D'Anvers, Stephen Danvers; Jacques de Franquemont, James Franks;* and so of the rest; by which all the Flemish, Dutch, and Walloon names were presently turned into English.

Defoe's own father was still occasionally called "deu-foe" or "Du-foe" during Daniel's boyhood. Daniel himself was called De Foo as early as 1695 and 1696 in printed announcements of his official post in the royal lotteries. In an age when the name of the Queen was spelled in two ways and when so eminent a gentleman as Dr. Arbuthnot had his name spelled and pronounced in an almost unrecognizable variety of ways, it was hardly strange that Daniel Defoe should have been referred to even in the last thirty years of his life by such variants as Foe, Faugh, Du Foo, Du' Foo, D'Foe, DeFoe, De Foe, De Fooe, Dubow (a sexton's blunder), and Daniel Defoe, Esq. He repeatedly signed his initials either D. F. or D. D. F.; it is not certain whether he ever decided definitely whether his name was D. Foe or D. De Foe. In a legal document near the end of his life he signed himself Daniel Foe, Gentleman.[3]

His immediate paternal ancestors lived in the east midland county of Northamptonshire—in the village of Peakirk and later in Etton. His grandfather Daniel Foe was described as a "yeoman" when he died at Etton (March 8, 1631), leaving the bulk of his little property to his wife, besides £230 divided almost equally among his three sons (Daniel, James, and Henry) and his daughter Mary.[4] Probably he died as a young man, for his oldest child was only six and his widow remarried two years later. It has been conjectured that he was an Anglican because he left ten shillings to the parson of the village church. But in a region so strongly inclined toward Puritanism, the small legacy to the Rev. Mr. Temple may indicate that the local clergyman was himself sympathetic toward the faith which had brought the Flemish weavers into exile.

Of the five members of Daniel Foe's family who survived him, his widow and daughter and oldest son passed out of the known records before Defoe's birth. The youngest son, Henry, was a saddler who died in the parish of St. Botolph, Aldgate (sometimes called St. Botolph's without Aldgate). In 1666 he was listed as a tax collector in the Barrs precinct of St. Botolph's. His burial on February 28, 1675, was recorded on the church register, and his brother James was his sole legatee and executor. Henry attained a shadowy immortality as "H. F.," the saddler who remained in London throughout the terrors of 1665 and 1666, upon whose real or imagined observations Defoe erected the superstructure of *A Journal of the Plague Year*. It is certain that Henry Foe was active as a citizen of London during the plague year and that he did not die until his nephew Daniel was fourteen years old.

James Foe soon moved from Northamptonshire to London; and after his apprenticeship to John Levitt, citizen and butcher, he set up as a tallow-chandler in the parish of St. Giles, Cripplegate.[5] Levitt, who was also styled "tallow-chandler" in the register of St. Botolph, Aldgate, made Henry Foe his executor in his will of February, 1666, when the plague was at its height. Defoe had much to say of the customs of London butchers; and he was intimately acquainted with the ways of graziers from the East Midlands who brought cattle and sheep down to the grazing lands near London, fed them through the winter, and sold them at high prices in the spring. If James Foe was first employed by an Essex grazier, his removal to London and his later career as tallow-chandler, citizen and member of the Butchers' Company, and presumably as an active butcher, would be partly explained.

About 1656 James married a girl named Alice. Nothing is known of her family except from Defoe's anecdote to illustrate the bitter name-calling among the factions of church and state, which has been taken to suggest that her father was a country squire of royalist sympathies who fell into distress during the civil war. The fact that Goring and Waller are mentioned, rather than more important generals, has suggested, as do a number of slight bits of evidence, such as Defoe's reference to a relative near Martock, that her family lived in Somersetshire or in one of the neighboring counties: "I remember my grandfather had a huntsman that used the same familiarity with his dogs, and he had his Round-Head and his Cavalier, his Goring and his Waller, and all the generals of both armies were hounds in his pack; till the time turning, the old gentleman was fain to scatter the pack, and make them up of more dog-like surnames."[6]

If Alice's father was actually a royalist country gentleman, he was obliged to scatter more than his pack of hounds; his daughter Alice went to London and was married to a Puritan tallow-chandler. There is no known record of their marriage or of her death; but the fact that she was named in the will of Lawrence Marsh in 1665 and not in that of his widow in 1671 suggests that she died in the interim. The assessment lists name a James Foe who was living with his wife in Coleman Street Ward in 1667 and 1669, but by 1683 James Foe (apparently the same man) was a "lodger" and presumably a widower in Jones Court in that ward. I see no adequate reason to identify him with the James Foe who was living with his wife Elizabeth in St. Benet Fink in 1695; there is nowhere any suggestion that Defoe had a stepmother, and no reference was made to her in the will of James Foe (March 20, 1706). Defoe learned of his father's death in December, 1706, while he was representing Harley in Edinburgh.[7]

The as yet unpublished discoveries of my friend and collaborator Mr. F. Bastian of Trowbridge, Wilts, provide additional facts and suggest unexplored possibilities. There were Foes in Leicestershire, and the recurrence of certain family names such as Tuffley which were significant in Defoe's life suggests a possible center of relationship. In 1665 Lawrence Marsh of Dorking left funeral rings to his cousin Foe and his wife. Marsh was a wealthy landowner, a former member of the Barebones Parliament and a justice of the peace in Dorking. After the death of Lawrence's widow Elizabeth in 1671, James Foe was named sole executor of the Marsh estate; and in 1706 he bequeathed £20 to James Marsh, a son of Lawrence and Elizabeth.

It would be rash to lay great stress on the fragmentary information which is available as yet. However, it seems probable that Alice Foe had been brought up as a Puritan, that she (more likely than her husband) was closely related to the family of Lawrence Marsh of Dorking, and that it is at least not unlikely that she inherited enough property to have aided the family in its increasing prosperity before Defoe's bankruptcy in 1692.

James and Alice Foe had two daughters and one son (our Daniel). Of Mary (born November 13, 1657) nothing further is known except that she was married to a shipwright (Francis Barham, Jr., later spelled Bartham) and that their son Francis received a silver watch by the will of his grandfather Foe.[8] (James Foe's own gold watch, which was willed to Defoe's son Benjamin, was quite possibly the one which had been bequeathed to James Foe by the will of Henry Loxam of Belgrave, Leicestershire, February 23, 1676 [probated March 11, 1678]: "To James Foe citizen of London I give my watch.") Elizabeth (born

June 19, 1659) became the wife of Robert Davis, an engineer and shipwright who invented a diving engine for salvaging wrecks; until he settled as a shipbuilder in Leith in 1706 he was the frequent companion on Defoe's journeys and sometimes Defoe's confidential messenger to Harley or to the Earl of Halifax. Davis must have acquired some means, as he furnished £250 bail for Defoe in 1703. The daughters of Robert and Elizabeth Davis, Elizabeth (Davis) Roberts and Anne Davis, were legatees in the will of James Foe. A modern American variant, which supposes an entirely different marriage for Elizabeth and tells of a daughter who emigrated to Maryland, is derived from the semifictional narratives of Mary E. Ireland late in the nineteenth century.[9]

In his first letter to the Earl of Halifax, Defoe apologized for his brother who acted as his messenger but "whose head" was "not that way," so that he brought Defoe an imperfect account of what Halifax had recommended for his perusal. This messenger was Robert Davis, whom Defoe called both brother and brother-in-law.[10] The guess that Davis was very dull or subject to mental alienation is wide of the mark; as an engineer he would hardly be qualified to bear an oral message from Halifax on the abstruse subject of paper credit. Still further, Halifax had preferred to give only cautious hints; Defoe was asking for explicit instructions. It was a dexterous stroke to lay the blame on his brother-in-law's memory rather than on the vagueness of Halifax' message.

Defoe had a relative who kept school at Martock, in Somersetshire; he mentions another in or near Sherborn, in Dorsetshire; he refers to another who served under the Earl of Orrery in Flanders about 1674;[11] his father remembered in his will a cousin John Richards, who owed him money in 1704. Perhaps few of these had any considerable influence on the life of Defoe, who declared in the concluding lines of *The True-Born Englishman,*

> Fame of Families is all a cheat,
> 'Tis personal virtue only makes us great.

The most significant factor in his childhood development lay in his home. Throughout his writings he shows respect, even reverence, for a woman's part in the family. He grew up during the Restoration, and he was a careful reader of the cynical plays and poems of the court wits—but this seems never to have warped his judgment. Perhaps he had his own mother in mind in one of his similes: "like the child that threatens the mother that if she corrects it it will go drown itself." He refers to her directly in one anecdote: *"If you vex me, I'll eat no dinner,* said I, when I was a little boy, till my mother taught me to be wiser, by letting me stay till I was hungry."[12]

Nowhere does he refer to his mother except in these recollections of his early childhood. She was alive in 1665, when she was named in Lawrence Marsh's will; but she seems to have died before 1671, for she was not mentioned in the will of Elizabeth Marsh. When her young son was sent to a private boarding school in Dorking about 1671 or earlier, the home of the Foes was already broken.

But James Foe lived an active and useful life until his son was forty-six years old. All that we can learn of him suggests a pious and upright man who succeeded in business through patience, integrity, and hard work. Yet he seems to have been sympathetic toward his gifted son. He provided an education which was exceptional for a boy in his circumstances, hoping that Daniel would enter the ministry; but we have no indication that he was resentful when that expectation was unfulfilled. His relations with many of his fellow Dissenters must have been strained when Daniel failed to follow the line of action laid down by some of their leaders, but he secured his son's admission to his own livery company (the Butchers').[13]

In discussing a civic abuse, five years after the death of his father, Defoe paid tribute to his strength of character: "It shall never be said, that my father's son lived to see it, and feared to speak it." But perhaps James Foe himself read, two years before his death, an earlier tribute written by his only son: "the care, tenderness, love, and benignity of a true parent, cannot be returned; 'tis not of a kind that can ascend. It may descend, and be paid to posterity."[14]

III. ST. BARTHOLOMEW'S DAY

I am not to preach, but to relate.

Roxana (Aitken ed.), I, 52

F OR MODERN READERS it is difficult to understand Defoe's
loyalty to the Dissenters. Why should a man so broadly national in
feeling support a minority group outside the legal Establishment?
Why should a man who so often experienced the ingratitude of the
Dissenters, and who repeatedly declared that he would gladly subscribe to the Thirty-Nine Articles of the Church of England except
for a few dealing with episcopal power and ceremony, refuse the advantages of the compromise called Occasional Conformity?

To Defoe, as to most thoughtful men of his age, religion was the
central experience of human life. And to him it was the Church itself
which had gone into dissent from the principles on which it had been
founded.

Until he was two years old, his parents worshiped in the Church of
England as by law established.[1] Their pastor had been reappointed to
his living of St. Giles, Cripplegate, after the first rapid changes of
ecclesiastical reorganization. Charles II had seemed willing to choose
men of Puritan leanings as royal chaplains and even to offer them
bishoprics. It was widely believed that a compromise could be worked
out to make possible a truly national church.

Many clergymen of the High Church persuasion had suffered
wrongs during the interregnum of civil and religious strife; moderate
men hoped that the Restoration would right those wrongs without
turning the oppressed into oppressors. A few clergymen who had held
office under the Protectorate of Oliver Cromwell gave up their pulpits to their predecessors, but no general solution was possible on such
terms. The seeds of the old controversies which had brought Archbishop Laud to the block germinated for harvest after 1660.

At Breda in the Netherlands the King had declared in favor of "liberty to tender consciences," before he was brought home from exile

with the support of the Presbyterians. A few weeks after Defoe's birth, Charles promised a national synod to settle religious differences. In the following April such a group met in the Savoy at the lodging of Gilbert Sheldon, the politic Bishop of London and soon thereafter Archbishop of Canterbury.

According to Defoe, Sheldon would have tricked the Puritan ministers into raising new scruples against a religious union if their old ones had been surmounted. But there was no need of this. The conference ended in July, 1661; in November work was begun on a revised Prayer Book; in April, 1662, this new Prayer Book was adopted by a Parliament far more royalist than the King; and on May 12 the Act of Uniformity received the King's assent. This act required of the clergy episcopal ordination, unconditional acceptance of the new Prayer Book, repudiation of the Solemn League and Covenant, and subscription to the doctrine of nonresistance to the King. Such conditions were not meant to be complied with by the Puritan wing of the clergy. Most of these men had never received ordination by a Bishop, many had had no chance to see the new Prayer Book, perhaps not one of them could honestly have accepted the doctrine of passive obedience to the royal will. "So the bishops had their pound of flesh."[2]

By grim irony the date for the eviction of the nonconforming clergy was Sunday, August 24, 1662—St. Bartholomew's Day, the ninetieth anniversary of the most famous religious massacre in history. The choice of the day was perhaps suggested by the tithes which fell due shortly thereafter; nonconformist clergymen were to be deprived of their livelihood as well as their pulpits.

Samuel Pepys, no martyr for religious enthusiasm, was caught in the fervor of the parting sermons. He inquired eagerly what was happening elsewhere in the city, and he attended church more often than usual. Early on the Sunday morning before "Black Bartholomew" he was at St. Dunstan's, where Dr. William Bates was to bid farewell to his congregation: "At eight o'clock I went, and crowded in at a back door among others, the church being half-full almost before any doors were open publicly . . . and so got into the gallery, beside the pulpit, and heard very well. His text was, 'Now the God of Peace———;' . . . he making a very good sermon, and very little reflections in it to any thing of the times." To be sure, Pepys had to add: "Besides the sermon, I was very well pleased with the sight of a fine lady that I have often seen walk in Graye's Inn Walks, and it was my chance to meet

her again at the door going out, and very pretty and sprightly she is."
But he soon went on:

After dinner to St. Dunstan's again; and the church quite crowded before I came, which was just at one o'clock; but I got into the gallery again,
but stood in a crowd and did exceedingly sweat all the time. He pursued
his text again very well; . . . I hear that most of the Presbyters took their
leaves to-day, and that the City is much dissatisfied with it. I pray God
keep peace among us, and make the Bishops careful of bringing in good
men in their rooms, or else all will fly a-pieces; for bad ones will not go
down with the City.

When Pepys attended the service on the next Sunday, the religious
apathy of the next century and a half had already set in: "Here we
had a lazy, dull sermon."[3]

Relatively few of the "Bartholomeans"[4] starved to death; not a
great many actually died in prison. But they were deprived of their
pulpits, and all learned professions were closed to them; only con-
formists were admitted to private chaplainships, tutorships, school-
teaching, law, or medicine. On August 17 the "silver-tongued" Bates
was the most popular clergyman in London. Thereafter (until he took
the oath of allegiance) he was hunted from one secret conventicle to
another, in constant danger through the paid informers of an Archbishop who preserved the purity of the Church by methods which
had once been adopted to prevent the spreading of the Christian religion. On July 13, 1664, Oliver Heywood wrote: "Stephen Ellis our
church-warden came to demand four shillings for my absence from
church four sabbaths. My servant answered that if I came he would
put me out of church. 'Yes,' saith he, 'and so I will too'; the law must
be enforced, both to keep me away and punish my absence."[5]

Defoe was fond of quoting a text in Ecclesiastes, "Surely oppression maketh a wise man mad." Oppression proved disastrous to victor
and vanquished alike. Clarendon, the wise statesman and observer of
historical events, had helped to draw up the liberal Declaration of
Breda in 1660; after 1663, he was forced into alliance with bigots, accepting responsibility for the coercive acts known as the Clarendon
Code. There had been similar oppression under the Commonwealth;
but now an opportunity for generous appeasement was lost, and the
animosities of civil war were revived in an era of good will. The
sacred office of the bishops had been reaffirmed at the Savoy Conference; by the eighteenth century, bishoprics had become political
spoils.

15

The heaviest blow to the Church was the loss of so many of its ablest ministers. The religious fervor, the learning, even the common morality of the clergy were lowered at the very time when the power of the clergy was increased. By a lax interpretation of the law which required the ownership of freeholds as a qualification for voters, the livings of beneficed clergymen were now regarded as freeholds; and in the extremely limited body of electors, the thousands of beneficed clergymen were a relatively large group. The Church soon became the most powerful of political organizations, and a cry of "the Church in danger" was likely to silence any proposal for political or ecclesiastical reform.

At first, efforts were made to retain a few leaders among the Bartholomeans. Dr. Annesley was promised promotion if he would conform. Dr. Edmund Calamy related that his famous grandfather was "not a little courted by persons of distinction to come into the national church, upon its establishment in 1662, and could he but have complied, might have had his own terms, and any preferment he had desired, and an opportunity of making and enriching his family, as they did who were then dignified and distinguished, by the renewal of church leases, which were at that time generally expired, which brought in immense sums of money to those then made bishops." The Bartholomeans who were lost to the national church "were men known all over the whole world; their general character was owned even by their enemies; generally speaking, they were men of liberal educations; and they had a vast stock of learning; were exemplar in piety; studious, laborious, and unexceptionably capable of carrying on the work they were embarked in."[6]

The Dissenters lost even more heavily. Many Presbyterians hoped to be reunited to the Church of England, and in this hope they were encouraged by many Episcopalians. Gradually their leaders died away; the names of these leaders were long remembered, but no adequate provision was made to train successors. As the fervor which had borne them up under persecution subsided with the Act of Toleration under William III, their followers fell into rival camps over Occasional Conformity, and later over the controversy regarding the Trinity. Defoe remained a nominal Presbyterian (although he seems to have rejected predestination in favor of free grace or even justification by works). In his last years, although Presbyterianism remained the national religion in Scotland, it had ceased to be a vital influence in England, where its special form of church government had not been realized in practice, its dogmas were not widely held with conviction, and its followers were drifting back into the Church of England or becoming Congregationalists or Unitarians.

The Foes' family pastor, Dr. Annesley, was never mentioned as one of the more intellectual of the Bartholomeans. But he was devoted to his calling from childhood, when he dreamed that "he was to be a minister, and should be sent for by the Bishop of London, to be burnt as a martyr."[7] According to a tradition which still lingers in historical writing, he was a nephew of the first Earl of Anglesey. It seems certain that he was from a private family of country gentlemen in Warwickshire, unrelated to the nobleman who is said to have offered him promotion at the Restoration and whose countess is said (through confusion with a different clergyman) to have esteemed his sanctity so highly that she desired to be buried in his tomb.

It has been supposed that Annesley removed almost immediately from St. Giles to his own meeting house in Little St. Helen's; but that chapel was not built until a few years later. While the Great Plague raged in London, many of the conforming clergymen fled from their parishes, although the most uncompromising foes of the Dissenters—Archbishop Sheldon and Bishop Henchman—remained at their posts, and Henchman threatened the forfeiture of the livings of those who failed to return to their duty. Dissenting ministers who had been driven into hiding also remained in London, and many came out from their secret meeting places to take over the pastoral duties of deserters. In its safe retreat in Oxford, Parliament passed a still more oppressive law: "The Five Mile Act" required all nonconformist ministers to take the "Oxford Oath," affirming their acceptance of complete nonresistance to the King and their repudiation of any desire to alter church or state by any lawful means whatever.

Meanwhile Annesley and his congregation moved from place to place, evading as best they could informers and officers who sought to break up their assemblies. By 1669 he was preaching "in Spittlefields at a new house built for that purpose, with pulpit and seats" which afforded room for a congregation of eight hundred—by far the largest Presbyterian chapel in the London area. Even after 1672, when he was licensed to hold meetings in his house in Spittlefields (Little St. Helen's), he was not free from persecution. In November, 1682, informers broke into his house and seized his goods for "several latent convictions"; a month afterward the same people entered his meeting-house and broke the seats in pieces, after which worship was suspended for a while. Dr. Edmund Calamy recorded that one justice of the peace died in the act of signing a warrant for Annesley's arrest. An apologist for the Church of England has remarked that the Clarendon Code was less barbarous toward the Protestant Dissenters than Louis XIV had been toward the Huguenots, not even as severe as the existing statutes against Roman Catholics in England.[8] Such comparisons would have given little comfort to the Dissenters who suffered.

Annesley belonged to the wing of the Bartholomeans who refused to take the Oxford Oath; but there was much sweetness in his character. An early American diarist recorded his own impression of a communion service in Annesley's chapel (at which Defoe was very likely present):

Sabbath, May 5, 1689. Went to Dr. Annesley's in little St. Helen's, with Capt. Hutchinson, where the Lord's Supper was administered. The Dr. went all over the meeting first, to see who was there, and spake something of the sermon, then read the words of Institution, then prayed and eat and drunk himself, then gave to every one with his own hand, dropping pertinent expressions. In our pew said—Now our spikenard should give its smell, and said to me, Remember the death of Christ. The wine was in quart bottles. The deacon followed the doctor, and when his cup was empty filled it again; as at our pew all had drunk but I, he filled the cup and then gave it me; as he gave it—must be ready in new obedience, and stick at nothing for Christ.[9]

Some writers, confusing Defoe with John Dunton, have stated that he married a daughter of Annesley's, whose sister married Samuel Wesley and became the mother of John and Charles Wesley. Annesley was a man of private means, and his great service to the Dissenters was largely at his own cost. In later controversies he stands out as a peacemaker, a man of strong principles but moderate temper. Whatever faults the Dissenting clergy had, he was notably free from most of them. He had enjoyed a liberal education at Queen's College, Oxford. Afterwards he served as naval chaplain to the Parliament's admiral, the Earl of Warwick, accompanying him on two cruises. Perhaps the chaplain of Cromwell's navy was not without use to Defoe, the future historian of seafaring and piracy.

Annesley was not a brilliant preacher, but he drew larger congregations than most of his brethren. He represented the great tradition of the Bartholomeans. When James Foe and his family went with him in exile from St. Giles, Defoe was cut off forever from the Church of England. Through his childhood attendance at Annesley's services in

Little St. Helen's, Defoe grew up near the center of Presbyterian worship in London.

However, this does not tell the whole story. Defoe was always more Christian than Presbyterian, more lover of the Church of Christ than Dissenter. In his earnest plea against the religious dissensions of 1717, he maintained that diversity of faith should never lead to disunity of purpose or effort:

if some seditious and turbulent spirits should raise a division and mutiny in the army, by spiriting up the Troopers to say, the Dragoons are not soldiers, and the Musquetiers to say that the Grenadiers were not soldiers, because the discipline of the former is more ancient; this practice instead of stirring up some bodies of the army to unsoldier others, would soon make the bravest army a prey to the enemy. Wherefore let not the Dragoon envy the Trooper his more sightly horse and accoutrements; neither let the Trooper despise the Dragoon for the size of his horse, and the meanness of his boots; and let not the Musquetier repine at the portly stature and embroider'd cap of the Grenadier; neither let the Grenadier look with an eye of contempt upon the more lowly appearance, and plainer habit of his fellow soldier, the Musquetier. But let the one and the other strive in unity, who shall be most punctual in obeying the commands of their leader. But above all, let not the officers treat with disdain, nor impress hardships upon the common soldiers; as knowing, that they are jointly engaged in the same warfare, that their lives are equally dear to them, and that in the day of battle the officers can do nothing without their assistance.[10]

IV. BOYHOOD

*I was always ... asking questions of things done in public
as well as private; particularly, I loved to talk with the
seamen and sailors about the great seafights, or battles
on shore, that any of them had been in; and, as I never
forgot anything they told me, I could soon ... give almost as good an account of the Dutch war, and of the
fights at sea, the battles in Flanders, the taking of
Maestricht, and the like, as any of those that had been
there; and this made those old soldiers and tars love to
talk with me too, and to tell me all the stories they could
think of, and that not only of the wars then going on, but
also of the wars in Oliver's time, the death of King
Charles I. and the like.*

*By this means, as young as I was, I was a kind of an
historian; ... I knew the names of every ship in the navy,
and who commanded them too, and all this before I was
fourteen years old, or but very soon after.*

Colonel Jack (Tegg ed.), pp. 9–10

IN DEFOE'S LONDON entertainment and instruction came from
seeing things made or done, from meeting men who had been active
in the world. London was the capital of the sea; a forest of masts
towered in the deep stretch of the river below London Bridge. Defoe
always preferred street scenes to high society; in the streets one met
what Dr. Johnson called "the full tide of human existence." Life had
not yet begun its retreat into skyscrapers or subways or into inclosures shut in by plate glass and ferro-concrete walls.

As a boy, walking through the narrow ways, Defoe saw almost
every handicraft known to civilized man. *Robinson Crusoe* presents
not only the hero's difficulties with basket-weaving and bread-making
and the firing of pottery, the shaping of boards and the building of
boats; it records Defoe's memories of his native city. In *A New
Voyage Round the World,* in his account of a volcanic eruption
which alarmed his hero one night in Chile, he reminds us of the terrors

of night fires in London. When his Robert Drury tells of the screams of wild boars slain by hunters and their dogs in the thickets of Madagascar, he is recalling what a London butcher's son remembered from the hog-killings he had seen in childhood.

Streets and inns and booths were a constant show of wonders. The pageantry which delights sightseers today in a few treasured survivals (like the Lord Mayor's Procession and the mounting of the Guards) was common experience in the city which still stood

Open unto the fields, and to the sky.

The Tower had not yet dried up into a museum; when Defoe was six years old, on the level grounds outside its walls the sailors of Pepys' navy demonstrated for redress of their grievances.[1] It was still the armory of England; and it afforded a substitute for a zoo, with its lions and leopards presented by African potentates—to the gratified embarrassment of the English king. Here was the Royal Mint; here was the observatory used by Flamsteed until accommodations at Greenwich were available. Here Defoe's youthful choice for king, the handsome Duke of Monmouth, was soon to be beheaded; here Defoe's patron, the Earl of Oxford, was to lie imprisoned two years, awaiting the expected trial for his life.

One could learn from books, though there were no modern libraries; Defoe read omnivorously long before he built up his remarkable collection of books, manuscripts, and maps. But the best chroniclers of the time were men who had traveled. Abraham Cowley had just proposed a college in which a fifth of the faculty were to be always traveling beyond seas, to report on the learning and the natural experiments to be heard of in foreign parts. The Royal Society soon developed a method by which captains of merchant vessels were to bring home scientific data as well as indigo, sugar, and rum.[2]

The most inquisitive of boys had worked out his own system of investigation long before he heard of the projects of his elders. Later, when Defoe came to write of the design to seize the West Indies in Cromwell's time, he explained it "from a very authentic, though verbal, relation, from a member of the very Council of War, to whom it was referred." When he defended William's plan for a standing army, he quoted what a veteran of the civil war had told him about raw militiamen.[3]

Some of Defoe's early biographers, supposing that he was born as late as 1662, denied that he could have remembered events of 1665–66.

But he was five or six years old then, and his personal recollections of plague and fire and the terrors of a naval war with the Dutch were vivid as long as he lived. Many years afterward he wrote:

> I am loth to remind our people of that sad particular of the City, in the time of the last infection or visitation, as it was called: How grass grew in the streets of London, and on the Exchange; how the most frequented places were abandoned; how all commerce was interrupted, and few shops in London were kept open: How a purse of money lay on the pavement in the Post-House-Yard, and no body durst take it up for some hours, till a man that had the plague, and was recovered, came with a pail of water, and a pair of red hot tongs, and took it up, and burning the purse dropped the money ino the pail.
>
> I remember very well what I saw with a sad heart, though I was but young; I mean the Fire of London. That all endeavors having been fruitlessly used to abate the fire, the people gave it over, and despairing citizens looked on and saw the devastation of their dwellings, with a kind of stupidity caused by amazement. If any people, still forward for the public good, made any attempts, the water they cast upon it made it rage with the more fury and boil like a pot; till scorched with the flames from every side, and tired with the fruitless labor, they gave over, as others had done before them . . . and the whole City was laid in ashes.[4]

When the middle-aged Defoe heard younger men ridiculing the danger of another war with Holland, he was troubled by childhood memories of what he had learned from maimed sailors:

> Fighting with the Dutch has always had a difference in it from fighting with other nations: These fight at a distance, and lie and pelt one another while they are a quarter of a mile or half a mile off, and pour in their small shot upon one another, to pick off their men; but when the English and Dutch formerly used to meet . . . the squadrons lie yard-arm and yard-arm, pouring in their cross-bar, double-head and round, and tearing one another with that dreadful fury, that nothing on earth can be spoken of to describe those sea fights by. Let those who remember the last Holland wars tell us whether the hottest action we have had at sea during this war can be compared to the way of fighting between us and the Dutch.[5]

Perhaps James Foe removed his family to the safety of the country for a time; but probably Defoe saw something of the plague at first hand, and later he talked with many whose personal narratives were absorbed into his memory. He was too young to understand the increase of trade between 1667 and 1670 resulting from "War, Pestilence, and Fire," but he saw his father's growing prosperity as he became a prominent member of the Butchers' Company. In his old age he bitterly twitted those who wished for another public calamity to bring good times. He recalled the widespread dram-drinking after the Dutch wars, when petty distillers blended crude spirits and sold them in glass bottles "with innumerable hard names to set them off" in such shops as his father's had once been:

> Here, as at a fountain, the good wives furnished their little fireside cupboards with a needful bottle for a cherishing cup: And hence, as from wholesale dealers, all the little chandlers' shops, not in London and its adjacent parts only, but over the great part of England, were furnished for sale; and to the personal knowledge of the writer hereof, and of thousands still living, not the chandlers' shops only, but . . . the barbers' shops . . . were furnished with the same, and sold it by retail, to the poor people who came under their operations.[6]

As a boy he saw the evils of coercive restrictions on trade; as a man he denounced the petty tyranny of "a certain Justice of the Peace, . . . the terror of butchers and poulterers, who presumed to sell such things of a Sunday morning as would not keep till Monday." It is not certain that James Foe grew into one of the notable "wholesale butchers, who sell it out to the butchers in the outparts and in the villages and towns near the City." But he did not stint expenses for his son's health or enjoyment; about 1668 the boy had begun his travels with a visit to the east coast at Ipswich, and a little later he was drinking the waters at Bath.[7]

Young Defoe saw a highwayman hanged at Tyburn who complained that he was undone by his gentleness; if he had shot the man he had robbed, there would have been no witness against him. He saw how the navy's press gangs started fights in the street to gather a crowd and then swept up the men from both sides. Later he spoke confidently of "my own knowledge of the river, which I have some reason to pretend to."[8] As a boy he was fascinated by the watermen on the Thames and by the fishwives in Billingsgate Market, whose language was unequaled for profusion and variety in terms of abuse. He never forgot (as an example to be avoided) the virulence he had heard so often; in the pages of no other writer does the term *Billingsgate* appear so often or so reproachfully.

In the streets no divinity hedged the King. When Defoe was eleven, the equestrian statue of Charles II was unveiled; a conduit spouted wine for hours, and there was public rejoicing. A little afterward, when the favorite royal mistress of the moment gave birth to a son, young Defoe shared the popular delight over the pillion which appeared behind the saddle of the King's statue, with the placard, "Gone for a midwife."[9]

The mad rejoicings over the Restoration ceased during his childhood. In later life he referred contemptuously to the time when "the excesses and transports of the clergy and people run out into revels, may-poles, and all manner of extravagancies." But if the young Puritan disliked maypoles, he had an extraordinary fondness for most games and sports.

He did condemn cocking and cricketing as childish; as an outsider in Cornwall he saw nothing but brutality in the interparish war called "hurlers"; he laughed at fox-hunting as a useless sport.[10] But he spoke of cards as an innocent pastime, unless one got entangled in gambling. On the bowling green he objected to nothing but the profanity. He used figures of speech from bullbaiting and football. On at least one English tour he carried a spaniel for hunting. His great endurance as a walker and horseman must have been developed early in life; later he suggested that the national character had decayed through the neglect of sport. Of swimming he declared that "no man ought to be without it." His love of boats grew so keen that it was with difficulty that he reasoned himself out of his project to circumnavigate Great Britain with a single companion (his brother-in-law Robert Davis), going up into every bay. His references to "the manly, noble diversions of . . . horse-races" betrayed an expertness acquired from jockeys and stables. Some of his recorded visits to the races occurred in middle life, but his taste went back to his boyhood.[11]

His early love of boxing and wrestling was shown as "a young boxing English boy" who was taught not to strike an opponent when he was down. Less attention has been given to his expertness with the sword, so rare an accomplishment among his literary contemporaries. His journalistic rival John Tutchin was beaten by political adversaries so that he died of his injuries. Defoe's life was often threatened; on at least three occasions he was attacked, and on another he walked into a room where five men were planning to kill him. His lifelong practice of defending his head with his hand gave force to his political courage: "He that will be known to speak truth impartially must do it in the face of danger." In a condemnation of dueling, he recalled his own sensations in the hours before such an encounter. As a fencer he objected to the brutal taste of the Bear-Garden spectators, who wanted only to see blood fly upon the stage, whereas to those who understand the art, or, as the back-sword men called it, the Noble Science of Defence, the best sight is to see two bold fellows lay heartily at one another, but to be so dexterous, and such exquisite masters of their weapons, as to ward off every blow, to parry every thrust, and after many nice closes, and fine attempts, not to be able to come in with one another, or so much as to draw blood. This shows them to be good swordsmen, and perfectly skilled in their weapons; whereas if either of them was to fight with a person less skilled, he would be cut down presently.[12]

It is unlikely that Defoe took lessons under a fashionable master, but he had much to say about his early acquaintance with Cromwellian officers. The boy could have learned the art of self-defense in no better school.

It is not certain when he began attending the theater. He knew Restoration drama exceptionally well, and he quoted passages long after the authors had lost their vogue. In a political pamphlet he introduced an act (supposedly from an unpublished play of his own) on the purchase of a seat in Parliament; his grandson recorded the tradition that he was one of the men suspected of writing Cibber's comedy *The Careless Husband.* Defoe objected to the licentious lives of many actors and actresses, to the profanity and indecency of many spoken lines, to the emptiness of many plays, to the stupidity of audiences, to the waste of time in habitual attendance at the theater. He condemned *The Beggar's Opera* (as did such shrewd observers as Hogarth and the Fielding brothers) for casting a glamor over vice and crime. But he admired tragedy, the more moral comedies, and good pantomime.[13] Defoe's attitude of partial disapproval and active personal interest can be seen when we discover that the moralist who condemned licentious plays was quick to read—and to indorse nearly two years in advance of performance or publication—a tragedy which he liked. Early in 1715 *The Fears of the Pretender turn'd into the Fears of Debauchery* expressed his disappointment over the low moral tone of Drury Lane under the patentees headed by Sir Richard Steele. But in a political pamphlet published May 16, 1717 (*The Conduct of Robert Walpole, Esq.*), his title page quoted six lines from the manuscript of Dr. George Sewell's tragedy *Sir Walter Raleigh,* a play which was not acted at Lincoln's Inn Fields until January 1718/9 and not printed until 1719.

To say that the boy was a Puritan and therefore hostile to drama and other art is to run counter to all we know of him. He grew up in the century which gave birth to Milton, Rembrandt, and Bach. Bach's explanation of his music—"for the glory of God, and a very pleasant recreation"—sounds remarkably like what Calvin wrote of the value of the invention of musical instruments by Tubal Cain—"so long as it is used in the fear of God and in the service of mankind." As a Puritan, Defoe insisted that *art must serve mankind*. But he was the only prominent literary man of his age who did not look down on music as the inferior sister of poetry or who had a genuine interest in and understanding of opera (itself an importation of Cromwell's time). In various places he showed his enthusiasm for vocal and instrumental concert music, drama, painting, statuary, architecture, and landscape gardening. To critics who complained that St. Paul's Cathedral was heavy and gross, he replied by a spirited defense of painting and statuary as aids to architecture, unfortunately ruled out here by the necessity of adhering to "protestant plainness."[14]

He labored under no musical handicap in his early travels on the Continent, where (according to a comtemporary) "there was no keeping of good and virtuous company . . . without as much of the practice of music as to enable one to bear a part in a concert." In his younger days he "was accounted no despicable performer on the viol and lute, then much in vogue." When he thought of music in the larger sense, it became almost synonymous with harmony, and therefore with the divine plan; for "Harmony, and the Beauties of Sound, which are the foundation of music, these are the Daughters of God." Elsewhere he refers to a treatise on *The Harmony of the Divine Attributes* by the Bartholomean Dr. Bates, and he continues: "thus there is music in every beautiful building, every delicious prospect, every fair object; all the regulated life of a just and pious man is music to the eye of the observer; the eloquence of the orator, the lines of the poet make music in the soul. Who can read Virgil, Horace, Milton, Waller, and Rochester, without touching the strings of his soul, and finding a unison of the most charming influence there?"[15]

His coupling of the profane Rochester with Milton may strike one oddly, but it is characteristic of Defoe. Early in life he learned to see both sides of every shield. He accepted facts and opinions as he found them, and he sought to live in peace and charity with his neighbors. Later he was involved in more controversies than most men have ever known; but he was perfectly honest in his lifelong effort to "allay the heats of faction."

Among his fellows Defoe was almost unique in his ability to laugh at his foibles and to repent of his shortcomings, to see the faults of his friends and the merits of his foes. His correspondent the Rev. Cotton Mather would never admit that he had helped to murder the women condemned in Salem as witches; his compatriot Dr. Edmund Calamy accepted for himself and his fellow clergymen an annual bribe, which he received unctuously as a reward of merit and an impartial expression of King George's good will. Defoe made no such mistake about the motives of others, and (as James Russell Lowell said of Samuel Pepys) he stood unbuttoned to himself. We cannot know all the causes of his open-mindedness, but it began somewhere in his boyhood.

V. MORTON'S ACADEMY

My pedagogue was very diligent, and proved an extraordinary man indeed.

Colonel Jack (Tegg ed.), p. 173

WHEN DEFOE was about ten years old, he came to one of the many turning points in his life. His mother was dead, and his careful father was all too busy with his thriving shop in the rapidly rebuilding city of London. The active little boy was becoming sickly, and London physicians had no remedy to offer. In his serene old age Defoe could struggle at leisure against such ailments as gout and the stone. But about the year 1670 he was sent off to the west of England to drink the waters at Bath.

Near the same time, provision was made for his education as well as for his health. The region around Dorking, in Surrey, was known as one of the most salubrious in England. An Independent minister, Rev. James Fisher, who had been ejected from his living at Fetcham in the same county on the fateful St. Batholomew's Day, was now keeping a private school in his new home in Dorking, where he boarded those of his pupils who came from a distance. The community was a strong center of Nonconformity; in the previous year it had been reported that four Dissenting meetings were held there, with three hundred Presbyterians, one hundred Independents, fifty Baptists, and an unspecified number of Quakers. Best of all, the pastor of the Foe family, Dr. Annesley, the wealthy patron of rural Dissenting congregations who was later called on to provide a minister for the neighboring village of Godalming, was a man of influence in the community.

So it happened that the frail boy was packed off from the unwholesome air of Cripplegate to begin his career amid the sunny and windswept downs southwest of London. The exact location of Fisher's school in Dorking is unknown, but it was very likely in one of the two buildings on a piece of land belonging to Lawrence Marsh, which (as Mr. Bastian has discovered) ran down to the river Mole at the foot of Box Hill. This would explain Defoe's extraordinary interest in the geography of the region, with which he seemed intimately familiar in winter as well as in summer.[1] More than half a century later, in the second letter of his *Tour thro' the Whole Island of Great Britain*, he drew on his boyhood memories for a minute refutation of the statements of such authorities as Camden and John Evelyn regarding the disappearance of the stream underground:

Now after all these plausible stories, the matter of fact is this, and no more; and even of this, the thing is wonderful enough too: But I say, it is thus, and no more, (viz.)

The river Mole passes by Beechworth Castle in a full stream; and for near a mile farther on the west of the Castle, it takes into its stream Darking-Brook, as they call it, and has upon it a large corn-mill, call'd Darking-Mill; below this it runs close at the foot of Box-Hill, near that part of the hill, which is call'd the Stomacher; then, as if obstructed by the hill, it turns a little south, and runs cross the road which leads from Darking to Leatherhead, where it is apparently rapid and strong; and then fetches a circuit round a park, formerly belonging to Sir Richard Studdolph, and which is part of it, within sight of Leatherhead, and so keeps a continued chanel to the very town of Leatherhead; so that there is no such thing as a natural bridge, or a river lost, no, not at all; and in the winter, in time of floods the stream will be very large, and rapid all the way above ground, which I affirm of my own knowledge, having seen it so, on many occasions.

Three paragraphs later, he affirmed that he had never seen the road near Mickleham entirely dry even in the dryest summer, "tho' I liv'd in the neighbourhood several years."

The one considerable mistake which runs through Defoe's description of the region only confirms his familiarity with it; for he does not trouble himself to look at a map, and he consequently locates places by his vivid but somewhat distorted memory—at an angle of ninety degrees from the true line from north to south, just as he recalled them from boyhood.

Education was emphasized by seventeenth-century Dissenters. Rev. Oliver Heywood declared that "if men neglect to sow good seed, the devil will not fail to sow tares." Children were "born blind," and could be enlightened only by training. Men pruned plants, broke horses, brought up hawks to the lure; it was far more important to educate children "in their tender years."[2]

The widower James Foe was not qualified (like many Dissenting clergymen) to undertake the education of his son at home; he had left the Church of England, which controlled education from the parish schools through the universities; and he was not a member of one of the five great livery companies which maintained schools in London. Besides, all such charitable enterprises in London were crippled by recent devastations of plague and fire. Nearly fifty years later a rival of Defoe sneered at the "house education" and "free school" of which Robinson Crusoe was so proud—and which was probably based on Defoe's recollections of his own instruction in the house of James Fisher at Dorking.

Fisher was the second of the Bartholomeans who influenced Defoe so deeply. It was fortunate that Fisher did not force the boy like a hothouse plant—or like an Isaac Watts, who was learning Latin at four, attending a Latin school at six, and taking up Greek at nine and Hebrew at thirteen.[3]

Lawrence Marsh's widow, Elizabeth, died in the summer of 1671, and in her will (probated December 15) she left the entire Marsh property to the sole care of James Foe, citizen of London. Defoe's father was no doubt a careful executor of the large but deeply in-volved estate. However, he was obliged to be in London most of the time, and he could not prevent the pranks which Daniel and his class-mates at Fisher's school played in the untenanted mansion which had been rated in the tax books for its twelve hearths.

In a book which he published fifty-six years later, Defoe gave a detailed account of what seems to have been the first example of his lifelong interest in ghosts and apparitions. He told the story to illus-trate popular credulity. But when he identified himself as "one of these unlucky boys" and accidentally referred to the culprits as "we," his mischievous boyhood stands momentarily revealed to us:

I remember a delusion almost as gross, the memory of which I believe remains for a truth to this day. Not far off of the town of Dorking in Surry, the people, or some people rather, entertained a notion, from the following passage, that a ghost walked in such a place; that she (for it was an ancient lady lately dead) was seen hovering about the mansion-house which was left uninhabited for some time, that she would be up and down in the house very often in the daytime, making a rumbling and clattering noise; and in the night-time she walked in the neighbouring fields with a candle in her hand, and that though the wind blew ever so hard, it would not blow the candle out; that sometimes she would appear in the open field, sometimes up in the trees, and, particularly, there was a little heath near Dorking called the Cottman Dean, where it was said she was fre-quently seen.

There was a boarding-school of boys in that town, where there was in particular some roguish London boys, who contrived all this walking from the beginning to the end:—First, they got a small rope, and tying one end of it to an old chair which stood in an upper room of the house, (for they had found means to get in and out of the house at pleasure) they brought the other end of the rope down on the outside of the house in a private place where it could not easily be seen, and by this they pulled the old chair up and then let it fall down again, and made a great noise in the house, so as it might be easily heard by the neighbours; then other boys of the same gang took care to call out to the old women in the next houses, that now they might hear the old lady a playing her pranks; and accordingly they would all assemble in the courtyard, where they could plainly hear it, but not one would venture to go up stairs. If any offered to go up a little way, then all was quiet again; but as soon as ever they retired, the rumbling would begin again. This was for the day.

In the night, one of these unlucky boys had gotten a dark lanthorn, which was a thing the country people did not understand, and with this he walked all about the orchard, and two or three closes near the house, sometimes showing the light on this side, and then his comrades calling all the old women about 'em to see it, on a sudden the light would go out, the boy closing up the lanthorn; and then he would run swiftly across the whole field, and show his light again on the other side. Now he would be up in a tree, then in the road, then upon the middle of the heath; so that the country people made no more question, but that the old lady walked with a candle in her hand, than that they saw the light of it; and in a word, it passed for an apparition as certainly as we, on the other hand, knew what knavery agitated it all.

It must be confessed that a dark lanthorn, joined with an enthusiastic head, might prevail to make such a sham take, with weak and bigoted people, and they were mighty willing to say beforehand that they were sure something walked.

When they heard the chair tumble about in the chamber, though pulled by a string, and nobody near it, no, nor in the whole house, the people who came together in the courtyard, fancied often they saw heads of people moving up and down the room where the noise was, and one said positively she saw a white headdress.

But to realize the delusion, one cried out, There's the spirit, there's the ghost, just at such a place of the window; and affirmed it stood close to the glass, and described it; another, as moon-blind as herself, says, Ay, so it does, and points peremptorily to the place, declaring that she sees it plainly; and thus they run away with it all together, that the ghost walks, and the house is haunted; and for a long time it was believed no other, when here was nothing but the mean contrivance of a few boys.[4]

A visitor in Dorking today may have great difficulty in locating any vestige of the once-haunted Marsh mansion. Even the neighboring almshouses where the credulous old women lived have been largely obliterated by modern alterations. But the open field at the southeast edge of the town is clearly identified by a signboard which reads "Cotmandene."

In the years after he had moved on from Fisher's school, Defoe must have returned sometimes to revisit his old friends in the neighborhood. About October, 1676 (if his often inexact indications of date are to be trusted), when autumn floods had overflowed the river Mole, he was one of a "young company" employed by the son of Sir Adam Brown of Beechworth Castle to recover the fish from his inundated pond. They damned up the water so that it could not return to the main stream, and then they built huts or booths, made fires, and sent for refreshments, while they waited two nights and a day until the overflow sank away in the field and left a great number of fish open to their captors. About the same time, "a certain set of young men, of the town of Darking" (Dorking) used gunpowder to blow up a wine cellar and frighten off the rakish young ladies and gentlemen who came there on Sunday nights. Defoe was always fascinated, as here, by the force of subterranean explosions;[5] but in this prank we have the first known example of his enthusiasm for the reformation of manners.

In the country homes near Dorking he came to know several Roman Catholic families, inoffensive people who were forced to scatter and hide a few years later in the wild panic of the Popish Plot. Perhaps his lifelong sympathy for the Catholics dated from boyhood acquaintanceship; the young Londoner who heard the accusations of Titus Oates did not altogether forget early friendships among the Howards and Browns and other Romanist families in Surrey.

Defoe's education would normally have ended in the boarding school at Dorking. As a Dissenter he was ineligible to attend Oxford or Cambridge, as a butcher's son he would ordinarily have been apprenticed to a trade. But a decision was made to prepare him for the Presbyterian ministry. Perhaps he mistook his religious zeal for the mysterious "call" to preach the Gospel; perhaps his father wished to dedicate his only son; even more probably the family pastor Dr. Annesley (who had great influence in the selection of candidates for the Dissenting ministry) recognized something of the boy's abilities and urged that he be trained for the pulpit.

Once higher education had been agreed on, plans were made to give Defoe the best available. He was entered in the foremost Dissenting academy in England[6]—Morton's, in Newington Green, a healthful village just north of London and close to Defoe's future home in Stoke Newington. It seems that he was in attendance there from about 1674 to 1679.

Rev. Charles Morton was a distinguished graduate of Oxford, and (like James Fisher) an Independent clergyman and a Bartholomean. But like Dr. Annesley, Morton had the advantage of possessing private means. Even a hostile writer testified that he planned to make no more from his academy than the bare cost of maintenance, "designing what he thought the glory of God more than his own private profit."[7] After he had been deprived of his parish in Cornwall, he devoted himself mostly to teaching. His large home in Newington Green soon provided classrooms and dormitories for his students. Accounts of the lax discipline given by Samuel Wesley, after he had gone over to the Church of England, deal with the period after Defoe had left, when Morton was being persecuted by the Bishop of London for alleged violation of the medieval "Stamford Oath" which required Oxford and Cambridge graduates not to give collegiate instruction elsewhere.

But, at best, there was little chance for social intercourse in a community of fifty boys and their master in a suburban village, in conflict with the bigoted rector of Stoke Newington and faraway from the great libraries and the eminent men of the universities. It is no wonder that Samuel Wesley deserted his old comrades when he breathed the heady air of Oxford, or that Samuel Parker turn against the Dissenters after he had defended their system of education. Recalling his own early exclusion from the universities, Defoe wrote bitterly:

> The disadvantages of private academies, being without public libraries, without polite conversation, without suited authority, without classes to check one another and, above all, without time given to finish the youth in the studies they apply to, are unavoidable. . . . Here and there one, a youth blessed with an extraordinary genius, strong parts, and great application, may outstrip others; and these, under all the discouragements and difficulties above, may rise to a pitch beyond the common rate: But, like David's second rate worthies, they may be great; howbeit they do not come up to the rate of the first.[8]

In later life Defoe was an alumnus of an academy which had ceased to exist, whose founder had died in exile, and many of whose promising graduates had fallen in Monmouth's Rebellion or had deserted from the Dissenters. Here, as so often elsewhere, he came to stand alone.

But for Defoe the advantages of Morton's academy were greater than its handicaps. Most good teaching was done by tutors, and Morton was incomparable as a tutor. Two famous universities and one college attempted to silence his competition. Jealousy of his success at Newington Green turned Oxford and Cambridge against him. After he had removed to America and had been denied the expected presidency of Harvard College (for fear of resentment by the English authorities), he accepted a pastorate across the river in Charlestown. Here he gave private lessons which attracted so many students that Harvard appointed him vice-president and later made him chairman of a committee to "draw up some proposals for the enlargement of the college by new buildings."[9]

It was a time of pedantry in the universities; rarely has instruction been so remote from the common interests of life. But Morton, whose work in mathematics at Wadham College had won the notice of the famous Dr. Wilkins, used his fine garden for instruction in botany, and he equipped his house with "a laboratory . . . with air pumps, thermometers, and all sorts of mathematical instruments."[10] When equipment was lacking, his ingenuity as an instructor served his turn. Fifty years later Defoe wrote:

I knew a philosopher that was excellently skilled in the science of astronomy, who told me that he had some years studied for some proper allusion to explain to his scholars the phenomenon of the sun's motion round its own axis, and could never happen upon one to his mind, till by accident he saw his maid trundling her mop; surprised with the exactness of the motion to describe the thing he wanted, he goes into his study, calls his pupils about him, and tells them that Betty, who herself knew nothing about the matter, could show them the sun revolving about itself in a more lively manner than ever he could; accordingly, placing his scholars in a due position, opposite to her left side, so that they could see the end of the mop when it whirled round upon her arm, they took it immediately; there was the broad-headed nail in the center, which was as the body of the sun, and the thrums whisking round, flinging the water round about every way, by innumerable little streams, describing exactly the rays of the sun darting light from the center to the whole system.[11]

Again and again Defoe referred to Morton's powers as a teacher. In the *Review* we have an outline of the course of study under Morton; we meet with a defense of his political theories in a tract; we find indirect praise of his instruction in applied mathematics in the scorn expressed for the inability of England to produce military engineers; we trace his methods as they were applied by Colonel Jack's tutor in Maryland; we recognize him in the gunner who undertook Captain Singleton's education in the wilds of Africa.[12] There are echoes of his teaching in *The Compleat English Gentleman*, where Defoe recounts the difficulties which Peter the Great faced when he began his reforms in Russia:

Their best surgeons knew nothing of anatomy; their best astronomers knew nothing of eclipses; they had not a skeleton in the whole empire, except what might be natural in their graves; their geographers had not a globe; their seamen not a compass (by the way, they had no ships), even their physicians had no books. Experiments were the height of their knowledge, and so we may suppose when a practitioner had killed four or five hundred he might pass for a doctor.

In the same book we are told of a young man who realized his own ignorance too late to overcome it by formal schooling. For four and a half years (about the length of time Defoe spent in Morton's academy) he followed the directions of a private tutor:

He run through a whole course of philosophy, he perfectly compassed the study of geography, the use of the maps and globes; he read all that Sir Isaac Newton, Mr. Whiston, Mr. Halley had said in English upon the nicest subjects in astronomy and the secrets of nature; he was extremely delighted with Sir Isaac's optics and all his other nice experiments, separation of colors, and other writings; for what he could not come at in English, his laborious teacher translated for him in lessons and abridged lessons, so that in a word in those four years and a half he was a mathematician, a geographer, an astronomer, a philosopher, and . . . a complete scholar; and all this without the least help from the Greek or the Latin. However, not content with all this, the last half year of his studies his diligent tutor formed a compendious method to teach him Latin, and made such progress in it, that the gentleman, my friend, began to understand it tolerably well.[13]

Morton, likewise, was always the tutor. He taught in English, he was interested in philosophy and the natural sciences, and he wrote out manuscript compendiums to be copied by his students as syllabuses for his lectures. Defoe had a collection of these manuscripts, Morton brought a complete set to America in 1686, and at least one of them passed into use in the classes at Harvard. The *Compendium Physicae* was adopted as a textbook before Commencement in 1687, introducing a new phase in the teaching of natural science at Harvard and remaining the basic text for forty years. During those years Harvard was in advance of the rest of the world in its instruction in natural sciences—because of Morton's re-examination of the teachings of Aristotle.[14]

Defoe's critical observation of nature began under Morton. Long afterward Gilbert White mistook the Cornish chough and employed boys to search barns and muddy bottoms of ponds to prove that swallows hibernate. Defoe described the chough with precision, and he observed the swallows on Suffolk roofs waiting to make their seasonal flight to Holland when their food in England failed.[15] While ex-collegians might be racking their brains for a Latin quotation, Defoe was walking the floor of the Royal Exchange or attending at the bar of the House of Commons or riding over the English and Scottish countryside.

Morton's other manuscript syllabuses have been lost, but the *Compendium Physicae* has been published by the Colonial Society of Massachusetts. This gives an insight into the instruction Defoe received. Forty years before Defoe's first account of the destruction of the Isle of St. Vincent, Morton was theorizing about the nature and effect of earthquakes. Nearly forty-five years before Defoe wrote of the whispering place in Gloucester Cathedral, Morton analyzed its acoustic properties. The supposed influence of comets on human life was dismissed by Morton long before Defoe ridiculed it. Defoe liked to clinch an argument or a strong statement with a brief passage in verse; Morton used ragged couplets to fix in memory the principles he was explaining. Dunton's account of Morton's teaching suggests Defoe's own method of enlivening his writings: "his discourses were not stale, or studied, but always new and occasional, for whatever subject was at any time started, he had still some pleasant and pat story for it."[16]

Morton lectured in English, and he required his students to write often and carefully in their own language. Aspiring young clergymen favored the affectations ridiculed by Echard in his witty tract on "The Grounds and Occasions of the Contempt of the Clergy and Religion." Those who made no attempt at cleverness suffered from training in which Latin was substituted for their native tongue. Of such men Defoe wrote: "they have no style, no diction, no beauty or cadence of expression, but are so dull, so awkward and so heavy in delivering themselves, that 'twould be a shame to hear one of them declaim in English, who, perhaps, would gain an universal applause if it were performed in the Latin tongue." Defoe's teacher Morton had set about to see that his pupils could live in the world around them and could converse with mankind:

To rectify this great mistake of the schools, he set up his little academy, wherein he taught Physics . . . with a system of Astronomy . . . he taught also Geography and the use of the maps and globes . . . he taught his pupils all the parts of academic learning, except Medicine and Surgery. He also had a class for History, ecclesiastic and civil. And all this he taught in English. He read his lectures upon every science in English, and gave his pupils draughts of the works of Khiel and Newton and others, translated; also he required all the exercises and performances . . . to be made in English.

He had a class for eloquence, and his pupils declaimed weekly in the English tongue, made orations, wrote epistles twice every week upon such subjects as he prescribed to them or upon such as they themselves chose to write upon. Sometimes they were ambassadors and agents abroad . . . and wrote accounts of their negotiations and reception in foreign courts directed to the Secretary of State and sometimes to the Sovereign himself.

Sometimes they were Ministers of State, Secretaries and Commissioners at home, and wrote orders and instructions to the ministers abroad, as by order of the King in Council and the like. Thus he taught his pupils to write a masculine and manly style, to write the most polite English, and at the same time to know how to suit their manner as well to the subject they were to write upon as to the persons they were to write to; and all equally free and plain, without foolish flourishes . . . or dull meannesses of expression. . . . In a word, his pupils came out of his hands finished orators, fitted to speak in the highest presence, to the greatest assemblies, or even in Parliament, Courts of Justice, or anywhere; and several of them came afterward to speak in all those places and capacities with great applause.[17]

Morton lacked the humor, the irony, the rhythm, the glowing phrase, the endless verve which one comes to expect in Defoe. But in clarity and simplicity of expression, in naturalness and ease of writing, he was one of Defoe's models. An eminent authority on literary history[18] has told me that he considers Defoe supreme in the art of making one read his printed page; it is easier to keep on with the book than to lay it down. Defoe learned much of that secret from the precept and example of the Rev. Charles Morton.

VI. CALLED, BUT NOT CHOSEN

. . . the pulpit is none of my office. It was my disaster first to be set apart for, and then to be set apart from, the honor of that sacred employ.

Review, VII, 341

THE YEAR 1681 was one of crisis in Defoe's private life. He was approaching his twenty-first birthday, and he had come to a time of decision. It seems that he was in communication with the French Huguenots at Charenton (if he did not actually cross the Channel to attend their famous gathering). From February 20, 1681, to some time in the autumn, he heard six sermons by the Rev. John Collins, an Independent (Congregational) clergyman educated at Harvard, the fourth Bartholomean who influenced his life. He left a manuscript record of these sermons, copied from his own shorthand notes and followed by ragged poems on intensely personal reflections called "Meditations."[1] Throughout the series Collins took his text from the one passage in the Bible which had most significance for Defoe at this time (Mark 16: 15–16):

And he said unto them, Go ye into all the world, and preach the gospel to every creature.
He that believeth and is baptised shall be saved; but he that believeth not shall be damned.

In the central Puritan tradition, the "preacher mounted the steps of his pulpit as if he were Moses ascending the mountain of Sinai." When he spoke, he was "opening the Scriptures"; what he said was "the revelation of God, confirmed in the hearts of his hearers by the interior testimony of the Holy Spirit." An Anglican might consider the Sacraments more sacred, the Homilies less subject to errors of human ignorance, the oratory of a Jeremy Taylor more beautiful. A Puritan divine spoke as "a dying man to dying men."[2]

From boyhood Defoe had been trained to look forward to such a career as a Protestant minister. But now, perhaps not long after his twenty-first birthday, in the autumn of 1681, he realized that he was not meant for that high vocation. Others might ascend Mount Sinai; he was no Moses—or at best only the Moses of Mount Pisgah, permitted to look on the promised land he was never to enter. When he came to search his own heart, he realized that he had not been "called."

In Defoe's England there were four principal groups of Protestant Dissenters. The Presbyterians tended to stress predestination and to prefer extemporaneous prayer; they practiced baptism of adults and infants alike; they rejected the authority of bishops; and (at least in theory) they sought a close-knit organization like that which became the national church of Scotland. The Independents differed from the Presbyterians primarily in giving wide discretion and power to the individual congregations. The Baptists also stressed the authority of the congregations; but they had special tenets of their own, such as the refusal to baptize infants. The Quakers desired no church organization more binding than their informal meetings, but sought to be guided by the inner light of divine revelation in their own lives. Defoe was a Presbyterian, he had been educated by Independents, and later he had some friends among the Quakers, including William Penn himself. It is not clear that he was influenced by the Baptists, unless that staunch individualist John Bunyan can be classed among the Baptists.

After Defoe had made his great renunciation, he seemed to feel that he owed a debt to the Presbyterians who had selected him and to the Independents who had educated him for the ministry. He suffered much on their account—from the hostility of their opponents and from the suspicion or ingratitude of many of themselves. But he continued throughout his life to serve them whenever he could, especially in representing their interests to the public, to the government of the day, and at times to the sovereign.

Although he remained a layman, it is possible that he preached occasionally, years after he had abandoned the hope of being ordained. Tradition names him as organizer of the Dissenting congregation at Tooting, in Surrey.[3] Dr. Edmund Calamy, who frequently attended the meeting with his grandfather Gearing, mentioned the Rev. Joshua Oldfield as the minister in charge, but he had nothing to say of Defoe as a lay preacher. However, this silence is not conclusive evidence; Calamy would be one of the last to say anything to Defoe's advantage. When Defoe was in hiding in 1703, a hostile pamphleteer urged the government to track him down by his scriptural language: "Follow him by the Scent of his Scraps of Scripture, and you'll find him at *Salter's*, or *Pinner's-Hall*, there needs no farther Pursuit, and whether you ask for Mr. *Fo* the Hosier, or Mr. *Fo* the Preacher; 'tis all one, there is no occasion to spend more time in search after him. There's your Man, I mean, there was your Man, before the Queen's Messengers made him *Lope* with his Divinity."[4]

This bitterness against the preaching of a layman recalls the contempt which the Rev. Samuel Wesley (a former Dissenter who had taken holy orders in the Church of England) expressed for all who listened to John Bunyan: "I remember several of us, if not all our pupils, went to hear Friend Bunyan, when he preached at Newington-Green. I'm pretty confident Mr. Morton himself heard him, for I'm sure he commended him; and 'tis notorious that nothing's more common among those Dissenters . . . than to hear persons, and that daily, who have no form of ordination."[5] People thronged to hear Bunyan while many ordained clergymen addressed empty pews. Later, when Wesley's son John spoke in a direct manner that drew thousands, the old family church at Epworth was locked against him (although he was ordained by the Church of England), and he preached in the churchyard standing on his father's grave.

Again, Bunyan was condemned as illiterate. The same charge was raised (with vastly less justification) almost endlessly against Defoe. Somehow it hurt him more than any other taunt, although he realized that integrity is more important than formal learning: "really, Gentlemen, a little reading, a little learning, will serve either to speak the truth, or to understand it." He loved Horace; but it was in self-defense that he boasted of "the right edition," "the edition printed at Leyden." He had a working knowledge of Latin, possibly a very slight acquaintance with Greek; but he felt the scorn of contemporaries who knew little else but the classical languages.[6] In *The Compleat English Gentleman* he cried out, "Will nothing make a man a scholar but Latin and Greek?" He told of the real learning of an acquaintance (probably himself, or an idealization of himself):

1. He speaks French as fluent as the English. He speaks Spanish and Italian and something of the Slavonian, for he has conversed very much among the Poles and Muscovites, and he has something of the Portuguese; and yet he is NO SCHOLAR.

2. He is as good a proficient in Experimental Philosophy as most private gentlemen, and has a nice collection of rarities; yet he is NO SCHOLAR.

3. He is a master in Geography, has the situation of the world at his fingers' ends. You can not name any country in the known part of Europe

but he can give you extempore an account of its situation, latitude, rivers, chief towns, its commerce, and, nay, something of its history and of its political interests: yet he is NO SCHOLAR.

4. He is as well skill'd in all astronomical knowledge, the motions and revolutions of the heavenly bodies as most masters in that science, that ever I have met with . . . but he is NO SCHOLAR.

5. He is a master of History, and indeed, I may say he is an universal historian, especially in all the histories that are written or translated into the English tongue, and those that are not, he has read them in French or Italian; but he is NO SCHOLAR.

6. For his own country he is a walking map; he has traveled through the whole island, and through most parts of it several times over; he has made some of the most critical remarks of several parts of it, so that he could not be charged, when he went abroad, to have known most of other countries and nothing of his own as is the just scandal of most English travelers; and yet this man is NO SCHOLAR. . . . A man may be a scholar in their sense and be good for nothing, be a mere pedant, a Greek and Latin monger. I think our mere scholars are a kind of mechanics in the schools, for they deal in words and syllables as haberdashers deal in small ware. . . . They are mere pedagogues; they seem to be formed in a school on purpose to die in a school.[7]

Probably Defoe heard Bunyan preach; there is no doubt of Bunyan's literary influence. Benjamin Franklin remarked that "Honest John" was the first who mixed "narration and dialogue, a method of writing very engaging to the reader, who in the most interesting parts finds himself, as it were, admitted into the company and present at the conversation." Franklin added that "Defoe has imitated him successfully in his *Robinson Crusoe*, his *Moll Flanders*, and other pieces." Defoe himself coupled *The Pilgrim's Progress* with a work of his own, *The Family Instructor*, and he cited Bunyan's example in defense of his own allegorical use of fiction.[8]

The homeliness and concreteness of Defoe's prose, his preference for idiomatic usage and for the rhythms of his native speech, his love of the Anglo-Saxon word, the ease with which he employed biblical language in a tract or in a fictional narrative, his blending of moral and religious reflections with realistic details of life, his keen awareness of the local background and of the common humanity of his characters—these came from many sources, but Bunyan was one of the most important. To Bunyan's detractors, *The Pilgrim's Progress* and *Robinson Crusoe* were equally worthy of contempt. But when Dr. Johnson named the three books "ever written by mere men" which anyone would wish to have longer, he mentioned these two among them; and when Robert Louis Stevenson recalled the four supreme moments in imaginative literature,[9] his only modern examples were drawn from from *The Pilgrim's Progress* and *Robinson Crusoe*.

In the cut and thrust of pamphleteering for readers who knew and revered the Bible, Defoe's skill in scriptural allusion must have proved remarkably effective. His method appears most clearly on the title pages of many of his books and tracts, where the central issue is often presented at first glance with great clarity, often with passion, and not infrequently with wit. When the Jacobites professed to read a prophetic warning in the sky after the execution of the rebel lords, he quoted from Matthew: "O! Ye Hypocrites, ye can discern the Face of the Skie, but can you not discern the Signs of the Times?" *Due Preparations for the Plague* was introduced by a passage from the Psalms: "There shall no Evil befall thee, neither shall the Plague come nigh thy Dwelling." The title page of his account of the Great Storm has a sentence from Nahum: "The Lord hath his way in the Whirlwind, and in the Storm, and the Clouds are the dust of his Feet." The more compliant Dissenters who practiced Occasional Conformity were countered with a quotation from the First Book of Kings: "If the Lord be God, follow him: But if Baal, then follow him." The factious High Churchmen were rebuked from First Corinthians: "Brethren, be not Children in Understanding: Howbeit in Malice be ye Children, but in Understanding be Men." And when some of the landed Tories were threatening to avenge themselves on the mercantile Whigs by buying and selling only among themselves, Defoe ridiculed their proposal in his *Review* by citing a passage from Revelation: "that no man might buy or sell, save he that had the mark, or the name of the beast."

The influence of Puritan pulpit oratory on Defoe's style is less obvious. A modern reader forgets that there must have been an emotional appeal in sermons which held an audience motionless on the uncushioned benches while the sands ran through the hourglass on the pulpit—in sermons delivered to men who stood in arms on a field of battle, or to men, women, and children who crouched in cellar or barn or on fog-shrouded hillside while the informers sought their place of hiding. The Rev. John Jenings, Master of Arts, might print his lecture after his parishioners had twice failed to come out to hear it.[10] But the Bartholomeans had to hold the attention of their audiences.

It was for this reason that Defoe objected to the exclusive study of

Hebrew, Greek, and Latin in the education of ministers: "the Gospel, which is the end of our study, is done in English, and it seems absurd to the last degree that all the time should be spent in the languages which it is to be fetched from, and none in the language it is to be delivered in." In the early eighteenth century he looked back from the foppish young city ministers to recall the fervor of their predecessors:

> If a true primitive Gospel preacher happens, from some remote corner, to rise among us, as one from the dead, and puts us in mind of our ancestors, the excellency is so intrinsic and the power so irresistible . . . the people are under a surprise; they are affected with it as a kind of miracle, and they inquire as men amazed; just as the Jews, in another case: is not this such and such a man? Does he not come out of Devonshire, or Wales, or Lancashire, or Scotland? Whence had this man these gifts?[11]

Many years later John Wesley was accused by a sophisticated gentleman of acting "ugly enthusiasm." But Benjamin Franklin was moved beyond his own control by the passion of Whitefield. We catch something of the same fervor in the bolder passages of Collins's sermons which Defoe transcribed in his youth. Later in life, the rhythm and fire of the pulpit speaker recurred many times in Defoe's pamphlets. In his masterpiece of irony, *The Shortest Way with the Dissenters*, where this rhythm and fire lead up to the blasphemous prayer of bigoted hatred, the effect was as appalling to the Dissenters as it was said to be delightful to the most frantic of their oppressors.

VII. MARRIAGE

The reader is desired to prepare not to be too much surprised at an unusual digression in our next.

Review, II, 71

I N T H E A U T U M N of 1681 Defoe had been an obscure young man of barely twenty-one engaged in making his painful decision against entering the Presbyterian ministry. Two years later he was already a successful young merchant, with his own place of business in a high-rent district in the heart of London. More important for his future career, he had just published his first political pamphlet. Most important of all, he was about to take a wife.

The winter of 1683–84 was long remembered as the coldest anyone had ever seen in England. A contemporary of Defoe left his boyhood recollections of the season:

December:—There was a very hard and severe frost, that lasted from the beginning of that month to the 5th of February following. During this time the roads in all parts of England were as good and firm as they used to be at midsummer, and the river of Thames was so frozen over, and the ice so firm and strong, that there were several hundreds of booths and shops upon it. Coaches plied as freely from the Temple-stairs to Westminster, as if they had gone upon the land. There were also conveniences provided for several diversions, such as bull-baiting, fox-hunting, billiards, and nine-pins, &c. Even an ox was roasted whole upon the river, over against Whitehall.[1]

Defoe must have spent some of the last days of his courtship on the frozen river. He was not one to miss such sport; and Mary Tuffley was a vigorous young woman who lived forty-nine years thereafter with a spirit worthy of her husband. Theirs was certainly a love match—none the less so because Mary was a considerable heiress and Daniel was one of the most promising young merchants in London. The frustrated ministerial student of a few years before had risen rapidly—partly through his own efforts, no doubt, and perhaps partly through the influence of wealthy relatives on his mother's side.

In the application for their license, which was granted by the vicar-general of the Archbishop of Canterbury on December 28, his age was given as "about 24" and hers as "about 20." Such marriage allegations usually gave only the approximate ages; Defoe was then twenty-three years old and Mary was probably somewhat younger. The application was signed by Charles Lodwick, of whom we know little except that he was a London merchant of Flemish extraction, related to a prominent Presbyterian minister and to the Mrs. Bargrave to whom the apparition of Mrs. Veal was later said to have appeared.

Four days afterward, on Tuesday morning, January 1, 1684, Mary became Defoe's wife at the old church of St. Botolph, Aldgate. The wedding was performed according to the ritual of the Church of England by Richard Hollingsworth (soon after Dr.), curate to the incumbent, brought up in Lincolnshire as a Presbyterian but now an ardent Anglican—one who would soon be hotly engaged as a pamphleteer in his efforts to glorify the memory of Charles I.[2]

The fact that the wedding was held in so large a church by the High Church curate of the parish indicates that it was (for young Dissenters) an unusually elaborate and ceremonial affair. We have no indication of Mary's appearance or of her taste in dress—except in the fact that Defoe, who was very critical in such matters, admired her greatly. She was an intelligent young woman of means, and this was no time for parsimony. Defoe himself was always fond of good clothes, and his rivals sometimes sought to ridicule him as a dandy. We know that he was sensitive about the large mole at the left side of his mouth, but the sharp lines of his lips must still have indicated a humorous rather than a sarcastic temper. A dashing young man, of a brown complexion and already sunburned by his travels, with a frank and open face and with keen gray eyes and an aquiline nose, rather slight and spare of build but now grown unusually athletic in frame, he must have been a handsome bridegroom. His gift for making an immediate and favorable impression, so marked throughout his life, was no doubt evident even then.

We can guess at the relatives most likely to have been present. Mary's father (said to have been a wine-cooper, surely a substantial business man to have given Mary a dowry of £3,700) was still living. So was Mary's mother, who survived her husband. Aunt Sarah Tuffley might have been present, besides Mary's three brothers—Giles,

Charles (who died as an impoverished sailor), and Samuel (who became a prosperous merchant, and who remained a staunch friend of Defoe). James Foe was almost certainly at his son's wedding—a vigorous widower of fifty-three who had outlived his sister and his two brothers—one of them the saddler Henry Foe who had lived in this same parish during the plague year. Defoe's older sister, Mary, had been married to the shipwright Francis Barham (Bartham) for nearly five years; perhaps their son Francis was old enough to attend the wedding of his Uncle Daniel. Probably Robert Davis had already married the younger sister, Elizabeth, and his close friendship with Defoe had begun. Some of the relatives of Defoe's mother were likely to have been present, especially if she had belonged to the Marsh connection with its branches in and near London.

It is a relief to come out from these broken shadows, cast by wills and licenses and church registers, by contemporary pamphlets and fragments of correspondence, into the clear light of Defoe's observations. As he and his young bride left the old church of St. Botolph which had been spared by the Great Fire which had raged around it, they walked through the chancel to the steps leading down to the level floor of the nave. On they went, below the lofts with which the church had been "pestered," as a local annalist quaintly said, to accommodate the parishioners who had "mightily increased." They passed out under the rectangular tower surmounted by four spires and a lantern, through the door and under a dial which extended over the street.[3] Perhaps they stood for a moment in the cold winter light.

Across Whitechapel Street, facing the church doorway where they stood, was the northern end of the street called the Minories, along which the "dead carts" of the Plague Year had come; and at the right-hand corner across from the church had stood Pye-Tavern, where the rioters had laughed at the victims of the plague, until they themselves were "every one carried into the great pit."[4] Around the side and back of the church itself ran the mark which still showed where the great pit had been, in which 1,114 bodies had been thrown until it was so full that it had to be covered over. For when the plague had arrived thus far eastward, as Defoe later wrote in his *Journal of the Plague Year*, "there was no parish in or about London where it raged with such violence as in the two parishes of Aldgate and Whitechapel."[5]

Defoe the father of the English novel was dogging the footsteps of the young bridegroom; but Defoe the political pamphleteer was already treading on his heels. Daniel had recently published the first of his hundreds of tracts; and by attacking many of his fellow Whigs for favoring the Turks against the Roman Catholic defenders of Vienna, he had ranged himself (as so often later) against the majority.[6]

For the young couple there would be no wedding trip. Instead, there would be a ride in a hackney coach half a mile to the westward, where they would start their housekeeping in Freeman's Yard, Cornhill, in rooms above the shop and warehouse (such as those which so often served the London merchant for a home). During their forty-seven years of married life, it is not known that Mary was ever twenty miles beyond the confines of the old walled city. By the early 1690's they enjoyed a country home near Kingsland (although that was apparently the property of her widowed mother). About 1700 they lived in the neighborhood of Defoe's brick and tile works, a score of miles to the eastward on the Thames, near Tilbury in Essex. About 1704 or 1705 Defoe was said to be making his home with Mary's stepfather at Newington Green. At different times (as in 1701 and 1707) they were living in Hackney,[7] perhaps with her brother Samuel Tuffley. Contemporary references to Defoe's residence in Hackney, Kingsland, Stoke Newington, and Newington Green are often baffling. Hackney was a far-flung suburban region which included twelve villages east and north of London, and in it Kingsland lay between the older part of Hackney and the Newingtons. For the last twenty-two years of their life together, Daniel and Mary were in Stoke Newington, occupying two different houses successively.

Defoe shared all these residences with his wife, but he had many other quarters for his varied undertakings. He was on the Continent at times, at least once for a lengthy stay. He was often in Scotland, and he took steps toward moving his family to Edinburgh for permanent residence. He toured England repeatedly, and he was in Halifax and Bury St. Edmunds and Canterbury long enough to give rise to local legends. He owned a house in Westminster (which he rented out, but perhaps never occupied). He probably lived in or near Kensington Palace and Hampton Court at times under William III, and he applied (unsuccessfully) for a private apartment in Whitehall during the reign of Queen Anne. At least seven times he was confined in Newgate, the Queen's Bench Prison, some debtors' prison, or the house of a Queen's messenger—once for a continuous period of four months. In 1706 he was meeting his creditors in Robert Davis' chamber in the Temple. He had secret lodgings in the Old Bailey and near

Greenwich in Kent.[8] When he was arrested in May, 1703, he was concealed at the home of a French weaver in Spittlefields.[9] He was in lodgings in Ropemaker's Alley, Cripplegate, when he died.

In spite of his financial vicissitudes, Defoe managed to bring up his children. Of the six who lived into adult life, all were well placed in the world except Benjamin (who made his own path rougher by breaking with the family as a young man and by attacking his father's political views in print). Defoe wrote near the end of 1714, after two daughters, Mary and Martha, had died in infancy or childhood: "I have six children; I have educated them as well as my circumstances will permit, and so as I hope shall recommend them to better usage than their father meets with in this world." In 1726 he reminded his readers of the importance to the nation as a whole of rearing children: "The father of three children in Rome, of four in the rest of Italy, and five in any of the more remote colonies, was entitled to more privileges, benefits, and liberties than a member of the House of Commons with us; and by those means . . . [Greece and Rome] preserved themselves entire for many generations, notwithstanding the vast numbers which war and luxury must have drafted away from them."[10]

His satiric poem *Advice to the Ladies* was thought to discourage marriage, so that he was forced to make a defense in which he blamed the piratical publishers for issuing his works without authorization; but this was no denial that he had written the poem. However, as he had declared in the Preface, he was not attacking marriage, but only the "wits and beaus, the plagues of the nation," men unworthy to be husbands. In other writings he declared that a husband had no right to object to his wife's behavior before her marriage to him; that only a cruel husband would refuse to forgive a repentant wife; and that good husbands got the wives they deserved. According to the imaginary Club which answered the questions submitted to his *Review:* "They are not fit either for husbands or wives who do not resolve beforehand to disband all humors and ill tempers, and sacrifice every inclination to their family peace. . . . The special interest of all such who attempt matrimony is to study each other's humors, and to endeavor so to match their tempers, that the marriage may unite their souls as well as bodies." Marriage seemed to him too important a relationship for trifling, "all that we call happiness in this life depending upon it."[11]

Mary was a good wife, and Defoe meant to be a good husband. In spite of his almost overpowering love of travel and adventure, he managed to stay quietly at home until something which seemed to him urgent necessity set him on the road again. Robinson Crusoe remained in Bedfordshire while his wife lived; it was only her death which started him off around the globe. Likewise, Defoe "corrected his wandering fancy," and he was becoming a snug citizen of Tilbury (except for voyages up the river to advise King William or to run his errands over England and Scotland) when imprisonment and renewed bankruptcy and the public shame of the pillory drove him "upon a deep relapse of the wandering disposition."[12] and set him adrift again as a citizen of the world.

Most authors of Defoe's time did not rank high as family men—whether we think of the cautious and loveless marriage of Addison, of the gross infidelities of Steele, or of the bachelors Congreve and Prior (with their mistresses) and Swift (with his one hastily withdrawn proposal of marriage, and his long and secret friendships so jealously guarded). Pope without illness or physical deformity might have been more like Defoe.

For nearly fifty years Daniel and Mary lived together in a censorious age, without public scandal and (as far as we can learn now) with no private recrimination. Perhaps she felt badly about the sinking of her dowry and the losses incurred by her mother in supporting one of Daniel's investments. Possibly she was uneasy about a proposed brick and tile factory on their daughter Hannah's estate. According to a fantastic misinterpretation of one of his anecdotes, Daniel went for more than twenty-eight years without speaking to her. This supposition ignored not only the obvious facts of his career but even his frequently expressed contempt for matrimonial differences: "I have often thought, 'tis the foolishest thing in the world for a man and his wife to quarrel, especially about trifles—when they know they must come together at night."[13]

Not only did Mary intercede with the Earl of Nottingham, correspond with Defoe when he was in Scotland, and handle his affairs with Harley in his absence; her brother Samuel Tuffley seems to have taken Defoe's family into his own home in Hackney during some of their financial difficulties. In September, 1711, when Defoe was in high favor as the official pamphleteer of the Earl of Oxford's Ministry, Tuffley fought a duel with a Jacobite pewterer who abused

Defoe in his presence—a bully known as Captain Silk, a muster-master in the London trained bands. Three years later, in October, 1714, when the Oxford Ministery had fallen from power and Defoe's own future seemed dark, Tuffley had a will drawn up which was carefully stated so as to provide for both his sister and her husband to the best of his ability. He bequeathed his entire estate to his "dear and only Sister Mary Defoe" with the explicit stipulation that any of her children were to be disinherited who failed to show respect for father and mother alike. In the same will, Tuffley took steps to prevent Defoe's real or pretended creditors from seizing Mary's inheritance; and he did this in words which expressed his own high personal regard for Defoe.[14]

Perhaps Mary knew Defoe from childhood, in the days of religious persecution when she lived in his Uncle Henry's parish in London. She was his wife when he underwent nearly every one of his dangers and hardships. Possibly she was not at his bedside when he died; but death came suddenly, when he was in hiding from persecution, and when a visit from her would have pointed the way to his arrest for alleged debt.

The letters they are known to have written to each other have long been lost, not being preserved (like nearly all of Defoe's letters which have survived) in public archives or in private libraries. But we have proof that he spoke of her with deep admiration and respect. He knew that money could be trusted in her hands with perfect security, and he declared: "my wife, who is my faithful steward, will not diminish it one penny." It was of her that he wrote to Harley in 1704: "a virtuous and excellent mother to seven beautiful and hopeful children, a woman whose fortunes I have ruined, with whom I had £3700, and yet who in the worst of my afflictions when my Lord N[ottingham] first insulted her, then tempted her, scorned so much as to move me to comply with him, and rather encouraged me to oppose him."[15] Doubt has been expressed whether Nottingham was the sort of man who would have "tempted" Mrs. Defoe; but the passage has no such equivocal meaning. Nottingham, the typical bigot, tried to persuade Mrs. Defoe to influence her husband to betray the Whig leaders. Failing in that, he was willing to see Defoe in the pillory and Mrs. Defoe and their seven children in danger of starvation.

In Defoe's reference to her, the key word is not "tempted" but "scorned." She had the two qualities which he held in highest regard—

moral and physical courage. She was the wife for a man who was to defy his persecutors as he stood in the pillory. His love for her and for their home enters into his constant emphasis on affection in family life: "How little is regarded of that one essential and absolutely necessary part of the composition, called love, without which the matrimonial estate is, I think, hardly lawful, I am sure it is not rational, and, I think, can never be happy."[16]

VIII. "KING MONMOUTH"

...the cause...I never doubted of, and freely ventured for.

The Succession to the Crown of England, Considered (1701), p. 32

DEFOE HAD MARRIED on January 1, 1684. In June of the next year London was overawed by soldiers. James II had succeeded his more popular brother Charles II less than four months before, and now he learned that his nephew the Duke of Monmouth had landed in the west to lay claim to the throne. Some of the rebels believed that Monmouth was the legitimate (although unacknowledged) son of Charles. Others regarded him as a bastard, but a useful pawn in their own game. To Defoe, Monmouth (whether a legitimate prince or not) was the nation's hope for ending the reign of a tyrant.

Soldiers were moving everywhere to prevent a successful rising for the once idolized Monmouth. Many Whig gentlemen in the country were imprisoned on suspicion alone. Sir Edward Harley, the father of Defoe's future patron, was stripped of the hunting implements he loved—two fowling pieces and a javelin.[1] But the young merchant Defoe was not the man to be kept out of action by a show of military force. He said goodbye to his wife in Freeman's Yard and rode westward through the by-lanes which led to Somerset, avoiding the pickets who guarded the main roads.

The army that Defoe joined had something of the appearance of a Crusade. Its banner of deep green bore Monmouth's motto in letters of gold: "Fear nothing but God." But like the armies of most crusades, this one was badly organized and badly led. Monmouth made no real provision for enlisting Englishmen in his service, and he soon abandoned the 1,500 useless breastplates he had bought in Holland with money which might have purchased muskets.

In the judgment of Lord Wolseley, the leading military expert who has written on the campaign, "Had William given him arms and accoutrements for, say, 20,000 men, the rebellion might have had a very different ending." But William was too much concerned with his own future prospects as successor to the English throne to furnish aid to the expedition of a rival claimant. Monmouth boasted that he could equip thirty thousand men;[2] but his artillery consisted of four small pieces, and many of his followers had no arms but scythe blades affixed to long poles. His only first-rate soldier shot a fellow rebel in a personal quarrel, and he had to be spirited away on shipboard. Monmouth's only nobleman, Lord Grey, who commanded all mounted troops, was certainly a coward and perhaps a traitor, losing the initial success at Bridport and throwing away the final chance for victory at Sedgemoor.

Monmouth had been a daring junior officer with disciplined troops, and Defoe had admired him in several of his gorgeous appearances at races.[3] But this was a dispirited Monmouth, with no confidence in his undrilled volunteers, no patriotic feeling for their cause, no share in their religious enthusiasm. His first impulse was to get back to his mistress in Amsterdam; just before his last battle he planned to desert his foot soldiers and ride off to try his chances in the north. The handsome rake made a sorry figure as the leader of a crusade.

Even under such leadership the rebels won some early advantages. King James feared that his militiamen might join Monmouth's army, and he distrusted his native Protestant officers. He soon replaced Lord Churchill (later the great Duke of Marlborough) as chief in command with his own French favorite, the Earl of Feversham. Defoe shared in the victory at Phillips-Norton (which he remembered long afterward by the name of the better-known Chipping-Norton, a mistake one might easily make if he had been there with a horse pistol instead of a guidebook). Two thousand desertions followed Monmouth's refusal to push his advantage, which Defoe thought might have led to a complete victory.[4]

Defoe lingered nine days longer, in the wearisome and endless rain, to share in the rout at Sedgemoor. He describes the battle twice; but his vivid details are borrowed from other writers, for he was in the mounted troops, swept off the field at the first encounter by Lord Grey's panic flight. At half-past three in the morning, small parties of Monmouth's horse were scattering in all directions.[5]

The victorious royal cavalry searched the roads and the countryside, shooting or hanging fugitives and bystanders or dragging them off to overcrowded prisons to await the semblance of a trial under the notorious Lord Jeffreys. Executions might soon have run into the thousands but for one restraining fact: money could be made by selling rebels (or even friends or relatives of rebels) to the West Indian plantations as slaves, so that well-dressed ladies of the court were soon demanding their share of the English farm boys who were to be offered for sale. From those few who had wealth, even more money could be made by holding them for ransom or securing the forfeiture of their estates. Active rebels were gladly pardoned—if they could be used as witnesses against an inoffensive old man who could pay £15,000 for his life, or against a gentle old lady who had only given shelter to a rebel but who had an estate to be confiscated for the Earl of Feversham.

When Mr. Muddiman remarked that the long-overlooked jail records "were first printed in 1716 as 'An Account of the Proceedings against the Rebels,'" he was unaware that this *Account* was compiled by Daniel Defoe and that it was meant to justify the severity of George I to the Jacobite rebels by showing how much more severe James II had been in his treatment of the Whigs. When Muddiman complained of the conclusions drawn by the author of the *Account*, he was only saying that the man who supplied his facts did not support his preconceived opinions.[6]

Most impartial writers were cowed into silence; but we have one contemporary report from a man always well informed on current events and rarely accused of emotional overstatement. On October 10 Robert Harley wrote to his father: "Lord Jeffreys is not yet made Earl of Flint. Three hundred and fifty are already executed in the west, above eight hundred condemned for the plantations, not one pardoned."[7]

Defoe escaped pursuit, although three of his classmates from Morton's academy became "Western Martyrs." Perhaps he found temporary refuge with a relative who kept a free school at the nearby village of Martock.[8] Certainly he knew the county better than most Londoners, he excelled at disguising himself and mingling in a hostile crowd, and he was a fine horseman. Most of all, he was not known as one of the "Western Men," who had appeared openly in the early stages of the rebellion and who were marked out for slaughter. If he could get back to London, no questions would be asked.

Why had a merchant not quite twenty-five years old left his young wife to follow an adventurer in battle more than a hundred miles away? The most recent investigator of the original documents decided that Monmouth was Charles's legitimate son, born to Charles's wife Lucy Walter before Charles solemnized a more public marriage with the Infanta of Portugal, and that only the execution of Monmouth's friends and his ill-success in battle silenced his claim to the throne.

If true, this would have been a secondary consideration with Defoe. As a student of history, he knew that there was no such thing as an unbroken royal line. As a lover of freedom, he considered the public welfare more important than the claim of any prince:

> Perish those poets, and be damn'd the song
> Which with this nonsense charm'd the world so long,
> That he who does no right can do no wrong.

If James had ruled justly, Defoe held that not even a legitimate son of Charles could have put in a valid claim *after his coronation*. Monmouth had "published a declaration not so much founded on his right by birth as upon the maladministration of King James." If Monmouth's invasion had succeeded, it would have served to overthrow the tyrant, and hence to the English public it would have seemed as justifiable a revolution as the glorious one of William three years later.[9]

Long afterward, Defoe declared that only the lack of five thousand regular troops kept Monmouth from beating James out of his kingdom, and he spoke contemptuously of the professed friends who had failed him: "I remember how boldly abundance of men talked for the Duke of Monmouth, when he first landed; but if half of them had as boldly joined him sword in hand, he had never been routed at Kingssedg-moor." He condemned James for refusing a parliamentary inquiry into the legitimacy of his son, allegedly brought into the royal bed in a warming pan. He contrasted this with Monmouth's declaration leaving his own birth to be determined by Parliament.[10]

Defoe was never exiled. But like many other active opponents of James, he may have found it safer to go abroad after the collapse of Monmouth's Rebellion. Between 1685 and 1688 he seems to have spent considerable time on the Continent as merchant and traveler. Perhaps he was back in England in 1686 when he "had the honor to see a calculation made to the Privy Council" regarding the balance of trade with France. About 1687 he published a tract to protest against addresses of thanks to James for "his illegal liberty of conscience, founded upon the dispensing power." If the King could dispense with one law, he could dispense with all laws. Late in the summer of 1688

Defoe issued his third political tract, ridiculing James's attempt to win the Dissenters' support for abolishing the Test Act.

In the open fields below Southwark, in the autumn of 1688, he saw James reviewing his cavalrymen (some of whom had ridden over Grey's mounted troops at Sedgemoor) in his preparations for resisting the expected invasion by William of Orange.[11] Before the end of the year James was an exile in France, and William had been welcomed in London as a deliverer.

Soon after the death of Princess Anne's only surviving son, Defoe wrote the most daring of all his tracts, *The Succession to the Crown of England, Considered* (1701). In this he argued that the Constitution of England stands upon the right of people to make and declare kings and successions; that "some people have affirmed" that the marriage contract between Charles II and Monmouth's mother would have been produced in Parliament if the witnesses had not perished in the general destruction of Monmouth's party in the last years of Charles; and that although Monmouth had submitted his legitimacy to the examination of a free Parliament, no such examination had been made. Monmouth had died to assert English liberties; the English people enjoyed those liberties, and they should do justice to Monmouth's son by examining the title of his father. The Union with Scotland would be preserved by choosing a prince so acceptable to the Scottish people as the Earl of Dalkeith, oldest surviving son of Monmouth and his wife, the Duchess of Buccleuch. James's pretended son would then "have no more title to the Crown than the Lord Mayor of Dublin."[12]

Princess Anne was still mentioned as heir apparent, but it must have been obvious that a parliamentary recognition of Dalkeith as the legitimate grandson of Charles II would displace her from the direct line of succession. There was a frank recognition of the claim of the Princess Sophia and her son, the Elector of Hanover—followed by a long discussion of the disadvantages any foreigner would have as ruler of England. Dalkeith—if accepted by Parliament—would be chosen "to succeed to his present Majesty, both at the head of the English armies, as well as at the helm of English councils." This incredibly daring tract was no random shot by an obscure journalist; it must have had the approval of men high in authority.

In the late summer and fall of 1701, rumors were in the air about an attempt to change the succession. According to some of the Tories, Somers, Charles Montagu (soon elevated to Baron and later Earl of

Halifax), and perhaps other Whigs favored a commonwealth, or at least a further limitation on the power of the crown. On the other hand, the Tory leader (the Earl of Rochester) was uncle to Princess Anne and father-in-law to Dalkeith. Why had that mercenary and ambitious nobleman married his second daughter to an impoverished young man of dubious ancestry in 1693, when William regarded Dalkeith with jealous eyes after his fine record in the campaign in Flanders in the previous year? What did Rochester seek for his own family after December 12, 1700, when he was Lord Lieutenant of Ireland and head of the Ministry and of the Church party? If Princess Anne succeeded to the throne, he would be one of the uncles of the queen; if Dalkeith succeeded, his daughter would be queen.

A bitter reply to Defoe appeared almost immediately, in which the author sought to ridicule Dalkeith's claim but seemed deeply concerned about Rochester's attitude. This Tory pamphleteer appeared to be distrustful of the motives of his own party leader.[13]

To some bold politicians Defoe's proposal offered solutions to the most pressing needs of the moment. The unpopular tie with Hanover would be dissolved; the gout-crippled and now childless Princess Anne would be set aside (with her advisers, the distrusted Marlboroughs); a handsome young man of military experience against France would be in line for the throne. Once recognized as the legitimate heir, Rochester's son-in-law might win over the Church party and the Legitimist wing of the Tories who had scruples about rejecting the exiled king. As Monmouth's son he would inherit much of the legendary affection of Whigs and Dissenters in the western counties. As heir to the Duchess of Buccleuch (even though her vast estate was in confusion through the mismanagement and the disaster of Monmouth) he could wield great influence in Scotland. To the rapidly aging William, whose heart was entirely set on organizing military resistance to France before he died, Dalkeith *might* have seemed attractive in 1701 for the very reasons which had aroused his distrust in 1693.

But the recognition of Monmouth's birth as legitimate required a favorable Parliament, and the new Parliament was not favorable. In the preceding autumn and early winter Robert Harley (now acting with the Tories) had carried on a furious correspondence, often unintelligible through the use of ciphers, but at least partly concerned with the disputed succession. The new Tory Parliament was more interested in attacking William's Second Partition Treaty and in impeaching the Whig lords than in doing justice to Monmouth's son. The Act of Settlement finally adopted (by which Anne was to succeed William, and to be followed by the Hanoverians) was stated in such a fashion that William gave the royal assent on June 12 only because he had no choice.

But William's real choice had already been made. Perhaps it had been made as early as 1698, when he appointed Marlborough governor of the young Duke of Gloucester, the last surviving child of the Princess Anne and at that time second in succession to the throne. On May 31, 1701, William named Marlborough commander-in-chief of the English forces destined for the Netherlands; on June 28 he named him ambassador extraordinary to the United Provinces; on July 1 William and Marlborough sailed together on the royal yacht. The Earl of Dalkeith died four years later—but any possible hope of making him king of England had passed away in the Tory Parliament of 1701.

Defoe made no further claim for Monmouth's family. In a confidential paper addressed to Harley in 1704 he remarked that Monmouth "really had not a great deal of personal merit." In *The Consolidator* (1705) he alluded to him as a natural son of the former king. But in the concluding book of *Jure Divino*, perhaps written as early as 1703 although not published until 1706, in listing the young noblemen who promised to continue the patriotic services of their fathers, he recalled Monmouth's heir, James Scot, the now almost forgotten Earl of Dalkeith:

And Scot his Monmouth's gallantry succeed.[14]

Here the key word is *gallantry;* Defoe was nearly as much interested in warfare as in politics. Was this interest due to his brief soldiering under Monmouth, or did he ride with Monmouth because he was already a student of warfare?

He was in the troop of horse led by the future Earl of Peterborough which escorted William to the Guildhall banquet in 1689. A few years later his hopes for a regiment of Dissenters were set aside by the failure of the government to remove the restriction on their service to the nation. In January, 1703, while he was hiding to avoid prosecution for *The Shortest Way with the Dissenters*, he wrote to the Secretary of State to say that if the Queen ordered him to serve a year or more at his own expense, he would surrender himself as a volunteer to any colonel of horse at the head of her armies in Flanders. He added that if the Queen would grant him a total remission of his offense, he would raise a troop of horse (sixty to one hundred men) at his own charge and would serve her at their head as long as he lived. A special student of military history has suggested that it is perhaps unfortunate that this offer was not accepted.[15] Posterity would have lost *Robinson Crusoe*, but the wars of Marlborough would have been recorded by the man who ought to have told them.

Few subjects interested Defoe so persistently as military affairs. His two favorite heroes, Gustavus Adolphus and William III, were both soldiers, and he knew their campaigns intimately. He argued the necessity of military training and experience for soldiers, and he outlined a plan for "A Royal Academy for Military Exercises." He wished that national sports could be changed to provide better material for the army. He wrote a tract defending soldiers against the contempt of civilians.[16] Robinson Crusoe stops in his travels to think of the ease with which European soldiers could overrun the armies of the Chinese; Defoe wrote few passages with more zest than his account of Crusoe's fortifications. In *Memoirs of the Church of Scotland* he forgets religious history long enough to attribute the Covananters' defeat at Dunbar to their folly in assuming the offensive. He speculates at length on the probable conquest of Scotland in 1708 if the French fleet had been lucky enough to overshoot Leith. In the *Tour* he is tempted to linger at any battlefield to discuss the tactics employed there, as when he blames the Duke of Argyll for his generalship at Sheriffmuir. *The History of the Principal Discoveries* discusses the changes in warfare wrought by the introduction of firearms.[17]

In *Memoirs of Dr. Williams* Defoe remarks that if the undisciplined Irish troops had been replaced by French soldiers, James could have subjugated Ireland long before William could possibly have arrived. Derry (later called Londonderry) could have been taken sword-in-hand in five days: "None but such infatuated counsels would have let a little unfortified, sorry, and indeed scarce defensible place, hold out for four months and baffle 22,000 men." In *A View of the Scots Rebellion* he argues that by "the difference in the very nature of a sword, which all [who] pretend to be called swordsmen must know," the Highlanders are no match for English soldiers trained to use the point rather than the edge. He explains the advantages of a defensive war against the insurgent clans, whose only chance lay in immediate victory. He refers to the practice of the Romans in keeping the Picts within bounds, and to that of the Duke of Alba in allowing the hired armies of William the Silent to waste away in indecisive warfare.[18] He often cites the failures of Hannibal and of Prince Rupert, to show the futility of winning onsets and battles without improving the opportunities they afforded. Military or naval adventures form the staple of his stories of the Cavalier and Captain Carleton and Captain Singleton; they appear also in *Colonel Jack* and *A General History of the Pirates* and *Robert Drury's Journal*. Defoe wrote a life of Peter the Great and two lives of Charles XII (with expert criticism of his battles by "a Scots gentleman in the Swedish service").

Only two writers have seriously questioned Defoe's reputation as a military historian. Boyer reprinted *An Impartial Account of the Late Famous Siege of Gibraltar* with many sarcastic asides. But his objections can be reduced to three. He knew that Defoe was the author; he pointed out that Defoe omitted or misrepresented some details and let slip some contradictions; and he remarked on a few errors in terminology. He could say little against the liveliness, the realism, and the essential truth of Defoe's narrative.

Colonel Arthur Parnell, a worshiper of German military organization, devoted some years to attacking English accounts of the War of the Succession in Spain, especially *Captain Carleton*. But his attempt to assign this book to Swift has met with ridicule, and better military historians have continued to regard the book as invaluable. Viscount Wolseley quoted it, Brigadier General Ballard used it freely, Sir Winston Churchill is indebted many times to its lively pages. As for the *Memoirs of a Cavalier*, a military officer praised the description of the passage of the river Lech by Gustavus Adolphus in the face of Tilly as "probably the most scientific operation of military engineering ever performed," and he went on to "appeal to the military engineers of the whole world to say whether such an operation could have been invented by Defoe."

Much of this controversy could be dismissed in a few words: Defoe was both historian and journalist, who knew how to tell of military affairs as of other things. He could laugh at himself when he corrected Prince Eugene's fantastic error in underestimating his own casualties at Belgrade by more than tenfold.[19] But what shall we say of his anticipating Marlborough in what has been considered the most brilliant plan of Marlborough's campaigns?

In a remarkable chapter called "The Thwarted Invasion (1708, July–August)," Sir Winston Churchill shows how nothing but Prince Eugene's incapacity to understand amphibious warfare prevented

Marlborough from shifting his attack to the rear of the French lines
by using the Channel for a supply route. What Churchill calls Marlborough's "greatest strategic design" would have forced the French
to abandon their almost impregnable fortifications and to battle on un-
equal terms in the open fields before Paris.

This identical plan had been presented by Defoe more than two
years earlier in his *Review* for May 28, 1706, and again one year
earlier in the *Review* for July 19, 1707. In 1717 Defoe came back to
the subject, when he represented a French observer as condemning
Marlborough for his failure to take advantage of the opportunity.
Defoe had no possible way of learning Marlborough's secret plans
two years in advance, whereas it is known that Marlborough sometimes read the *Review*.[20] Defoe had far less military experience than
Marlborough; but there is no recipe for genius.

IX. YOUNG PATRIOT

I told the Dissenters I had rather the Church of England
should pull our clothes off by fines and forfeitures, than
the papists should fall upon both Church and Dissenters,
and pull our skins off by fire and faggot.

An Appeal to Honour and Justice
(Hazlitt ed.), p. 15

TODAY THERE IS a tendency to attribute to James II liberal motives for which his shrewdest contemporaries never gave him credit. To the ablest observers in 1687 and 1688, James aimed not at religious freedom for his fellow Roman Catholics but at despotism by which his royal sovereignty would be made absolute and his own faith would be established as the state religion.

His methods were not approved of by the Pope or by most of his fellow religionists in England. When a large standing army remained on the outskirts of London in years of profound peace, the majority of the Roman Catholics in England were frightened almost as much as the Anglicans and the Dissenters. To critical observers, the illegal Declaration of Indulgence was a threat to the Constitution. If the Test Act could be set aside by the King, any other law could be set aside as easily. And if Anglicans and Dissenters could be turned against each other, a well-disciplined minority (with the aid of the executive power and the army) could dominate the nation.[1]

On April 4, 1687, James issued his notorious Declaration of Indulgence, granting dispensation from all religious obligations and tests. John Evelyn recorded the immediate effect of this in church attendance on the Sunday following: "There was a wonderful concourse of people at the Dissenters' meeting-house in this parish, and the parish-house [the Anglican church at Deptford] left exceeding thin." Subsequent issues of the official *London Gazette* showed the King's desire to represent his Indulgence as highly acceptable to the nation as a whole; long announcements were printed, repeating the effusive addresses to the King which poured in from London and from the country—from Anabaptists, Quakers, Congregationalists, distressed orphans, burgesses, Presbyterian ministers of Scotland, corporations, grand juries, even chapters of the Church of England, in thanks for James's "extraordinary and unlessened favors."

Defoe must have been back from Spain at this time; and although he was younger than any of the recognized leaders among the Presbyterians, his prompt rebuttal of these addresses appeared in a tract written to serve "honest blinded men," those of his fellow Dissenters who believed that their cause would be aided by a declaration which injured the nation as a whole. Perhaps this now-lost tract included the doggerel couplet (apparently the first specimen of Defoe's political verse), "these famous lines . . . which everybody had in their prints and discourse":

> The Declaration's but a Trojan Horse,
> The form's illegal, and the matter's worse.[2]

As an unusually active young Dissenter, Defoe may have received personal overtures from James "when the late King caressed the Dissenters, when he used all possible artifices to draw them in to side with him against the Church of England." In one of his last tracts Defoe speaks of a written communication from James which he possessed: "I have the honor to have seen the handwriting of five sovereigns, and to have in my possession the handwriting of most of them, as of King James, of King William, of Queen Anne, and of King George." An appeal from King James to the Dissenters might have been addressed to the respected James Foe, and thus might have come to Daniel by inheritance; but Defoe was always more active in politics than his father. King James liked to promote his interests by "closetings." It is amusing to think of Defoe as perhaps one of the Dissenters who received royal encouragement to seize on "the hook Tyranny . . . covered with the bait Liberty, as in all ages of the world it has been."[3]

In recent years Defoe had often been abroad or away on his travels over England. Now his position in London was more firmly established by his becoming a member of his father's livery company, the Butchers': "In the minutes, under date January 12th, 1687 [1688], is found this entry:—'At this Court Daniel Ffoe, son of James Ffoe, a member of this Company, came desiring to be admitted by virtue of his father's freedom, which was granted; and he further desired to pay a fine to this Company, and to be discharged from all offices, which was also granted—he paying £10 15s. fine for that purpose.'" Here, as in his later life as a citizen of Stoke Newington, we find Defoe paying a fine to avoid the routine tasks of minor offices. Time was always more precious to him than money. In an anonymous tract Defoe once compared himself to Shakespeare "as a person of little learning, but prodigious natural parts" who "had but a small share of literature." When the members of his own livery company in the nineteenth century decorated their hall with eight stained glass windows, two were in honor of the sons of English butchers who achieved fame as writers —Shakespeare and Defoe.

Once he had been admitted to membership, Defoe seems never to have taken an active part in the affairs of the Butchers' Company. In August, 1688, his father subscribed two pounds toward paying off the £500 indebtedness on the company's hall; and in January, 1700/1, James Foe voted in the company's poll for a new member of Parliament. The records of these polls were rather carelessly kept, so that more than three years after his death James Foe was still listed as a non-voting member of the company. But in none of the printed polls is there any indication that Defoe voted, and I have not found his name listed even as a non-voting member after 1710. It is likely that, at some time after the death of his father, Defoe ceased to be a member of the company.[4]

In the late summer of 1688, when James was instructing his agents how to secure a packed Parliament to support his measures, Defoe issued *A Letter to a Dissenter from his Friend at the Hague*. This was one of the ablest and most daring of all his tracts, an exposure of the King's insincerity in offering temporary religious freedom as a preliminary to overthrowing the Constitution. Like most political tracts of the day it was published anonymously, but it was also given a fictitious and impossible imprint. Defoe did not exaggerate the danger he incurred, when he wrote, twenty-three years later, that in this tract he had "opposed at the utmost hazard the taking off the Penal Laws and Test, and had the discouragement to be told by some grave, but weak good men, that I was a young man and did not understand the Dissenters' interest, but was doing them harm instead of good; to which, when time undeceived them, I only returned the words of Eliphas to Job, for which God never reproved him—*Old men are not always wise, neither do the aged understand wisdom*."

Near the same time occurred the first known death in Defoe's family. The parish registers of St. Michael, Cornhill, preserve the stark little record of all we know of his wife's namesake, probably their first-born daughter: "Sept. 7 Mary Foe, dau. of Daniell Foe & Mary his wife; in the lower vault in S. isle."[5]

Defoe was an affectionate parent, with little of the spirit of a Roman father who would sacrifice a child for the public good. But in spite of all his careful plans for the welfare of his family, private concerns were always being submerged in the stream of public interests. Political leaders in England had invited William of Orange to invade the country on their behalf, "the Glorious Revolution" was coming on, and Defoe moved about in the neighborhood of London.

Sometimes he was an eager observer, sometimes a participant in events. He saw James reviewing his troops in St. George's Fields below Southwark, to prepare to resist William's expected invasion. On Tuesday night, December 11, when William was advancing in triumph from the west and the first attempted flight of James became known, the London apprentices rose—as they had done nine years before during the wild days of the Popish Plot. Defoe had grown too sober a man to walk abroad with a Protestant Flail, but he was out on the street to watch the proceedings. He has told of one mob which he saw at work a little to the west of the Charterhouse:

Let me give you a short story to which I am a living witness—In the great rising of the mob at the late Revolution, they came to demolish a mass-house, or rather seminary of Popery, in an old building, I think, they called Berkely house near St. John's Street—They had assaulted the house with stones, and staves, and such tools as they had, but could not get the doors open—Some of the most forward call aloud for crows or sledges to split open the gates. Away run a knot of fellows down towards Cow-Cross to find out a smith's, and bringing along with them his great hammers and sledges, they soon got entrance—When they were broke in, and all hands busy to pull down and demolish, and as every one strove to be foremost, it was not likely the smith should get his tools again. Hey, Jack, says one; Tom, says another; you won't rob the poor smith! Come away, let's carry home the poor man's sledges. Away they go, a little troop, leave their spoil, and carried home the poor man all his tools, every one. He did not lose one; nay, two or three of them lugged away a great hinge, with a piece of the gate hanging to it, to give the smith the iron for the use of the sledges.[6]

Such violence threatened to sweep over the almost ungoverned nation. Not only were the Protestant majority turning against the Catholic minority; the unpaid and ill-fed soldiers were turning against the citizens. Among his large army encamped outside London, James had assembled two or three thousand Irish soldiers who were virtually foreigners in England, obeying no will but his own and that of his officers. Now that some of their military leaders had deserted to the oncoming army of William and others were shifting for themselves, the troops sought to provide for themselves by looting.

The next night Defoe rode to Windsor, on his way to join the army of William advancing from the west. At Windsor he heard more news of the rising of the Irish dragoons which had begun Sunday morning at Reading, when they had locked many townspeople in the principal church and had threatened to burn them inside. When an advanced guard of William's Dutch horse and dragoons came to the rescue, the mutineers broke and fled.

This confusion was spread by the inexcusable order of the Earl of Feversham, who (acting on what seemed to be explicit instructions from James) disbanded the royal army without paying or disarming the soldiers. Hugh Speke later claimed credit for having organized the report of an "Irish Massacre," by which he "hoped then to make the Irish Papists in the army useless to King James." As the Irish dragoons scattered eastward, they aroused wild panic wherever they stopped to demand quarters. On Thursday (December 13) Defoe traveled westward from Windsor to investigate for himself:

> I rode the next morning to Maidenhead: At Slough they told me, Maidenhead was burnt, and Uxbridge, and Reading, and I know not how many more, were destroyed; and when I came to Reading, they told me Maidenhead and Okingham were burnt, and the like. From thence I went to Henley, where the Prince of Orange, with his second line of his army, entered that very afternoon; and there they had the same account, with the news of King James's flight.[7]

At Henley-on-Thames, possibly Defoe himself confirmed the report. According to a nobleman in William's company, "somebody told the Prince how . . . the soldiers were all running up and down, not knowing what course to take." But Defoe missed the capture of James by fishermen at Faversham late at night on December 11. He did not see how patiently James bore the insults of a wealthy grocer who raised the mob, but he was soon interviewing some of the men who had been present. Nearly forty years later he recalled how he had "immediately inquired" what the fellow had said to the King, and so he was able to tell the story in minute detail as one he knew "personally to be true." For the only time in his career, James won Defoe's approval by rising superior to misfortune; and we find him credited with the same smiling serenity which Defoe attributed to such heroes as Gustavus Adolphus and William.[8]

For nearly two months after this, England was in confusion, with the Prince of Orange remaining as an invited guest at the head of foreign troops (and yet not regarded as a conqueror), and with a Convention serving in place of an elected Parliament. The throne was obviously vacant, but there was no agreement on how it was to be filled. Casuists tried to formulate a statement acceptable to all factions, explaining why James (a refugee in France) was not king and why William (in England) and Mary (still in the Netherlands) were about to be crowned in his place.

We do not know how often Defoe left his place of business in Freeman's Yard to attend the meetings of the Convention. Certainly he was present in the House of Lords on January 29, 1689:

I cannot forget what I happened to hear delivered at the bar of the House of Lords, in a message from the Commons, in Convention just upon the Revolution—

Mr. [Richard] H[amp]den carried the message, and the words were as follows:

"My Lords, I am commanded by the Commons of England, assembled in Convention, to acquaint your Lordships with a resolution, passed *nemine contradicente* by them, and ordered to be delivered to your Lordships, *viz.*

"*That it is inconsistent with the Constitution of this* Protestant *Kingdom, to be governed by a Popish prince.*"

The *Commons' Journals* and the *Lords' Journals* do not quite agree with each other on the text of this resolution. Defoe's version is both clearer and more dramatic than either of the others.[9] The young merchant had already taken his place as a political observer.

X. FRIEND OF WILLIAM

The best of Monarchs, and of Men to me.
Jure Divino (1706), Book I, p. 26

To THE WORLD AT LARGE William III was an unattractive person. Charles II and James II and the Duke of Monmouth had endeared themselves to the people by their love of dogs or horses or English sports, but William was a solitary even in his passion for the chase. Before he was legally established as King of England he had already proclaimed the full severity of the old laws against killing the deer or abusing the royal forests. His enemies recalled that his death had been hastened by a fall from his horse while he was hunting. In *Windsor Forest*, Alexander Pope suggested as characteristic of his reign the terrors of the forest laws and the massacre of Glencoe.[1]

Aspiring young Whigs like Steele and Addison might write occasional praise; but when Dryden was offered a large reward to dedicate his translation of Virgil's *Aeneid* to William, he preferred poverty and silence. The King's death was almost unnoticed by the poets, his funeral was huddled up at night, and soon his successor was thanked for having "retrieved" the national honor in a victorious war.

The exception was Defoe. During William's reign he published at least twenty-seven tracts or poems to support his policies; after his death he issued four others to defend his memory. In five of its nine years, the *Review* which appeared next after William's birthday celebrated his character and his achievements. On the slightest opportunity, from the Revolution to his own death, Defoe brought in William's name for praise.

His first long political tract (1689) ended with a plea "that we may all with one heart and one mouth bless God for his wonderful deliverance, and pray for the prosperity and long life of King WILLIAM and Queen MARY, whom God grant long to reign. Amen." About a year before the King's death, Defoe dedicated a tract to him in a tone of personal friendship. In a book left unfinished at Defoe's death, he recalled what he had heard "from the late ever glorious King William."

68

Long after the military splendor of his hero had been eclipsed, for other eyes, by the brighter light of Marlborough's fame, he still wrote of what "has been famous or valuable in the world, . . . from the siege of Jerusalem to the siege of Namur, and from Titus Vespasian to the greater King William."[2]

Defoe himself is chiefly to blame for the misconception that his acquaintance with William dated from the publication of *The True-Born Englishman* (January, 1701). In *An Appeal to Honour and Justice* (1715) he wrote:

> During this time [1700] there came out a vile abhorred pamphlet, in very ill verse, written by one Mr. Tutchin, and called "The Foreigners," in which the author . . . fell personally upon the king himself, and then upon the Dutch nation; and after having reproached his majesty with crimes that his worst enemy could not think of without horror, he sums up all in the odious name of FOREIGNER.
>
> This filled me with a kind of rage against the book, and gave birth to a trifle, which I could never hope should have met with so general an acceptation as it did; I mean "The True-Born Englishman." How this poem was the occasion of my being known to his majesty; how I was afterwards received by him; how employed; and how, above my capacity of deserving, rewarded, is no part of the present case, and is only mentioned here, as I take all occasions to do, for the expressing the honor I ever preserved for the immortal and glorious memory of that greatest and best of princes, and whom it was my honor and advantage to call master, as well as sovereign; whose goodness to me I never forgot, neither can forget; and whose memory I never patiently heard abused, nor ever can do so; and who, had he lived, would never have suffered me to be treated as I have been in the world.

But the *Appeal* must be read cautiously. In February, 1715, Defoe was not attempting to give a history of his relations with William, but to seek ground on which he could stand together with the Whigs and the Dissenters under Queen Anne's successor George I—and at the same time (if possible) to save the life of Robert Harley, his former patron, whose enemies were seeking to impeach him for high treason.

We are too likely to forget the personal dangers which a few centuries ago surrounded a public man who had fallen from power. In seventeenth-century England, Strafford was beheaded and Clarendon banished. In the next century Bolingbroke fled for his life, and Robert Harley, Earl of Oxford, was imprisoned for two years awaiting his trial. The inoffensive Prior suggested that Godolphin would have to escape from England after the fall of his Ministry in 1710;[3] five years later he was himself a prisoner of the House of Commons. Walpole was sent to the Tower, was restored to honor by George I, was driven into the ranks of the Opposition, and was received into high favor as virtual prime minister—all within nine years.

Often Defoe showed a martyr's zeal for religious or political freedom; but after the death of Queen Anne in 1714 he sought to avoid personal tragedy in what seemed to him a mere change of party alignment. On the whole, the *Appeal* is a rather accurate bit of autobiography; but it suggests that his connection with William was late and accidental, instead of being one of the profoundest and most enduring experiences of his lifetime.

It is possible that Defoe had met William on the Continent before 1689, as did so many other Whigs and Dissenters who went abroad. The two men would have found much in common: the paternal strain of Dutch or Flemish blood, the Calvinistic background tempered by the desire for religious toleration, the rather small stature, the piercing glance with the hooked nose and sharp chin, the ceaseless energy, the forgetfulness of self in the consideration of public affairs. When the Prince of Orange sought a shrewd appraisal of the English political scene, he might have secured it from the most observant of English travelers.

But on February 13, 1689, Defoe did not need to stir many paces from Freeman's Yard to mingle with the rejoicing throng before the Royal Exchange, after William and Mary had accepted the instrument from the Lords and Commons which declared them king and queen. On the next Lord Mayor's Day (October 28) the popularity of the new sovereigns was still running high in the city. The last celebration had been thinly attended, and any festive spirit had been quenched when James summoned the Lord Mayor and the sheriffs to Whitehall to give an account of the mob which had pulled down a mass house. Now in 1689 came the greatest Lord Mayor's Day which had ever been known. A contemporary writer declared, "never was there heard so loud and unanimous acclamation in the streets of this populous city, as attended our royal pair from their palace, all the way to Guildhall."[4]

Oldmixon gave a description of the procession in Cheapside and of the banquet in the Guildhall (most of it taken from White Kennett's history, but with an added slur against Defoe): "what deserved to be particularly mentioned, says a reverend historian, was a Royal Regiment of volunteer horse, made up of the chief citizens, who being gallantly mounted and richly accoutred, were led by the Earl of Monmouth, now Earl of Peterborough, and attended their Majesties from Whitehall. Among these troopers, who were for the most part Dissenters, was Daniel Foe, at that time a hosier in Freeman's Yard; the same who afterwards was pilloried." Kennett's account tells of "a magnificent feast" at the Guildhall, after which, "at their Majesties' return in the evening, the soldiers had, at convenient distances, lighted flambeaus in their hands; the houses were all illuminated, the bells ringing."[5]

The leader of this escort reappeared long afterward as Lord Peterborough, the hero of Defoe's fictional memoirs of Captain Carleton. Defoe was one of the "chief citizens" who made up this "Royal Regiment of volunteer horse." Several such regiments of Dissenters were projected for service against France—if William could persuade Parliament to repeal the Test Act (which James had attempted to set aside by his illegal Declaration of Indulgence). Defoe was to be an officer among the first volunteers. His only reference to this has a note of sadness: "But the King saw there was nothing to be done, and was obliged thereby to refuse the offers which divers Dissenters had made him, to raise regiments for his service, and to serve in person in the war then coming on."

Charles Gildon—blind, diseased, frustrated, and intensely jealous of his literary success—later ridiculed Defoe as claiming to be Sir Richard Steele's equal as a military authority:

I must do myself that justice to let you know that I too have been a military man. Soon after the Revolution there was a body of zealous Dissenters, who got to be incorporated into a Regiment under the name of the Royal Regiment, who declared their resolution to defend King William against all his enemies. In this Regiment I had the honor to be an officer. 'Tis confessed that we were never in action, nay, that as soon as we heard the first rumor of being designed for such, we with much fear and solicitation got ourselves to be disbanded. However, we were so often exercised during our standing, that I think I may put in for an equal share to a military speculation, as well as the noble Knight who spoke last.[6]

And so, because Defoe could not conscientiously take the Sacramental Test which would have qualified him to be an officer in Flanders, a writer who had never served his country accused him of cowardice.

It is true that one of the few men in England who rivaled Defoe in political acumen and in his intimate acquaintance with William held an altogether different opinion of the proposed employment of Dissenters in the army. In his secret record of conferences with the King in 1689 and 1690, the Marquis of Halifax reported that William saw in Peterborough an unstable demagogue, in the Royal Regiment a body sometimes dangerous because of its powerful supporters and sometimes contemptible because of its scanty numbers, and in the Irish Presbyterian volunteers men undesirable as recruits in Ireland because (as Halifax conjectured) they "would be less ready than others to go to France, in case of success."

Probably these contradictory views of Defoe and Halifax both had much truth; William himself wavered between the rival factions which sought his exclusive patronage. What Halifax wrote of William's judgment about employing Irish Protestants in his army might be repeated for many another subject: "he changed his mind several times upon that article."[7]

It was not as a volunteer soldier but as a pamphleteer that Defoe was to serve William best. His pamphleteering methods were developed by advocating the King's measures, which had to be presented so as to win the approval of an unwilling people. In April, 1689, he could still write such an old-fashioned tract as *Reflections upon the Late Great Revolution*, with Scripture texts to controvert the texts used by James's adherents in favor of the divine right of kings. In 1691 he could still rely on diffuse and imitative verse satire instead of his later concise, hard-hitting prose. But by 1697 he was proving himself more than a match for the best rival political writers in England. Of *An Argument Shewing, That a Standing Army, with Consent of Parliament, Is not Inconsistent with a Free Government*, an unfriendly critic has written:

> None of his subsequent tracts surpass this as a piece of trenchant and persuasive reasoning. It shows at their very highest his marvelous powers of combining constructive with destructive criticism. . . . He cuts rival arguments to pieces with dexterous strokes, representing them as the confused reasoning of well meaning but dull intellects, and dances with lively mockery on the fragments. . . . To persuade the mass of the freehoders was his object, and for such an object there are no political tracts in the language at all comparable to Defoe's. He bears some resemblance to Cobbett, but he had none of Cobbett's brutality; his faculties were more adroit, and his range of vision was infinitely wider.[8]

Of the thirty-six books or tracts Defoe is known to have published during William's reign, most advocated the King's foreign and domestic policies. Several others were favorable to William. Only two can conceivably be regarded as attacks on him, and these expressed views which William himself may have shared. *Reasons against a War with France* (1701) makes a shrewd appeal for Tory support of the impending war, suggesting that it could be largely fought at sea, and proposing a profitable war against the Spanish colonies and vulnerable regions like Italy instead of bloody frontal attacks on the French fortresses in "the cockpit of Europe." *The Succession to the Crown of England, Considered* (1701) must have been authorized by someone high in Whig counsels who was hesitating before making the final commitment in favor of the succession of Princess Anne and—after her—the Hanoverians.

We can trace Defoe's friendship with the King throughout the reign. Defoe gave William credit for introducing into England two of his own hobbies: the love of gardening and the love of painting. He recalled that William (like Gustavus Adolphus) was an exception to the rule that great personages act only for money. Defoe smiled often and laughed rarely; and he attributed the habit of smiling to William, as to so many of his other principal characters in history or in fiction. William's dry wit was congenial to him; he is almost the only observer who has much to say about William's smiles. He could speak a little Dutch; unlike some of the English ministers, he could certainly converse with William in French. Occasionally he recalls the French words which William spoke (inexactly, as usual in Defoe's foreign languages, but always intelligibly).[9]

About 1689 he observed William's enjoyment of his first visit to Sir Stephen Fox's estate near Chiswick or Islesworth, Middlesex. In 1689–90 he knew at firsthand that the Duke of Schomberg advised William not to invade Ireland without twenty thousand men. In the late autumn of 1689 or early 1690, when Nottingham House was being remodeled as Kensington Palace, the gardens were laid out "in something of the Dutch fashion which the King loved," according to which plan "the walks were straight, and converged upon vases or busts which terminated vistas." Defoe's only allusion to his acquaintance with Queen Mary occurs in a reference to this work: "The first laying out of these gardens was the design of the late Queen Mary, who finding the air agreed with, and was necessary to the health of the king, resolved to make it agreeable to herself too, and gave the first orders for enlarging the gardens: the author of this account having had the honor to attend her majesty, when she first viewed the ground, and directed the doing it, speaks this with the more satisfaction." Five years later, when Mary lay dead from smallpox, William astonished Europe by shutting himself up in her familiar residence in a long agony of grief; and his attachment to the palace and garden is said to have been strengthened by the recollection that she had loved them.[10]

In June, 1690, Defoe followed William as far as Chester on his way to Ireland and the Battle of the Boyne, and he seems to be alone in attributing William's first stop for dinner to his interest in gardens. On June 8 William was in Chester, which Defoe saw for perhaps the first time. Three days after that, William embarked for Ireland, and Defoe—in pursuit of his oft-neglected interest in trade—went on to Liverpool, which he had not visited for ten years.[11]

This neglect of business no doubt aggravated Defoe's losses in wartime marine insurance, which culminated in 1692 in his first bankruptcy. William himself was terribly pressed for means to carry on the war, and he could do little for a young merchant who had failed for £17,000. As a bankrupt, Defore was for a time better acquainted with fugitive debtors than with the King. But about 1694 he was standing by when John, Lord Strathnaver, the future sixteenth Earl of Sutherland, brought his clansmen to serve under William in Flanders. Near the same time, he was invited by merchants in England and on the Continent to settle at Cadiz. Later he explained his unwillingness to leave England: "Providence, which had other work for me to do, placed a secret aversion in my mind to quitting England upon any account, and made me refuse the best offers of that kind, to be concerned with some eminent persons at home in proposing ways and means to the government, for raising money to supply the occasions of the war then newly begun."

Sometime before 1695 he appeared before the Privy Council and the House of Commons to testify in favor of opening the trade with France (which he considered injurious to England in the earlier years of the reign, but beneficial afterwards).[12] It has been surmised that he was associated even thus early with Charles Montagu in devising means to support the government's finances; but for the middle 1690's we can be sure only that in some of his financial proposals Defoe was allied with Dalby (later Sir Dalby) Thomas. It was through Thomas that Defoe secured the only official posts he is known to have held during William's reign—as manager-trustee for the royal lotteries and as accountant for the commissioners of the Glass Duty.

Defoe knew that William spoke favorably of the diplomatic services of John Robinson and Lord Raby in 1697; and on November 16, when William entered London in triumph after obtaining the Peace of Ryswick, Defoe heard his remark about the bad omen of the eclipse of the moon. In the same year, "in a day when I could be heard," he testified in favor of abolishing the extralegal districts of London (like Whitefriars and the Mint) which were used as sanctuaries for fugitive debtors.[13]

Outside of William's inner circle few men in England realized that the Treaty of Ryswick offered only a breathing space before a world war. Most Whigs thought a war would not come; nearly all Tories thought war could be fought more cheaply at sea, without Continental entanglements. Whigs and Tories alike hated William's Dutch guards, the veterans of service against France; and both shared the distrust of any standing army. But the childless King of Spain was dying a lingering death, and the vastest empire in the world would soon be claimed by the rival royal families of France and Austria. The War of the Spanish Succession was about to begin.

The Hapsburgs would become too strong if their German Empire was consolidated with that of Spain, but France was already the most powerful military state in Europe. If Louis XIV's grandson became King of Spain, the bullion from Spanish American mines might pay for the army and navy of France, and the garrisons of all the fortresses in the Spanish Netherlands might be turned northward against Holland instead of southward as a barrier against France. If that were allowed to happen, the Dutch states would fall in a short time, and England could not hope to survive as an independent nation.

Since Louis was not sure his grandson would be named heir to the vast empire of Spain, he was eager for the compromise of the First Partition Treaty (1698). By this the Electoral Prince of Bavaria was to be King of Spain and the Indies, and the numerous Spanish provinces in Europe were to be divided. When the Electoral Prince died unexpectedly, the Second Partition Treaty was substituted (1699), naming the Archduke Charles of Austria as future King of Spain and the Indies, and giving better terms than before to Louis's grandson.

But the dying King of Spain upset these careful calculations to insure peace by willing all his dominions to the grandson of Louis. Louis broke the treaty by allowing Prince Philip to accept the inheritance. When the exiled James II died in France (September, 1701), Louis seemed to seek a war by proclaiming the young son of James as the new King of England, in direct violation of his pledge at the Treaty of Ryswick. William knew that his own frail and overtasked little body was failing. But in the few months that he had left, he arrayed most of the free states of Europe against the military despotism of France.

It is impossible to know just how far Defoe served as William's adviser in this crisis; we can only be sure that he was intimately acquainted with the King's plans. The Second Partition Treaty had been a secret from the world at large; even the Ministers and Marlborough testified that it was presented to them only as an accomplished fact. Defoe alone affirmed on his own knowledge that William inserted the ninth article, which specified that the Spanish monarchy was never to be held by the Emperor; he heard William give his reasons for accepting the treaty; and he "had the honor to hear his Majesty say, too prophetically, that England would be glad to make peace, upon worse terms, after seven years' war." Eleven years later, when he supported a new proposal for the partition of the Spanish dominions as a condition for peace with France, he argued from his personal experience in the drafting of William's treaty (which he "had the honor to see, and something more in its embryo"): "These schemes are drawn from, and with very little difference, are a faithful abstract of those original drafts, from which the late Treaty of Partition, which he had the honor to see formed, was after many consultations and alterations concluded; and which he has still by him to produce."[14] Early in 1701, he had "some more than common reason to know" that William was uneasy over Parliament's delay in authorizing ten thousand troops to assist the Dutch.

Attacks on William and his friends could not be easily answered by Defoe when they were made under the immunity of parliamentary privilege. But when Tutchin, a disgruntled Whig, wrote a satiric poem called *The Foreigners*, Defoe became for the moment the unofficial poet laureate. He defended the King by ridiculing national snobbery in *The True-Born Englishman* (January, 1701), the most widely sold poem that had appeared in the English language. Tutchin's poem had been called Part I, but Part II was never published.

After this triumph, Defoe was more openly employed by the King as adviser, friend, and advocate. Four years afterward Defoe informed Harley of the successful advice he had given William in the difficult winter of 1700–1701, when he had persuaded the King to weaken the Tory opposition by dividing it: "Your majesty must face about, oblige your friends to be content to be laid by and put in your enemies, put them into those posts in which they may seem to be employed, and thereby take off the edge and divide the party."[15] Later, when the Tory House of Commons delayed making preparations for war with France in 1701, Defoe presented to Speaker Harley his incredibly daring *Legion Letter*, defended the Kentish Petitioners for addressing the House, and urged the dissolution of the Parliament.

In the last months of the reign, we find Defoe drawing up for the King's approval elaborate plans for trade with Spanish America and for conquest of the Spanish colonies in the West Indies—plans which he retained in manuscript copies and which he continued to present (or to offer to present) as long as he lived. Years after Defoe's death, Lord Marchmont recalled how the Secretary of War, early in the reign of Queen Anne, had been impressed by one of these proposals:

Lord Bolingbroke told me, that about forty years ago, he had read King William's plan for making war in the West Indies, which had been formed in concert with the ablest seamen in Holland, and with Sir George Rooke and others in England; that in general it was to let loose all our buccaneers, privateers, &c., on the West Indies, and to assist them with the King's ships and land forces, to take post only in proper places, so as to secure their retreat; and in the manner to ravage the country, and interrupt their trade; and he believed, the French would not be able to prevent their Martinico men from joining us.

Bolingbroke's biographer has given joint credit for a later variant of this proposal to "St. John and Defoe." But the idea arose before St. John (later Viscount Bolingbroke) held high office; and it was suggested by Defoe—not by Dutch seamen or by the bullheaded Sir George Rooke. As early as March, 1698, William outlined it to Heinsius (who, like other Dutchmen of the time, had no desire to expand English trade or territorial possessions in the West Indies). The plan was revived in 1703, but it was quickly dropped by the Ministry for fear of offending the Spaniards and thereby hurting the prospects of the Allies' claimant for the Spanish throne.[16]

We cannot always be sure whether Defoe suggested an idea to William or whether he worked out the details of a plan which the King had suggested. The two men seemed to be in complete harmony on Continental diplomacy, military strategy, and the South Sea trade. Sometimes Defoe spoke of his proposals as William's plans, sometimes as his own. Both held that Louis could be impoverished by cutting off Spanish imports from the West Indies and breaking French domination of the Mediterranean; yet both were inclined to regard a direct invasion of Spain through Catalonia or Portugal as likely to prove wasteful and ineffective, except as a diversion to break the deadlock on the northern front. Both held that a great victory in Flanders might prove decisive; yet both had lost confidence in the slow process of invading France by besieging Vauban's masterpieces of fortification.

Defoe defended William's earlier wars of attrition by saying that they had worn down French resources; a long succession of such victories as Louis had won would eventually turn the scale against France. But he held that the constant lack of money and men and supplies had left William no chance to undertake some variant of his own master plan of strategy—masking the frontier fortresses by a minor show of strength, supplying the main army through the Channel ports, and striking directly at Paris through the open fields back of the French lines. He declared that William would have prevented the war of the Spanish Succession if he had not been blocked by opposition in England, and that before his death William had laid plans for the earlier stages of Marlborough's war.[17]

It is sometimes alleged that Defoe flattered the King and that he bragged about their friendship. The sardonic William was the last man in the world to be deceived by flattery, and Defoe said very truly that panegyric was not his own talent. Even the death of Queen Mary, which brought poetical tributes from venal pens, did not stir Defoe to write. But when William and his measures were slandered after his death, Defoe continued to declare his obligation to his old master: "a debt that I am almost alone in paying, to the shame of an ungrateful nation be it spoken." From their long association Defoe got no permanent advantage except an intimate acquaintance with a first-rate political mind. The money he received from William was soon swept away in his second bankruptcy—which came on him because he refused to betray William's secrets in the early years of the reign of Anne. Afterward no return was to be expected but partisan abuse: "Has the King any more bounties to give, any more favors to bestow on me?—Any more smiles to animate me by?—no, no—but I abhor turning from point to point, and forgetting when he is dead the wisdom, the prudence, the anxiety which he exerted for us when alive." Occasionally he brought in William's name to strengthen his arguments; more often he recalled the King's memory only because it was slighted, and he was determined to prevent such neglect.[18]

Few of Defoe's contemporaries had any real idea of how well he had known the King or of how faithfully he had served him; but no one doubted that the two had been closely associated. When Defoe urged Harley to weaken the Opposition by placing some of his enemies in the government, he was only one year out of Newgate Prison, and he must have recalled that Harley had been a leader in the attack on William's advisers three years before. But he told Harley that the advice he now gave was the same he had formerly given to William; and Harley knew that Defoe was saying no more than the truth. When the Whig leaders attacked the proposed partition of Spain in 1711, Defoe reminded them that he knew—and that they knew that he knew—that the policy had been adopted by William himself.[19]

The fury of Defoe's attacks on John Tutchin and on Lord Haversham was due to one thing: they had been rewarded by William, and they had betrayed him. It was not in self-praise but in contempt of Haversham's ingratitude that he wrote: "If I should say I had the honor to know some things from his Majesty, and to transact some things for his Majesty, that he would not have trusted his Lordship with, perhaps there may be more truth than modesty in it." It was in scorn for their misrepresentation of William that he cried: "I am not at all vain in saying, I had the honor to know more of his Majesty, than some of these that have insulted his character knew of his horse."[20]

Defoe offered no criticism of Queen Mary except that (in her innocent love of china and East Indian calicoes) she had introduced a taste for exotic luxuries which tended to impoverish the nation. He offered no objection to King William except the licensing of hackney coaches on Sundays for added revenue in wartime, and the errors (such as the massacre of Glencoe, of which he had heard William's defense from his own mouth)[21] resulting from dependence on ministers and agents.

All else was friendship, admiration, almost adoration. According to Defoe's theory of constitutional government, it was the King's duty to summon the Parliament. It was the Parliament's duty to serve as "the supreme authority of the nation." If Parliament failed, all authority reverted to "that other original of power, the collective body of this nation." William was the first parliamentary King; much as he disliked many of the acts of the legislative assembly, he abided by them. Defoe never admired William more than when the King refused a proposal to establish himself as superior to Parliament by military force.[22]

Apparently he was alone in regarding William as the equal of his adored Gustavus Adolphus. Among the elegies appended to one of his favorite books, *The Swedish Intelligencer* (Third Part, 1633), was a poem "Upon the King of Sweden" which began with the couplet:

> The Youth, hereafter, when old Wives shall chat
> *Gustavus* high deeds; will aske *What Giant's that?*

Defoe recalled these lines as long as he lived; but he modified them to be applied to William, as in *The Mock Mourners* (1702):

> Posterity, when Histories relate
> His Glorious Deeds, will ask, *What Giant's that?*

He realized that William's life in England had been virtual exile from Holland. From his own knowledge he spoke of William's secret practice of piety. He admired William's desire for Church union, his tenderness toward the Dissenters, his courage in calling in the debased coinage while the nation was in desperate need of revenue, his interest in the navy, his steadiness amid the selfish turnings of Whigs and Tories, his brief hours of glorious victory, his fortitude in the long years of defeat. The highest praise he could give to Louis XIV was to admit that, if the fortunes of war turned against him, he would perhaps emulate William's constancy, and "lose his country by inches, and like a true hero die in the last ditch."[23]

The subtlest representation of Defoe's friendship with William appears in a book offered as the supposed memoirs of a French diplomatic agent, Monsieur Mesnager. Here Defoe was drawn into portraying the close association of the King of France with the merchant who became his confidant. The reader discovers that Louis XIV is William as William would have been at Versailles, and that Mesnager is another name for Defoe. Like William, Louis is called "the late King, of glorious memory"; like William, he smiles; like William, he discusses with his confidant a plan for conquest of the West Indies; like William, he has his West Indian plan balked by jealous allies. The instructions which Defoe received when he set out on a journey for William must have been much like those which Louis wrote for the obscure French merchant Mesnager with his own hand ("the shortest that ever any agent received on a business of such importance"): "Place yourself at the Hague incognito. Acquaint yourself with persons as you see occasion. Correspond with nobody but myself. You know your business." Defoe was the only Englishman who said that he had been "BELOVED by that glorious Prince." This claim of affection might have aroused derision among some who had known the King; but Defoe spoke from experience, and he never said it of anyone but William.

On February 20, 1702, the King's horse stumbled in a molehill as his master hunted in the park at Hampton Court, and the rider broke a collarbone in his fall. Apparent progress toward recovery was followed by an acute pleurisy, complicated by inflammation of one lung and a constitutional tendency to asthma. Soon came an unexpected collapse of the exhausted little body. On March 8, 1702, William was dead. On March 29 the Rev. John Pigott preached a sermon on "The Natural Frailty of Princes Considered."

But in the remaining twenty-nine years of his own life, Defoe never forgot. In his ragged verse he continued to praise his friend and master:

> *William*, the Glorious, Great, and Good, and Kind,
>   Short epithets to his just memory;
> The first he was to all the world, the *last to me*.

In his fervent prose he did not cease crying out: "If you insult the name, reproach the memory, lessen the merit, forget your obligation to, or raise slander upon, the actions of *the Glorious King WILLIAM*, who (however unworthy) I have the honor to say was my master; whom I faithfully served, by whom I was beyond my capacity of merit rewarded, and whom I cheerfully suffered [for] because I would not betray—I MUST SPEAK, *I should be an ungrateful dog if I should forbear.*"[24]

XI. MERCHANT

... a merchant ... I had the misfortune to be bred.

Review, VIII, 754

IT WOULD BE EASY for a biographer to forget that during most of his career Defoe made his living as a merchant. However often he might volunteer as a soldier, or write political pamphlets, or give advice to sovereigns or prime ministers, it was usually by trade that he sought to support his growing family. His political and literary rivals (who professed to regard merchandising as degrading) liked nothing better than to remind him of this.

About 1679 he left Morton's academy with an outlook much like that of the youthful Crusoe: "I was now eighteen years old, which was too late to go apprentice to a trade, or clerk to an attorney." Soon afterward he could have said, as Crusoe did in his old age, "I begin to be a convert to the principles of merchandising."[1]

Defoe denied that he had ever been an apprentice, and his frequent travels and his crowded life do not allow the necessary seven years for such a purpose. He did become an expert bookkeeper, but the most likely explanation is that of Lee: "young Defoe was not under articles or in any menial capacity, but was instructed in book-keeping, management, and such other duties as would fit him to conduct a similar business on his own account."[2]

For the young student of merchandising in the London of 1679 the greatest distraction lay out of doors. There were reports of a gigantic Popish Plot against the national church and even the life of the King. Defoe himself, then eighteen or nineteen years old, was one of many who undertook to copy the Bible into shorthand, so that it could be concealed from spies and informers whenever its reading was prohibited. He added, "At which task I myself then, but a boy, worked like a horse till I wrote out the Pentateuch, and then I was so tired I was willing to run the risk of the rest."[3]

Long afterward he recalled his exploits as one of the brisk young fellows who had roamed the streets in 1679 with the jointed clubs called "flails" to scatter any loiterers who threatened pedestrians:

Now this Protestant Flail is an excellent weapon; a pistol is a fool to it. It laughs at the sword or the cane, for you know there's *no Fence against a Flail*. For my part, I have frequently walked with one about me, in the old Popish days; and though I never set up for a hero, yet when armed with this scourge for a Papist I remember I feared nothing. . . .

I remember I saw an honest stout fellow, who is yet alive, with one of these Protestant Instruments exercise seven or eight ruffians in Fleet Street, and drive them all before him quite from Fleet Street into Whitefriars, which was their receptacle, and handled it so decently that you would wonder, when now and then one of them came within his reach and got a knock, to see how they would dance. Nay, so humble and complaisant were they that every now and then they would kiss the very ground at his feet . . . if they received but the word of command from this most Protestant Utensil.

When rumors circulated that high officials were trying to silence the witnesses against the Plot, he attended "a meeting of some honest people in the City." There he heard pretended revelations from the informer Bedloe, and he saw Titus Oates, "whose zeal was very hot." Defoe believed (as later historians have agreed) that some conspiracy was afoot. But he came to distrust Oates and to realize that the overthrow of the government by a small minority was out of the question. He saw the absurdity of swallowing every rumor, like the yarn that six Frenchmen had tried to steal away with the towering monument erected to commemorate the Great Fire. And he came to distrust the politicians who profited by the commotion, like the Earl of Shaftesbury, who had betrayed the Dissenters after he had persuaded them to accept the Test Act.[4] Throughout his life he was usually a non-party man; perhaps his first disillusionment regarding party politicians came when he realized that the great Earl was playing for his own stakes.

But in spite of such distractions, Defoe progressed rapidly as a young merchant. He seems to have dealt in haberdashery at first, making journeys in various part of Great Britain and the Continent, perhaps to buy his goods at the great country fairs and to find markets for them abroad. Already he was observing as an economist, not as a mere traveler. Forty years later he recalled the disastrous effect of bountiful harvests during the eight years before the Revolution, which caused such abundance that farmers sold their wheat at a heavy loss.[5]

In December, 1683, he was well established as a merchant of St. Michael's, Cornhill. His home and his place of business were on the north side of Cornhill, in Freeman's Yard, twenty-five yards east of the Royal Exchange: "a large open court, with a free-stone pavement, well built, and well inhabited." According to a contemporary, Cornhill

is very spacious, and replenished with lofty houses, graced with good fronts, and inhabited by traders of good note, and chiefly with linen drapers (who also deal much in India silks and muslins) on the north side, and upholsterers on the south; and many booksellers about the Exchange. . . . Not only this street but all the adjacent parts are of a great resort, and crowded with merchants and tradesmen, insomuch that the taverns, coffee-houses, eating-houses, and other such like places of public reception, as they make considerable gains, so they pay vast rents.[6]

There are two great mysteries about Defoe's career as a merchant: how he got the experience and the capital to set up so early for himself, and in what lines of trade he engaged and where and how he transacted business.

The question about experience runs through his whole life. He required little experience to verify his theories. The one thing he needed to learn was caution—and he never acquired that from a lifetime of experience.

As for his capital, the £3,700 dowry which his wife brought him in 1684 was engulfed in his ventures. As James Foe's only son he was probably able to count on considerable support. He perhaps inherited something from his mother, who had died before 1671. His instinct as a projector and his great powers of persuasion perhaps induced substantial Dissenters to extend credit far beyond his capital resources. His extraordinarily rapid advancement in the wine trade indicates the possible influence of family connections: Lawrence Marsh, the cousin of one of his parents, had as his first wife a daughter of a member of the Vintners' Company, and Defoe's own father-in-law was apparently a prosperous wine-cooper.

From the fragmentary records of the commercial lawsuits in which he was engaged, and from his own writings on trade, it is clear that he must have transacted business on a greater scale than his capital justified. He played for high stakes. In the troubled conditions of war and the fear of war, a few lucky ventures as exporter and importer might have made success seem easy.

His political enemies rarely admitted that he had ever made any considerable success. According to one, "he had never been a merchant, otherwise than peddling a little to Portugal, and was for some years secretary, as he styled himself, to the tile-kilns and brick-kilns at Tilbury." According to another, "he run through the three degrees of comparison: pos[itive] as a hosier; compar[ative] as a civet-cat merchant; and super[lative] as a pantile merchant."

Two favorite charges were repeated again and again: that he had been "a civet-cat merchant" and that he had been "formerly a hosier," "a broken hosier," "a predicating hosier," "a hosier, in Freeman's Yard, Cornhill," or "hosier in Newgate Street." This last phrase, meaningless except as a slur at Defoe's imprisonment in Newgate, parallels Swift's innuendo against Defoe in his account of the early career of Lemuel Gulliver: "I married Mrs. Mary Burton, second daughter of Mr. Edmund Burton, hosier in Newgate-street, with whom I had four hundred pounds for a portion."[7]

The civet cat allusion has been cleared up by the discovery that in 1692 Defoe purchased an establishment of civet cats, whose glandular secretion was still an important basic material for the manufacture of perfume. He always denied the charge that he was a hosier, and he prided himself on being a wholesale dealer rather than a retail merchant of any sort. But the supposed absurdity of dealing in hosiery lingered in the minds of his more snobbish opponents. In Dr. Thomas Dibben's Latin verses on Defoe in the pillory, the culminating insult is an invitation to "become again a fashioner of footwear."[8]

Recollections of Defoe's residence as a merchant in Spain and of his trade with Spain and Portugal and the American colonies recur throughout his writings. While he was living abroad, he detected an inferior brandy which had been substituted in the casks he had agreed to purchase for his London importer. When he exported goods to Portugal and Spain, it would be natural for him to bring back wine on the return voyages. In his own business he imported as much as seven hundred pipes (about seventy thousand gallons) of Oporto wine in a single year. He tells how merchants' letters used to take twenty-two days to reach Cadiz or Lisbon when they were sent through France and Spain, whereas the new packet boats carried them directly in nine or ten days. He refers to proverbs learned, or to observations made, while he lived in Spain. He declared that if the trade to Spain were reopened, he would settle there as a trader, and that he would receive better treatment than he had met with in England. He tells a long anecdote of a merchant whose agent in Boston saw the apparition of his elder brother who had been murdered in London. Through similar agents in Boston, New York, and Maryland, he engaged in carrying merchandise to America and in bringing home tobacco. When his Colonel Jack became established in that part of Maryland which is now the District of Columbia, he reversed Defoe's arrangement by dealing with his own correspondent in London.[9]

The merchant's life was not without personal danger as well as financial hazards. In 1704 Defoe wrote: "I had the honor, disaster, or what else you please to call it, of losing the first ship that was taken upon the breach of the last war, and before it was declared." He was with the merchants on a large yacht which ran past the customhouse at Gravesend and on to Caen in Normandy; and as the cargo included a great quantity of block tin, besides other goods which had not been entered at the customhouse, this reads like a bit of wartime smuggling of contraband.

He recalled an Algerian rover which took a Dutch ship bound from London to Amsterdam about the year 1686. He told of a similar experience of his own during the latter years of Charles II, when he must have been less than twenty-five years old: "I myself had an adventure in a ship bound to Rotterdam, that was taken by an Algerine man of war in the mouth of the River Thames and in sight of Harwich."[10] Presumably he was soon ransomed or released by another vessel; otherwise he might have experienced Crusoe's captivity among the Moors, instead of staying in London to write about it.

As long as he lived, he continued to be a merchant. When he was accused of writing for bread, he replied that he made his living by trade. According to one legal record, he was involved in a transaction regarding land at Tilbury as early as 1678; and although it has been urged that the date must be a scribal error for 1698, the explanation would not greatly change our impression of his career. As the Secretary of State's secret representative in Edinburgh in 1706 and 1707, he was active in promoting the Union of England and Scotland; but he was also engaged in the manufacture of linen, the exportation of salt, and the shipping of codfish from the Hebrides. He made occasional investments in the African Company and the South Sea Company. In 1721, 1723, and 1726 he trafficked in wool or woolen goods in Trowbridge and at Blackwell Hall, London. In his mid-sixties he was buying large quantities of cheese and oysters.[11]

The reputation he established as a wholesale merchant in Freeman's Yard must have been very considerable. Throughout 1711, newspaper advertisements record a running controversy between two rival wholesalers of gowns—a Mrs. Baker (or someone else carrying on a business from Baker's Coffee-House) and Henry Bright, who had removed from that place to set up for himself in Freeman's Yard. There was some confusion about the respective locations of the two establishments, and on July 9 Bright sought to inform the public of the exact site of his "Gown-House": "N. B. This was the Ware-House of Mr. Daniel Defoe." On July 28 he was even more explicit: "*N. B.* The Ware-House stands in Freeman's Yard, where Mr. D. D'Foe Liv'd. My Customers may go in and out, without going through any House, or Coffee-House."

It is a striking fact that the warehouse in Freeman's Yard was popularly remembered as Defoe's nineteen years after the bankruptcy of Defoe and long after he had removed to other quarters and transferred to other activities. Even so, the traditional ill-fortune of the place continued. On March 24 of the next year Henry Bright was advertising a clearance sale of the goods at his "Gown Ware-House in Freeman's Yard, near the Royal Exchange" before Lady-Day, "The Ware-House then to be Lett."[12]

In one of Emerson's poems we are told that a field affords two different crops: one to the farmer who carts off the load, one to the poet who bears away his song. It is not certain that Defoe ever profited for long as a merchant; there can be no doubt that his experience aided him as economist and author. The great fortunes of the world may be acquired by the John Jacob Astors and the Hetty Greens. The Arthur Youngs and the Daniel Defoes often suffer financial distress, despite the wisdom with which they enlighten mankind.

Defoe always wrote well on trade—in his novels as in his economic tracts and his periodicals. Whenever he started to "launch out on this vast ocean of trade," he was a social philosopher and not infrequently a literary artist. To him the beauty of the heavenly bodies was not more remarkable than the diversity of nature which was the foundation of trade. He could not mention Spanish fruits without a rush of poetic feeling. In a mere account of the use of cotton among the ancients, his joy in the sonorous names might have won the approval of Milton himself: "the rich atlases, and flowered silks; the light painted chints, and fine Maslapatans . . . of Bengal, and Golconda, and all the calicoes of the East Indies, that part between the Ganges and the Indus; and which were brought into Europe, either by the Red Sea,

to Suez and Alexandria, or by the caravans to Aleppo and Smyrna."
When his love of history and of geography was enlisted in his account
of merchandising, the dry facts of commerce were given (as if by the
poet of Shakespeare's Duke Theseus) "a local habitation and a name":
"The fine linen of Egypt is removed to Holland and Flanders, and the
dyeing of purple and scarlet, for which the Phoenicians were so
famed, is lost to that part of the world."[13]

XII. BANKRUPT

I am fit for nothing but a memento mori, *a beacon or buoy,*
to show where the rock lies that I have split upon.

The Family Instructor (Tegg ed.), II, 16

DEFOE RODE in 1689 with the "Royal Regiment" escorting the King and Queen to the Guildhall. Three years later he was a bankrupt. In the next ten years he paid off all but £5,000 of the original £17,000,[1] but he was never again free from old debts. In 1703 his affairs were thrown into confusion once more, when he was hunted down by the Tory Government.

Many writers have suffered great financial reverses. To most of them such losses have come late in life, and the blow has frequently been softened by public sympathy or by the benevolence of a grateful nation. Defoe wrote the most popular book in the language, but as a bankrupt he received none of the courtesies extended to Sir Walter Scott—a generous composition agreed on by his creditors, the claim which would have sent him to prison bought off by a friendly banker, a pension provided for his unmarried daughter, a warship assigned to bear him to Italy.

Admirers of Scott have sometimes expressed regret that he had not died before the bankruptcy became known, so that he could have closed his life in the glory of the earlier novels without knowing the drudgery of the later ones. But if Defoe had died before his first bankruptcy, we would have only eight of his more than five hundred books and tracts and periodicals, and his public career would scarcely have begun.

Defoe's bankruptcy was not largely due (like Scott's) to living beyond his means or to discounting notes to realize capital before it could be earned. The "post-obits" on expectations from his grandfather's estate which Shelley floated so gayly had no counterpart in Defoe's difficulties. England was engaged in commercial expansion through the widespread use of unlimited credit. Any individual could be dragged down by another who failed to meet his own obligations; and he could be savagely punished for inability to pay back what he should never have been allowed to borrow. Debtors were illegally assumed to be fugitives, and arrest was used to prevent the abuse of credit. In one of his last tracts, Defoe pointed out that England (like no other nation in history) punished debtors by making them incapable of paying their debts. When he heard that one of the men responsible for the law of perpetual imprisonment for debt was confined in Newgate, he saw in such retribution the guidance of Providence.[2]

No doubt he had entered the world of business as a very young merchant, so that he could say with Robinson Crusoe, "I bought all my experience before I had it." No doubt he ventured in what Crusoe called "projects and undertakings beyond my reach; such as are indeed often the ruin of the best heads in business." He gives the frankest testimony regarding his own subterfuges to stave off the collapse in 1692:

> If I were to run through the infinite mazes of a bankrupt, before he came to the crisis; what shifts, what turnings, and windings in trade, to support his dying credit; what buying of one, to raise money to pay another; what discounting of bills, pledgings and pawnings; what selling to loss for present supply; what strange and unaccountable methods, to buoy up sinking credit! What agonies of mind, does the distressed tradesman go through, I appeal to those gentlemen, that have gone through the labyrinths, and entangled in the toil of failing credit, have struggled themselves out of breath, and at last like a deer, hunted down, are driven to stand at bay with the world![3]

He did become too deeply involved in land speculations and in diving engines and in civet cats and in cargoes freighted for overseas trade. He did lose by wrecks and by looting at Deal or on the coast of Biscay. In discussing the inadequate protection of English shipping, he pointed out that the loss suffered by trade at sea was supposed to have amounted to more than a third of the entire cost of the last war. But to emphasize such details would be like treating the symptoms and not the disease. The immediate and overwhelming cause of his bankruptcy was that he was one of nineteen English merchants ruined by insuring vessels during William's long struggle with France.

Today such risks are recognized as national obligations, to be covered by national insurance. Even in 1693 and 1694 the House of Commons realized that the nineteen "merchants insurers" had suffered for the general welfare. The "Merchants Insurers' (War with France) Bill" as it was carried up to the House of Lords named Daniel Foe as eighteenth among nineteen "who have been known merchants and traders beyond the sea for many years past, and have paid great sums of money to the Crown for customs upon goods exported and imported, and always honestly and duly discharged their several credits as well in this Kingdom as in parts beyond the sea." The bill went on to recognize the public service which the insurers had rendered:

And whereas the interest of trade hath for many years past and since the beginning of the present war with France been promoted and carried on by assurance upon ships and goods outwards and homewards; And whereas in all trading nations the custom of assurance hath been always esteemed necessary and useful and practised by the best of merchants, and that it hath been as much encouraged in this nation as any foreign parts, appears by Acts of Parliament made in favor thereof, and which hath greatly encouraged and promoted the trade and navigation of this Kingdom and advanced the revenue of the Crown, many of which ships and goods, so assured by them the said merchants aforenamed, have been taken and made prizes by the enemies of this kingdom, by which means they have sustained such losses as tend to their utter ruin, having paid since the war with France very great sums of money for losses by assurance as aforesaid, by which means the greatest part of their capital is exhausted, which was very considerable, and they stand yet indebted unto divers persons divers sums of money, which at present they are incapable of paying, and are now forced to withdraw themselves from their habitations and leave their families in great distress; . . . And whereas most of their several creditors being satisfied that the many great losses that have befallen them did not happen through their own neglect or default, but were chiefly occasioned by the miscarriages of the sea affairs, and are contented to take such proportions of their several and respective debts as are hereby directed and required, but others of the creditors, fewer in number and for much the lesser part of their respective debts, insist upon their full debts or the severity of the law.

The bill further declared that some of the debtors had already attempted to make arrangements with their creditors, and by far the greater part of the latter had come to terms; but the small minority of creditors who refused to sign made the composition useless. The bill provided that each debtor was to be allowed to make terms with the creditors who held two-thirds of his debts. When this composition was made and carried out in good faith, it was to be equally binding on all creditors, preventing future claims against the debtor for the obligations so covered.[4] There can be no doubt that the bill stated the facts, and that Defoe was entitled to relief under its provisions.

A brief history of the bill is necessary to explain its rejection by the House of Lords. On November 22, 1693, a petition of "Merchants and others, concerned in the foreign trade and navigation," was read in the House of Commons, stating that "the petitioners have suffered very great losses by the mismanagement of the sea affairs; for want of ships of war for cruising, by the long detention of ships here, by many irregularities in pressing, by embargoes, and many other particulars, which tend to the ruin of the trade of this nation: . . . And praying relief in the premises." Apparently nothing could be done to improve the wretched system of convoys or to stop the seizure of the crews of merchant ships for naval duty. But steps could be taken to prevent the unhappy merchants insurers from being made life-prisoners by a small minority of their creditors, for debts which they had incurred because of "the mismanagement of the sea-affairs."

On December 9, 1693, leave was granted "to bring in a Bill to enable divers Merchants Insurers, that have sustained great losses by the present war with France, the better to satisfy their several creditors." On December 13 Mr. Edmund Waller presented the bill; and next day it passed its first reading. On December 21 some of the creditors petitioned to be heard in opposition, the bill passed its second reading, and the bill and the petition were referred to a select committee of thirty-eight members, besides "all the members of the House who are Merchants; and all who serve for the sea ports." This committee was to meet at four that afternoon in the Speaker's Chamber, to hear the petition of the minority creditors.

On January 15, 1694, six additional members (some of them very eminent merchants) were added to the original committee. On February 6 Mr. Waller reported that they had made several amendments to the bill. But as some of the creditors had not yet been heard, the bill with the amendments was referred back to the committee for further consideration, "to the end that the several creditors be heard before the said Committee." On February 8 still another creditor sought to be heard by counsel before the bill was passed, and his petition was referred to the committee.

On February 9, 1694, appeared a new applicant for relief under the bill:

A petition of Daniel Foe Merchant was presented to the House, and read; setting forth, That the petitioner having sustained divers losses by insurances since the war with France, and having met and proposed to his creditors a means for their satisfaction, some few of them would not come into those proposals: That there being a Bill, depending in this house, to enable some Merchants Insurers the better to satisfy their creditors, the petitioner prays that his name may be inserted in the said Bill, to have the like benefit with them.

The House ordered that the consideration of this petition be referred to the committee. As Defoe was the latest comer among the applicants for relief, in the face of the creditors who opposed the bill, his affairs must have received very close scrutiny. Any oversight or misstatement would have been mercilessly exposed. But when on February 22 Mr. Waller reported that the committee had "examined and considered" the bill and the petition, he presented the bill and its amendments, reading them once throughout and a second time one by one. Both the bill and its amendments were passed by the House: "And an Amendment being proposed, by inserting the name of Daniel Foe into the Bill; The same was, upon the question put thereupon, agreed unto by the House." It was then ordered that the bill, with the amendments, be engrossed. On February 27 the bill was read the third time, and passed; and Mr. Waller was ordered to carry it to the Lords to desire their concurrence.

On February 28 Mr. Waller and others brought the merchants insurers' bill up to the House of Lords. On March 1 this passed its first reading, and the Lords ordered that its second reading should come at ten o'clock in the forenoon of March 8, and "that this order be fixed on the doors of this House." But on the next Thursday morning, March 8, the leisurely pace of the Lords was impeded by a number of private bills. The great bill, with the name of Daniel Foe added by a special amendment, was not brought to a vote. Next day (Friday, March 9) the bill did come to its second reading:

> The Question was put, "Whether this Bill shall be committed?"
> It was Resolved in the Negative.
> The Question was put, "Whether this Bill shall be rejected?"
> It was Resolved in the Affirmative.[5]

The lords who were present that morning could hardly be expected to realize that they had wrecked the hopes of a young London merchant named Daniel Foe. But what explains their sudden rejection of the bill on its second reading? The bill was an eminently fair one, it had been approved by the House of Commons after three months of exceptionally close scrutiny and revision, it had passed its first reading in the House of Lords, and no new evidence had been brought against it.

The *Journals of the House of Lords* usually tell us nothing of the votes cast, and very little about debates in the sessions of two or three centuries ago; but they do give the name of every member of the House attending on each day. When the bill was first offered to them (February 28), sixty-six lords were in attendance. When it passed its first reading (March 1), sixty-four were present. But on March 9, when they rejected it, only fifty-one were present.

Some of the staunchest supporters of the government (like the Archbishops of Canterbury and York, some of the bishops of William's creation, and the Earls of Bridgewater and Portland) were present on March 1, when the bill passed its first reading. They were also present on March 8, when it was scheduled to be read the second time. But they were not in the House on March 9, when the bill was defeated. On the other hand, most of the staunchest Tories, who had not attended on the other days, appeared in their places on March 9. Only twenty-six votes were needed on that day for a majority. From the list of those who were present, it would be easy to pick out that many who stood for the rights of "men of property" and who might well have opposed relief for merchants who had failed through insuring vessels during the foreign war of the "Dutch King." If even the two archbishops, a few more of the Low Church bishops, and Bridgewater and Portland had been in their seats on March 9, 1694, Defoe's bankruptcy might have been ended by a favorable composition with two-thirds of his creditors.

Defoe's disappointment must have been intense, but he rarely mentions it. In *An Essay upon Projects* he remarked that "The losses and casualties which attend all trading nations in the world when involved in so cruel a war as this, have reached us all, and I am none of the least sufferers." In the *Review* he recalled, as one of the evils of the last war: "The ruin of our merchants, the number of which, upon the first [rupture], was so great, that the House of Commons passed a bill to give certain Merchant Insurers a limited time to make up with, and satisfy their creditors; but the Bill was afterwards rejected in the House of Lords, for reasons too long to insert here."

Less than three years later a more comprehensive bill was brought in to relieve debtors from the exactions of a minority of creditors who insisted on having from the debtors more than their all. On April 1, 1697, this bill received William's assent as "An Act for Relief of Creditors, by making Composition with their Debtors, in case Two-Thirds in Number and Value do agree." But a year later (April 21,

1698) the Commons passed a bill of repeal, and on June 20 the Lords agreed on the amendments.[6]

Thereafter Defoe sometimes referred wistfully to the advantages of an act, such as the one which had stood for a short time under William, permitting a composition with the creditors "two-thirds in number and value." But he could never again be sure when his work would not be stopped by some claimant for a real or imaginary debt. At a time when his services were almost indispensable to the government, he was begging Harley for two or three hundred pounds to free himself from his most furious creditors, so that he could continue his work for the Ministry.

If a Tory or High Church agent (or, later, a secret Jacobite or a Whig opponent of the Peace of Utrecht) wished to silence the pamphleteer whose arguments were unanswerable, he had only to procure (or forge) an old claim for debt, and he could demand Defoe's arrest. If a minority creditor was dissatisfied with the terms accepted by the majority, he could stand out from the composition and demand payment of his own claim in full. Of the few creditors who refused his offer of composition, Defoe wrote: "the remarkable compassion of some creditors, after continued offers of stripping myself naked, by entire surrenders upon oath, have never given me more trouble than they were able, or less than they knew how; by which means most of the debts I have discharged cost me 40s. in the pound to pay, and the creditors half as much to recover."

If through generosity the debtor gave a creditor any payment above the amount stated in the terms of composition, he could be betrayed to a new inquisition. Defoe warned a friendly correspondent that he ran this danger because of a report that he had paid the people at Yarmouth more than the law required. All that he asked was an opportunity to go about his work, with time to pay off his obligations. To one correspondent he replied in the *Review:*

1. He that cannot pay his debts may be an honest man.
2. He that can, and will not, must be a knave.
3. He that can pay his debts at leisure may not be able to do it all at once; and if it were required of all men, the Lord have mercy upon half the tradesmen in England.[7]

In 1705, there was introduced in the House of Commons "A Bill to prevent Frauds, usually committed by Bankrupts." In 1706 a clause was proposed to protect those who had become bankrupts before December 25, 1705, or who had a commission of bankruptcy issued against them before June 24, 1706—if they voluntarily gave notice before July 1 that they would surrender themselves for examination. But on its second reading (March 5) this clause was defeated. The next day a similar clause in favor of those who had become bankrupt before March 25, 1706, and who surrendered themselves voluntarily before June 24, was passed by a majority of a single vote.

It was said that the principal consideration of one speaker was to exclude Defoe from the provisions of the clause. This speaker was a linen-draper near Covent-Garden (whom Defoe called W—— or W——r, but who is named in the *House of Lords Manuscripts* as John Water). We recognize Defoe's account of W——r in the blustering testimony which John Water gave at the bar of the House of Lords when he appeared with the petitioners against the bill on March 11. According to the *Review* of September 15, 1711, Water's own prosperity did not last much longer:

A certain draper not far from his neighbors had it always in his mouth, such a man was a rogue, such a villain, such a cheat—Why, Sir, says one?— Why, he can't pay his debts—If he had said won't pay his debts, I had joined with him; but to prevent my asking about his abilities, he always added, every man was a rogue that was a bankrupt; and in six months, I found his father's name in the *Gazette*. This made him a little modester, and now he finds as much difficulty to keep his own out, as any man in the street has done this seven year—[8]

After its passage by the Commons, the bill was carried up to the Lords. On March 19 the Commons accepted the two amendments which the Lords had added. One of these (Defoe had "pressed hard in Parliament for an amendment" to this) left the commissioners entirely free to decide whether a bankrupt had complied with the law. The other (which he heartily approved) required that the commissioners pay for what they ate and drank at their meetings, and not charge the expense to the bankrupt or to his creditors. Although Defoe had suffered no personal loss from greedy commissioners of bankruptcy, he had distributed charity to a shipwright who was later driven to suicide by the exactions of such commissioners.[9]

Defoe had been very active in the passage of this, "one of the best Bills that ever was produced in Parliament, since the Habeas Corpus Act, for securing the liberty of the subject." A contemporary said that Defoe had appeared at the bar of the House of Lords to reply to a petition against the bill (apparently on March 11, when John Water opposed it). When his enemies charged that he hoped to be a bene-

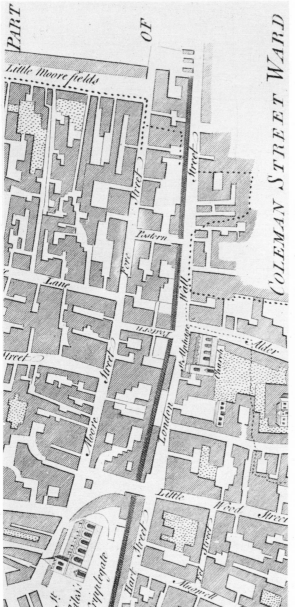

FORE STREET, WITH ST. GILES'S AND LONDON WALL

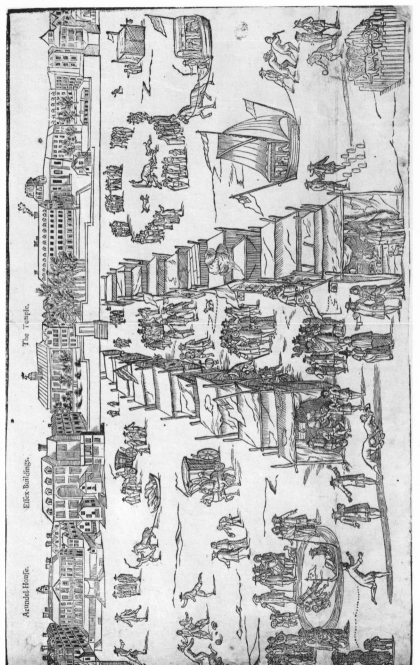

Arundel House.   Essex Buildings.   The Temple.

Ice Fair on the Thames, December, 1683

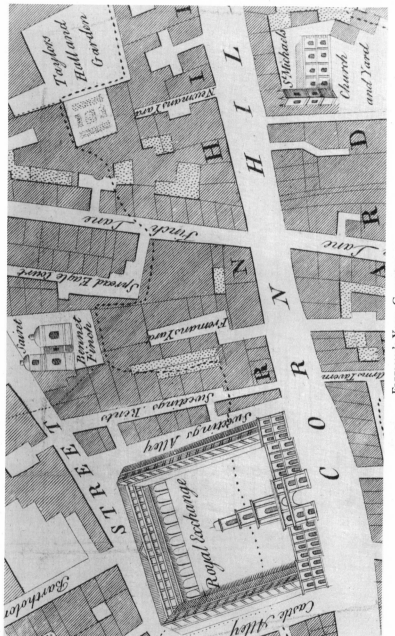

FREEMAN'S YARD, CORNHILL

(Defore's daughter Mary was buried in St. Michael's Church. Daniel Jr. later lived in Finch Lane)

CORNHILL, WEST OF FREEMAN'S YARD

Mercers' Chapel

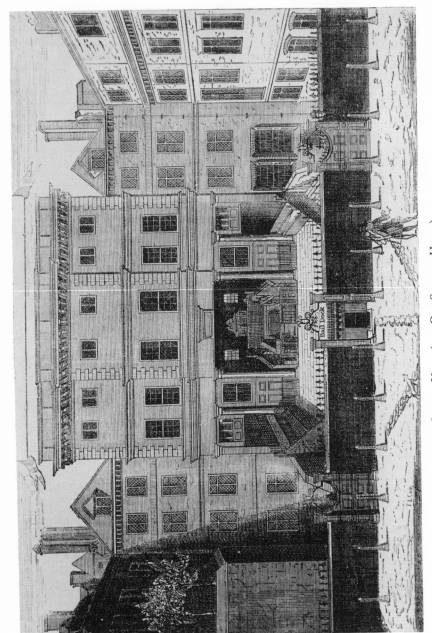

JUSTICE HALL. (THE OLD SESSIONS HOUSE)

DEFOE IN THE PILLORY (after Eyre Crowe's painting)

Laudatur et Alget
.*Iuven . Sat . I.*

M.V.ᵈʳGucht Sculp:

DEFOE IN 1706 (Von der Gucht's engraving)

ficiary, he offered to forgo any personal advantage in order to secure its passage. On May 24 he wrote to a correspondent that he might be obliged to leave the kingdom, for he was not certain that the law would aid him.

For a time he continued his effort to clear his affairs under the new act of Parliament. During the summer of 1706 he was examined four times by the commissioners and whatever creditors chose to attend the sessions, in the chamber of Robert Davis, his brother-in-law. In the *London Gazette* for July 18 to 22 the following advertisement appeared: "The Commissioners in a renewed Commission of Bankrupt against Daniel Foe, late of London, Merchant, hereby give notice, that he hath surrendered himself to the said Commissioners, and been twice examined; and that he will attend again on Tuesday the 6th of August next, at 4 in the afternoon, in order to finish his examination; when and where his creditors may attend, to show cause why a certificate should not be signed pursuant to the late act of Parliament."[10] In the *London Gazette* for August 5–8 the advertisement was repeated with slight changes. Defoe had now been examined "thrice," and he was to attend again on August 22 in Davis' chamber in the Middle-Temple. For some reason this last meeting was advanced to August 21. But after "four severe trials upon oath" and "the full free and honest surrender" of all his affairs, he found even on August 21 so much opposition among some of his creditors that he postponed asking for a certificate until his mission to Edinburgh for the Ministry was completed. As he had to conceal the official purpose of this mission, in Scotland even more than in England, there was an advantage in the false report that he had fled north on account of private debts.

On September 11 Benjamin Bragg (formerly Defoe's principal publisher, now his political enemy and the piratical publisher of some of his works) advertised that "Yesterday was publish'd, Observations on the Bankrupts Bill, occasion'd by the many false Misrepresentations and unjust Reflections of Mr. Daniel de Foe, in his several Discourses on that Head, humbly offer'd to the Consideration of all fair Traders: By a well Wisher to Trade and Credit." Two days later Defoe wrote to Harley that he was "just taking horse" for Scotland (where he was to serve the government as a secret agent in promoting the Union and in reporting on the course of events). Perhaps he hoped that the success of this important mission would enable him to settle his financial difficulties in London. But he received from Harley barely enough to provide for his subsistence; and before his return to London at the close of 1707, Parliament had added a clause requiring the signatures of four-fifths of the creditors (in number and in value). Defoe could have secured the signatures of two-thirds, but not of four-fifths; and so he made no further attempt to secure the certificate which would have given him relief.[11] After 1708, claims might be brought against him, even if they had been satisfied long before.

In his *Review* Defoe printed a letter from a correspondent warning that canceled bonds might sometimes be brought up again for a second payment. When he was driven from home about a year before his death, Mrs. Mary Brooke was making claims for debts which he had provided for thirty-five years before, at the time of his first composition for bankruptcy, with Samuel Stancliffe, long since dead. The first three executors of Stancliffe's estate had brought no such claims against Defoe. In fact, one of them (James Stancliffe, a creditor in his own right and an administrator of the estate of Samuel Stancliffe) had been actively engaged as Defoe's friend when he was released from Newgate (November, 1703). In 1706 Defoe called his creditors together a second time and agreed to surrender everything, assigning all property to James Stancliffe, who was to act as trustee for the satisfaction of all claims.

But when the widow of James Brooke succeeded her husband as administrator for James Stancliffe, who had been executor for Elizabeth Stancliffe, who had been executor for her late husband Samuel Stancliffe, Defoe was called on (in January, 1728, and in April, 1730) to pay for the long-forgotten and surely long-since-canceled "bonds and pretended debts."[12] In its cumulative detail, this legal claim resembles a nursery jingle like "The House that Jack Built" rather than a serious account of the honest administration of an estate.

We cannot now unravel all the details from legal briefs nearly two and a half centuries old. But one is struck by three indications that Mrs. Brooke knew nothing about the possible legality of her claim and that in all probability she was a tool acting on the instigation of some of Defoe's political opponents:

1. She was totally illiterate, so that she signed the administration of Defoe's affairs given her on September, 1733, with her mark alone.

2. The statements made in the application for that administration show that she did not know the name of Defoe's wife, or the comparative ages of their daughters, or the fact that Benjamin was the older brother. She did not even know that Defoe himself had been dead nearly a year before she heard of it.

3. If there had been just claims against Defoe from the Stancliffe estate,

it is incredible that they would not have been presented until after the lapse of more than a third of a century, when they fell into the hands of an illiterate woman who knew almost nothing about the Defoe family.

Defoe often pointed out that commercial claims were most easily settled out of court by impartial referees. Mrs. Brooke gained nothing by her litigation—although perhaps her instigators served their immediate purpose by handicapping one of the Ministry's principal journalists. Even so, Defoe continued to edit the *Political State of Great-Britain* in Walpole's interest through October, 1730—about seven months after Mrs. Brooke's demurrer of April, 1730, during part or all of which time he was driven into close hiding to escape Mrs. Brooke's persecution.

The confusion involved in such a suit was not due entirely to the complexities of legal proceedings or even to the false or misleading statements of some of the principals. Professional witnesses were constantly hanging around the law courts, "knights of the post" who stood ready to offer perjured testimony for "half a crown." A contemporary of Defoe was warned that he could be sent to prison for an imaginary debt. He wagered that this would be impossible, but his adversary hired "knights of the post" to swear him into Newgate. The prisoner was then obliged to hire other witnesses to swear that they had seen him repay the non-existent loan, and after that he was freed.

We do not know that Defoe ever suffered in just this way. But on August 28, 1706, after he had surrendered everything to his creditors, a stranger wrote to tell his brother-in-law Robert Davis that a gentleman of his acquaintance (*if he were paid enough to make it worth his while*) would bring proof that Defoe had withheld an estate of £400 a year—a crime which would have called for capital punishment. Defoe replied that if he had owned any such estate, he would not have gone into bankruptcy.[13]

Defoe seems to have spent only eleven days in prison for debt, but he must have gone about in constant fear and uncertainty. In his *Review* for August 20, 1706, just before his last meeting with his creditors, he wrote that whisperings had been spread of a plot against his life. Writing from Edinburgh early in the next year, he devoted parts of three *Reviews* to an account of a creditor whose sufferings were much like his own. This man had failed for £17,000 about 1692. He had made a composition with all but three or four of approximately 140 creditors, for fifteen shillings in the pound for £15,000 of the debts. He had a place in the government worth £200 a year, the income from which he offered to the creditors if they would let him go on with his work.

After his bankruptcy, he "had several times gotten into public business, but as soon as ever it was known, [he] was so constantly pursued with arrests, escapes, judgments, etc., that he was forced from them, and as if they had pursued him not for their debts but for his own destruction." Up to this point the story could be regarded as Defoe's own; but he provided a different conclusion. After this Defoe-like debtor had been imprisoned for years, the judge released him when he discovered the malice of the creditor chiefly responsible for his confinement.

In two other significant passages Defoe spoke indirectly of his own bankruptcy. He represented an angry Dissenter as fixing on the charge that "he had broke and can't pay his debts." To this the Observator (ostensibly John Tutchin, but here only a spokesman for Defoe) replied:

If you had said he had broke and won't pay his debts, you had said more to the purpose.

But I must do one piece to justice to the man, though I love him no better than you do, that is this: That meeting a gentleman in a coffee-house, where I and everybody else was railing at him, the gentleman took us up with this short speech.

Gentlemen, said he, I know this D'Foe as well as any of you, and I was one of his creditors, and I compounded with him, and discharged him fully; and several years afterwards he sent for me, and though he was clearly discharged he paid me all the remainder of his debt voluntarily, and of his own accord. And he told me, that as fast as God should enable him, he intended to do so with everybody. When he had done, he desired me to set my hand to a paper to acknowledge it, which I readily did, and found a great many names to the paper, before me, and I think myself bound to own, though I am no friend to the book he wrote, no more than you.

The generous effort to pay creditors more than he had compounded for (of which he was so proud in 1703) became a source of distress to Defoe when he was in danger from creditors to whom he had given fullest satisfaction.[14]

More than a century and a half ago, the first considerable biographer of Defoe discovered in Defoe's *Mercator* a clear explanation of his bankruptcy. But as Dr. Chalmers did not know that Defoe wrote *Mercator*, he gave little attention to the narrative, condensing part of it in a few lines for his own use.[15] Later biographers have relied on Chalmers' brief summary without consulting the original.

In the protectionist journal *The British Merchant*, Henry Martin had accused Defoe of writing for money when he supported the liberal commercial clauses of the Treaty of Utrecht (1713). In the early eighteenth century the pious fiction still prevailed that all good writers were wealthy amateurs, and that no patriot needed to earn a livelihood. If *Mercator* was to serve its purpose, Defoe had to deny his authorship and the receipt of any reward for writing it. A century later, when the prejudice against professional writers had dwindled, a man so honorable and so well-versed in the law as Sir Walter Scott denied that he had written the Waverley Novels, adding that (as no one had any right to ask him such a question) he would have felt free to deny the authorship even if he had written them.

In No. 101 of *Mercator* Defoe lets an imaginary correspondent tell how he interviewed Defoe himself on the subject, and in so doing he provides the most accurate account we have of his financial troubles. His explanation may be summed up as follows:

About 1692, when Defoe was ruined by the disasters of the war with France, an angry creditor took out a commission of bankruptcy against him. Immediately thereafter his creditors (including even the man who took out the commission) employed an attorney named Parkins to set aside the commission, after Defoe had convinced them that he would pay them in full if they gave him time. On his own initiative he attempted to satisfy his creditors; but finding his debts very heavy and some creditors impatient, he paid off such as were willing to accept part payment in composition. Defoe showed a paper on which several acknowledged that after they had received such compensation they had fallen into personal distress and he had paid them the full remainder of the debts from which they had discharged him.

At this time, through the favor of King William, Defoe was in rising circumstances, and he was certain of paying off his other creditors. But he was once again ruined, this time by the neglect of his brick and tile manufacture while he was being prosecuted and imprisoned for writing *The Shortest Way*, so that in the end he lost over £3,500. In 1706 he sought to obtain a discharge by reviving the old Commission of Bankruptcy. At that time he made a full and faithful discovery of all the estate and effects he had in the world, offering to surrender them according to the act of Parliament. But he met with opposition from some of his creditors, and he deferred asking for a certificate until his return from Scotland nearly a year and a half later. After the next Parliament added a clause to the act which made it impossible for him to meet the requirements, he ceased his efforts to secure a certificate.

A slanderer reported that Defoe had given a deficient account upon oath and had fled from the commissioners; but when Defoe returned to London he advertised a reward of £20 to anyone who would prove any deficiency in his oath and account.

Henry Martin had charged that in March, 1713, Defoe had been taken up on a judge's warrant for £1,500, and that he had paid the money the next day—suggesting that Defoe must have received the £1,500 for writing *Mercator*. Defoe referred to the attorney employed against him (Mr. Evans of Fleet Street) for confirmation of his statement that this arrest happened nearly seven years after his surrender of his effects, that *Mercator* was not begun until some months later, that the payment was not made until Defoe had been confined for eleven days, and that the creditor accepted one-tenth of his claim for £1,500, receiving only £25 of that amount in actual money.

There is no evidence to support the legend that he was a fugitive in Bristol, and no proof that he took shelter in the extralegal territory in Southwark where a mint had been operated under Henry VIII. But he must have spent some time as a refugee from his creditors until a composition could be agreed on, probably in one of the few remaining places which afforded immunity from arrest for debt. Twenty years later he recalled a cynical proverb he had "heard much among the Alsatia-men, viz., the Knights-Shelterers of the Mint, Whitefriars, &c." In 1723 he regretted that "the Mint" had been suppressed by the last session of Parliament; for as long as a debtor could take refuge, he could make terms for paying his creditors. After a debtor was confined in prison, both he and the creditor lost through his prolonged distress.

About this time Defoe interviewed Sir John Morden about his proposed asylum in Kent for broken men "upwards of fifty years of age, bachelors or widowers, and members of the Church of England," "poor, honest, sober, and discreet merchants who shall have lost their estates by accidents, dangers, and perils of the seas, or any other accidents, ways, or means, in their honest endeavor to get their living by way of merchandising." He would have been ineligible for Morden's project, both as a Dissenter and as a young married man. But he must have recalled it when he wrote his own proposal for a Protestant monastery, where aged men could be secure from the ingratitude of their children.[16]

Several times he speaks of the peace of mind a bankrupt enjoys after he decides to make a complete surrender. A tradesman had told him of his relief when he was no longer "obliged to stand in his shop, and be bullied and ruffled by his creditors, nay by their apprentices and boys, and sometimes by porters and footmen, to whom he was forced to give good words, . . . he was now no more obliged to make promises, which he knew he would not perform, and break promises as fast as he made them, and so lie continually to God and man; . . . the ease of his mind which he felt upon that occasion was so great, that it balanced all the grief he was in."

But to a Dissenter and a merchant, "bankruptcy was not only a disgrace but almost a sin." A gentleman of fashion might borrow money to supply his pleasures, and he might play pranks on his creditors to postpone the day of reckoning. The orthodox view of Dissenters was stated in a letter from Dr. Philip Doddridge to Dr. Isaac Watts: "We do hereby declare that if any person in stated communion with us shall become bankrupt or as it is commonly expressed *fail in the world*, he must expect to be cut off from our Body."[17]

Defoe felt the stain of failure. But he felt that his difficulties were a challenge to his character, not a mere token of defeat; and he rejoiced in his ability to shift for himself. "The scholar, got into misfortune, is good for just nothing but to scribble for bread," he declared. "The English tradesman is a kind of Phoenix, who often rises out of his own ashes, and makes the ruin of his fortunes to be a firm foundation to build his recovery." The merchant deserved disaster if he allowed reverses to prostrate him: "'A man that will lie still should never hope to rise; he that will lie in a ditch and pray may depend upon it he shall lie in the ditch and die."

Courage—which Defoe considered the most essential part of character—was as necessary to a merchant as to a hero of the wars: "A tradesman is never out of hope to rise, till he is nailed up in his coffin and six foot under ground."[18]

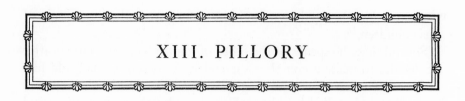

XIII. PILLORY

He that betrays his Master, tho' dead, or exposes his memory when he can no longer reward him, tho' it be to escape a pillory, or come out of Newgate, let his reputation die the death of a traitor.

Review, V, 586

I

ABOUT NOON on Thursday, July 29, 1703, a rather smallish figure stood on a wooden platform before the Royal Exchange in Cornhill, in the financial center of London. His neck and wrists were held rigidly in the openings of a cross-shaped frame, so that he stood in almost the same posture which has been made familiar by countless paintings of the Crucifixion. But although his hands were held painfully up in the slots at either side of the crossbar, they were not nailed. And although there was an inscription over his head, it did not ridicule him as a king, but recited the accusation that he had written *The Shortest Way with the Dissenters*.

There was no shade from the July sun, and an hour was a long time to stand in so cramped a position. Few men had ever died in the pillory, but many had fainted or had been maimed by objects thrown from the crowd in the street below. The suffering was always intense, and the shame was the greatest which could be inflicted under the law. No man in England but Defoe ever stood in the pillory and later rose to eminence among his fellow men.

The onlookers in the street who moved past the platform were, many of them, old business acquaintances of Defoe—on their way to or from their noonday meal. Twenty-five yards to his left was the entrance to Freeman's Yard, where he had brought his bride nineteen years before and where he had been one of the most daring of young merchants—until he had been swept into bankruptcy by the hazards brought on by the foreign war of King William. Eastward beyond the entrance to Freeman's Yard, and across the street, loomed St. Michael's, where the infant namesake of his wife had been buried in the lower vault of the south aisle. If his eyes twitched, he could not move a hand to wipe them. One could remember many things in an hour.

Six years ago, there had been a truce called the Peace of Ryswick, by which France and England tacitly agreed not to go to war again until the invalid King of Spain should die and leave his vast empire to the strongest claimant. The House of Commons would not allow William troops enough to resist Louis XIV. When he sought to prevent the impending war by his treaties of 1698 and 1699/1700 which called for a partition of the Spanish Empire, isolationists denounced them as secret pacts made without parliamentary approval. The Whig lords who had approved those acts were in danger of impeachment.

After the House of Commons had illegally imprisoned the Kentish Petitioners who demanded preparations for national defense, Defoe appeared at the door of the House the next morning (May 14, 1701) with his *Legion's Memorial*, which asserted the right of the people to control their representatives and concluded with a note of defiance:

Our Name is LEGION, and we are Many.

Postscript. If you require to have this Memorial signed with our Names, it shall be done on your first order, and personally presented.

The extraordinary memorial was inclosed in a letter to Robert Harley, Speaker of the House, commanding him in the name of two hundred thousand Englishmen to deliver it to the Commons.

Rumor was busy about this first meeting of Harley and Defoe. It was reported that as Harley entered the door of the House, Defoe, disguised as an old woman, handed him the paper. Defoe did take the precaution to write "in a hand that stood the wrong way," but he delivered the memorial in person and alone, although about sixteen gentlemen of quality were ready to defend him against violence.

Two brave men faced each other at the door of St. Stephens' Chapel that morning. The Kentish Petition had been treated with scorn, but *Legion's Memorial* was not slighted. It has been surmised that Harley was impressed by the unusual man who faced him and by the unusual memorial which he presented. Harley and Defoe came to know each other well in the years which followed.

In the House there was something like panic. Harley did not alter "his usual haughty tone"; but many members were frightened and dropped off into the country before the session ended on June 24—after a timid gesture of good will encouraging William to strengthen his hand through foreign alliances.

Soon the Kentish Petitioners, freed from imprisonment by the rising of Parliament, were "being invited to a noble entertainment at Mercers-Hall in Cheapside, at the charge of the citizens of London, where above two hundred gentlemen dined with them together with several noble lords and members of parliament." A medal was struck to celebrate the Kentish men who had not "sold their country for gold." And Defoe sat beside them as a guest of honor—whose triumph a hostile pamphleteer sought to ridicule but could not conceal: "Next the Worthies was placed their Secretary of State, the author of the Legion-Letter; and one might have read the downfall of parliaments in his very countenance."[1]

A Tory writer might remind his readers (from the miracle in the New Testament) that those were devils who called themselves Legion. But the great lawyer Lord Somers reiterated Defoe's legal theory in his own next tract, and he was not unwilling "to use the words of *Legion*." Tory writers alleged that the Kentish Petition and *Legion's Memorial* were both designed "to divert the House from their intended prosecution" of four Whig lords. In the next month all four were freed—Somers and Orford on acquittal by the House of Lords, Halifax and Portland when the Lords dismissed their impeachments. *Legion's Memorial* had proved the most influential of the Whig "libels," of which a Tory complained that they were "dispersed not only all over England, but even through Holland, Germany, and the West Indies."[2] "Legion" because almost as proud a title as "The Author of *The True-Born Englishman*."

Defoe had also supported the reformation of manners which King William proclaimed in 1692. Magistrates, selected to strengthen their party in elections, were frequently the worst offenders under the laws against vice and profanity which they were asked to enforce; and the Anglican clergy were often as hostile to Puritanism as the magistrates.

In *The Poor Man's Plea* (1698) Defoe had declared that magistrates often laid severe penalties on men less guilty than themselves. In *Legion's New Paper* (1702) he had charged the High Church and High Tory members of the House of Commons with failure to suppress vice. In *Reformation of Manners* (1702) he had invited his readers to go with him through London "to see how lewd our Justice-Merchants are." Whigs as well as Tories, clergymen as well as laymen, all who had offended against public morals, had fallen under the lash of this City Juvenal. The High Church lawyer and the alderman-judges had their say about Defoe—when he came before them in Justice Hall on July 7, 1703.[3]

But the immediate excuse for the government's prosecution of Defoe grew out of the controversy over the Occasional Conformity of Dissenters. The Test Act, which required communion with the Church of England as a qualification for public office, had been passed in 1673. Ostensibly intended to check the growing power of the Roman Catholics, it remained as a barrier against the employment of a far more numerous minority—the Protestant Dissenters. However, in practice a working compromise had at last been reached. Saintly Dissenters might sometimes feel free to conform to the ritual of the national church, as an expression of Christian brotherhood. More worldly Dissenters might argue that there was no real breach of faith if they conformed, because the Test Act was designed to keep Papists out of office. Ambitious Dissenters might conform "occasionally" to qualify for public offices.

Defoe saw both sides of the problem, and in his unsparing honesty he offended leaders of both parties in the dispute. As a political observer, he recognized that the Dissenters were treated unfairly and that the nation needed their services. As a conscientious Dissenter, he allowed no room for "playing Bo-peep with God Almighty."

It would have been easy for Defoe to change sides when he found that the Dissenters would not defend him and that the High Fliers (the extreme advocates of royal prerogative and of ecclesiastical power) would prosecute him unless he gave up his allegiance to his own faith. Some leaders of the High Church party had grown up as Dissenters. It was even reported that Samuel Wesley, an ex-Dissenter who had attended Morton's academy shortly after Defoe left there, wrote the speech delivered by Dr. Sacheverell at his famous trial. The Jonathan Swift who (as a Whig) had defended Somers' theory of government in 1701 was welcomed by the Tories when he went over to their party in 1710. Defoe was fond of quoting from "the incomparable *Hudibras*,"

> He that hangs, or beats out's brains,
> The Devil's in him if he feigns.[4]

No test of faith is so convincing as the willingness to undergo martyrdom. By that test Defoe was one of the most loyal of Dissenters.

Queen Anne had hoped for a government above party. In an evil hour (May 25, 1702) she concluded a speech to her first Parliament with words which were taken to imply gross partiality: "I shall be very careful to preserve and maintain the Act of Toleration, and to set the minds of all my people at quiet: My own principles must always keep me entirely firm in the interests and religion of the Church of England, and will incline me to countenance those who have the truest zeal to support it." One week later Sacheverell preached his notorious "Oxford Sermon," in which he urged the Church to "hang out the bloody flag, and banner of defiance." As Defoe said, "the dread monsters revived, and, like Cadmus's field, all the bones of the slaughtered furies stood up in bands of armed men."

A national issue was brought to a crisis through a sermon by one of the dullest preachers who ever mounted a pulpit stair to sound an alarm on the "drum ecclesiastic." Dr. Henry Sacheverell was, according to the Whig Duchess of Marlborough, "an ignorant and impudent incendiary, the scorn of those that made him their tool." According to the High Churchman Thomas Hearne, who knew him well and who agreed with his politics, he was "conceited, ignorant, impudent, a rascal and a knave."

But Sacheverell put himself forward as the symbol of a cause. With the aid of the men who wrote his best speeches, he gave bold expression to the favorite ideas of extremists and thereby helped to direct the course of events. According to the historian Feiling, "from the date of the Kentish Petition, the back-benchers in the Commons got entirely out of hand." Sacheverell was a mouthpiece for those Tory backbenchers, who for a while dominated the party which ruled England. In the reign of Anne, as in the time of Balaam, an ass was permitted to speak with the voice of prophecy.

When the new Parliament convened on October 20, 1702, the moderate Harley (a former Whig who was now allied with the Tories) was chosen Speaker of the House of Commons; but it was said that only the fear of a split in the party kept the High Fliers from opposing his election.[5] Soon the House got down to its serious business of breaking the working alliance between Low Churchmen and Dissenters which gave the Whigs much of their strength.

On November 1 the House of Commons granted leave to Bromley, St. John, and Annesley to prepare and bring in a Bill to Prevent Occasional Conformity. Of these three chosen defenders of the national church, Annesley was a secret Jacobite, Bromley was suspected of strong leanings toward Roman Catholicism, and St. John was a Deist who rarely attended any religious service.

The government of the day, totally unconcerned about the fate of the Dissenters, was willing to let the bill pass—if it did not delay the Land Tax necessary for the war against France or imperil the grant of a dukedom and pension for Marlborough, Lord Treasurer Godolphin's ally and his relative by marriage. On November 7 Godolphin wrote to Harley: "The votes of yesterday with the assurances which I have had that no angry thing shall be stirred in the House of Commons, give a fair prospect of a speedy and quiet end of the sessions, of which I am extremely glad for many reasons." But an "angry thing" was being stirred in the House. On November 14 and 17 the Bill to Prevent Occasional Conformity passed its first and second readings, and on November 23 it was engrossed with its amendments. On November 24 Godolphin could still write confidentially to Harley: "if the House of Commons suffer no new incident to interfere with the dispatch of the supplies I am not out of hopes but the session may yet end with the old year, which I think would be a better new year's gift to the whole kingdom than they have had to brag of this long time."[6] On Saturday, November 28, the bill was read the third time and it was ordered to be carried up to the House of Lords. Defoe reported that "about the Bill the press swarms with pamphlets; the pulpit sounds with exaltations on one hand, and deprecations on the other."[7] But no writer for the Dissenters had been able to get a hearing, and the bill had been passing triumphantly through the House of Commons.

For nearly five years Defoe had been involved in a controversy with those of his fellow Dissenters who complied with the Test Act in order to qualify for public offices. In a broadside recently discovered in the Huntington Library, *The Opinion of a Known Dissenter* (published late in 1702 but postdated 1703), he repeated for the man in the street the most telling arguments which he had used previously in three full-length pamphlets against Occasional Conformity.

But now he suddenly ceased to appeal to the conscientious scruples of his fellows, and he struck at what he regarded as tyranny. On Tuesday, December 1—the very day before the bill was to be carried up to the House of Lords—appeared *The Shortest Way with the Dissenters*. Here he no longer attacked individual Dissenters who had proved too weak to undergo oppression, but the organized power which used oppression as an instrument of national policy.

A few years later a pamphleteer for the High Fliers charged that

The Shortest Way was instigated by Harley, who rose to power by overthrowing the High Church wing of the Tories. It was widely believed that Defoe was serving Somers and Halifax and that the tract was meant to forestall their threatened impeachment. It has been suggested that Defoe wrote as a good journalist, because he was a specialist and the subject interested him. Harley did profit by the reaction against the High Church leaders, but he was as much alarmed by its first effect as anyone else. Somers and Halifax were strengthened in their fight against the Tory House of Commons, but the tract was not written primarily to support them. Defoe did enjoy one of his greatest triumphs as a journalist, but there is no reason to reject his own statement of his purpose: *He sought to put the High Church party hopelessly in the wrong by an ironical statement of views which they held but dared not proclaim.*[8]

The Shortest Way had an immense sale, and thereafter Defoe was "Shortest Way" as often as "Legion" or "True-Born Englishman." His enemies charged him with using rhetorical methods learned at Morton's academy; certainly *The Shortest Way* is one of the finest examples of the debater's method of *reductio ad absurdum*. No one but an intense bigot would have wished to express himself so; but the most extravagant High Flier would have said this, if he had been honest enough to utter his real feelings and able enough to write such glorious prose. Sacheverell's ravings tended in the same direction; but they no more equaled Defoe's tract than the muddy waters of a back stream equal the white fury of Niagara.

The Dissenters were panic-stricken by Defoe's proposal to hang them unless they recanted. When they discovered that the author was one of themselves, they turned wildly on the man they regarded as their betrayer. The High Fliers were even more angry, when their first rejoicing was exposed to ridicule. One of their number, Moore (a fellow of a college at Cambridge according to Oldmixon, "an eminent clergyman in the country" according to the story which Defoe referred to several times), received a copy from a London bookseller. He was so grateful for this expression of his feelings that he wrote to give thanks for *The Shortest Way*, which he prized above any book he owned except the Holy Bible and the Sacred Comments, praying to God to put it into the heart of Queen Anne to carry out the methods presented in it. Even as late as October 9, 1703, a High Church pamphleteer still admitted that his party had approved of the pamphlet until they discovered the hoax, and he advised Defoe to avoid further difficulty by naming the man who had set him on to write it.[9]

The High Fliers' position was obviously untenable, though a few pamphleteers fought a rear-guard action by claiming that Defoe's tract said much that was true about the Dissenters, and that some persecution might be a good thing for them. An Old Whig suggested that persecution would only strengthen the faith of those who might be drawn into the Church if they were allowed to taste the sweets of office. He urged that the most effective way to weaken the Dissenters was to let them alone. But the Tory extremists desired nothing less than to allow Dissenters to taste any such sweets; legal toleration seemed to them more than sufficient, and *The Shortest Way* a blasphemous attack on Mother Church.

Throughout most of December, January, and February the controversy over the Occasional bill rocked Parliament. The Commons (overwhelmingly Tory) insisted on the bill as it stood. The Lords (in whose House the Low Church bishops appointed by King William provided a slight Whig majority) did not dare to oppose it openly, but they refused to pass it without amendments which they knew the Commons would reject as invasions of their exclusive control over financial legislation.

There was wide difference of opinion regarding the purpose and probable effect of the bill. According to Bishop Burnet, it was introduced in 1702 to dishearten the Whigs from lending money to the government, and thereby to block the war itself. According to Robert Harley's brother Edward, the bill as it was finally passed in 1711 had little effect, "not more than five persons through the whole Kingdom having quitted any place of profit under the Government."[10]

An oversimplified statement may present the situation more clearly. Lord Treasurer Godolphin cared little about the Dissenters or the bill, but he needed the co-operation of the House of Commons in order to support his ally Marlborough and to finance the war. Speaker Harley wished to bridle the Tory extremists and to lead the majority in a moderate course; and so—indifferent to the welfare of the Dissenters or to the fate of the bill—he sought to aid Godolphin in getting on with the war. Nottingham and his High Church allies had no heart for the war; they sought to shackle the Dissenters and, later, to break the power of the Whigs by successful impeachment of the lords who were held responsible for the Second Partition Treaty. Halifax, Somers, and Orford were disposed to be friendly to the

Dissenters; but they had escaped from the perils of an impeachment too recently to be eager to risk their own safety. Even while Halifax was a leader in the Lords' committee whose insistence on amendments wrecked the bill, the Commons reopened their attack on him by voting him guilty of breaches of trust as William's Chancellor of the Exchequer. The Lords had to come to his rescue by resolving that he had delivered the imprest rolls according to the ancient course of the exchequer.

If *The Shortest Way* was a bold maneuver in favor of the Whig lords, it was one in which Defoe took all the risks, for no apparent advantage to himself.

On December 9 the Commons got completely out of the Ministry's control, voting 171 to 99 against considering the all-important Land Tax, and proceeding immediately to a discussion of the Lords' amendment to their own bill. Next day Godolphin wrote in distress to Harley: "If you would be at liberty this night I would come to you after Council is done to talk a little about the madness of yesterday, and to have your opinion of a thought I have had concerning the matter. Does anybody think England will be persuaded that this Queen won't take care to preserve the Church of England? And do they forget that not only the fate of England but all Europe depends upon the appearance of our concord in the despatch of supplies?"[11]

On December 17 the House of Lords agreed to a conference, but no compromise was to be expected. The House of Commons sought the enactment of its favorite bill. Among the managers for the Lords were the Bishop of Salisbury and Somers, Halifax, and Orford—the most hated of Low Church bishops and three of the four Whig lords whom the Commons sought to strike down. On December 10 the Lords ordered Carmarthen and Halifax not to proceed to a challenge about some words regarding the bill. On January 9 Sir Richard Onslow disarmed another member of Parliament in a duel arising out of a committee meeting. On January 14 Godolphin wrote to Harley, "I find by the stopping of the money bills the Queen's servants in both Houses are vying who shall be maddest."[12]

As Defoe recalled the events nine years later, "nothing was more strange than to see the effect upon the whole nation which this little book, a contemptible pamphlet of but three sheets of paper, had, and in so short a time too." According to his most hostile critic, "it stirred up the common people to that degree that the clergy were insulted in the streets and on the highways, and were in danger of being mobbed all over the nation." In late December Godolphin wrote rather desperately to Nottingham: "I had last night some talk with the speaker, and he has had a mind to speak to you about a book lately come out, called, *a short way with the Dissenters.* He seemed to think it absolutely necessary for the service of the Government that your Lordship should endeavor to discover who was the author of it."[13] This brought the matter into the realm where the Earl of Nottingham was supreme. As the more active of the two principal secretaries of state, he had taken charge of regulating the press, and he had at his command the Queen's messengers and the power to issue warrants for arrest.

As the so-called "Secretary of the Party" on whom all effective writings for Whigs or Dissenters were likely to be fathered, Defoe was under suspicion as the probable author of any such tract. Near the end of December he was apparently taken up to be questioned, but he got away. On January 2 the *Observator* reported that "one person" was taken into custody on account of *The Shortest Way,* but made his escape from the messenger. A few weeks later a hostile pamphleteer reminded Defoe that "they are in search of him, and if he does not provide himself with ways and means to jump out of windows as he did, he may keep company with his printer, who has got a stone-doublet to fit close on his shoulders for changing parties, and when he had some reputation in the world by conversing with honest men, for losing it of a sudden by keeping company with those that had none." This suggestion that Defoe's printer was a deserter from the High Fliers accords with Dunton's remark about George Croome: "some would insinuate as though he favored the Jacobites, but I take him for a man of more sense." In 1702 one of Harley's agents reported that Croome was printing seditious books. In 1705 another reported that he was a non-juror (one of those who refused to take the oath of allegiance to the government as established by the Revolution of 1689).

Nottingham was the "Don Dismal" of Defoe's later writings—a tall, thin, dark, proud, and dull man, whose one great virtue was his loyalty to High Church. He was not the man to allow Defoe to slip out of his hands so easily. On January 2 it was reported that "A warrant is out for taking up one Bellamy for handing to the press a libel called A Short Way with the Dissenters."[14]

According to a Tory writer, the man sought in 1703 was "Mr. Bellamy, the Party's agent, both in England and Holland." Seven years later Defoe represented the Pope as referring to "my old friend Bellamy," "a true son of our Church," who had once published a book asserting that it was impossible for subjects to be Presbyterians and not rebels. An Edward Bellamy is listed in the British Museum Catalogue as the translator of a Spanish book in 1698. In 1690 a Southwark hosier named Bellamy had called Sir Peter Rich the murderer of the Whig martyr Lord Russell, and a sympathetic jury had allowed Rich only nominal damages. A Bellamy of Southwark can be traced as early as 1686 as a principal witness at the trial of "Julian" Johnson, the clergyman who was sentenced to an even more severe punishment than Defoe's for writing against the tyrannical plans of James II. The three men who signed the indictment on which Defoe was brought to trial on July 7, 1703, were Robert Stephens (the Queen's messenger), Geo. Croome (the printer of *The Shortest Way*), and Edwd. Bellamy.

We cannot be certain that the same Edward Bellamy was referred to in all these statements. But it is very likely that the Whig agent who betrayed "Julian" Johnson in 1686 by testifying that he had distributed Johnson's pamphlet was identical with the Whig agent who informed Nottingham in 1703 that he had delivered Defoe's manuscript to the printer Croome. A few weeks later Defoe wrote a dialogue in which both speakers used *Bellamy* as a synonym for *informer*.[15]

On Saturday, January 2, 1703, Bellamy named Defoe as the author of *The Shortest Way*. On the next day Nottingham issued a warrant "to Henry Allen, one of her Majesty's messengers in ordinary":

These are in her Majesty's name to authorize and require you taking to your assistance a constable forthwith to make strict and diligent search for Daniel Foe, and him having found you are to apprehend and seize, together with his papers for high crimes and misdemeanors, and to bring him before me to be examined concerning such matters as shall be objected against him touching the premises and to be further dealt with according to law. In the execution hereof all mayors, justices of the peace, constables, and all other her Majesty's officers civil and military, and loving subjects whom it may concern, are to be assisting unto you as there may be occasion, for which this shall be to them and you a sufficient warrant. Given at the Court at Whitehall the 3d day of January 1702/3.

NOTTINGHAM.

In this warrant four points are of special interest. Defoe was charged with high crimes and misdemeanors for restating in banter what Sacheverell and others had declared in earnest. Nottingham wished to examine Defoe in person before he was committed to prison; from the first his chief concern was to learn what Defoe could tell him. He also wished to examine Defoe's unpublished manuscripts. Perhaps through respect for Defoe's recently proved agility in escaping from a Queen's messenger, perhaps through fear of a rescue, Defoe was to be dealt with by at least two men.

According to Defoe's own account of the arrest, he was seized by two men. Ten years later, when he was led on horseback from his home as a sick man, great precautions were taken to prevent his escape or his rescue by the crowd. In Nottingham's warrants of January and July the three messengers named to have custody of Defoe were Henry Allen, Samuel Hill, and Mr. Dagley. Apparently the Queen's principal messenger for the press, the fat and gouty Robert Stephens, so often ridiculed by Defoe and others as "Robin Hog," was not to be trusted to capture a gentleman so nimble at escaping by jumping out of windows—though Stephens was called on to search Defoe after his arrest.

Defoe was in hiding, but he could not remain concealed indefinitely. A day or two after the warrant had been issued, his wife made an unsuccessful journey to Whitehall to ask Nottingham for terms.[16] As the hot search continued, Defoe fell back on his last and greatest resource—his pen. In an earnest letter on January 9 he volunteered to answer Nottingham's questions without subjecting himself to cross-examination and to offer himself and his financial resources to the Queen for her military service. In the second paragraph of this letter Defoe seems to deny writing *Legion's Memorial*, which was his own work; but his ambiguous denial applies even better to such things as the Kentish Petition, *The Black List*, and *Jure Populi Anglicani*, which were really not his.

Defoe's letter to Nottingham (with modernized spelling and punctuation) is as follows:

My Lord,

I am exceeding sensible that I have given her Majesty and the Government offence; and several poor and some innocent people being in trouble on my account, moves me to address your Lordship in this manner, for which rudeness I humbly ask your pardon.

I had long since surrendered to her Majesty's clemency, had not the menaces of your Lordship's officers possessed me with such ideas of her Majesty's and your Lordship's resentments, as were too terrible, and such as respected former things which I have had no concern in, though I have had the misfortune to pass for guilty by common fame.

To flee from her Majesty's justice seems, my Lord, to be a kind of raising war against her, and is very irksome to me. I beseech your Lordship to assist me in laying down these arms, or at least in making such a truce as may through her Majesty's condescension obtain her pardon.

My Lord, a body unfit to bear the hardships of a prison and a mind impatient of confinement have been the only reasons of withdrawing myself. And, my Lord, the cries of a numerous ruined family, the prospect of a long banishment from my native country, and the hopes of her Majesty's mercy moves me to throw myself at her Majesty's feet, and to entreat your Lordship's intercession.

I beseech your Lordship to assure her Majesty that I am perfectly free from any seditious designs, and however I have unadvisedly offended, I am and ever was entirely devoted to her interest and service.

With the lowest submission I entreat her Majesty's pardon for this mistake, for which I am ready to make any public acknowledgment, and further humbly beseech your Lordship's pardon and patience in making a proposal on my own behalf. For though it must be an unusual condescension in her Majesty to capitulate with an offending subject, yet offences differ in their nature, and her Majesty's mercy is unbounded.

I was informed, my Lord, that when my distressed wife made application to your Lordship, you were pleased to direct that I should surrender, and answer to such questions as should be asked me. My Lord, would your Lordship condescend to permit any questions you think fit be writ down, and sent to, or left at my house, I will as soon as I can receive them, give your Lordship as plain, full, direct, and honest answers as if I were in immediate apprehensions of death from your resentments; and perhaps, my Lord, my answers may be so satisfactory as may incline you to think you have been misinformed concerning me.

But, my Lord, if after this I should still have the misfortune to remain under her Majesty's displeasure, I am then her most humble petitioner that she will please to remit the rigor of prosecution, and that pleading guilty I may receive a sentence from her particular justice a little more tolerable to me as a gentleman than prisons, pillories, and such like, which are worse to me than death.

I beg leave to observe to your Lordship, that felons and thieves, whose punishment is death, are frequently spared upon entering into her Majesty's service. If her Majesty will be pleased to order me to serve her a year or more at my own charges, I will surrender myself a volunteer at the head of her armies in the Netherlands, to any colonel of horse her Majesty shall direct, and without doubt, my Lord, I shall die there much more to her service than in a prison. And if by my behavior I can expiate this offence and obtain her Majesty's pardon, I shall think it much more honorable to me than if I had it by petition.

And lest I should seem to prescribe to her Majesty's mercy, my Lord, if her Majesty, abating prisons and corporal punishments, shall please to pass any sentence upon me that I am capable to put in execution, I resolve cheerfully to submit to it and throw myself upon her native clemency.

But if her Majesty shall extend her grace to a total remission of this offence, and if I may presume to say shall further be pleased to accept my service, I will raise her Majesty a troop of horse, at my own charges, and at the head of them I'll serve her as long as I live.

At least, my Lord, this may assure you I am ready with my hand, my pen, or my head to show her Majesty the gratitude of a pardoned subject; and to give her Majesty all the satisfaction I am capable of, being extremely grieved that I have offended her. Humbly entreating your Lordship's favor and intercession which possibly your Lordship will not repent, when you shall find you have granted it to a zealous, thankful, and faithful subject, and to

> May it please your Lordship
> Your most obedient, distressed
> Humble petitioner and servant
> DE FOE.[17]

In this remarkable letter two features are most noteworthy. Here for the first time we have an example of the sort of letters which the student at Morton's academy had learned to compose, when he and his classmates were taught "to know how to suit their manner as well to the subject they were to write upon as to the persons they were to write to" and when their classroom exercises were often "directed to the Secretary of State." Secondly, although Nottingham was fond of his own eloquence, such refinements of style in a Whig journalist were not to his taste. Highwaymen might be allowed to escape hanging through military service in Flanders; but satirical writers for the Opposition could expect no mercy if they refused to betray their party leaders. For the first and last time in his long career, Defoe offered his services to the government only to be treated with scorn.

The history of the reign of Queen Anne might have been very different if this Secretary of State had welcomed Defoe's support—as King William had done, and as Harley, Godolphin, Townshend, Stanhope, Sunderland, and Walpole were to do later. But Nottingham had no desire to win the gratitude of an able political writer. All he sought from him was information which would enable him to discredit the reign of King William and to impeach Halifax and his allies. Failing in this, he could still punish the man who had refused to give him the evidence he sought.

Nottingham answered Defoe's letter by advertising, in two successive numbers of the official *London Gazette*, a very large reward for the discovery of a mere journalist. Both announcements were dated January 10, but the second was rewritten from new information. On January 11 the notice read: "St. James's, Jan. 10. Whereas Daniel de Fooe is charged with writing a scandalous and seditious pamphlet entitled The shortest way with the Dissenters, whoever shall discover the said Daniel Fooe to one of her Majesty's Principal Secretaries of State, or any of her Majesty's Justices of the Peace, so as he may be apprehended, shall have a reward of £50 which her Majesty has ordered immediately to be paid upon such discovery." The type for this advertisement was entirely reset for the *Gazette* of January 14, so as to correct the spelling of Defoe's name and to give a description of his appearance and some account of his commercial activities:

St. James's, Jan. 10. Whereas Daniel de Foe *alias* de Fooe is charged with writing a scandalous and seditious pamphlet entitled The Shortest Way with the Dissenters. He is a middle sized spare man, about forty years old, of a brown complexion, and dark-brown hair, but wears a wig, a hooked nose, a sharp chin, grey eyes, and a large mole near his mouth, was born in London, and for many years was a hose-factor in Freeman's-yard in Cornhill, and now is owner of the brick and pantile works near Tilbury-Fort in Essex. Whoever shall discover the said Daniel de Foe to one of her Majesty's Principal Secretaries of State, or any of her Majesty's Justices of the Peace, so as he may be apprehended, shall have a reward of £50 which her Majesty has ordered immediately to be paid upon such discovery.

Biographers are in debt to the informer Bellamy for the best description of Defoe in existence. But Defoe was annoyed. It was well enough to be likened to William III—quite another thing to be reminded of a sharp chin and a Dutch nose. In Defoe's next tract a speaker grumbled about these marks of identification: "Read the *Gazette;* there you have the man with the sharp chin, and a Dutch nose. . . . I have no mind to have my nose and chin described, . . . the man with the hook nose and sharp chin, . . . if you would turn informer, you might hook their noses into the *Gazette* too." As late as July he still recalled the slight in his account of a victim of party interest:

All men would say the picture was thy own,
No *Gazette* marks were half so quickly known.[18]

Five days after Nottingham announced the reward, he issued a warrant for arresting Defoe's printer and for raiding his dwelling and printing house. All manuscripts and printed copies of *The Shortest Way* were to be seized, marked sheet by sheet, and brought to Nottingham or to the Queen's Attorney-General. Justices of the peace would not serve the turn now; Nottingham had brought in the Attorney-General, and he was preparing for a state prosecution. On

January 25 the Solicitor to the Treasurer gave Godolphin a list of persons for whose prosecution £200 was set aside, and one entry read: "The Queen against De Foe and others for a libel entitled 'The Shortest Way with the Dissenters, &c.' "

At the same time, Nottingham was showing no such eagerness to suppress treasonable Jacobite pamphlets. Seven years later Bishop Burnet told how one was openly sold at the door of the House, plainly calling William a usurper and urging the Queen to possess the throne only until she could deliver it to the rightful heir: "At that time there was quick prosecution of a paper published with the title of The Shortest Way with the Dissenters; and upon that I brought that pamphlet [*The Exorbitant Grants of William III*] to a great minister [Nottingham], and offered to show him this passage in it, to see if there should not be a prosecution of this ordered. He turned from me; so whether he heard me or not, I cannot tell: I am sure, if he says he did not, I will believe him."

Angry Dissenters and Tories did not need to fear a man in hiding. One challenged Defoe to a duel. Mr. S——, at the head of a club of Dissenters, declared that if he could find him he would deliver him without the reward. Another Dissenter, Col. W——ll, voluntered to serve as hangman rather than let Defoe escape. Still another wished to betray him for the reward; but Defoe "drew upon him, frightened him out of his wits and made him down of his knees and swear that if ever he met him again, he should shut his eyes till he was half a mile off him."[19]

Perhaps Defoe's actions at this time suggest a spirit of frenzy, but the Tory leaders were not calm. On January 19 the Lords voted sixty-five to sixty-three to adhere to their amendments. A little later, old John Evelyn recorded in his *Diary:* "The Bill against Occasional Conformity was lost by one vote." On February 27 Parliament was prorogued, and it did not meet again until November 9. All attempts to impeach Halifax had failed, and the Occasional bill could not be brought in again until late November. But something could still be done. On February 24, before the Justices of Oyer and Terminer at Justice Hall in the Old Bailey, Defoe was indicted for writing and publishing a seditious libel.[20]

II

It was near noon on Friday, July 30. The scaffold for the pillory had been moved to the widest thoroughfare in London—in Cheapside, near where the great Conduit had stood before the Fire. All up and down the broad paved way were the most luxurious shops in the City. Here it was that one could see the foremost spectacle of London every autumn—the gilded coach of each new Lord Mayor as he moved in procession to Westminster. Here it was that nearly fourteen years earlier Defoe and his comrades in the Royal Volunteers had held lighted flambeaus when they rode as escorts to King William and Queen Mary on their return from the banquet in the Guildhall.

Northward across the street stood the handsome building called Mercers' Chapel, with its "beautiful front of stone towards the street, with a balcony, and the figures of Faith and Hope artificially wrought in stone, and above them the larger figure of Charity."[21] Only two years before, in the great hall which extended behind that balcony, Defoe had dined in glory with the Kentish Petitioners, as one of the patriots who had resisted the tyranny of a House of Commons which attempted to stifle freedom of speech. The two hundred gentlemen who had honored him that evening were all scattered; and there were no more banquets to look forward to, now that one's home was Newgate Prison.

The original indictment was lost for more than two and a half centuries; but it survives in the City of London Records (Oyer and Terminer Roll for February 22 and 24, 1702/3). The "Memorandum" is too long to be reproduced in full, but its substance is as follows:

On February 24, 1703, in Justice Hall in the Old Bailey, before Sir Samuel Dashwood (the Lord Mayor), Sir John Holt (Chief Justice), Sir Littleton Powis (a judge), John Smith (a Baron of the Exchequer), Sir Robert Geffrey and Sir Thomas Lane (aldermen), and (Sir) Salathiel Lovell (Recorder of London), "and other their associates, justices of the said Queen appointed by letters patent under the Great Seal," an indictment was brought in against Defoe. This was sworn to by Robert Jeffes, James Bardoe, Edward Round, John Britton, Thomas Waters, James Baker, Robert Owen, George Hurst, Thos. Browne, Thos. Rogers, Nathaniel Jarvis, Charles Herle, William Woolley, John Wade, Chas. Harvey, Henry Greenaway, and Thos. Newman, "honest and lawful men of the City of London."

The indictment alleged that on December 22, 1702, copies of *The Shortest Way* had been offered for sale in the parish of Bow in the ward of Cheap, and that Defoe had sought to keep Protestant Dissenters from enjoying religious toleration and to prevent the Union of England and Scotland. To support this charge, selected passages were quoted almost verbatim from certain pages of *The Shortest Way* (2, 3, 4, 6, 10, 11, 12, 13, 15, 16, 17, 18, 19, and 21).

The memorandum concluded by stating that the Sheriff of London was ordered to bring Defoe before the justices at the next session of Oyer and Terminer (April 7, 1703). On the following day a complaint was made to the House of Commons, several paragraphs were read from pages 11, 18, and 26, and *The Shortest Way* was ordered to be burned the next morning (February 26) in the New Palace Yard, Westminster. These three pages denied the necessity of a union with Scotland, suggested the use of force against the Scotch to preserve the succession, argued that it was equally kind to destroy a Dissenter and a poisonous snake, and declared that the Church must be established while a perfect combination existed to carry out the desired reform—with Parliament, Convocation, the gentry, and the Queen united in the common purpose.

The treasury books record payments to the Treasurer's solicitor for "swearing the witnesses before the grand jury" in finding a bill against Defoe "for a libel," for "other expenses and inquiries after Daniel D'foe in order to [his] being prosecuted," and "for costs in the proceedings to outlawry (the defendant De Foe absconding)."

For the fourth consecutive day Defoe remained the primary object of the government's attention. On the very next day after *The Shortest Way* was burned in the open space before Westminster Hall, the Queen's address to both Houses of Parliament urged an even stricter censorship of such pamphlets as the famous one by Defoe: "I think it might have been for the Publick Service, to have had some further Laws for restraining the great License which is assumed, of publishing and spreading scandalous Pamphlets and Libels; but as far as the present Laws will extend, I hope you will all do your Duty, in your respective Stations, to prevent and punish such pernicious Practices."

This appeal did not go unheeded. While Defoe remained in hiding, prosecution in the courtroom was impossible; but it went on freely in the press. Defoe reissued *The Shortest Way* with a supplement, in which he explained that he had never aspersed Parliament or meant that the Occasional bill was intended to lead to persecution. He declared the author's intention, "if the people now in trouble may be excused, to throw himself upon the favor of the Government, rather than others should be ruined for his mistakes."[22] But he received no promises from the government to induce him to free his printers by surrendering his own person; and even in this hour of danger he could not resist reminding his readers that the tract was "By the Author of the True-Born Englishman."

On April 7 the Session of Oyer and Terminer convened again, before much the same group of officials. But still no action could be taken against Defoe while there was no prisoner to be brought up for trial, and the session was adjourned to May 12.

Sometime early in 1703 Defoe issued *A Dialogue between a Dissenter and the Observator, Concerning The Shortest Way with the Dissenters*. In this tract he reviewed his writings on current issues, and he remonstrated against Tutchin and other Dissenters who had left him in the lurch. Defoe had to omit the tract from his *True Collection* a few months later because he could not possibly have acknowledged that he had written such a defense of himself; but Tutchin's publisher John How knew that it was his, and he inserted it in his unauthorized collection of Defoe's writings which was published in April.

The name John How continues to recur among Defoe's opponents, representing three different men (at least two of them related to or closely connected with John Tutchin). There was John [Jack] How, the fiery member of the House of Commons who turned bitterly against King William and all his measures. There was the Rev. John How, said to be Tutchin's uncle, a leading Dissenting clergyman and the object of Defoe's attack as an Occasional Conformist. There was also John How of Talbot Court, Gracechurch Street, Tutchin's printer and perhaps a relative, who won Defoe's scorn by printing the first collection of his writings while he was still hiding from the law. Two years later, in an attack on little printers who pirated single works for sale on the street, Defoe turned on How as a far worse offender.[23]

The collection Defoe objected to was advertised in the *Observator* for April 17, 1703, and How was still advertising it in 1705. By 1709 How had become so notorious that he issued privately *Some Thoughts on the Present State of Printing and Bookselling,* in which he attacked other booksellers for piracy and sought to vindicate himself.

There were three special reasons why Defoe resented the publication of How's pirated collection. He could not admit the authorship of his self-defense in *A Dialogue between a Dissenter and the Observator;* another reissue of *The Shortest Way* could not be helpful while he was trying to make peace with the government; and he was in dire need of money—in hiding, unable to appear openly in business of any sort, with his brick and tile works going to ruin. To secure a few guineas from booksellers he was sorting through his unpublished manuscripts. Some old writings were being furbished up with new prefaces; even *More Reformation* and *A Hymn to the Pillory* (composed in Newgate while he awaited trial or the execution of his sentence) contain passages which were certainly written earlier. Near the end of July he issued the first volume of his *True Collection* at six shillings. How's unauthorized *Collection* was being advertised in bound copies at two shillings and sixpence, so that Defoe protested that his own more expensive *True Collection* had his portrait and more tracts and that it was more accurately printed on better paper.[24] Although How's "spurious edition" was published by a pirate, it is important as the first collection of Defoe's writings. It included two important tracts which Defoe did not choose to reprint, and every line in it is Defoe's.

On May 12 the Session of Oyer and Terminer was held again. Defoe was still at large when the session was "further adjourned until Wednesday July 7th."

But Defoe knew that he could not support his wife and seven children while he remained a fugitive. From the prosperity of a successful brick and tile manufacturer who was rapidly paying off his old debts, he was being plunged into utter poverty. After his letter of January 9 he made further applications to Nottingham or other officials. In April he appealed to Harley through Paterson, whom he had come to know during William's reign and who now served Harley as news correspondent and occasional adviser.

Defoe's long letter to Paterson made a handsome apology for his *Legion's Memorial* episode as an error which would not have occurred if Defoe had known Harley personally. It blamed the Dissenters for ingratitude, told of his unsuccessful overtures to Nottingham, and expressed sorrow and dismay that the government had been offended by an attack meant only for such men as Sacheverell and Stubbs. It implied that Defoe was faced with exile and that he would gladly serve the government (and Harley) if he could remain in his native country. In its circuitous course from Defoe's place of hiding, the letter did not reach Harley until nearly eight days after Defoe's arrest. Harley indorsed it, in his ominously methodical style which so often reads like the subtlest irony: "Received from Mr. Wm. Paterson Friday May 28, 1703 at one o'clock."

By that time Defoe had already been run to earth at the house of Sammen, a French weaver in Spittlefields (in modern usage, Spitalfields). Dyer's *News-Letter* referred to Defoe as "Sammen's tenant," a sneer at his place of arrest. In the next year Sir Charles Hedges, in reporting Sammen's own arrest for distributing Defoe's *Legion's Humble Address to the Lords*, paid unwilling tribute to his loyalty to Defoe: "I have taken up the dispenser of the Address, one Sammen, a weaver, a tool of De Foe's. I can get nothing out of him against others, but I have sufficient evidence against him."

According to a semiofficial tract, the discovery of Defoe was accidental. For over four and a half months he had eluded the Queen's messengers. But there had been suspicion of a widespread plot in which he was not concerned, some people had been committed to Newgate, and on May 15 there was a general search in Spittlefields for disaffected persons. On May 20 an informer discovered Defoe's hiding place, two of the Queen's messengers were notified, they strengthened their party "with other assistants," and that night (or more probably early the next morning) they apprehended their man.[25]

But to Defoe few events ever seemed accidental. His arrest had resulted from his failure to act on a warning from the spirit world. Twenty-four years later he gave an account of this experience, with no apparent error except his forgetfulness (or his intentional vagueness) about the precise year:

A person, whose name it is not so proper to mention here, but who may be produced if there should be occasion, being still living, was under the disaster, about the year 1701, to fall under a party censure (the occasion is needless to the present case). In hopes, upon the recess of the house, which was not far off, he should, as is usual, be at liberty, he withdrew himself, and avoided being taken up as much as he could; but the house resenting it, a vote was passed, ordering the secretary of state to prosecute him at law; which obliged him to resolve to leave the kingdom, and in the mean time to conceal himself with more exactness, the government having issued out a proclamation for apprehending him, with a reward to the person who should discover where he was, so as he might be taken.

In order to conceal himself more effectually, he left his lodging where he had been hid for some time, and removed to Barnet on the edge of Hertfordshire; intending, as soon as he had settled some family affairs, to go away north into Scotland; but before he went away he was obliged to come once more to London, to sign some writings for the securing some estate, which it was feared might be seized by outlaw, if the prosecution had gone on so far.

The night before he had appointed to come to London, as above, being in bed with one Mr. R[obert] D[avis], he dreamed that he was in his old lodgings at London, where he had been concealed as above, and in his dream he saw two men come to the door, who said they were messengers, and produced a warrant from the secretary of state to apprehend him, and that accordingly they seized upon and took him.

The vision surprised and waked him, and he waked Mr. D[avis], his brother-in-law, who was in bed with him, and told him the dream, and what a surprise he was in about it. Mr. D[avis], seeing it was but a dream, advised him to give no heed to it, but compose himself, and to go to sleep again; and he did so.

As soon as he was fast asleep again, he was waked again with the same dream, exactly as before; and he awaked his brother again, as before. It disturbed them both very much; but being heavy to sleep, they both went to sleep again, and dreamed no more. It is to be observed, that he saw the very men that apprehended him, their countenances, clothes, weapons, &c., and described them in the morning to his said brother, D[avis], in all the particulars.

However, the call to go to London being, as he thought, urgent, he got ready in the morning to go, resolving to stay but one day, and then set forward for Scotland. Accordingly he went for London in the morning, and that he might not be known, walked it on foot, that so he might go by more private ways over Enfield-chace, and so to Southgate, Hornsey, &c.

All the way as he walked, his mind was heavy and oppressed; and he frequently said to his brother, who walked with him, that he was certain he was going to London to be surprised; and so strong was the foreboding impression upon his mind, that he once stopped at Hornsey, and endeavored to get a lodging, intending to send his brother to London to see if nothing had happened there to give him any alarm.

As he had just secured a convenient lodging, he accidentally saw a gentleman standing at the next door, whom he knew very well, but durst not venture to trust on that occasion; and finding on inquiry that he dwelt there, he concluded that was no place for him, and so resolved to go forwards.

The impression upon his mind continuing, he stopped again at Islington, and endeavored to get a lodging there, but could not; so at last, when his brother brought him word he could not get a lodging, except where it was too public, Well, says he, then I must go to London, and take what follows; or to that purpose; and accordingly did go, and the next morning he was taken by the messengers, just in the very manner as he had been told in his dream.[26]

Here, as elsewhere, Defoe called Robert Davis both brother-in-law and brother. He said that the arrest was made in the morning (on the morning of May 21, not on the evening of May 20, as it was sometimes reported). Perhaps an arrest undertaken in the previous evening was completed after midnight. Confirmation of this is suggested by the fact that he remained in the custody of a Queen's messenger until Saturday morning, when he was taken to Whitehall.

Defoe has given several accounts of his interviews with Nottingham. Let a Tory pamphleteer describe the first one, that of May 22:

[He]was carried before Right Honorable the Earl of Nottingham, her Majesty's principal Secretary of State, who examined him strictly about the said libel; telling him how he had incurred her Majesty's displeasure by so malicious and factious a pamphlet. His Lordship laid the matter home to him, alleging the ill offices he did the nation by such a scandalous and malicious libel. Mr. De Fooe answered with some kind of prevarication, endeavoring to extenuate the matter, but little in his defence; upon which his Lordship, after some time spent in his examination, committed him close prisoner to Newgate, and there to be kept in safe custody till he was discharged by due course of law. Pursuant to which commitment, he was conveyed in a coach, under a guard, from the Secretary's office to Newgate, in order to take his trial at the next ensuing sessions.[27]

Nottingham considered himself a very busy man, but he had time for a close examination of Defoe. Furthermore, he feared an attempt to rescue Defoe as he was carried through the streets. While Defoe complained that his friends had deserted him, there had been rumors that he was securely hidden by his party or (later) that a great sum was being raised to free him from prison.

Both men came through the first inquisition with some triumph. Nottingham showed the power of his office, and Defoe refused to betray his friends. One dirty little business remained: the informer (fearing reprisal from the Dissenters or the French weavers) claimed his reward secretly through Mr. Armstrong of Nottingham's office. On May 25 Nottingham wrote to Lord Treasurer Godolphin: "The person who discovered Daniel Fooe (for whom a reward of £50 was promised in the Gazette) sends to me for his money, but does not care to appear himself; if therefore your Lordship will order that sum to be paid to Mr. Armstrong, I will take care that the person shall have it who discovered the said Fooe, and upon whose information he was apprehended." Next day Godolphin minuted this letter: "Recd 26th May 1703. £50 out [of] secret service to be paid to Mr. Armstrong for apprehending Mr. Fooe."

After the interview Nottingham sent the warrant for Defoe to the Keeper of Newgate, with this instruction: "you are to keep him safe until he shall be delivered by due course of law." The *Diary* of Lady

Cowper describes the courtly manners of the tall, gaunt Nottingham eleven years later under George I, telling how he "harangues the King every day for one hour and a half (concluding always, with his hand upon his breast, and these words: 'Sir, I have done my duty and discharged my conscience, after having told the truth before your Majesty. If your Majesty will not follow my advice, I have nothing to do but submit with resignation to your Majesty's better judgment')." This Polonius-like counselor sought to pluck the heart out of Defoe's mystery. His messengers had seized Defoe's books and papers. The treasury books record payments made for "expenses at several meetings (by order as is alleged of my Lord Nottingham) for examining the many papers and libels found in De Foe's custody when taken."[28]

And yet two years later Defoe was able to boast that the sheets of his *Advice to All Parties* were "a standing monument of the dexterous management of a certain most exquisite statesman, whose strictest scrutiny all these papers passed, and yet came home as things relating to the author's private concerns, and with them several other manuscripts, which nobody but such an over-vigilant minister would have parted with." In 1711 Defoe sent Harley a draft of his own South Sea project, with the explanation: "the originals were always in my own hand, till my Lord Nottingham's fury forced me to burn them with other papers to keep them out of his hands."

But at least one of Defoe's manuscripts did not escape Nottingham's vigilance. The extremists among the Tories had ridiculed William's claim to the throne, and Defoe had an unpublished reply which carried the argument farther than they intended. When Nottingham brought him before the Privy Council at the end of May or the beginning of June, he was asked to explain this manuscript: "I well remember, I was once questioned before the Privy Council of England, in the beginning of the Queen's reign, for a paper of some questions which they that brought me there never thought fit to let the world know what they found fault with— And one of the questions was this, *viz.* Whether her Majesty was not as much an usurper as King William. A great many objections were made to the rest of that paper; but when their Lordships came to this, and it was read, not a word was said."[29]

There were other examinations in Nottingham's office—at least one of them on a Tuesday or Friday night, when the official mails were going out to the Channel fleet and to the Netherlands. Defoe warned Harley against the carelessness in handling confidential papers he had seen at the office of the Secretary of State—a carelessness which continued after Harley had become a secretary of state, until it cost Harley his place in 1708 and led to the hanging of his clerk Greg for betraying secrets to France.

After the examination by Nottingham and the Privy Council, Defoe made what overtures he considered honorable. Nottingham played cat-and-mouse by allowing him liberty on bail. On June 5, according to another previously undiscovered Old Bailey document in the City of London Records, Richard Warre released Defoe on the extraordinarily high bail of £1,500. Five hundred pounds was subscribed by "Daniel De Foe of the City of London, Gentleman." The four others who offered bail, each responsible for £250, were as follows: Joseph Whitaker of Chicklane, in the parish of St. Sepulchre's, London, broker; Robert Davis of Tilbury, in the county of Essex, shipwright (Defoe's ever faithful brother-in-law); Thomas Powell of the parish of St. Andrews Holborn, in the county of Middlesex, gentleman; Nicholas Morris of Turnmill Street, in the parish of St. James, Clerkenwell, in the county of Middlesex, baker. After the signatures to this recognizance was appended the stipulation that Defoe must appear at nine o'clock on Wednesday, July 7, in Justice Hall in the Old Bailey.

The government's case against Defoe was not a strong one, and he had given no information which justified the great effort made to arrest him. Perhaps Nottingham hoped that he would attempt to escape. Some years later, when Defoe upbraided Ridpath for flight under somewhat similar circumstances, he reminded his own readers that he and his family had been ruined because he had kept faith with his friends:

I was under bail and at liberty. The danger was as terrifying as possible, insomuch that when I went to see an honest and good man for advice, all he would say was in the words of the disciple to our Blessed Lord, *Master, save thy self*. My friend[s], for some few friends I had then too, and who were engaged deeply enough as bail for me, were so apprehensive for me, and for my family, that they earnestly pressed me to go away, and offered to give it me under their hands that they had given me their free consent. But the honor and justice of the cause I was embarked in, the character of the good people I was embarked for, the reputation of my own integrity, and the reproach of running from my bail; these outvoted fear, and outvoted the compassion of my friends, and obliged me to resolve to bear the utmost indignities rather than quit the cause I had undertaken.[30]

What Nottingham sought to discover would not be divulged in a courtroom. If Defoe could have employed such an expert lawyer as

James (later Sir James) Montagu, he might have been rescued from Solicitor-General Harcourt. In November of the next year Montagu brought off the far less defensible Tutchin from the same Harcourt. As one reads Montague's defense of Tutchin in the *State Trials*, he asks himself what such counsel might not have done for Defoe, when he could have paralleled from sermons by High Churchmen the phrases in Defoe's tract which had been singled out as most false and libelous.

But Defoe had no Montagu to defend him. Almost penniless as he was, he was glad to accept the volunteer assistance of William Colepeper, an amateur of the law, unqualified by temperament or ability or experience for such a task, and already in great disfavor with the government as one of the Kentish Petitioners.

For six months Defoe had sought to make an honorable surrender, holding that "to flee from her Majesty's justice seems to be a kind of raising war against her." Now, early in July, Nottingham gave him the promise he asked for. Defoe determined to "submit to the clemency of my superior, with this resolution, *It is the Queen, let her Majesty do with me what seems good in her eyes.*" He would free the government from its difficulty in securing a conviction; he would plead guilty, and the government would keep its promise to treat him as a gentleman.[31] Montagu would never have allowed a client to fall into such a trap; but to the sanguine Colepeper, "both as a friend and a lawyer," this seemed a happy solution. Colepeper had bitter memories of his own illegal confinement by an irate House of Commons; he believed that Defoe would win favor through a generous surrender.

In an evil hour Colepeper advised his client to come in and throw himself on the mercy of the Crown. Afterward the Queen declared that she had left all that to Nottingham and that she did not think he would have treated Defoe in such a manner. But Nottingham had no fear now of a reversal in the courtroom. The prisoner had pleaded guilty, and his conviction was certain. Solicitor-General Harcourt—no such lawyer as Montagu, but a powerful speaker—could work on the prejudices of the judges. Nottingham, the bigot and precisian, had perhaps felt no malice; but now he showed no mercy. He gave Harcourt permission to display the full terrors of his office and his extraordinary courtroom delivery.

On the morning of July 7, the first day of the Court of Oyer and Terminer, the case came up in Justice Hall in the Old Bailey, next door south of Newgate Prison where Defoe was confined. The only surviving official accounts of this trial seem to be in the City of London Records, in two hastily scribbled summaries of the sentence, written above Defoe's name on the Sessions Roll for July 7 and at the end of his indictment. The British Museum formerly owned a printed account of the three days' session: *The Proceedings on the Queen's Commission of the Law . . . held . . . in the Old Bailey . . . 7th, 8th, 9th of July, 1703* (press mark 6495. k. 5). This was destroyed in wartime by an incendiary bomb, and I have been unable to locate a copy of it elsewhere.

But we can recover much of the tone and manner of the prosecution from later remarks by Defoe or by his friends or enemies. Harcourt bullied him and declared that *The Shortest Way* paved a way over skulls of the Churchmen. His vehemence impressed some observers least sympathetic to Defoe. One High Church pamphleteer soon afterward represented a Dissenter as not daring to plead guilty in court: "Not guilty, my Lord. Catch me pleading guilty as my friend Daniel de Foe did, if you can. I have more sense than that." Eight years later a pamphleteer reminded Harcourt that in Sacheverell's trial he defended exactly the same doctrines which he had assailed when Defoe presented them ironically. When (according to the pamphleteer's satirical statement) he was asked how a lawyer came to contradict himself so flatly in two trials, he replied, "I suppose he was paid for both, and such a change at the Bar is no miracle."[32]

Harcourt was well paid for his brief service against Defoe. The treasury books show that £42 7s. 6d. was allowed for the prosecution. As one third of Defoe's fine of two hundred marks was also granted to the prosecutor, the total came to almost £87, only £21 less than was paid for the famous prosecution "against Lord Halifax by order of the House of Commons." For a man so notoriously in need of money as Harcourt, £87 for so easy a morning's work must have been very welcome.

The Recorder, Sir Salathiel Lovell, was a very old and a very staunch Whig. But Defoe's satiric poems had singled him out for vice, dishonesty, brutality, and incompetence; and he was as savage to the prisoner as the Tory Harcourt. In two burlesque titles of the day, assigned to imaginary books, the names of Lovell and Sir Simon Harcourt are blended into one: "Two treatises, the one of fair dealing, the other of good breeding, by Sir Sim——ll. Dedicated to Mr. D. Defoe."

Defoe insisted that he had been promised mercy and that he had never agreed to reveal secrets. The Tories told two contradictory stories: sometimes they said that he had not been offered anything; more often they declared that he had failed to divulge the secrets for which mercy had been promised. It is unlikely that Defoe would have surrendered unconditionally or that he would have reminded the government of promises which had never been made. It is clear that Nottingham expected to make him talk freely, and (failing in this) that he resorted to violence. Harcourt demanded—and secured from a bench of judges predisposed against Defoe by personal animosities—an extreme sentence which was widely regarded as having no relation to the laws of England or to the nature of the alleged offense.[33]

According to the summary of the trial appended to the memorandum of the original indictment in the City of London Records, the following officials presided at the Assizes in Justice Hall on July 7: Sir Samuel Dashwood (Lord Mayor of London), Sir Edward Ward (Baron of the Exchequer), Sir John Fleet, Sir Edwin Clarke, and Sir Thomas Abney (aldermen), and (Sir) Salathiel Lovell (Recorder). Before them stood "Daniel de ffooe alias de ffoe in his own person to hear judgment." That judgment was severe beyond all expectation and almost beyond all precedent:

for a fine of 200 marks of the lawful money of England, and to stand upon a pillory, one day in Cornhill by the Exchange, London, and another day in Cheapside near the Conduit there, the third day in Fleet Street by Temple Bar, for one hour between the hours of eleven before noon and two after noon, whichever one he likes, with a paper on his head on which his offences are written, and that the said Daniel de ffooe alias de ffoe should find good sureties to be of good behaviour for the space of seven years then next following.

Meanwhile the prisoner was "committed to Her Majesty's gaol of Newgate to be kept safe in the custody of the sheriffs of London."

This sentence was intended not only to silence Defoe for seven years. To a man deserted by his party and reduced to destitution by the prosecution which had wrecked his business, it might easily have been equivalent to life imprisonment.

Nottingham had Defoe completely in his power at last, but he seemed almost as far from his end as ever. He had secured no evidence which would enable him to impeach the Whig lords. On June 1 the Attorney-General was reported to have entered an information against Halifax as auditor of the Exchequer, but on June 15 (obviously for lack of evidence) this prosecution had been postponed until the next term. How easy Nottingham's course would have seemed—if only Defoe could have been made to talk!

On July 10 Tutchin's *Observator* made a biting attack on the government's severity, implying that Defoe had been ruined in defiance of the laws of England. But the Ministry was too busy now to fly at such small game. A prosecution was brought in against Tutchin, but the case did not come to trial until November of the next year.

On July 11 Defoe sent Colepeper to Windsor with a petition to Nottingham, who said that he was Defoe's friend and that he would forward the petition to his utmost. But while the unlucky messenger stood outside the council-chamber door, awaiting the adjournment of the session, an express passed through with news from the fleet. The tactless Colepeper inquired whether Sir George Rook (the Tory admiral) was with the fleet or at Bath (a tender subject, as Rook had left the fleet very early in a summer notorious for abuses in naval administration). Soon afterward Sir Jacob Banks, disregarding the privileges of the royal palace, assaulted Colepeper; and this attack was later followed by a series of attempts to murder Colepeper or to force him into duels with bravoes. According to Defoe's narrative of the quarrel, "Mr. de Foe suffered by this accident, which is a very extreme hardship upon him, since it could never appear there was any resentment either in Sir G. R. or Sir J. B. against Mr. De Foe, or that he was so much as personally known to them. . . . After this accident, his Lordship [Nottingham] abated of his civility and good will when he was applied to on Mr. De Foe's account."[34]

From his cell in Newgate Defoe made a very different attempt at conciliation. This was aimed at three of the most eminent Dissenting clergymen who disagreed with him about Occasional Conformity, and who held that he had done an injustice to the High Church faction by overstraining Sacheverell's doctrine. John How, John Spademan, and Robert Fleming stood at the head of their calling. All were men of liberal education, all had suffered exile in Holland, all had risen to eminence under King William. How had delivered the address of the Dissenting ministers to William, Spademan had traveled abroad under Wharton, Fleming was an intimate friend of Somers. Spademan was How's copastor in Silver Street; Fleming was pastor of the Scots Church in Founders'-Hall. Defoe invited these three eminent ministers to pray with him; but they refused to see him, although How had visited the highwayman Whitney in Newgate before his hanging ten years before. Whitney had been a robber and a murderer, but he had never offended the Rev. John How by a disagreement on church discipline.

His abandonment by Whigs and Dissenters now seemed so complete that Defoe could say of himself, "thy too well served allies are fled." Newgate was a place of filth and disease, of brutality and noise, almost unendurable to a sensitive man who lacked money to pay for such luxuries as food and bedding, candles and fire, or, most of all, a cell affording some degree of cleanness and privacy. Charges had become so high that prisoners were allowed temporary freedom to procure money to pay the exactions of the officers. In 1706 a reward of £20 was offered for the apprehension of any prisoner set free by his keepers—as Swift phrased it, "Duly let out a-nights to steal for fees."

But in prison or out of it, Defoe was a keen observer of men and women and a projector of new undertakings. It was in Newgate that Defoe came to know highwaymen and pirates, on whose lives he was later such an authority. Here he began his most ambitious poem; here he revised and expanded several of his older tracts for publication; here he edited the first authorized collection of his writings. Here "*in tenebris*" he felt the prompting of "that secret hand" which directed him to undertake the *Review*.[35] Miserable as he was in Newgate, his stay there was perhaps the most stimulating in his career.

But his large family remained unprovided for. His admired De Laune had died in prison as a martyr to religious convictions, but Defoe had no wish to suffer martyrdom for a cause in which he stood almost alone. All through July the fear of the pillory hung over him. At least four different dates—July 19, 23, 26, and 29—were set for his first day's exposure.

He made another appeal, this time through the great Quaker William Penn—a fellow sufferer as a Dissenter and himself the author of a paper on the Occasional Conformity bill, but one who had known the ways of the Court from boyhood. As a man of wealth and great personal influence, Penn was in high favor at that time with Speaker Harley and well acquainted with such officials as Godolphin, Nottingham, and the Duke of Buckinghamshire and Normanby.

According to Lord Dartmouth, Penn "was much employed by Lord Godolphin when he was treasurer, in carrying messages to people he did not think proper to converse with himself." Three years later Penn upbraided Harley with the government's ingratitude for his secret and public services. On July 5 we find Penn seeking a pardon for some unnamed prisoner, inclosing a letter to Godolphin, who desired to be present at the examination with Nottingham—which could not be if the prisoner suffered on July 6. The situation of this prisoner suggests Defoe's; but Defoe was not tried until July 7.

Probably Penn was a stranger to Defoe until they met in Newgate. It has been suggested that Penn and his son were on their rounds to convert prisoners when they called on Defoe in his cell. This is unlikely for the father, utterly incredible for the dissolute William Penn, Jr., the only son then old enough to have been concerned.[36] It seems clear, rather, that Penn had sent his oldest son to make overtures on behalf of Nottingham and that Defoe rejected those overtures and begged Penn to intercede for him in person. In modernized form, Defoe's letter of July 12 reads:

SIR,

Though a long apology suits neither your own temper nor my condition, yet I can not but let you know with all the thankfulness I am capable [of] the sense I have of your extraordinary kindness, concerning yourself for me, so much a stranger to you. Nor can I doubt whether, to one who appears so much my friend as to attempt being my savior from this distress, I should scruple to use the utmost freedom with relation to the present case.

Sir, the proposal you are pleased to hint by your son from my Lord Nottingham of discovering parties is the same which his Lordship has often put upon me before.

Sir, in some letters which I have sent his Lordship I have answered him with the same assurance I did to the Privy Council; viz., that in the manner which they proposed it I really had no person to discover: that if my life were concerned in it I would not save it at the price of impeaching innocent men, no more would I accuse my friends for the freedom of private conversation.

It has been my character, Sir, among those who know me, that I scorn to lie, and by God's grace I'll preserve it while I live. I take the freedom to give you the trouble of repeating it, only to affirm to you with the more confidence the protestation I make. I solemnly affirm that other than what passes in conversation (and perhaps there is ill blood among people of my opinion more than enough), but other than that I have no accomplices, no set of men (as my Lord called them) with whom I used to concert matters of this nature, to whom I used to show or receive hints from them in order to these matters; and therefore to put it upon condition of such a nature is to offer me nothing at all.

But, Sir, my case is this. I came in upon the honor of the Government, being under bail that (at least some of them) consented to let me go away [from], and pressed me to it. I agreed to give the court no trouble, but to plead guilty to the indictment, even to all the adverbs, the seditiouslys, the maliciouslys, and a long rhapsody of the lawyers' et ceteras; and all this upon promises of being used tenderly. I am ready to do the Church of

England any justice by vindicating her in the same public manner they suppose her affronted—I mean in print.

This is what I thought fit to give you the trouble of, for which I ask your pardon, and entreat the continuance of those kind offices you have so generously undertaken for

An unknown captive, your distressed servant

DANIEL DE FOE.[37]

In the following April Defoe wrote to an unnamed correspondent (surely Penn) the most warmly personal letter we have from him. He had come a great way to wish this man a good journey and to shake his hand; but his friend had left so suddenly that he was "obliged to supply [his] absence by putting it into writing": "This I thought myself obliged to in return for those many and kind visits you bestowed on me in a house of bondage and affliction."[38]

Penn acted quickly for Defoe. By Friday he had got in touch with the two chief Ministers of the Crown, so that Godolphin wrote to Nottingham:

WINDSOR July 17, 1703

MY LORD

After I had the honor to see y[r.] L[p] yesterday M[r.] William Penn, came to mee to tell mee he had acquainted my Lord Privy Seal that *De Foe* was ready to make oath to y[r.] L[p] of all that he knew, & to give an Account of all his Accomplices in whatsoever he has been Concerned, for the information of the Queen, & the Lords of the Councill, provided that by so doing, he may bee excused from the punishment of the pillory, & not produced as an Evidence against any person whatsoever, & upon my acquainting the Queen with this just now at noon, her Ma[ty] was pleased to tell mee she had received the same Account yesterday from my Lord pr. Seal, & seemed to think, that if there were no other, occasion, would make it reasonable for the Cabinett Councill to meet here tomorrow & has commanded mee to tell you soe, because, she says, you seemed to think yesterday, that it might be an unnecessary trouble, but perhaps your meeting with the D. of Schomburg this morning, may have furnished you with occasions you did not foresee, & besides, it is high time to consider what shall be done about Diepp & either to give over wholly the thought of that matter, or to adjust ye necessary measures for putting it in Execution;

I must be the fav[r.] of y[r.] Lp. to send the enclosed to y[r.] neighbors M[r.] Nairn from

My Lord
Y[r.] Lps
most humble &
obedient servant
GODOLPHIN.[39]

The private affairs of Daniel Defoe were considered worthy of a special meeting of the Cabinet Council, even if they had not been brought up with such weighty matters as the plans for the Duke of Schomberg's military expedition to Portugal or some mysterious Jacobite conspiracy communicated through the French harbor of Dieppe. But strangely enough, this letter is one of the documents misused to represent Defoe as a trickster or turncoat. The historian Burton expressed amazement that Defoe had "succeeded in sending the sternly earnest Quaker on such an errand." Defoe's own letter to Penn five days earlier discredits any such interpretation. Perhaps a chain of oral communication had introduced confusion. We do not know what young Penn told his father, or what Penn told the two Ministers, or what Godolphin and the Lord Privy Seal (the Duke of Buckinghamshire and Normanby) came to imagine that Penn had told them. We do know that the man who wrote to Penn from Newgate on July 12 was in no mood to play the traitor, and that Nottingham never secured the information he sought from Defoe.

Penn did not rest content with the uncertainties of oral communication. On July 18 he wrote an urgent letter to Godolphin:

NOBLE FRIEND
FOR THE QUEEN'S SERVICE

I beg this mans disgrace may be deferr'd if not pardon'd. I inclose a lett^r to Lord p^r Seal who desireing to be by at his examination wth Ld Nottingham, before he suffers the sentence wch cannot be if he suffer to morrow.

Thy very Resp^{ll}
& thankf^l Frd
WM. PENN[40]

18. 5^m [i.e., July 18]
1703

Godolphin moved rapidly. Nothing in this strange correspondence is more remarkable than the speed which Defoe's affairs aroused in such unlikely actors—the stout and formal Quaker William Penn, the lean and formal Tory Nottingham, the indolent and formal Lord Privy Seal, the fat and formal Lord Treasurer (so gouty that he was often unable to write with his own hand), the rotund and formal Queen (so gouty that she pined for the healing waters of Bath, to which her visit was being delayed). The names of two of the Queen's messengers who bore these missives in such haste—Samuel Hill and a Mr. Dagley—have been preserved for us in the margins. On the same day Godolphin saw the Queen, and Nottingham wrote to Sheriff Bedingfield: "I am commanded by the Queen to signify her pleasure to you that you must not put in execution the sentence for setting Mr. De Fooe in the pillory until Friday next [i.e., July 23]."

But on July 19 a new difficulty arose for Nottingham. He learned that the sentence would be voided if Defoe left London; and Nottingham had no desire to visit Newgate in person if he could help it. On July 20 he asked the Lord Keeper (Sir Nathan Wright) for a writ of habeas corpus to cover the emergency:

I sent yesterday to Newgate to the Keeper to bring me De Fooe, who came to me and told me he could not bring him out of London, for it would be an escape and a discharge of his fine and he could not compel him to return back with him to Newgate. So that I can't speak with him without going to Newgate or an habeas corpus to bring him to me, which last in many respects is best for the Queen's service; though it has the appearance of some ease to me. This I acquaint your Lordship with, that you may please to order an habeas corpus to bring him before me.

Once again the lords of the committee were disappointed in the expected revelations, so that on July 22 Godolphin wrote to Nottingham: "as to Defoe, the queen seems to think, as she did upon your first acquainting her with what he said, that his confession amounts to nothing. However, she is willing to leave it to the Lords of the Committee to let his sentence be executed tomorrow [i.e., July 23], or not till after Sunday [i.e., on Monday, July 26], as they think proper."

But Nottingham was one of the most persistent of men, and he still had a high regard for his own powers of persuasion. He and the exquisite Lord Privy Seal (a favorite of the court ladies) would risk the smells and the jail fever of Newgate in person. On Friday morning, July 23, he talked with the Queen and secured a tentative promise to defer Defoe's sentence once more, so that he was encouraged to write to the Sheriff of London (in great haste again, as Defoe would otherwise be exposed in the pillory near the noon hour): "You may expect her Majesty's orders concerning Mr. Fooe this morning but I doubt not time enough to prevent his standing in the pillory today if that should be her Majesty's resolution, and therefore unless you hear from me again this morning, you will do well not to execute this sentence till Monday, by which time I shall acquaint you with her Majesty's final determination."[41]

Nottingham's visit to Newgate with the Lord Privy Seal was a most unusual proceeding. The historian Oldmixon wrote, in some uncertainty: "The Earl of Nottingham sent to, if he did not go to him in Newgate, to offer him Tory mercy, if he would discover who set him on to write his *Shortest Way*." Defoe alluded to the visit in his satirical account of "the Man in the Moon" who had been prosecuted for writing a tract called *The Shortest Way with the Crolians:* "the great scribe of their country, with another of their great courtiers, took such a low step as to go to him in the dungeon where they had put him, to see if they could tempt him to betray his friends. . . . Neither by promises of reward or fear of punishment they could prevail upon him to discover any thing, and so it remains a secret to this day."

The strange visit was confirmed by one of the Tory pamphleteers:

> Witness the Court that heard his guilty fears,
> And what he said in Newgate to two peers;
> He'll tell you likewise promises were broke,
> That lawyers grants of mercy could revoke,
> But ne'er give credit to the shuffling knave,
> Till he proves that was broke they never gave.

It would be impossible now to resconstruct the interview between the two lords and Defoe in Newgate. Defoe referred to it in his satirical account of the Man in the Moon, who was visited in prison by "the grand scribe . . . with another of their great courtiers": "The comical dialogue between them there the author of this has seen in manuscript, exceeding diverting, but not having time to translate it, 'tis omitted for the present, tho' he promises to publish it in its proper season for public instruction."

Certainly one subject they discussed was the Second Partition Treaty. Nottingham not only attempted to pry out of Defoe information against the Whig lords who were held responsible for it; he even condescended to attack the treaty itself. A year and a half later Defoe recalled this extraordinary debate between men so unequally situated:

I remember when a certain Nobleman, in Great Office in this Government, did me the Honour to force me to hear him Reproach the Memory, *of my dear and Glorious* Master, King *William*, who, tho' a Foreigner, not only pursued, but understood the Interest of this Kingdom, better than any of her Kings that ever went before him—His Lordship entring upon the Article of the Treaty of Partition, was pleas'd to be very Witty upon His Majesty in saying, That *he purchased our Peace with the Ruine of our Trade.*

Perhaps in his long public career Nottingham never again allowed himself to appear quite so ridiculous. He had ventured into Newgate to argue with an authority on the Second Partition Treaty, and he "had forgot to bring his maps." Defoe had not only been a merchant in the Mediterranean and had gone over the subject in his examinations before the Cabinet Council, "some of the greatest men in this kingdom, and the greatest enemies to that treaty." He had written a tract to prepare the public for the First Partition Treaty. He had defended William's standing army—the sudden reduction of which had emboldened Louis to violate the Second Partition Treaty. He had attended William when he had discussed partition. He had seen the draft of the Second Partition Treaty. He could vouch for William's having added one clause himself. He recalled having heard the King say that Europe would be glad to make such a peace after a seven years' war. He remembered the Whig lords who were present when the treaty was being formed. Years later, when there seemed to be a prospect of peace with France during the War of the Spanish Succession, Godolphin had called him into conference about the partition. When the Whigs later reversed their own policy, in order to oppose the partition of Spain in the Tory Peace of Utrecht, Defoe reminded them that he had not forgotten their stand in favor of partition a dozen years before.[42]

But whatever satisfaction Defoe derived from the superiority of his arguments in his long interview with Nottingham and the Lord Privy Seal in Newgate, they retained the arm of power. Defoe felt that the government's promise of mercy had proved a lie; he could hope for no mercy without a betrayal more shameful than the pillory. Years later he said in retrospect: "I have passed through the severest trial of this kind, and would I have been treacherous, what work should I have made with families: Nay, perhaps what blood might I have been the occasion of?" In this last interview with Nottingham, he came to his decision as one "who dares stand in the pillory, rather than betray his friends." As he said afterward: " 'tis well known, he would have delivered himself from that ignominy if he would have sold all his friends for his liberty, and betrayed the memory of his master King William."

Tory pamphleteers might ridicule him as "the prophet Dan" in "the lions' den" of Newgate, but he had made his choice. His lawyer had failed him, his party leaders had deserted him, his clergymen had refused to kneel beside him in prayer. The sheriff who would preside was Sir Robert Bedingfield, whom he had attacked twelve years before for his obscene conversation. Now the satirist could say what he pleased, when he stood at last in the wooden frame with "the paper on his head" naming his crime of writing a seditious libel. Sometime after his last interview with Nottingham, he gave the printer's messenger the manuscript of *A Hymn to the Pillory*, with the lines:

> And yet he might ha' been secure,
> Had he said less, or would he ha' said more.

Even the persistent Nottingham had come to realize that Defoe's decision was final. On Tuesday, July 27, he sent a brief order to the Sheriff of London: "I must acquaint you that her Majesty does not think fit to delay any longer the execution of the sentence upon Mr. Fooe, so that you must cause it to be inflicted without any further order."[43]

III

It was near noon on Saturday, July 31. The long month was at last coming to an end—the month which had brought the ruin of Defoe's private business, a savage trial and sentence in Justice Hall after he had thrown himself on the Queen's mercy, and now the three daily exposures to public shame. This was the last of the three.

The platform for the pillory had been removed to the west end of Fleet Street, on the east side of the old city gateway called Temple Bar. Behind the platform were the stone effigies of Queen Elizabeth and James I—perhaps also the dried head of a Jacobite conspirator on a spike. Two doorways for foot passengers led through Temple Bar toward Westminster, where the Earl of Nottingham might still be holding solemn conferences in his office in Whitehall. Defoe knew that office very well—he had been taken there several times in a little over two months; but he could not turn his head to look back toward it. Before him, eastward on the cobblestones of Fleet Street, surged the mob.

In his famous painting of this scene, Eyre Crowe caught the air of detached observation with which the future novelist looked down on the people. Among some modern publishers it has become the fashion to introduce authors at literary parties; never in the annals of English literature was there another reception like this. The proud face which had been almost unknown except among his business associates had suddenly been held up before the public in the three most crowded centers of the greatest city in the Western world.

And somehow, as he stood there unable to move head or hands, he seemed completely free at last—and no longer alone in his resistance to oppression. Londoners had always admired courage, even among the brutal highwaymen who "died game" at Tyburn. But this was a far braver man than most of them had seen before. The mob recognized, in its rough but quick sense of justice, that this was no criminal who deserved punishment, but a man who had defied unjust authority to preserve their liberties. The throng which swarmed below him was now a friendly one—apparently none of the Whig lords for whom he had dared so much, but what hostile writers called "knights and aldermen," "city friends," "the Dissenting tribe," and the great mob— "That dirt themselves protected him from filth."[44] Virulent Tories began to regret that Harcourt's demand for a whipping sentence had gone unheeded and that they could not have their enemy "at a cart's-tail; where the mob could not defend him." Now their victim could declare, "I can triumph on a pillory."

Six months before, *The Shortest Way* had been burned by the common hangman. Now copies of it were rushed out in barrows from the printer's, and "with other of his books were hawked about the street, round the pillory while he stood upon it." Bundles of a poem written in Newgate (just off the press) were cried by women and boys. Its twenty-four pages were handsomely printed, in spite of the slips made by printers who had set type long after their usual hours. Looking down from his station, Defoe could not read the lines. But he knew *A Hymn to the Pillory* almost by heart, as he knew so many of his own poems:

> Hail hieroglyphic state machine
> Contrived to punish fancy in:
> Men that are men, in thee can feel no pain.[45]

King William had been dead for less than seventeen months; already his confidential adviser had "tasted the difference between the closet of a King, and the dungeon of Newgate."[46]

The heavy bar of the pillory rested on his head and neck in the July noonday:

> Thou are the State-trap of the Law,
> That neither can keep knaves nor honest men in awe.

His hands held high in the slots of the pillory—even that tireless hand with the smudge of ink—grew numb; yet the lines kept running through his head. He had written most of them very rapidly, but they said what he had meant to say to the world:

> And thus he's an example made
> To make men of their honesty afraid,
> That for the time to come they may
> More willingly their friends betray;

Tell 'em the men that placed him here
Are friends unto the times,
But at a loss to find his guile,
They can't commit his crimes.

At last the two large figures of Hercules with his club, eastward on Fleet Street at St. Dunstan's Church, struck the fourth quarter of the hour on their bells. The Sheriff's party opened "the wooden ruff," and they took the benumbed figure back to Newgate. But the hour of shame had passed, and the people "expressed their affections, by loud shouts and acclamations, when he was taken down." Even a hostile writer observed that the crowd "hallowed him down from his wooden punishment, as if he had been a Cicero that was exposed and declaimed against there."[47]

IV

Defoe's exaltation of mood died within the dreary stone walls of Newgate. On September 16 it was reported that the Queen had pardoned twenty-seven condemned prisoners in Newgate, but for one innocent man there was no such hope. On that day his only living patron, his old friend Sir Dalby Thomas, left England forever to serve as governor-general of the African Company in Guinea.

London was deserted by the world of politics and fashion. Harley could not leave for his remote country home until after September 20, but the Queen had gone to Bath in mid-August, and Lord Treasurer Godolphin had followed her at the end of the month. At Bath soon afterward appeared two of the leading High Fliers, Sir Edward Seymour and Jack How. But the tide was now beginning to turn against them; for on September 8 Queen Anne was joined by her confidante, the Duchess of Marlborough.

At this time Anne's greatest pleasure was to gratify the Duchess, the Duchess was devoted to the interests of the Duke, and the Duke had found his career in the war against France. In the last session of Parliament the Occasional bill had delayed supplies for the war of the great Duke; in the next session a similar measure might be "tacked" to a money bill and block supplies altogether.

The ambitious Harley, still obscure in his post as Speaker of the House, but the ablest parliamentary strategist in England, seized his opportunity. To the prime manager of the Occasional bill he assigned the task of guiding the money bills through the Commons. While the unsuspecting Nottingham worked serenely in his favorite role as a party spoilsman, by placing his friends in minor offices of profit, Harley was writing mysterious letters which aroused Godolphin's deepest interest, and which were often communicated to the Queen.[48]

Harley always preferred to work underground, but this time we can trace some of his burrowings. He was winning over a few of Nottingham's allies and learning secrets from them. With the next session of Parliament at hand, Marlborough and Godolphin had begun to depend on Harley to "allay the heats" of the contending factions, in order to rush their money bills through the Commons. Godolphin was soon asking Harley for private conference twice a week or oftener.

A third undertaking was even more in Harley's own line. Marlborough realized the importance of military information, and he used spies lavishly in warfare; but neither he nor Godolphin understood the political necessity of domestic news or the growing power of the press. Harley was unique among English statesmen of his time in seeing the need of securing information and maintaining good public relations. Under William he was said to have spent half of his private income for copies of all the papers handed in to the House of Commons, so that while he was in the Opposition the King's people were afraid to speak before him. Under Anne he promoted the best system of semiofficial publicity ever known in England up to that time. As early as August of the previous year he had been urging the reluctant Godolphin to do something to improve the government's use of the press: "I cannot but, upon this occasion, again take the liberty to offer to your L^{op} that it wil be of great service to have some discreet writer of the Government's side, if it were only to state facts right; for the Generality err for want of knowledge, & being imposed upon by the storys raised by ill designing men."[49]

Since May 28 Harley had apparently done nothing about Defoe's appeal through Paterson. Even after Defoe had become his devoted servant, Harley's enemies could not agree on an explanation of the new relationship. A hostile Whig wrote that "Mr. Harley's genius was so near akin to Foe's that he could not but take him into his confidence as soon as he got acquaintance with him." Another Whig charged that Harley "had helped to set him in the pillory." A Tory alleged that Defoe had met slyly with Harley to write the Legion Letters, that his name was changed by Harley's advice, and that he had been the tool to raise Harley to eminence. There is much truth in the last of these five statements, but the two preceding ones are absurd.

The first Legion Letter, largely an attack on Harley, was delivered to him as an ultimatum; Harley sometimes wrote "Foe"[50] long after "De Foe" was the usual spelling, and "De Fooe" was the alternative form even in Nottingham's notices to the sheriff or the jailer.

Defoe had begun by regarding Harley as a renegade Whig, one of those who "found themselves not rewarded according to their merit, turned popular, champions for the people's liberties, and railers at the Court." He had attacked Harley as Speaker of a House of Commons which seemed pro-French. But later he had come to wonder whether Harley might not be William's successor as a statesman above party, the calm man steering a national course between the rival claims of faction. He was always a hero-worshiper, inclined to refer every public act to the standards set by Gustavus Adolphus and William. After William's horse had thrown his little rider to the earth, Defoe had no white plume to follow. He despised the High Fliers; three Dissenting ministers had refused to pray with him; the Whig leaders had failed him utterly.

During this anguished period of indecision, sometime in July after he was sentenced to the pillory, a cryptic message from Harley was delivered to him in Newgate: "Pray, ask that gentleman what I can do for him." Defoe, whose life was full of what seemed to him secret promptings and miraculous dispensations, thought of the blind man's answer in the Gospel of St. Mark. When the messenger had gone, he took up his pen and wrote his reply: "Lord, that I may receive my sight."[51]

Harley's communication was unsolicited, and it came to Defoe as a surprise. To bear such a message, which might have compromised Harley with the leading Ministers at the very time when he was moving with supreme caution, an intimate of his own or a very discreet neutral would have been chosen. By far the most likely person was William Penn—a close friend of Harley's, an expert and trusted intermediary, and a man in touch with Defoe in Newgate at that time.

Nottingham continued his inquisition until he abandoned Defoe to the pillory. Throughout August the court thinned out, and still nothing was done for Defoe. But in September Godolphin and the Duchess of Marlborough were at Bath to remind the Queen that Parliament must convene soon, and that the High Fliers were likely to hold up appropriations for the war. An able political pen was still locked up in Newgate when Harley wrote to Godolphin on September 20:

I find Foe is much oppress'd in his mind with his usage, and particularly the two lords who examined him in Newgate. I do find he lays the harshness he has suffered upon particular persons, and would be willing to serve the Queen. Your Lordship can judge whether he be worth it; there is a private attempt among his friends to raise the 200 marks for his fine; he is a very capable man, and if his fine be satisfied without any other knowledge but that he alone be acquainted with it that it is the Queen's bounty to him and grace, he may do service, and this may perhaps engage him better than any other rewards, and keep him under the power of an obligation.[52]

Harley was famous for his skill in reading character; and here we find him seeing that Defoe was to be appealed to through gratitude, not through hope of financial reward. Harley was equally famous for his skill in making other men accept his thoughts as their own, but this was unusually good even for him. *"A very capable man"*—with a deep personal resentment against Nottingham and the High Fliers! *"Willing to serve the Queen . . . under the power of an obligation"*—but perhaps about to be released by his own friends! Even the unimaginative Godolphin was roused to prompt action. Six days later he replied from Bath: "I have found it proper to read some paragraphs of your letter to the Queen. What you propose about Defoe may be done when you will, and how you will."

Harley was already vacationing at his distant country home in Herefordshire, but he could have freed Defoe quickly if that had suited his purpose. He was to be away nearly a month longer, while his temporary allies and his enemies alike were returning to London. It was all very well to assure Defoe that he owed his release to the Queen's bounty; it would be a very different thing to let him fall into the hands of Harley's rivals. Defoe recalled that "Her Majesty was pleased particularly to inquire into my circumstances and family, and to send to me [in] the prison money to pay my fine and the expenses of my discharge." That was no doubt arranged by Godolphin in Harley's absence. But Defoe remained in Newgate until early November; and there was no haste to get a pardon signed by the Queen before July 31 of the next year,[53] by which time he was completely committed to the service of Robert Harley.

In the autumn of 1703 the pamphlet war against the High Fliers was already beginning. In the previous winter Nottingham had ignored Bishop Burnet's request for investigation of a Jacobite pamphlet called *The Exorbitant Grants of William III*, and in July the Queen's desire for such a prosecution came to nothing. Now, in October, that tract was presented by the grand jury of London, with other libels reflecting on the memory of King William. Still Harley was not quite ready to unleash the journalist whose abilities soon roused the Tory complaint

> That twenty thousand cut-throat libels
> Shall sell, before a score of Bibles;
> And Low-Church satires move much faster
> Than sermons by a High-Church pastor.

On October 9 the Queen arrived at Windsor from Bath, and on October 12 Godolphin proposed that Harley "prepare the heads of what is proper to be said in Parliament." The relatively obscure Speaker of the House had now become the policy-maker and spokesman for the government. The Queen's speech from the throne which followed was a concise statement of the needs for war supplies, for equipment of new troops, for subsidies to the Allies, for holding down the price of coal in wartime, and for dispatch in granting the appropriations. Not one word was said about the Church's danger. Instead, the speech concluded with an innuendo against the introduction of another Occasional bill.[54]

The High Fliers were furious but undaunted. Soon they would be singing:

> When Anna was the Church's Daughter,
> She acted as her Mother taught her;
> But now she's Mother to the Church,
> She leaves her Daughter in the lurch.

On November 25 the same three members of Parliament—Bromley, St. John, and Annesley—were granted leave to prepare and bring in another bill for preventing occasional conformity. Defoe had already anticipated the new bill on September 18 (while he was still in Newgate) by one of his ablest pamphlets. In this he had reviewed the bill which had been defeated at the last session of Parliament and had undertaken to put the matter "into the best possible light, in order to frame a right judgment, how a Bill like unto that (if at any time hereafter such should be prepared) may affect the Commonweal."[55]

But Harley was secure of his place in the Government, now that he had made his alliance with Godolphin and Marlborough. At last he was ready to fight the High Fliers through the press—for on November 4 Godolphin had written, "I have taken care in the matter of Defoe." Fresh out of Newgate with tracts ready for publication, Defoe offered to hold back anything which did not meet with Harley's approval.

Not only could Harley rely on the services of the grateful Defoe; the venal—but still useful—pen of one of the ablest Tory writers was now at his disposal. In the previous May the Tories had supposedly secured the services of Dr. Charles Davenant for life by giving him a post worth £1,000 a year besides perquisites; but on November 16 he was announcing an attack on the Occasional bill in his forthcoming *Essays upon Peace at Home and War Abroad*.

In late December a correspondent expressed sympathy for Nottingham under the persecution he was suffering, and the hope that he would remain in office. At the same time Godolphin wrote to Harley: "I am glad to hear you talk of calming people in these holidays, and should be glad to have your directions what part I should be able to take towards making men a little more moderate."

On January 7, 1704, Defoe anticipated and helped to defeat a Tory bill for muzzling the press. In February he started the greatest of the twenty-six periodicals with which he was at one time or another connected—the *Review* (1704–13), which he continued as the principal organ of the government for many years. All through 1704 he poured out a stream of his most effective writing, uninterrupted by the proposed trip to the Netherlands or by the first of his political and journalistic tours for Harley through the English counties. In jest he declined to engage his *Review* in private controversy, on the pretext that he had just come out of a bloody war which had exhausted his ammunition; but his pen was always ready to serve the government as long as he could agree with its measures.

Godolphin's letter to Harley on July 31, 1704, implied that Defoe had already entered into some regular employment under the Queen, the precise nature of which is not known today: "I return you the blank warrant signed by the Queen for D[e Foe's] pardon. Her Majesty commands me to tell you that she approves entirely of what you promised him, and will make it good."[56]

But Defoe's old enemy Nottingham was no longer Secretary of State for the Southern Department. Now that the Ministry had agreed on a policy of moderation, there was no room for him in the government. On April 22 he had been obliged to resign; on May 18 Sir Charles Hedges had succeeded him as Secretary of State for the Southern Department (dealing with the south European nations), and Harley had replaced Hedges as Secretary of State for the Northern Department (dealing with Scotland and the north European states). In addition, Harley had taken over the control of the press and other home affairs which Nottingham had regarded as his own special province. In vain Nottingham had petitioned for leave to remain in a mansion belonging to the crown; what he had spent for repairs would be repaid him, but he was required to move out. The Lord Privy Seal, who had gone with Nottingham to badger Defoe in Newgate, clung on through court influence for another year, and then he too was displaced from office.

Harley was rapidly becoming the first man in England. Tory writers reminded him that Defoe had "been the tool that raised you up aloft"; but Harley sought to conceal their relations. When Defoe wrote on November 9, 1703, to give thanks for his liberation, he called himself a "stranger" to Harley, and he found it desirable to communicate through Stancliffe. In the following May he apologized to Harley because someone had discovered their secret meetings; and he offered a method whereby ill consequences could be prevented. In June someone who signed the initials "J. W." offered to betray Defoe to Harley for a reward, supposing that the government still sought to prosecute him. Harley's colleague, Secretary of State Hedges, knew so little of Defoe's actual position that as late as September 28, 1704, he was informing Harley of his own success in arresting "a tool of Defoe's" for dispersing *Legion's Address to the Lords*.[57]

But Defoe had nothing to fear from the Ministry now. The connection with Harley had become as necessary to the ambitious Secretary of State for the Northern Department as to Defoe. About the end of July, 1704, Defoe was advising Harley to become Prime Minister in fact by making himself master of public affairs, urging him to win over the Dissenters by claiming credit for the defeat of the Occasional bill. In November he urged Harley to encourage the introduction of a third Occasional bill in order to "blast it" and thereby to "ruin all the Confederacy" by alienating them from the Queen. We cannot be certain that in each instance Harley followed Defoe's advice. We do know that Defoe gave the advice, that Harley preserved the letters and memorandums which Defoe sent him, and that Harley owed his advancement to the defeat of the Occasional bill followed by the consolidation of a moderate Ministry.[58]

The Shortest Way had exposed Defoe to the High Fliers, but their persecution of him had opened the way for the overthrow of their party. The influence of this persecution on his own career was even more remarkable. The daring young merchant with a flair for politics and a love of literature became the hard-bitten journalist and the father of the modern novel. In 1704 and afterward he was a professional, the most prolific of English writers. The greatest books in his long list—*Moll Flanders, Colonel Jack,* and so many others which grew out of his sympathy for men and women and his deep understanding of human life and character—would never have come into being if he had not suffered in Newgate and the pillory. His first bankruptcy gave us *An Essay upon Projects;* his imprisonment and public shame gave us the travels, the histories, the periodicals, and the novels.

When Robinson Crusoe tells how his narrow life of growing contentment was shattered by the coming of the savages to his island, he reflects the personal experience of his creator: "How frequently, in the course of our lives, the evil, which in itself we seek most to avoid, and which, when we are fallen into, is the most dreadful to us, is often times the very means of our deliverance."[59]

XIV. REPORTER

I have been almost in every corner of England myself, and not been an idle observer of things neither.

Review, V, 515

U NTIL NOVEMBER, 1703, Defoe had never been a reporter of news. He had acquired shorthand, he had formed the habit of taking notes, he had traveled widely for himself and for King William, he had become a keen observer of men and affairs. He had even mastered a prose style of unusual simplicity and force. But the father of modern journalism had never written a news story for publication until he was forty-three.

Now, in the month of his release from Newgate, occurred an event from which we can date the beginning of his career as a reporter. He was living with his family "in a well-built house in the skirts of the City" (probably in Kingsland or Newington Green, with his wife's mother and her second husband). For two weeks the wind had blown exceedingly hard; but the weather was fair, and there seemed to be no danger. About four in the afternoon of Wednesday, November 24, the wind increased until it blew in violent gusts with squalls of rain. As Defoe approached his home that evening, tiles were flying off some of the roofs, and he narrowly escaped injury from the fall of part of a house.

For two days the high wind continued, but it caused no great apprehension to those who could remain indoors. On Friday night about ten o'clock it increased so suddenly as to arouse the curiosity of Morton's old pupil in physical science, although he admitted that in "natural philosophy" he was still "a mere junior, and hardly any more than an admirer." Defoe looked at the barometer, and he saw that the mercury was lower than he had ever known it to be—so low that he thought his children had handled the instrument and disturbed the tube.

Most families in the neighborhood went to bed as usual; but by one or two o'clock the wind became so furious that nearly everyone was up again. When their house was shaken by the fall of a stack of chimneys in the neighborhood, the Defoes opened a door to escape into a garden for fear the roof might fall on their heads. But when they looked out into the moonless night, they decided to await their graves in the ruins of their own home. Tiles were blowing almost horizontally through the air, sometimes thirty or forty yards until they were imbedded deeply in the earth. Some tiles flew across the broad suburban streets and broke windows on the other side. Sheets of lead and pieces of timber or iron were carried in the air for considerable distances.

Most of the family dared not look out again, but Defoe watched throughout the night, attempting to estimate the direction of the wind as it shifted in the southwest and west. About six o'clock in the morning it veered northward and blew louder, until an hour later it came more nearly from the south and gradually abated.[1] Friends and relatives began to look about them to see what had happened to their loved ones and to view the havoc of the storm. But that afternoon the wind became as violent as ever. Chimneys fell, houses that had been hastily repaired were untiled again, and the storm continued until Wednesday, December 1,[2] a full week after it had begun.

Defoe was concerned because the wind had come with the new moon and a high tide; he rejoiced to learn that the Thames had not risen a foot higher, to overflow both sides of the river. He took special note of a robbery committed in the height of the storm, when the victims could not get help from their terrified neighbors. As a Puritan he recognized the storm as a manifestation of God's power and his unrevealed purpose in the world. Most of all, he was concerned to preserve the exact record "to assist in convincing posterity that this was the most violent tempest the world ever saw." He set about to make a minute record of it, as "The Age's Humble Servant," who held that one who wrote should be even more careful of his words than one who preached from the pulpit, because "he that prints or publishes to all the world has a tenfold obligation."

The earlier biographers of Defoe were puzzled by this statement, for they supposed that he was confined in Newgate until his pardon was signed in the following July. As so often with Defoe, his precise statements of fact led to the mistaken supposition that he was not telling the truth. His vivid descriptions seemed examples of circumstantial fiction, not firsthand observations by a man whose acute natural powers were sharpened by his recent imprisonment.

One who moved about as freely as Defoe could do much of his investigating in person. In Islington he counted the chimneys which had fallen in a great mansion of a nobleman that had been let out in tenements; he walked in streets where "the houses looked like skeletons"; for several days he conversed with people in London about their experiences. On the day after the storm he walked alongside the Thames to see the great Pool blown clear of all shipping except four vessels, and nearly seven hundred ships driven helplessly upon each other between Shadwell and Limehouse. A month later he traversed Kent, where he counted 1,107 houses, outhouses, and barns blown down; but he was obliged to give over his attempt to reckon the destruction of orchards and trees.

He corresponded with maritime friends to learn of their experiences at sea. He read several contemporary accounts, and in his own later narrative he used at least one of them: *An Exact Relation Of the Late Dreadful Tempest* (1704). When he heard of an account of the storm which had been printed in Paris, he promised to translate it into English if he could procure a copy (a difficult thing to achieve during the war with France). He read what he could find on tempests in such works as the *Philosophical Transactions* and Ralph Bohun's *Discourses concerning the Origins and Properties of Winds*.[3] When some rival authors attacked his book because it contained borrowings from Bohun, they showed their failure to understand his scientific method of seeking both the data and the theories which had been offered to explain them.

For the first time in his life he attempted to organize a systematic plan of news-gathering from correspondents. Only five days after the storm was over, he inserted the following advertisement in the *London Gazette:*

To preserve the Remembrance of the late Dreadful Tempest, an exact and faithful Collection is preparing of the most remarkable Disasters which happened on that Occasion, with the Places where, and Persons concern'd, whether at Sea or on Shore. For the perfecting so good a Work, 'tis humbly recommended by the Author to all Gentlemen of the Clergy, or others, who have made any Observations of this Calamity, that they would transmit as distinct an Account as possible, of what they have observed, to the Undertakers, directed to John Nutt, near Stationers hall, London. All Gentlemen that are pleas'd to send any such Accounts, are desired to write no Particulars but what they are well satisfied to be true, and to set their Names to the Observations they send, which the Undertakers of this Work promise shall be faithfully Recorded, and the Favour publickly acknowledged.[4]

The cost of the proposed correspondence would be considerable, for the postage on incoming letters was then paid by the receivers. One of Defoe's correspondents apologized because "this account will hardly be thought worth the charge of passage."

The clergy were not slow in representing the storm as a preachment against the crying evils of the day. One notable sermon was "A Warning from the Winds," delivered on January 19, 1704, by the Congregational minister at Cambridge, Joseph Hussey, an old student at Morton's academy and perhaps a classmate of Defoe. On February 24 Defoe tried his own hand in *The Layman's Sermon upon the Late Storm;* but his main work on the subject went forward tardily because replies were slowly coming in from outlying parts of England and from ships at sea.

On June 27 he felt confident enough to advertise that the book was at last in press and that it would appear next week. On July 25 this announcement was repeated. Not until July 29 was he able to announce as actually published *The Storm: or, A Collection of the most Remarkable Casualties and Disasters which happened in the late dreadful Tempest, both by Sea and Land.*[5] The title page was deceptively like others of the day, for its sonorous motto was taken from the prophet Nahum: *"The Lord hath his way in the Whirlwind, and in the Storm, and the Clouds are the dust of his Feet."* But Defoe's book, for the first time in English literary history, attempted to give an elaborate factual account of a recent natural phenomenon—solely as recorded by reliable eyewitnesses.

As later replies slowly trickled in, Defoe promised his first sequel; he would hold back unused material and issue a second volume. But he rarely published any of his proposed sequels. Nothing more was said of this one, although letters continued to arrive while his earlier correspondents were clamoring for speedy publication. The book seems to have made a lasting impression on many serious-minded readers, but it was never a favorite with the general public. In January, 1713, unsold sheets of the original edition were offered by the same publishers with a new title.

Some replies which Defoe received were not used because of the triviality of their details; others were introduced with an apology for their homely style. Two poems were included—a sentimental pastoral from Oxford on the late storm and a versification of the 148th Psalm. The commodore of a squadron of men-of-war at Milford Haven reported what had happened on his station. But Defoe relied principally on letters from country clergymen—no doubt some of them High Churchmen who had accepted *The Shortest Way* as a reasonable proposal for rooting out the Dissenters and who had rejoiced when its author had been set in the pillory. Little wonder that Defoe remained anonymous as "the Author" and as "the Undertakers," so that in his lifetime he was almost never suspected of having compiled the pious record of the Great Storm.

On August 15 he did publish a satirical *Essay on the Storm* as a companion poem to *An Elegy on the Author of the True-Born Englishman;* but this new attack on the High Churchmen had no apparent connection with the nonpartisan prose collection which had been published a little over two weeks before.

Six years later, *The Storm* was still highly regarded by an Anglican family in faraway Yorkshire. In preparing a supplementary section of the book, which told of an earthquake that came a month later than the Great Storm itself, Defoe made use of parts of two letters to his publisher from the High Church antiquary Ralph Thoresby. Later, when Thoresby outlined his own plans for devotional reading, in his *Diary* for 1711, he named the exercises he had followed for the first day of the new year: "January 1. . . . I design for the future to read a chapter in the Bible, morning and evening, and in secret, besides the said other treatises; accordingly I began at the first of Genesis. Lord, give a blessing! Evening, son Ralph read us the conclusion of the account of the dreadful storm, anno 1703, with the earthquake." Here we find Defoe's compilation bracketed with the Book of Genesis.[6]

Among Dissenters the influence of Defoe's book was even more lasting. In the 1730's there was a yearly commemoration of the anniversary of the Great Storm in Little Wylde-Street, on an endowment "by the appointment of Mr. Taylor, deceased." In these annual sermons Defoe was drawn on by the preachers as the principal source of their illustrative examples. In several of their discourses a relation was "given of the manner and time of its rise and continuance." In 1733 Mr. Aaron Ward gave "an account of the damage that was done by it." In 1734 Mr. A. Gifford devoted his primary attention to recounting "some of those extraordinary instances of mercy the Lord was pleas'd to shew during that dreadful calamity." Mr. Gifford made use of many of Defoe's anecdotes in his sermon, and in the printed text he inserted a footnote specifically acknowledging them: "See the printed account of the storm, 1703, in which are many more particulars."[7] The ministerial student of Morton's academy had not altogether failed to serve in his intended calling.

Defoe's reporting of current events had begun accidentally, but it soon developed into one of his principal interests. On February 19, 1704, he inaugurated his *Review;* and although this journal remained primarily a commentary on public affairs rather than a record of news, it marks an important step in his career as a reporter. It was the first (except for Dunton's *Athenian Mercury*) and in many ways the most significant of the twenty-six periodicals in which Defoe had some share as contributor or editor.

Early in the same year he was admitted to those frequent and secret conferences with Harley which exerted such a profound influence on both men and on the nation's affairs as long as Harley held high office. In view of their confidential relations, it is ludicrous to read how on July 5 an anonymous informer sent Harley a report about Toland, Defoe, and Pierce, offering to discover more about them if his own activities in the matter were kept secret. After the official pardon was granted on July 31, 1704, Defoe had no reason to fear a renewal of the prosecution of the previous summer.

Since November, 1703, he had been putting out political tracts for Harley; but, as yet, little had been done about granting an allowance for his subsistence. His family affairs remained in desperate shape while he worked for the government, although he had already established himself as Harley's confidential agent, his adviser, and his most trusted writer. Nothing had been done—or ever would be done—to give him one branch of the auditor's office, for which he felt specially qualified. Nothing had come of the proposal in the spring to send him to Holland on a mission for Harley.[8]

By midsummer Defoe was convinced that the primary need of the new ministry was a skilful presentation of the news. On July 7 he was suggesting how Harley could employ the news of a military victory abroad for his own political advantage. Sometime in the same month he outlined to Harley his plan for a system of information whereby the new Secretary of State for the Northern Department would be supreme in the government through his unique acquaintance with affairs at home and abroad.

Still, no specific employment had been found for Defoe. On August 23 his friend James Stancliffe wrote to Harley: "I saw Mr. F. yesterday, and he seems to be much dejected by the deferring of hope, which, as the wise man says, makes the heart sick; but at the same time he and all men must know that your hurries of late have been such as are not ordinarily met with." Within the next month Harley finally agreed that Defoe was to have some regular appointment as an observer of national affairs. By September 28 Defoe was writing from Bury St. Edmunds the first of those many political reports which kept Harley better informed about public opinion than any other man in the government. In 1705, from July 16 to November 6, Defoe traversed a large part of England on one of the most extensive and interesting of all his tours for Harley.

But in the early part of 1706 he was under pressure from creditors, and he was engrossed with the Bankrupts Act and with his own possible chance of benefiting from it. He was in such dire financial straits that the system of correspondence which he had established in most parts of England (by Harley's orders) was dying for want of the promised assistance. He could hardly cross London to keep his appointments with Harley for fear of arrest by a bailiff, and he could no longer travel about over England with Christopher Hurt from the Custom House or with his favorite companion Robert Davis. On August 21 he was meeting with his creditors for the last time in Davis' chamber in the Middle Temple.

Three days later, on August 24, 1706, Harley was confiding to a correspondent his own perplexity regarding the critical state of affairs in Scotland, where the Scottish Parliament was about to decide whether it would accept the proposed Union with England. By September 13 Defoe was starting northward on horseback, in such haste that he was not allowed to stop for further conference with Harley. He used the precaution of adopting the traveling name "Alexander Goldsmith," he rode with two horses, and he was so well armed with pistols that he had no fear of highwaymen. Not until about October 24 did he receive Harley's personal instructions, which have survived among Harley's papers in a fragmentary draft:

1. You are to use the utmost caution that it may not be supposed you are employed by any person in England, but that you came there on your own business and out of love to the country.
2. You are to write constantly the true state of how you find things, at least once a week, and you need not subscribe any name but direct for me under cover to Mrs. Collins at the Posthouse, Middle Temple Gate, London. For variety you may direct under cover to Michael Read, in York Buildings.
3. You may confidently assure those you converse with that the Queen and all those who have credit with her are sincere and hearty for the Union.
[4.] You must shew them this is an opportunity that being once lost or

neglected is not again to be recovered. England was never before in so good a disposition to make such large concessions, or so heartily to unite with Scotland, and should their kindness now be slighted—[9]

For a messenger in such hot haste, English weather was unfavorable; on September 22 Defoe wrote from Leicester that he had been "locked up" for forty-eight hours by the rain. But in his travels he was always the reporter. His *Review* for October 8 told of his journeying with a rustic to whom Prince Eugene's relief of Turin from the French meant a rise in the price of wool: "Master, says an honest countryman to me the other day, as I was riding along, there's brave news, they say, at London about Prince HOUGIN; they say, he has killed all the French, and they say, we shall have a main trade, our wool rises already upon it. Pray what is this Prince HOUGIN?"

In the same issue of the *Review* Defoe confirmed his remarks on the wool trade by what he had heard in passing through Leeds: "this paper was wrote upon the spot, viz. at Leeds in Yorkshire, where I had the testimony of the whole community to make it good."

On the night of September 30 "Mr. Alexander Goldsmith" arrived at Newcastle, where he drew money from Harley's agent, the postmaster John Bell, drank a bottle of ale with him, and admitted that he was so publicly known in Edinburgh that it would be imprudent to go there under an assumed name. Bell—no man of letters—wrote doubtfully to Harley: "I have read part of a book under his name; it may be his own but be pleased to let that pass." Further conversation convinced Bell (as Defoe's conversation seems usually to have convinced the men he met) that Defoe was "a very ingenious man and fit for that business I guess he is going about." When Defoe attempted to leave Newcastle on the morning of October 2, one of his two horses failed (it is likely that his brother-in-law Robert Davis accompanied him on this journey). After securing a replacement from Bell, he pressed on to arrive at Morpeth that night. As his next letters to Harley are all lost, we do not hear from him directly until he was writing from Edinburgh on October 24. However, "several letters" which Defoe addressed to G. Mason for the eyes of Godolphin had been received in London before October 23;[10] and it seems clear that Defoe had arrived in the northern capital before October 12, the date of his first known communication as Edinburgh correspondent for the *Post-Man*.

Defoe was a confidential political reporter much of his life; but it was on his arrival in Edinburgh early in October 1706 that he first appears as the star reporter for a London newspaper.

Jean de Fonvive's *Post-Man* was generally regarded as the best written as well as the most widely circulated newspaper of the age. We cannot be sure just when or how Defoe's relations with Fonvive began. The two men had much to draw them together. Fonvive's journalistic ideals were much like Defoe's, and Fonvive was one of the French Protestant exiles (in whom Defoe had been interested from early manhood). Defoe's first known reference to him appeared on March 18, 1704, in a bantering account of Fonvive's supposed appearance before the imaginary "Society" of the *Review*. There it was charged that Fonvive made up news when the posts were slow in arriving, that he wrote long speeches and answers for foreign diplomats, and that he abused the English language: "And here Monsieur had little to say for himself, but that he was a Frenchman, and he thought it had been good English, which trivial excuse not availing him, he was voted guilty, and recorded in the Register of Impertinence, Fol. 6." On September 19 of the same year Defoe professed that Fonvive was again in difficulty with the "Society." Someone had reported Fonvive to the *Review* for inserting in the *Post-Man* verses stolen from Waller's poem on Oliver Cromwell. But this time Defoe let him off with a slight reprimand and some very high praise: "the author professes no greater desire than that wilful errors should be avoided and accidental ones acknowledged; and that gentleman being the most careful and most authentic of any of our writers, gives a testimony of it by owning that he has been abused, as any man might be in the like case." By April 19, 1705, Fonvive had won Defoe's favor so far that a group of supposed correspondents wrote to complain that the *Review* exposed the errors of other newspapers but allowed the *Post-Man* to escape without censure, adding the innuendo, "Perhaps there's a pecuniary understanding betwixt your Club and this gentleman." To this real or imaginary accusation Defoe replied by stating that the *Review* overlooked more errors in other newspapers than in the *Post-Man* and that Fonvive was above offering a bribe, just as the *Review* was above accepting it. He defended his refusal to print one attack on Fonvive on the ground that the *Post-Man* was the best newspaper in existence. By March 31, 1711, Defoe was praising the *Post-Man* as the only newspaper which carried out his own ideal of interpreting the news in addition to relating events.

On December 3, 1706, the *Review* named the *Post-Man* as the London newspaper which could be relied on to refute an antiministerial account of a tumultuous scene in the Scottish Parliament. The *Post-Man*'s account of this scene which Defoe praised, like most of its news from Edinburgh while Defoe was in residence there during part of 1706, 1707, and part of 1708, was transmitted by Defoe himself.

If we compare the *Post-Man*'s Edinburgh news with that of contemporary London papers, it is clear that the *London Gazette* leaned over backward to give only the safest official statements—the first meeting of the Parliament, a brief defense of the use of force to quell an Edinburgh mob, and the final acceptance of the Act of Union. The *Daily Courant* rivaled the *Post-Man* in its almost day-by-day accounts of the sessions of Parliament, but it gave very little more than the official minutes of those sessions. The *Post-Man* was likely to explain Scotticisms to the English readers, to condense or restate the minutes, or to omit them altogether.

Many of Defoe's reports were written on the following day, so that he was able to view the debates in retrospect and to analyze the reaction of the populace. He was inclined to omit or condense the repeated protests against the proceedings leading toward the Union (of which the *Daily Courant* said so much); and sometimes he pointed out that the protesters were few and unrepresentative and that the signatures to the protests were often secured by coercion. In his emphasis on the repeated defeat of the antiministerial forces, he gave a clear sense of the steady progress toward the accomplishing of the Union.

The *Post-Man* did not minimize the rioting in Edinburgh and Glasgow; but it suggested that the rioters were ruffians and idlers, tools of "the true authors of this uproar" who were themselves afraid to appear openly against the Union. When seven of the Edinburgh rioters were to be prosecuted, it observed that they were boys, the oldest about sixteen years of age. When Finley and Montgomery were arrested as leaders of the mob at Glasgow, it discovered that Finley was a professed Jacobite and that neither man had ever been an army officer as reported: Finley was formerly a maltman and Montgomery a tailor.[11]

The *Post-Man*'s Edinburgh correspondent was obviously not (like the *Daily Courant*'s man) a mere clerk whose chief duty was to see that the minutes of Parliament were sent to London by the next mail. He was a consistent individual deserving of the personal pronoun which he so often used. He shared Defoe's special interests and his personal connections. For instance, he was intimately acquainted with the proceedings of the Presbyterian Assembly. He had apparently sat up much of the night to observe the rioting in Edinburgh. He was interested in the taxes on beer and ale (regarding which Defoe was called in as a special adviser to the committee). He rejoiced at the prospect of improving trade in Scotland. He was a guest at the Duke of Queensberry's celebration of Queen Anne's birthday at Holyrood House. Apparently he saw the annual horse race on Leith Sands, attended a dinner at Leith in honor of Queensberry, and returned homeward through the north side of the city while a furious fire was blazing—surely a great day for such a lover of horseflesh, such a friend and admirer of Queensberry's, and such an observer of current events. He reported the passing of an act relating to the mines and minerals of the Duke of Queensberry; years later he told how he had visited the Duke's estate at Drumlanrig to advise him about the development of those mines.[12]

On April 3 the *Post-Man*'s correspondent wrote a glowing account of Queensberry's departure for London. On the same day, Defoe was writing to Harley to tell how the Great Man in Scotland had honored him on the preceding evening when Defoe had called to take his leave. On August 5 he reported (what Defoe loved to report from Scotland) a prodigious crop of corn. On October 22 he rejoiced that the supposed poverty of Scotland had been refuted when six hundred thousand dollars and ducatoons were brought in to be exchanged for new money. On December 2 he reported another great fire in the northern part of Edinburgh, which (according to a favorite method of Defoe) he estimated in terms of London: "they compute about 250 families burnt, which may be esteemed as in London about 60 houses."

The *Post-Man*'s correspondent sometimes paused to analyze the significance of measures or to indulge in shrewd prophecies like one of October 29, 1706: "all questions have been hitherto carried by such a majority, there is no reason to fear this." After the Act of Union had become a certainty, he could not refrain from a *Nunc Dimittis* to express his own feelings: "this grand affair is brought, God be thanked, to a happy conclusion, in spite of a vigorous opposition."[13]

While Defoe was traveling in Scotland during much of 1707, the *Post-Man*'s reports from Edinburgh ceased altogether, as they did when he returned to London at the end of December; but they were renewed in 1708. The unusually clear accounts of the attempted Jacobite invasion in March were mostly due to the full statements given out by the government; but perhaps Defoe's advice in London aided Fonvive in making better use of them than his journalistic rivals did. Soon Defoe was sent to Edinburgh by the new Ministry, and we find him writing to Godolphin from there on April 20. Again it becomes evident that the *Post-Man* had its own reporter in Scotland, and from June 18 until late September its news stories resembled Defoe's writing, as when he gave explanations for English readers of "The assembly, or meeting of the Lords" and of "The great stone buildings, called the Parliament-Close." But this was an age when strangers and all minority groups were under suspicion: English Dissenters were sometimes represented as conspirators against the government, and Roman Catholics were still accused of having burned London. So eager an observer as Defoe was in real danger in Edinburgh when opponents of the Union "industriously attempted to raise a report that [a] house was set on fire by some English men, which was spread in order to incense the people against the English."

During those periods, the *Post-Man*'s Edinburgh correspondence was written by Defoe, but the author remained in the background. However, on February 20, 1707, he allowed himself to come out into the open to rejoice over the discomfiture of a cantankerous adversary: "One Mr. Webster, a minister of this city, having written two libels against the English dissenters, the proceedings of that gentleman have been very much disliked by the other ministers of this city, and Mr. Daniel de Foe being in this place has fully vindicated the Protestant ministers in England against the aspersions contained in those pamphlets." But an agent for the Act of Union could not risk the loss of Scottish good will for so personal a triumph. Next day the *Post-Man*'s correspondent wrote to London to give the Rev. James Webster a comfortable line of retreat—if he chose to accept it: "We told you in our former of two pamphlets published against the English dissenters, and that they were written by one Mr. Webster: This was what all the town said, but upon enquiry, I must do that gentleman justice, and I do not hear that he owns those pamphlets, which I believe were written by an enemy of the Union, and would fain create differences between the Church of Scotland and the English Dissenters. If I can hear of any other particulars, I shall acquaint you therewith."[14]

Unless Defoe's gesture of conciliation is to be taken as a stroke of irony, it expresses a generous willingness to allow a beaten opponent to escape from the field. But when a writer is at the same time a star reporter, a pamphleteering controversialist, and a secret agent for the government, he must expect—at times—to make some concessions to his adversaries.

Defoe's confidential reports to Harley tell of the same horse racing at Leith, the same fire in the north side of Edinburgh, the same exposure of Webster, and the same care to avoid giving offense to Webster. As Defoe explained to Harley, he withheld an effective reply he had intended to publish: "when I considered my business here was peace, reconciliation and temper, I thought it was better to use him gently."[15]

Defoe believed that he had suppressed his reply to Webster. But one copy survives in the National Library of Scotland, with the title: *Passion and Prejudice, The Support of one another, And Both destructive to the Happiness of this Nation, In Church and State: Being A Reply to the Vindicator of Mr. W——r's Lawful Prejudices*. Its fourteen pages are called "The Preface"—apparently meant as a preface to *The Dissenters in England vindicated* (1707), after which it is bound up in the same volume of tracts.

If one has any doubt about how Defoe could write when he was angry, he should read this tract. Its tone is indicated by the first scriptural motto on the title page: "These things the Lord hates—Prov. 6. 16, 19. A False Witness that speaketh Lies, and he that soweth Discord among Brethren." When we remember the sacrosanct character of the Presbyterian clergy in Scotland, among whom Webster was eminent, it is clear why Defoe, as Harley's agent, decided not to publish the tract which had been printed for him as the injured representative of the English Dissenters.

Defoe's first reporting concerned a storm; he was always interested in storms, earthquakes, volcanoes, explosions, fires, and plagues. To the Puritan these were manifestations of God's power and his will; to the journalist they were always worth their space on the printed page. In a bantering account of the marvels narrated by his rivals, after he was established as the foremost journalist in London, Defoe professed that he was willing to indulge reporters in their flights of imagination —as long as they did not seek treasonable ends:

Let them try by degrees to get the better of themselves; and if, after their endeavors, they find it impossible for them to help telling wonders, let them tell such as, if they are not credible, are at least innocent. Let them turn the stream of their invention another way; let them shift the scene of it, and lay it at a greater distance. Let them now and then bring a few wild Indians down upon our Settlements; and, as often as the necessity of their affairs require it, let them dethrone or murder the Great Mogul. Let them now and then sink one island by an Earthquake, and carry another floating a thousand leagues from its original situation. This is certainly the safest method, both with regard to themselves, as well as the Government. For it is not an easy matter to detect them when their facts are laid so remote and tolerable well-circumstanced; at least, if anybody should be so malicious to go round the world to disprove them, that must be a work of time; their readers would first have swallowed and digested these occurrences as truths, and their papers would have had their run.

I am willing to give them still a larger scope, and, without confining them wholly to foreign affairs, allow them to sport their fancy with the other relators of Home Truths. They may once a month import leopards, tigers, and other strange beasts from the coast of Africa. As for lions, indeed, they must be managed with more caution; for being generally lodged in the Tower, the common people, who are fond of such sights, will require ocular demonstration. I wonder they don't sometimes, in a dry season, go a fishing for whales, which they may bring safe enough up to the mouth of the River Thames. I would not advise them to venture them much higher, because they would then become a perquisite of my Lord Mayor's and that would make the case subject to too nice an enquiry. But then, instead of it, they might easily, by the advantage of a stormy day, drown sixteen passengers at London Bridge, or overset a boat or two going to Lambeth. Methinks they should now and then let their imagination rove into the country, where they might, in the first county that comes into their heads, blast a parcel of tall oaks, burn several stacks of corn, and take off a steeple or two with lightning. And they might deal in meteors, coruscations, and armies fighting in the air, provided they did not draw State consequences from them, and place the Pretender at the head of one of the contending parties.

In such a city as this, they can seldom fail of a dreadful fire or horrid murder to help them out at a pinch. And if these subjects were pretty well drained, they might describe the rare qualities of the Indian Princes or the robust comeliness of the Hairy Tribesman; with innumerable other novelties of that kind, which might serve to elevate and surprise (as Mr. Bayes calls it), though (to speak in their own language) they might merit confirmation. But when that happens to be the case, and that the proofs are pretty strong against them, and too near at hand, they will do well not to be too circumstantial. I discovered this caution lately in a brother-writer, who informs the public that *A man dropped down dead in the street,* without any other particulars. Here is the surprise of sudden death, to keep up the attention of the reader; and yet, in case it were not a fact, I would be glad to know which way you would go about to confute it. This is Art in writing, without the Appearance of it; and that is the Great Secret.[16]

Here Defoe jibes at his rivals for lying about islands sunk by earthquakes. The subject was still a sore one for him; only a year and a half earlier (1718) he had been taken in by a very similar story. His accounts of the explosion which supposedly destroyed the West Indian island of St. Vincent have often been praised as extreme examples of his fictional journalism. But the story did not originate with him, and when he told it he did not suppose that it was fictional. His interest in the explosion (like his interest in the Great Storm) was to report it accurately and fully and to offer scientific explanations of the facts as reported. He was annoyed to learn that later accounts from the West Indies reduced the explosion of an entire island to a volcanic eruption.

The English reading public cared little enough for natural science, but its appetite for marvels was voracious. Interest in volcanic eruptions was so keen that the sober *London Gazette* had to cater to it at times. In no other period in the history of the world have a comet and an earthquake aroused such intense and widespread interest as in the first six decades of the eighteenth century.

In his approach to such natural phenomena, Defoe differed from his journalistic rivals in his careful attempts at scientific explanations. Several times he referred to the explosion of a foundry near Moorfields, when the molten metal poured for a brass cannon blew up because water had seeped into the mold. In so unlikely a place as *A Letter to the Whigs* (1714) he introduced a long analogy to describe political heats, which he likened to the explosions produced by underground streams pouring in on the gulf of subterranean fire. A year before the eruption of St. Vincent was reported in London, Mist's *Weekly-Journal* printed an account from Spain regarding a vast American earthquake in which several West Indian islands had disappeared. Defoe's known connection with Mist began two months later, but he reprinted the gist of this news story in his own monthly called *Mercurius Politicus*.[17]

In June, 1718, it was reported in London that the island of St. Vincent in the West Indies had been destroyed. The stages by which the story developed in print cannot be traced with precision because of the incompleteness of the extant files of London newspapers for that period. But on June 24 Applebee's *Original Weekly Journal* announced that "Letters from Barbados also give a deplorable account of damages done there by a tempest; and add that the island of St. Vincent is for the most part destroyed by fire and sulphurous matter emptious [*sic*] from the earth, in which conflagration great numbers of people and cattle perished." This statement was elaborated in Read's *Weekly Journal: Or, The British Gazeteer* for the same date:

By two ships newly arrived from Barbados we have an account that on Wednesday the 26th of March last about nine at night a very black cloud appeared to the eastward, and soon covered the Barbadians with showers of fine dark colored ashes or sand, driven on 'em like snow; with the wind it continued to fall three hours all which time it was exceeding dark, and very surprising on account of its suffocating quality. Capt. Calder coming from the leeward met the same twelve leagues off this island; and a vessel from Virginia bound to this island met the like about fifty leagues to the windward. 'Tis generally called here ashes of dust, but 'tis said, by such as have viewed it both dry and wet after they have washed it, with a microscope, to be fine sand. About the same time the island of St. Vincent was for the most part destroyed by a sulphur that took fire and blew up all before it, particularly several trees into the sea, which damaged many vessels on the coast, and such a quantity of dust was blown to Martinico that in several places the inhabitants were up to the knees.

On June 28 *St. James's Evening Post* was able to verify this and to amplify the account as follows:

St. Christopher's, April 18. By letters from passengers on board a sloop which sailed the 21st of March for Barbados, we have received advice that on the 26th of the same month, being about five leagues to the leeward of that island, they met with a calm, the weather being very black about twelve o'clock at night, when it looked dismally all round the horizon, as if it had been on fire, with a sulphurous smell, and they heard prodigious reports like cannon, which were followed by the continual showers of dry dust or ashes. About five the next morning there was such a darkness for three quarters of an hour that they could not see one another without candle light. It continued to rain dust upon them till seven at night, when it lay seven or eight inches thick upon the deck. There being at that time but little wind, they bore up the helm for Martinico with a design to get bread and other necessaries they wanted. It begun an hour after to rain dust, but not so violent. The night looked still terrible, but the weather pretty moderate, and on the 30th they arrived at Guardaloupa, where they heard the surprising news that the island of St. Vincent was blown up, and that they had an account from Martinico that from the Wednesday night, being the 26th of March, to the Thursday morning, they had heard above 1200 reports like cannon, and that St. Vincent was sunk. We hear since, by other advices, that the Governor of the Leeward Islands, having received the like information, sent a sloop to see if they could discover that island, but they could not see any land, but where they expected to have seen the same they saw the sea in a breach, so that it seems nothing remained of that island but a rock. One of our sloops coming from Barbados met with the same showers of dust or ashes, and brought some of it, which is like sand in the hour-glasses, but the color is like that of ink-powder. The island of St. Vincent was about eight leagues long and six broad, and inhabited by Indians.

On July 5 Applebee's *Original Weekly Journal* repeated the account of the *St. James's Evening Post*, with this significant addition: "The island of St. Vincent is blown up, which occasioned the shower of ashes so much spoken of by our sailors, who were so terrified thereat, and at the prodigious reports they heard at the same time, as if a thousand or twelve hundred great guns had been discharged, that the accounts we have received from them are very imperfect. We hear that nothing of that island is to be seen but only two small rocks."

So far Defoe had not shown the slightest interest in the story. But now it offered too striking a challenge to be ignored by a journalist who was an amateur of science. At long last, in Mist's *Weekly-Journal* for July 5, he recognized that this "piece of public news" was "of such consequence" that he laid aside the usual letters from correspondents and devoted more than two pages to a leading article in which he told of the destruction of the island, attempting to explain it as the result of exploded gases (sulphurous and nitrous particles exposed to the air) or of water poured in on subterranean fire (as at the foundry near Moorfields): "by either of these two ways, this terrible event of blowing up the island may be supposed possible in Nature; so we do believe that all the philosophers in the world cannot find a third."

Once Defoe had been aroused to investigate the reported explosion, he drew on his own previous knowledge of explosions and on his extensive reading, perhaps even on his recollections of his scientific studies at Morton's academy. As usual for him, he went far beyond the printed accounts and sought out "several other letters to other people"[18]—further source materials like those on which the newspaper stories had been hastily grounded. He was not acting here as the perpetrator of hoaxes, nor was he the stubborn journalist who was tardy in facing the facts. Once again he was "The Age's Humble Servant," as he had been when he had labored for seven months to record the devastation of the Great Storm nearly fifteen years before.

The elaborately organized foreign correspondence of modern newspapers was of course unknown in Defoe's time. Most of the real news from abroad was received by public officials, merchants, even men like the gamblers who bet on confidential tips from the battle front or private citizens of wide-ranging interests like Sir Hans Sloane. It was in a personal letter to Sloane that the best account of the great West Indian hurricane of 1722 was given to the world.

The brief report of the destruction of St. Vincent in *St. James's*

Evening Post was reprinted in Boyer's *Political State of Great-Britain* for June (but like all such digests of the news, actually published two or three weeks after the month had ended). When Defoe brought out his own monthlies for June, he again gave much fuller accounts of the explosion than anyone else had done, but he was obliged to vary the telling of it in the two rival publications issued under his editorship for different groups of readers. *Mercurius Politicus* repeated with slight additions Defoe's long analysis which had originally been written by him for Mist's *Weekly-Journal*. It added much new material; but it quoted a London news story dated July 1 including certain details to be found earlier in *St. James's Evening Post* or later in *Applebee's*, together with one significant detail not to be found in either.[19]

All three of Defoe's own reports (in Mist's *Weekly-Journal*, in *Mercurius Britannicus*, and in *Mercurius Politicus*) have two features in common: they show his great care to get behind current rumor to the basic facts, and they show his scientific interest in ascertaining the cause of the supposed explosion.

Defoe laid no claim to priority, "the business being not to contend who has the first account, but who can best relate the whole event, and give their readers the most perfect history of the thing it self." Throughout July other news from the West Indies continued to arrive, as of a destructive fire on Antigua and of a piratical attack off Puerto Rico and the surrender of pirates at Barbados. As late as July 26 *Applebee's* reported letters from New England giving support to the original story: "We have received a confirmation of the destruction of the island of St. Vincent, by the mighty Hand of Providence."

But one week later, direct reports from the West Indies were beginning to discredit the main features of the story. On August 2 the irresponsible *Applebee's* (which had been one of the first journals to report the explosion as an accomplished fact—and which had not yet passed under Defoe's control as one of the most interesting periodicals of the day) reversed its own stand by a contemptuous disclaimer, which was later reprinted (with slight modifications) by Boyer's *Political State:* "Letters from Barbados mention the eruption of a volcano, or burning mountain, lately in the island of St. Vincent; which generally happens once in fifty or sixty years. And this is the only ground of the whole island's being blown up, which was dressed in such formidable figures in some of our newspapers a while ago; the said island standing where it ever did."[20]

Defoe had been slow to accept the original account; but he was too careful a journalist to be ready to accept this sudden rumor in place of what seemed a well-attested fact. He replied to the latest news about St. Vincent (but not in response to the flippant recantation published in *Applebee's* on the same day): "They pretend to tell us a strange story, viz., that the island of St. Vincent is found again, and is turned into a volcano, or burning mountain; but we must acknowledge we do not believe one word of it."[21] Later in the month he was forced to admit, however reluctantly, that the original reports had been exaggerated: "But that which is most wonderful of all is, that there are some who pretend to tell us that all our stories from the West Indies which give us an account of the entire destruction of the island of St. Vincent are wrong, and that the island is found again, only a great volcano or eruption of a burning mountain is broken out in the midst of it: All which we must wait the confirmation of."

Defoe, the journalist with a flair for science, was left in a position much like that of an amateur scientist who has offered an attractive explanation for "flying saucers"—only to be informed that there are no "flying saucers" to explain. Naturally he was irritated because letters from the West Indies had led him astray. When earthquakes and volcanic eruptions were reported from the Canaries soon afterward, he refused to be drawn into any detailed statement without further confirmation: "as I have not yet any particulars, and that I do not think fit to invent any, as I am apt to believe others have practiced in the late dismal stories published of the island of St. Vincent, which it seems are not one tenth of them true; and also that I do not choose to be the messenger of evil tidings, I refer the reader to such information from Canaries as the next ships may bring, when it may be hoped better news may come to hand."[22]

Another remarkable narrative by Defoe has often been misunderstood as an extravagant fiction foisted on his credulous readers as sober truth. On September 8, 1705, the apparition of a Mrs. Veal was said to have appeared immediately after her death to her friend Mrs. Bargrave at Mrs. Bargrave's home in Canterbury, at noon on a Saturday when the town was thronged for the cattle market. The story is the most naturalistic and convincing of ghost stories, so that it has been explained in a wide variety of ways, from the supposition that it was based on a real happening to the suggestion that Mrs. Bargrave invented it.

The one thing that is quite certain is that Defoe did not make up the story. For nearly two months after the supposed happening (until

November 5) he was away on a long tour for Harley in the western, central, and northern counties of England; and his narrative is confirmed by three accounts. One of these is a private letter from Lucy Lukyn to her aunt on October 9, written nearly a month before Defoe had returned from his journey for Harley in regions remote from Canterbury. The second report was published in the *Loyal Post* for December 24, which may have been either a little later or a little earlier than Defoe's narrative. The third was an account of an interview with Mrs. Bargrave in 1714, jotted down in the form of manuscript notes in a copy of Defoe's *True Relation*.

Recently it has been suggested that still another account of the apparition confirmed, corrected, and improved on Defoe's story as late as 1766. But this negligible version was only the very late attempt of an obscure printer to pirate a valuable literary property which was controlled by a group of well-established publishers. Similar attempts were often made for others of Defoe's works. An edition of *Robinson Crusoe* professed to be corrected from Crusoe's own manuscript before it had been mutilated by Defoe, an edition of *Moll Flanders* was allegedly based on the heroine's papers after her death in Ireland, *Colonel Jack* was condensed and rewritten to fit into a history of the highwaymen, *Roxana* was continued from the point at which Defoe chose to end it. We can learn nothing whatever about Defoe's works from such irresponsible piracies undertaken long after his death.[23]

We can do little more than guess how Defoe came to hear of the apparition—which would certainly have interested him at any time, even if he had not already become a professional news reporter. In Kent there was a group of Dissenting families with wide ramifications in his life and writings and in later literary history. A clergyman named Veal conducted the school attended by Samuel Wesley before he entered Morton's academy; Mrs. Veal's brother-in-law was William Young, Jr., captain of the *Degrave* on which Defoe's Robert Drury was shipwrecked off southern Madagascar. The captain of the ship which carried Henry Fielding on his sad voyage to Lisbon was still another Veal. It is probable (but not certain) that Defoe knew the families concerned. It is also probable that he had received some written account of the apparition of Mrs. Veal (whether from the justice of the peace who supposedly vouched for it or from someone else). It is extremely probable that he interviewed Mrs. Bargrave in Canterbury for detailed confirmation, as he was in the habit of interviewing other informants.

Later editions of the tract were likely to mention, on their title pages, the fact that the "Apparition recommends the Perusal of Drelincourt's Book of Consolations." The famous story that Defoe wrote the tract to promote the sale of Drelincourt's "book on death" was given wide currency when Sir Walter Scott retold it in his critical essay on Defoe's writings. That story may well have been greatly exaggerated after a hundred years, but it perhaps contained a certain amount of truth. It is extremely unlikely that Defoe would have written the story only to sell the book; but in Lucy Lukyn's account and in the *Loyal Post*'s report the name of the author of the book on death was not given, whereas Defoe emphasized it more than most features of the story. What could be more natural than for the publisher of Drelincourt's *Consolations*—certainly by September, 1706—to have made the most of so favorable a reference?

Defoe's *True Relation* has been too often praised to call for further comment here. Perhaps the clearest analysis of Defoe's method is that of Sir Charles Firth: "Like a skilful journalist, he arranged, selected, developed, and to some extent dramatised what he was told."[24] It should not lessen our admiration to realize that the story is journalism rather than fiction and that it belongs in a class with Defoe's numerous other accounts of supernatural visitants. He probably believed in the apparition himself—as Dr. Samuel Johnson would perhaps have believed in it if he had not heard the denials set afloat by the brother of Mrs. Veal and others.

In his amusing account of Defoe's *True Relation*, Scott remarked: "Had Mrs. Veal's visit to her friend happened in our time, the conductors of the daily press would have given the word, and seven gentlemen, unto the said press belonging, would, with an obedient start, have made off for Kingston, for Canterbury, for Dover,—for Kamschatka if necessary,—to pose the Justice, cross-examine Mrs. Bargrave, confront the sober and understanding kinswoman, and dig Mrs. Veal up from her grave, rather than not get to the bottom of the story. But in our own time we doubt and scrutinize: our ancestors wondered and believed."[25] No doubt Defoe's readers were more credulous than Scott's. But the amazing thing is that Defoe used (as far as possible) the best reportorial methods of later times. He went almost everywhere; whatever could be learned by observation or by inquiry he was likely to learn. Many of his illustrative anecdotes (like an account of a trial which he attended at the Old Bailey) begin with a personal guaranty such as, "I can offer you an instance within my own knowledge." When such anecdotes can be checked, they are nearly always found to be authentic.

It is astonishing to see how often he can be proved to have seen the principal events between the Great Fire of 1666 and his death in 1731 and how often he can be proved to have interviewed some of the main actors in those events. It is a rare thing to find a sedentary man like Sir Richard Steele "scooping" Defoe by his interviews with Alexander Selkirk, whom Defoe perhaps never met. But Steele had the easy advantage here that he was a great frequenter of taverns, where Selkirk spent most of his time when he was in London. In the end it was Defoe and not Steele who used many of Selkirk's recollections in *Robinson Crusoe*.

The range of characters cited by Defoe for his firsthand information is as varied as it is essentially accurate. Among the multitude are these: "a gentleman who had lived many years in Muscovy"; "some merchants now living in London" who had bought in the market at Constantinople; Bishop Tillotson; Jonathan Wild; the crew of "a buccaneering pirate vessel"; English gentlemen who served the Germans in Upper Hungary; exiles from the German Palatinate; a banished Hungarian minister; and two men who had been accosted by street robbers, "as well the gentleman who had his sword pulled at over against Stocks Market, as the other who gave him the admonition in Lombard Street, and warned him of the gallows."[26]

Not all of Defoe's reportorial writing is as well organized as *A True Relation*. In November, 1714, the government and its supporters were concerned for fear that the carefully planned riots in several cities against George I meant the beginning of the expected Jacobite rising (which actually started in Scotland less than ten months later). *The Bristol Riot* gives an extreme example of rough notes which Defoe seems to have hurried back to London while the trial of some of the agitators was still in progress and while he was being jostled by younger reporters who sought to beat the elderly gentleman in getting their news stories up to London—"several persons sent down on purpose to pick up scraps of intelligence," "ordinary fellows of no acquaintance" who had "no opportunities to come at a perfect knowledge of the matter."

This pamphlet was printed off in London so hastily that in some copies it was bound with pages 7 to 14 preceding the rest of the tract. There are indications of a lapse of time in the writing and of a change in the writer's plans. Defoe suggested that the publisher Roberts have his accounts of fact "put into order by some friend of his"—but apparently this was not done. The pamphlet remains in great disorder, in spite of a reminder in the Postscript: "You will excuse my want of method, and get it mended by some more able hand, if you make use of what I write." Defoe promised to inclose a transcript of a letter which a Bristol friend had drawn up to be sent to a merchant in London, if he could get it copied before the post left; fifteen pages later he admitted that he had not found time to procure the letter and that he was obliged to substitute another one to an apparently different merchant in London. But the Postscript indicates that his report had not been sent three days later; and it remains doubtful how the two letters to London merchants really differed, especially since the letter as transcribed is in exactly the same style as the rest of the pamphlet.

We are told that the court sat on Friday (p. 26), and that the author was writing at ten o'clock (p. 27); three days later he wrote that the trial "is yet young" (p. 28). To complicate matters still further, Defoe's rough draft explains how he had become so quickly familiar with details about Bristol (details which he later incorporated in his own *Tour*): "You will wonder how I could collect so many particularities in so little time, but 'twill not surprise you when I tell you, that most of them were already methodized by the Reverend Mr.——, who had it done for helps to his memory, himself intending an account of this affair from the beginning to the end, and in most places of this letter, he not only assisted me with his memoirs, but with his hand."[27]

This is Defoe at his worst as a reporter, but—as far as one can judge from the existing evidence—it is still Defoe. He had sent in this news story too hurriedly to have time to make it entirely coherent. Yet even as it stands, it appears to be the unfinished work of an able political reporter, and it gives by far the most vivid existing account of the second largest city in England while a rebellion seemed to be developing in its streets.

Another advantage which Defoe had as a reporter was his skill in shorthand. So good a Presbyterian as Sir John Clerk of Penicuik might regret that his own handwriting had been spoiled by the custom in Scottish schools (where shorthand was almost unknown) of teaching pupils "to write long notes of sermons after the minister" (although he admitted that the practice "served a little to fix our attention, and to keep us from doing worse things"). Defoe regarded shorthand as a useful skill, whether one recorded a sermon or a trial or the dying speech of a criminal. In 1726 he regretted that the art had become very rare in England for lack of use: "the occasion lessens every day, for as to sermon writing, that is quite laid aside (as sermon hearing indeed seems also likely to be in a little more time); and as to trials in extraordinary cases, and speeches, people have so often been reproved for writing on such occasions, and put out of the courts and places where they have attempted it, that this also seems to be left off."[28] Defoe wrote this from experience. As "Mr. Applebee's man" he was the foremost writer of the lives of criminals in England. In 1704 he had apparently been ejected from the trial between Rook and Cole-peper as one of the writers "appointed by Mr. Colepeper" who took the trial "in shorthand, as far as permitted" until it was ordered that "the writers to be turned out of the court." He rejoiced that the ejection came too late to prevent the case from being recorded for publication almost in its entirety: "However, thus far the shorthand writers had proceeded with great exactness: and they are ready, by their handwriting and notes, to justify all before mentioned in this trial, which by this time was very near ended."[29]

Defoe had a third advantage as a reporter in his practice of reading foreign newspapers, which contained news and expressed points of view little known in England. Early in his career he was offered an annual sum to translate the *Paris Gazette* for English readers, but the government suppressed the undertaking. Later he began his connection with Mist as translator for the *Weekly-Journal*.[30]

His fourth advantage as a reporter lay in his carefully organized system of correspondence. Abel Boyer, who mailed his newsletters to the Continent for a guinea a month, relied mostly on current gossip and on accessible printed material; but Defoe had a news-gathering and news-distributing system of his own. In one communication to Harley he listed sixty-three agents in England alone who were to deliver his "Remarks" throughout the country. In his *Review* he made frequent allusions to his special sources of information from Scotland. He kept offering Harley an intelligence service which would make him supreme in the government, and he could not bear to think of giving up such an opportunity for lack of funds to maintain it. Shortly after Harley's return to power, Defoe wrote (September, 1710) to offer what seemed to him the most valuable help he could give: "I have since I served [you] (as you know) established a general correspondence, and at some charge maintained it by which I may have a fixed intelligence (I may say) all over Britain. But especially in the north I confess it grieves me to think of letting it fall, because I cannot fail of rendering it very useful to your service on every occasion; and shall, the next time I have the honor to wait on you, show you a proof of it."

While Defoe was writing for the government, he was often allowed to see the Customs books and many other official records. It is quite likely that he saw some of the Jacobite letters intercepted in the mail; but it was only a joke when he professed to publish a long letter from France expressing the French attitude toward the attempted assassination of Harley. The letter is extremely characteristic of Defoe, and it was published to suggest that Harley was hated by the French.[31]

As a reporter Defoe insisted on direct statement of the facts; on frank publicity, even when it revealed such unpleasant news as the nation's losses in battle; most of all, on impartiality and regard for the truth.[32]

The old notion of Defoe as an equivocator grew largely out of the failure of some of his critics to allow for two circumstances:

(1) When he sought to write fiction, he had to create a new public. Literal-minded readers of *Robinson Crusoe* often demanded that it be explained as either true or false, and they were as persistent as a cross-examiner in demanding an explicit answer of "yes" or "no." Long after his death, the novels of Defoe were often still confounded with his journalistic and historical works, and he was reproached (as no modern writer should ever be) because his fiction was only fiction.

(2) Many of his writings were in the field of controversy, where the easiest answer a defeated opponent could make was to call an argument a lie. Defoe was sometimes misinformed, sometimes partisan, rarely angry—but almost never false to the essential truth as he saw it at that time.

When he seems to be opposing his own honest judgment, he is writing playfully or indulging his all-too-dangerous love of irony—except when he is using casuistry for an honorable end. Writing as a supporter of the Hanoverians, he admitted that Harley (Lord Oxford) should be impeached and tried for his life; but he pointed out that some other members of the late government who still ranked high in court favor should be treated in exactly the same way. This was no betrayal of his late patron but the strongest defense of Harley which could then be offered.

As for the Defoe who had been called "a great, a truly great liar, perhaps the greatest liar that ever lived," he is an imaginary figure, born of a misunderstanding of so many of Defoe's honestly written narratives, like those which told of the destruction of the island of St. Vincent or of the apparition of Mrs. Veal. The Defoe who is more likely to be found by the unbiased reader is the reporter—a man with "the seeing eye, the immediate recognition of what is and what can be made to appear significant, the insatiable curiosity, and, perhaps above all, the honesty that preserves a completely open mind."[33]

XV. SCOTLAND

*Mr. De Foe is now returning to England, and really I can-
not but say he seems to have a pretty good knowledge
of our affairs and just enough notions of them.*

Rev. William Carstares to Robert Harley, November 18, 1707 (*H.M.C. Portland*, VII, 298)

DEFOE IS NOT KNOWN as a reporter in Scotland until October, 1706; but for many years after that he was such a specialist in the
affairs of Scotland that his activities in that country require a separate
chapter.

Until the Union in 1707, the parliaments of the two nations were
quite independent. There was no assurance that "the golden link of
the Crown," established in 1603 and re-established in 1660, would
continue unbroken after the death of Queen Anne, when the Scots
might refuse to acquiesce in the choice of the next sovereign. The
Church of Scotland was inclined to distrust even the English Dissenters. Rivalry between English and Scottish companies trading with
Africa and the East Indies was so acute that in 1705 it almost led to
war.

Before 1707, and at several critical periods after the Union, Defoe
was actually the closest tie between the two nations. He was an English businessman with interests in both countries; for several years he
gave English readers of the *Post-Man* the fairest report of Scottish
happenings; he was the Edinburgh agent of successive ministries under
Godolphin and Harley, Godolphin, and later Harley again; he was
the London spokesman for the Church of Scotland.

As a statesman Defoe sought the welfare of both nations; as a reporter he sought to tell the truth about Scotland for English readers.
As late as 1726 he was completing the volume of his *Tour* which
dealt with Scotland, in which he avoided "the most scandalous partiality" which had appeared in all similar narratives "written by natives of that country": "the world shall, for once, hear what account

an Englishman shall give of Scotland, who has had occasion to see most of it, and to make critical enquiries into what he has not seen." His account was unlike that of Scottish travelers; but it differed even more from that of English writers, who liked to fill their pages with jibes about the disposal of sewage in Edinburgh, the inadequate dress of the Highlanders, the sanctimonious cant and the provincial speech of the Lowlanders, the beggarly pride of the gentry and noblemen, and the lice and fleas and all-pervading poverty of the common people.

Before Defoe, no important English writer had ever visited Scotland except Ben Jonson, and that grandson of the Annandale Johnstons was perhaps only returning home when he came north to Edinburgh and Leith. Until some years after Defoe's death, no other important English writer ventured beyond Tweed except Sir Richard Steele—and he only as a Commissioner of Forfeited Estates, notoriously lax in attending the committee meetings.

Among men of public affairs in London the ignorance about Scotland was almost as great as among writers. London periodicals carried more news from Venice or Danzig than from the sister nation. Few government officials in Westminster knew much more about Scotland, except through the biased accounts of adventurers who came southward to seek their fortunes. William III became involved in the Glencoe Massacre because he relied on information and advice from his Scottish subordinates. George IV was the first sovereign, for more than 135 years, who had seen Scotland.

The future Duke of Marlborough, who attended the Duke of York in Scotland, never returned to the country where he received his first title as Baron Churchill of Aymouth (on the southeastern coast of Scotland); and Defoe remarked dryly, "I never heard that he did anything for the town, which is at present just what it always was, a good fishing town." Young Scottish gentlemen preferred military service on the Continent to peaceful industry at home; landlords frequently spent their rents in England or abroad. So good a patriot as Fletcher of Saltoun believed that his countrymen could not succeed as merchants, and he held that the misery of the lower classes could only be relieved by a modified form of slavery.

In contrast with the ignorance of most Englishmen and the narrow views of so many Scots, Defoe regarded Scotland with sympathetic understanding. Almost every line he wrote about the country was devoted to two ideas:

(1) Scotland and England must be united—on terms acceptable to the Scots.

(2) Scotland must be encouraged to develop its economic life—through agriculture, manufacturing, mining, fisheries, shipping, and trade—until it could share the prosperity of England.

Defoe did not write as a sentimental theorist, like so many humanitarians of the age. He knew Scotland better than any other Englishman, better than almost any native Scot before Sir Walter himself. He seems to have visited Scotland six or more times, for periods totaling at least three years. Before his arrest in 1703 he was preparing to shift his residence there. In August and September, 1706, he had a close correspondence with Scotland and was well known personally in Edinburgh.[1]

In his letters to Harley he might jest regarding the apparent diversity of his interests in Scotland, but those interests were far more than a mask for his political mission. He seemed equally at home with men of different religious faiths, political views, and economic interests. In Dumfriesshire he could sit with nearly seven thousand wild Cameronians on a hillside to hear John Hepburn preach for almost seven hours;[2] in Edinburgh he was an honored visitor at the sedate meetings of the Commission of the General Assembly of the Church of Scotland. In the Lowlands he could be a guest at the castle of the Queen's High Commissioner; in the Highlands he could accept an invitation from a chieftain who might have preferred to receive the Queen's exiled brother as his sovereign. He was a friend and admirer of that staunch old defender of the Protestant Succession, Lieutenant General Maitland; but he paid a kindly visit to Lord Belhaven when he was imprisoned in Edinburgh as a suspected Jacobite. He was an active member of the Edinburgh Society for the Reformation of Manners; yet when the vintages of France were being rushed into Scotland before the Union, he offered to serve Harley in his old capacity as an expert taster of wine. He brought his brother-in-law Robert Davis from London to undertake shipbuilding at Leith, he established periodicals in Edinburgh,[3] he wrote two ambitious poems in honor of Caledonia, and two of his most important writings were records of the Union and of the sufferings of the Church of Scotland.

Defoe regarded Scotland as a second home. Biographers have remarked on the parallel between his fondness for Scotland and Robinson Crusoe's interest in the other side of his island. From 1709 or 1710 to 1711 Defoe's older son Benjamin was entered in the University of

Edinburgh, partly no doubt because the English universities were closed to Dissenters, but very possibly to prepare the youth to carry on his father's connection with Edinburgh journalism. Several political tracts by Defoe are marked by his use of Scottish idioms, and (where he was not known in advance) he seems to have been successful in passing himself off as a native of the country. To Harley he proposed a plan by which he would divide the seasons between England and Scotland, spending eight months of each year in the north and one month on the less familiar roads between London and Edinburgh. He would have been satisfied to devote only three months of each year to London.

His longest and perhaps his earliest journey in Scotland was apparently undertaken some time during the reign of William III, when with four companions and two servants he rode up the east coast to the northern limits of the island and back along the extreme northwest shore and through the Highlands to Fort William. This was one of the most pleasant of his many travels, undertaken long before apoplexy or the stone made horseback-riding a painful necessity rather than a source of delight. In his *Tour* he was tempted to tell of the trip in detail, but he passed it over as he did all personal recollections that concerned his own experience more than the interests of the public:

> It would be no unpleasant account to relate a journey which five, two Scots and three Englishmen, took in this manner for their diversion, in order to visit the Duke of Gordon; but it would be too long for this place. It would be very diverting to show how they lodged every night; how two Highlanders who attended them, and who had been in the army, went before every evening and pitched their little camp; how they furnished themselves with provisions, carried some with them, and dressed and prepared what they killed with their guns; and how very easily they traveled over all the mountains and wastes without troubling themselves with houses or lodgings. But as I say the particulars are too long for this place.[4]

Defoe's enthusiasm for this trip probably suggested his plan for circumnavigating the island of Great Britain in a boat "with an able commander for that purpose" (apparently his own man Friday, his much-sharing and long-suffering brother-in-law Robert Davis). The trip gave him some of his personal familiarity with the "infinite creeks and coves" of the Scottish coastline, so favorable for the smuggling about which he warned Godolphin in the summer of 1707 when Defoe was being considered for Secretary to the Commissioners of the Customs in Scotland, and no doubt again on March 22, 1708, when Godolphin was dispatching him from London "as a person employed for the Queen's service in Scotland relating to the revenue, etc." It gave him an insight into the herring industry, which later interested him greatly.

The Highlanders "who had been in the army" might well have come from Fort William, commanded by the guardian of the Highlands—the humane Maitland, on whose conversation Defoe drew for much of his account of the earlier military cruelties against the Covenanters, and whom he urged on Harley as the best choice to command the nation's forces in Scotland. Years later, when both Harley and Maitland were no more, he paused in his account of the Highlands to pay tribute to the memory of his friend:

Lieutenant General Maitland, an old experienced general, who had signalized himself upon many occasions abroad, particularly at the great battle of Treves, where he served under the French and where he lost one of his hands.

I name this gentleman not to pay any compliment to him, for he is long ago in his grave, but to intimate that this wise commander did more to gain the Highlanders and keep them in peace and in a due subjection to the British Government, by his winning and obliging behavior and yet by strict observance of his orders and the duty of a Governor, than any other before him has been able to do by force and the sword; and this particularly appeared in the time of the Union, when endeavors were everywhere made use of to bring those hot people to break out into rebellion, if possible to prevent the carrying on the Treaty.

In Defoe's later life we have many echoes of this trip to the north, in his obvious familiarity with Scotland before 1703, in his intense and continuing interest in the difficulties of the Presbyterian churches of Ross and Sutherland, and in his high praise of the Duke of Gordon in his *Caledonia* and his personal acquaintance with the Duke's followers when the Act of Union was under consideration.[5]

Perhaps the most striking example of his confidence in his knowledge of the Highlands occurred in July, 1707, when there were reports of a meeting of Jacobite armed forces to prepare for the landing of the Pretender—forces assembled under the pretense of a vast deer hunt or "Highland Hunting." Defoe wrote to Harley from Fife: "If you think it may conduce to the public service I shall willingly hazard myself to go north, and make myself master of as much of those mysteries of iniquity as can be obtained in order to give you seasonable intelligence." No other Englishman at that period possessed the special knowledge required for success in so daring an undertaking. The ex-Jacobite spy Captain John Ogilvie, a Highlander with exceptional connections among the clans, wanted Harley's promise to provide for his wife and children "in case of death or other misfortune befalling me," and he declared after his return from a visit to the north that he would have been "murdered and never heard more tell of" if the chieftains had "but in the least suspected me."[6]

In the spring and early summer of 1704, when the "Scotch Plot" was in the air and Jacobite agents were being reported as on their way from the Pretender's court near Paris through Rotterdam to Scotland, Defoe was expecting orders to go on a secret mission to Holland, where his unusual knowledge of Scotland and of the Continent might have been most useful. But the excitement soon died down, and by the latter part of the summer he was preparing for the first of his trips over England as Harley's agent. In 1705 a hostile pamphleteer accused the *Review* of depending on a Scottish amanuensis to supply Defoe's deficiency in Latin.

In the same year, Defoe showed keen interest in the seizure of the English merchantman "Worcester" in the Firth of Forth, which brought ill will between the nations to a crisis. More than any of his contemporaries, he knew how Captain Green, his chief mate, and his gunner on the "Worcester" were legally murdered in Edinburgh on a trumped-up charge of piracy; and he wrote of that national crime for more than twenty years—sometimes as a government apologist who sought to save the Union when it was endangered by English resentment of the wrong or by the outburst of anti-English fury in Edinburgh, afterward as a detached historian recording controversial facts more clearly and impartially than they were recorded by anyone else.

But it was the proposed parliamentary union between England and Scotland which drew him into the open as an expert on Scottish affairs. To Scottish Nationalists today the Union may appear to have been a mistake; to Jonathan Swift it was only a move by Godolphin to save his head after his criminal blunder in allowing the Scottish Act of Security to be enacted; to the historian John Hill Burton it was "an act of statesmanship unprecedented in the history of man."[7] During the reign of Queen Anne, it seemed to most impartial observers the only means of preventing the landing of the Pretender in Scotland with a French army to support his claim to both kingdoms.

On December 11, 1705, after announcing that he had "always purposely avoided entering into the debates between the kingdoms," Defoe devoted most of one *Review* to developing his thesis: "a breach between the nations would complete the ruin of both; so an Union between them would fix their prosperity and strength in so many articles that I am frequently sorry to see all that have hitherto wrote of it touch so few of them, and those few so lightly."

From April 16 to July 22, 1706, the lords commissioners of the two nations met in Westminster to draw up the proposed Articles of Union, and these in turn were submitted to the Scottish Parliament in Edinburgh. The Union was a highly controversial issue, in Scotland even more than in England; and Defoe approached it cautiously. He began on the subject in his *Review* for April 27. On May 4 and 24 he published the first two parts of *An Essay At Removing National Prejudices Against A Union with Scotland. To be continued during the Treaty here*. When the scene of decision shifted to Scotland, the author changed his appeal from English to Scottish readers, and the place of publication from London to Edinburgh.

The summer of 1706 was a time of exceptional personal difficulties for Defoe, so that on August 20 he devoted one number of the *Review* to protesting against the barbarity of his creditors, which threatened his wife and seven children with starvation.

Harley had already proposed that Defoe "be employed abroad" (that is, in Scotland). On August 21 the decision was hastened by the arrival of a thirty-six-page manuscript brought by a special messenger from Edinburgh, an appeal from some Scottish Presbyterians to arouse English Dissenters against the terms of union agreed on by the commissioners. Defoe expected that he would be asked to arrange for its publication; to forestall this, he got hold of the manuscript and sent it to Harley (August 29) with "remarkable passages in it underlined."

Defoe's difficulties presented a situation to Harley's liking: a man so harassed by creditors that he needed to get out of England, so well connected that he could appear before the Scottish Presbyterians as a spokesman for the English Dissenters, and so well acquainted with Scottish affairs that he could represent the interests of the Ministry from the first moment of his arrival in Edinburgh.

The Scottish Parliament was to assemble to consider the Union on October 3. On September 13, Defoe left London on horseback for the first and longest of his three Scottish missions for Harley. In vain he protested that he needed detailed instructions regarding his task and the men he was to meet. He was not allowed to confer with

Harley, and his confidential instructions did not reach him until October.[8]

Harley often professed indifference toward Scotland and the Scots. In 1704 he declared in the House of Commons that he knew no more of Scotch affairs than of Japan. When twelve peers were created in 1712 to give him control of the House of Lords, he said it was done to let the Scotch lords know they were not needed as much as they imagined, for they had come to expect a reward for every vote they gave. But when he sent Defoe to Scotland in September, 1706, Harley knew that the survival of his coalition ministry depended on the adoption of the Treaty of Union.

It has been assumed by some scholars that Harley was Defoe's generous patron and friend. Defoe was grateful for the small favors he received, and after Harley's fall in 1714 he tried to save his old master (even after his efforts had been rejected).[9] But one has only to look at the record to see how coldly calculating Harley was in his choice of agents. Like Louis XI of France, he preferred obscure men whom he could safely use and easily cast aside.

It is true that some of his apparent neglect of his friends was due to his vice of procrastination or to the courtier's habit of putting off supplicants by meaningless expectations. It is also true that, as a collector of news from every possible source, Harley received letters from Scotland from anyone who would write to him—from the Dukes of Argyll and Atholl and Queensberry, from the Earls of Ilay and Leven and Mar and Stair, from the Earl of Kinnoull and his son (Harley's own son-in-law Lord Dupplin), from the Rev. William Carstares and many others. As a moderate Tory who sought to sustain a coalition government, he wished to secure news and aid from any quarter.

But Harley's personal agents in Scotland were broken men. One was D. Fearns, a pious Presbyterian, but so poor that he depended on meager payments through Harley's agent. Another was Captain John Ogilvie, an ex-Jacobite conspirator who owed his forfeited life to Harley. Another was William Paterson, an unsuccessful projector who often interrupted his plans to save millions for the nation by begging for a few pounds or some post for himself. Another was John Ker of Kersland, who became so suspected at home that he dared not revisit Scotland, and whose debts were so urgent that he could not venture out on the streets of London. Another was William Greg, who became so destitute that he once feared to risk arrest by coming to his post of duty in Harley's office. With him Harley overplayed his hand; extreme poverty led Greg to accept French bribes, and the treason of this clerk in the office of the Secretary of State overthrew the Ministry in 1708 and brought Harley himself into grave danger.

Harley would have been willing to use Defoe only as he used so many others: Newgate Prison, the pillory, and the pressure of debts made him an obvious choice as a secret agent. The astonishing thing is that Defoe remained so vastly superior to such tools as Ogilvie and Paterson and Ker and Greg and, as a correspondent, so superior to such high officials as the Dukes of Argyll and Atholl and Queensberry or the Earls of Kinnoull and Mar. Defoe dared to give the advice which seems to have shaped Harley's success. He helped to determine Harley's policies and supported them with his political writing. He knew how to appeal to the very people with whom Harley found it most difficult and yet most necessary to maintain his influence—the Scottish Presbyterians and the English Dissenters, the merchants and the moneylenders, the private citizens who had little concern for the prerogative of the crown or the Establishment of the Church.

Defoe knew that there were four main obstacles in the way of a successful Union. The Scottish Parliament must not be allowed to reject the commissioners' proposals; it must not be allowed to clog those proposals with amendments which would later be rejected in London; it must not be given an opportunity to delay action until effective opposition could be organized; and the Scottish people must not be roused to such resentment that the Union would fail even after its nominal acceptance.

On September 24 and shortly thereafter, Defoe approached the subject very gradually in his *Review*—partly because the leading articles for those issues had been written in London or on the road to Edinburgh. On September 26 he alluded to the controversial tract from some of the Scottish Presbyterians which had precipitated his own journey: "I shall not examine the virulence of a late libel handed about in manuscript, in order to persuade the Dissenters [i.e., in London] against the Union, and fill them with jealousies about it; I shall only tell them, the enemies of the Union can wish for nothing more than to draw the Dissenters into a dislike of it, and then fix the odium of its miscarriage, if anything so fatal should happen, upon them." He was unwilling to rush into the heat of controversy, and he filled large parts of three successive issues of the *Review* with a poem on

"Peace and Union" which he prefaced as follows on September 26: "Before I enter upon this, I shall sing you a song of Peace and Union, and introduce the serious subject as merrily as I can; that it may with the more easiness and pleasure sink into the understanding of the readers."

But such a carefree frame of mind could not be sustained after Defoe arrived in Edinburgh early in October. The Jacobites were determined to halt the proceedings by any means in their power. Although their premature violence actually strengthened the government and prevented a successful revolution which might later have been carried out, it did not make Defoe's situation either safe or comfortable in October and November. Soon his character was being libeled by the venal pen of James Hodges; the Edinburgh mob raised by the Jacobites to terrorize the government's managers found enough spare time to threaten him; and mounted troops had to be brought into the capital to prevent civil war in the streets.

But the patience and tact of the Duke of Queensberry and other managers for the government were rewarded. Step by step the articles of the Union received conditional acceptance, while its opponents registered their futile protests again and again, hoping for a favorable day of decision which never came. The armed clansmen from the Highlands never reached Edinburgh—supposedly because of the double-dealing or the excessive caution of the Duke of Hamilton which held them back at the last. By December 24 Defoe was openly announcing his proposal to write a history of the Union, and by January 26 he was apologizing for harping on the same subject so long: " 'Nothing but Union! Union!' says one now that wants diversion. 'I am quite tired of it, and we hope 'tis as good as over now. Prithee, good Mr. Review, let's have now and then a touch of something else to make us merry.' "[10]

On May 1, 1707, the Act of Union became effective and the primary reason for Defoe's stay in Edinburgh was at an end. But he remained there until late December, sometimes pleading with the Secretary of State Harley and Lord Treasurer Godolphin for the financial aid necessary to enable him to return home. Harley and Godolphin made repeated promises; but they seemed unable to agree on what post to assign him, or what compensation to allow him, or whether the cost of his stay was to be charged to Harley's secret-service money or to the nation. For five months Defoe received no financial aid from either of them.[11] Even as a journalist his position was becoming impossible: readers of the *Review* complained of an editor who wrote nearly four hundred miles away, and Fonvive's *Post-Man* had little need for a star reporter in Edinburgh, with so little there to interest its London subscribers.

From the first, the cause of Defoe's trip to Edinburgh had been variously understood. To conceal his connection with the government, he allowed the rumor to grow that he had fled north on account of his debts—a report that was partly true. When his return was so long delayed, he implied that only the barbarity of a few creditors in London had obliged him to remain away from home. While the Union was under consideration he jested to Harley about the various activities in which he was supposedly engaged:

> I talk to everyone in their own way, to the merchants I am about to settle here in trade, building ships &c., with the lawyers I want to purchase a home and land to bring my family and live upon it. God knows where the money is to pay for it!
>
> Today I am going into partnership with a member of Parliament in a glass house; tomorrow with another in a salt work, with the Glasgow mutineers I am to be a fish merchant, with the Aberdeen men a woolen, and with the Perth and Western men a linen manufacturer, and still at the end of all discourse the Union is the essential, and I am all to everyone that I may gain some.

Two months later he repeated some of these professed plans while he added still others:

> I have hitherto kept myself unsuspected, have whispered and caused it to be spread that I am fled hither for debt and cannot return, and this particularly that they may not suspect me. Under this reproach, though I get some scandal, yet I effectually secure myself against suspicion. Now I give out, I am going to write the history of the Union in folio, and have got warrants to search the Registers and Parliament books, and have begun a subscription for it. I tell them it will cost me a year's time to write it. Then I treat with the Commission to make them a new version of the Psalms, and that I'll lock myself in the College two years for the performance. By these things I effectually amuse them and I am perfectly unsuspected.
>
> Then I am setting weavers to work to make linen, and I talk of manufactures and employing the poor, and if that thrives I am to settle here and bring my family down and the like, by which trifles I serve the great end, viz. a concealment.

These passages were written to amuse Harley; but most of what Defoe told his Scottish friends was literally true. His multifarious activities in Scotland concealed his mission for the ministry all the better because each of them represented a very real interest of Defoe. He did seek to recoup some of his financial losses by success in linen-weaving, and he offered to have linen woven for Harley's own use as soon as Harley's agent would send him the pattern preferred by so great a lover of his family's heraldry: "My other request is that he would be pleased to let me have a short quartering of his arms, in order to make him a small present of this country's manufacture. Perhaps it may be to the honor of Scotland and to his own very good liking." More significantly, Defoe regarded the linen industry as one in which Scotland had boundless opportunities to excel. He did dabble in salt and herrings, and he had hopes for Scotland as the future center of the English fisheries. He did establish his brother-in-law at Leith, he was deeply concerned about shipbuilding as a Scottish industry, and he gave Harley an elaborate plan for the development of the upper Firth of Forth as a vast wet dock and harbor, thus anticipating the Royal Naval Base of the twentieth century. He did undertake a history of the Union, both as a private literary venture and as a public justification of the event. There were no words which he was prouder to quote than the thanks of Queen Anne to the men who had secured the Union: "That it should be mentioned hereafter to the honor of those who were concerned in bringing it to pass."[12]

Defoe's own share in enacting the Union would be difficult to overestimate. His qualifications were unique, and so were his achievements. With no vote in the proceedings, no public office, no power of wealth or family connection, his influence was due entirely to his ability, his energy, his integrity, and his courage. As an expert accountant and a student of economics, he was constantly sought after to advise a committee on such difficulties as equalizing the excise and fixing the "Equivalent" which was to be paid to Scotland to compensate for some sacrifices made under the Union. As the confidential correspondent of Harley and Godolphin, he was on hand to interpret the political scene in Edinburgh and to explain the necessity of granting the commercial concessions on which the trading classes had set their hearts. When it was all over, he was the man who wrote the semi-official record of the transaction, making use of his unequaled experiences and of all available records (such as the originals of the threatening notes which were sent to the Duke of Queensberry).

His *History of the Union* has considerable faults: it is badly organized and hastily written, and the Scottish printers made errors in setting type for some of the calculations. But it will always remain the principal source for one of the greatest events in British history. Sir John Clerk of Penicuik, a highly intelligent contemporary who had a share of his own in adopting the Union, was one of the first to do it justice:

> I need not narrate here what was done in this Parliament, there being a very exact History published by one Daniel Defoe, who was sent to Scotland by the prime minister of England, the Earl of Godolphin, on purpose to give a faithful account to him from time to time how every thing past here. He was therefore a Spy amongst us, but not known to be such, otherways the Mob of Edin. had pulled him to pieces. [*Marginal note:*] The History of the Union deserves to be read, it was printed in folio. There is not one fact in it which I can challenge.

Clerk's high estimate of the reliability of the *History* is only confirmed by the vehement strictures of George Lockhart and John Oldmixon. Lockhart, as a Jacobite conspirator, objected to Defoe's exposure of Jacobite intrigues. Oldmixon, as a bitter partisan for one clique of the Whigs, rejected Defoe's narrative as false and untrustworthy—and then proceeded (with no acknowledgment whatever) to base his own account of the Union in his *Memoirs of North-Britain* almost altogether on Defoe.

In the years which followed the enactment of the Union, Defoe protested earnestly against the attempts of English politicians and Scottish Jacobites to break some of the terms which he had done so much to persuade the Scots to accept as an inviolable agreement. As late as 1717 his *Memoirs of the Church of Scotland* (actually written some years earlier) was hurried to the press in an effort to aid three Presbyterian ministers who had come to London to seek the repeal of certain infringements against the Church of Scotland.[13] In the summer of 1726 the third volume of his *Tour* was being completed, urging the economic and social improvements in Scotland which he had expected to see made possible under the Union.

Two questions have been raised regarding Defoe's affairs in 1707. If he was engaged in so many commercial enterprises in Scotland, why was he in such desperate need of money from Harley and Godolphin? And why should Godolphin have written to Harley, in regard to the post of Secretary of the Scottish Commissioners of Customs, "I have not yet ventured to nominate De Foe for fear I should not get him to go down with Mr. Lowndes unless it be recommended from you"? But Defoe's enterprises in Scotland, however promising, were likely to call for additional capital rather than to pay early dividends. And William Lowndes, Secretary to the Treasury, was notorious for providing for his family out of the public purse. If a secretaryship in Scotland which paid £300 a year seemed worth picking up for a kinsman still unprovided for, Lowndes might have made the appointment of Defoe difficult.

When Defoe reached London again on December 31, 1707, he had served the state well. But his own affairs were more precarious than ever. New legislation had made a final settlement with his creditors impossible, and Harley was about to be displaced from his office in the realignment of the Ministry under the Lord Treasurer Godolphin. Defoe remained incognito as long as possible, and then—by an arrangement creditable to all—he parted on cordial terms from his old master and gave allegiance to the new Ministry. Again, as in August, 1704, he was introduced to the Queen, and again he had the honor to kiss her hand: "Upon this second introduction, her majesty was pleased to tell me, with a goodness peculiar to herself, that she had such satisfaction in my former services, that she had appointed me for another affair, which was something nice, and that my lord treasurer should tell me the rest; and so I withdrew. The next day, his lordship having commanded me to attend, told me that he must send me to Scotland, and gave me three days to prepare my self."[14]

On March 22 Godolphin wrote to the Earl of Leven, commander of the forces in Scotland, a "letter by the bearer, Mr. De Foe, only to recommend him to your protection as a person employed for the queens service in Scotland relating to the revenue, etc." And so after his short stay with his family Defoe was on his way back to Scotland, over deep roads and in rains that continued for the first eight days. Once again, there was much for him to report on in Scotland, and there were many things in which his influence was needed. A Jacobite invasion had been attempted, the General Assembly of the Church of Scotland was to convene for the first time since the Union, and Scottish peers and commoners were to be elected for both houses in the opening session of the new British Parliament.

From April 17 until mid-November Defoe represented Godolphin in Edinburgh (with a brief interval in early May when he was perhaps observing the electioneering in northern England, although his travels were more likely restricted to Scotland). His situation was a delicate one. He was expected to hold the Presbyterian clergy in line for the new Ministry, and yet Parliament was preparing to require an oath which some of the most loyal of the Scottish clergymen would refuse to take. Furthermore, Sunderland and the Whig Junto were seeking to overthrow Godolphin and Marlborough, as Godolphin and Marlborough had ousted Harley not long before.

In concert with the leading spokesman for the Dissenters in London, his friend Dr. Daniel Williams, Defoe was eventually able to appeal to Godolphin and to get the Scottish clergymen "dropped silently out of the Act then preparing."[15]

An even greater difficulty was raised by the attempted palace revolution of Sunderland and other "Old Whigs" in secret alliance with the Scottish Jacobites. In several of his later writings Defoe alluded to Sunderland's conspiracy, and two years after Godolphin's death he referred to the pages of the *Observator* and to the Duke of Marlborough for his justification:

> In this dispute my Lord Godolphin did me the honor to tell me, I had served him and his grace both faithfully and successfully. But his lordship is dead, and I have now no testimony of it but what is to be found in the "Observator," where I am plentifully abused for being an enemy to my country, by acting in the interest of my Lord Godolphin and the Duke of Marlborough. . . . My errand was such as was far from being unfit for a sovereign to direct, or an honest man to perform; and the service I did upon that occasion, as it is not unknown to the greatest man now in the nation under the king and the prince, so, I dare say, his grace was never displeased with the part I had in it, and I hope will not forget it.[16]

In the latter part of August, 1709, Defoe returned to Edinburgh for Godolphin. His connections with the clergy and the magistrates must have been particularly valuable. An agent in Scotland for the High Church party reported to his superiors in England that Defoe was being paid at least ten shillings per annum by every Presbyterian minister "for his good services by the Review," that he had received many gifts from the communion (particularly a considerable one from the sacrament at Leith in January, 1709), and that on New Year's Day in 1709 the magistrates of Edinburgh had given him about twenty guineas.[17]

But Defoe's services were in even more demand in England. Sometime before February, 1710, he was called hurriedly back to London to support the impending prosecution of the firebrand Sacheverell for the notorious sermon attacking the Revolution principles on which Queen Anne's reign and the Hanover Succession were grounded. Defoe would have preferred that Sacheverell be disgraced as a Jacobite who had lied when he took the oath of allegiance to Queen Anne, and as a clergyman of notoriously bad morals. But the Ministry had decided on a great public trial in Westminster Hall, which enabled the theatrical Sacheverell to pose as a martyr. The Church felt constrained to rally to the support of a clergyman, even when he acted as knave or fool; and Godolphin's government was doomed.

On August 8, 1710, Godolphin was ordered to break the white staff which he bore as Lord High Treasurer. On the same day, Defoe waited on Godolphin, who told him that he was the Queen's servant, and that he should apply himself now to the new Ministry. Harley succeeded Godolphin at the head of the government, and the pension which Queen Anne had granted Defoe "for services in a foreign country" (i.e., Scotland) was continued.

Once again the government considered Defoe's special knowledge of Scotland indispensable. The Presbyterian clergy were unhappy because of the overthrow of Godolphin's administration. Harley needed the support of every one of the Scottish representatives in Parliament who were to be chosen in the coming election. The situation became almost intolerable for Defoe. When Harley ignored his protests against the domineering of the lords who professed to represent the court in Scotland, he wrote his *Atalantis Major* to expose the bullying and the sharp practices of Argyll, Ilay, and Mar. But he dared not let Harley know that he had ventured to write this exposure of the party whips; and apparently Harley was deceived by his equivocal remarks about its authorship.[18]

Defoe returned to London not long before February 13, 1711, but his chief concern was still about the unhappy state of affairs in Scotland. Harley, who soon recovered from the murderous assault by Guiscard in March, refused for a time even to see Defoe, and he showed that his chief interest was in securing the acceptance of his own South Sea project which he expected to solve the financial crisis of his administration. Defoe must have found it increasingly difficult to persuade the Scottish clergymen that he was still their friend, and in his later proposals to Harley regarding another Scottish journey he was likely to speak of the uncertainty of his health. His trip near the end of October, 1712, was undertaken partly by direction of physicians for the sake of a mineral bath in Derbyshire. On October 20, 1713, his brother-in-law Robert Davis was still settled in Leith; but Defoe would hardly have ventured so far to join him, even if the bitter quarrel between the rival leaders Harley and Bolingbroke had permitted a journey for a Ministry divided against itself. He remained in London, occupied with the commercial clauses of the Treaty of Utrecht and with his own need for a pardon to protect him from the charge (by hostile Whigs who sought to destroy him or to force the Tory Ministry to defend him openly) that his ironical tracts in behalf of the Hanover Succession were treasonable.

But the mental strain of partisan strife was at last undermining a constitution which had survived so much fatigue on foot or horseback. On October 28, 1713, Defoe was carried home so ill that he was unable to keep an appointment with Harley. On December 25 he failed to keep another appointment, "being confined by a violent cold." On June 23, 1714, he apologized for his continued absence, "by reason of a lameness, which has long confined me."[19] Before the middle of August Harley had been ousted by Bolingbroke, Queen Anne had died, George I had been proclaimed King, and Defoe faced the incoming of a new Ministry.

Years after Defoe had discontinued his long journeys, he still represented Scottish interests in London. In 1716 he was collaborating with Dr. Carstares of Edinburgh and Dr. Williams of London in an attempt to stop the acceptance in England of Presbyterian ministers who had been rejected in Scotland. In the spring of 1717 he published *Memoirs of the Church of Scotland* at the time when it would give needed support to the representatives sent to London by the Church of Scotland.

We find indications of Defoe's interest in Scotland as late as the *Memoirs of a Cavalier* (1720), *Colonel Jack* (1722), the life of the Scottish pirate John Gow (1725), the retelling of the life of Gow in the second volume of *A General History of the Pirates* (1728), and the brief section on Scotland in *Atlas Maritimus & Commercialis* (1728). But Defoe, as the expert on Scotland, speaks out clearly for the last time in the third volume of his *Tour* (dated 1727, but actually published in August, 1726, from notes that were already becoming old).

For many years Defoe's communications with Scotland were so intimate that he was able to give the government (and sometimes the English public) information obtainable nowhere else. In late March, April, and early May, 1711, he had accurate reports from Scotland, especially in regard to the meeting of the General Assembly of the Church of Scotland. When that Church sent five ministers to congratulate George I on his accession to the throne in 1714, one member of their delegation, the Rev. James Hart of Grey Friars, Edinburgh, drew on Defoe through Adam Bell, a Scottish stationer and bookseller in London, for a total of twenty pounds. This transaction was recorded by Hart with no concealment. Defoe had many financial dealings in Edinburgh and in London, and Hart presumably found it convenient to draw money in London through one of Defoe's publishers who was himself a Scot.

There are many other indications of Defoe's close contact with the Scottish clergy, of which a letter from the Rev. William Carstares affords a delightful example. On February 10, 1713, Carstares was asking Defoe to use his influence with Harley in favor of a Scottish military officer who had been unemployed since the Union: "I know, sir, I may with confidence leave this affair to your discreet management. I trouble you with my hearty respects to your lady and the young ladies your daughters, not forgetting your sons." When the Scottish clergymen disagreed with Defoe (which they so often did, as with each other), they were likely to regard him as a well-meaning outsider who could not be expected to know the whole truth about their special interests. The Rev. Robert Wodrow, widely read in Defoe's historical and controversial writings, wrote to a friend in Westminster regarding what he considered errors of fact in Defoe's acceptance of the Covenanters' point of view about the Highland Host and the Indulgence in his *Memoirs of the Church of Scotland:* "Had I any acquaintance of his I would acquaint himself with his mistakes, since he appears a friend to liberty, and I think has erred not of design, but as people must do, who go not to records, through misinformation." And the Rev. William Adam apologized for publishing his own reply to Webster's *Lawful Prejudices against an Incorporating Union with England* on the ground that no one had replied to it but Defoe: "Mr. D. F. is a most ingenious person who gives a new and happy turn to every subject and argument he handles, but it cannot be supposed that a stranger, who has not applied himself to the particular consideration of our history, should be so well acquainted with it as to discover those mistakes which many even of our own writers who pretend to truth and exactness have fallen into. Had he not engaged in this debate with this disadvantage, all the attempts of others against his adversary would, no doubt, have been prevented."[20]

But Defoe's relations with the Scottish clergy were not always so friendly. He never quoted Milton's "New Presbyter is but old Priest writ large," but he was fond of an even more severe line from Dryden: "For priests of all religions are the same." Several times he recommended the Dutch method of getting rid of a minister who interfered in the concerns of the government: "if our divines were to be sent a pair of wooden shoes, a long staff, and half a crown, when they meddle in state affairs, our pulpits would soon be thinned, and our clergy believe themselves retrenched of a mighty privilege." Even when he was most anxious to preserve the terms of the Union, he expressed irritation over the stubbornness of "this terrible people the Churchmen."

The two worst offenders were the Rev. James Webster of Edinburgh, who sought to prevent the fulfilment of the Union by an attack on the English Dissenters as scandalous men with whom God-fearing Scots should hold no communion, and the Rev. James Clark of Glasgow, who attempted to deny his own share in stirring up riots against the Union. Defoe gained his ends, and he was generous enough to try to withhold from publication his severest reply to Webster. But in one defense of his *History of the Union* against the ravings of Clark he appeared as a native Scot rebuking Clark for his attack on the character of the absent Defoe. There were few times in his life when Defoe gave such free play to his love of banter as he did in "pulling the leg" of the pompous and irate clergyman for his

invective, unchristian, and opprobrious speeches against Mr. De Foe, whose writings make him famous, since in them is conspicuously to be seen *eminency of gifts, humility of spirit, elegancy of style, solidity of matter, height of fancy, depth of judgment, clearness of apprehension, strength of reason, and ardent zeal for truth, &c.* All sweetly met together, and truly (as well as piously) improved for the maintenance of pure religion, and that against bitter and powerful adversaries. To rail on and reproach such a Phoenix of this age, such a rare and precious gentleman, *the envy and glory of his sex*, is a sort of *indiscretion* (not to call it worse) that none would have thought Mr. *Clark* capable of. Now I think it needs give no offence for me to say I do most earnestly wish, and desire to hope, that Mr. *Clark's* thoughts on this practice, . . . so very unsuitable to his station, have by this time produced that very gracious effect so sweetly and cordially to constrain him to say with the *Psalmist David, Psal.* 39. 1. *I will take heed to my ways, that I offend not with my tongue.*[21]

Defoe had elsewhere called Clark "the warm gentleman" and "a gentleman of an unhappy temper." This hilarious rebuke was hardly calculated to moderate his fury; and Defoe, who so often smiled, perhaps for once indulged in loud laughter.

Defoe disliked many other features of Scottish life. The nobles, the more powerful gentry, and the heads of clans were often despots in their own domains. Clansmen were obliged to follow their leaders in war; and even in times of peace

> The little chiefs, for what they call their due,
> Eat up the farm, and eat the farmer too.

He protested to Harley against the expected pardon of a murderer related to a noble family. The law, which should have protected the common people, had been too often the instrument of tyranny. When commoners dared to resist, they had sometimes fallen into the religious frenzy of the persecuted Cameronians of the wild hill country in the southwest or into the blind fury of the Edinburgh mob.

Most of all, he was appalled by the slothful neglect in developing agriculture and industry, so that poverty became the result as well as a principal cause of the nation's backwardness. What he said of Kirkcudbright, he might have said of many other decaying towns:

Here is a very pleasant situation, and yet nothing pleasant to be seen. Here is a harbor without ships, a port without trade, a fishery without nets, a people without business; . . . I believe they are very good Christians at Kirkubry, for . . . they obey the text, and *are contented with such things as they have.* . . . The salmon come and offer themselves, and go out again, and cannot obtain the privilege of being made useful to mankind; . . . But to bid men trade without money, labor without wages, catch fish only to have them stink . . . is all one as to bid them work without hands, or walk without feet. 'Tis the poverty of the people makes them indolent.[22]

However, he rejoiced in many things which he found in Scotland: the honesty and morality and piety of the people, their love of learning, their hard common sense. He admired their hospitality, their independent character, their pride in their nation, their sense of the historic past. He praised their military courage, and he never forgot the share which the Scottish soldiers had in the glories of his hero Gustavus Adolphus. He had a high regard for the native ability of the Scots, although he saw in its misuse much of the same neglect which impressed him so unfavorably in the unused harbors and the uncultivated soil.

Many of these ideas are expressed in the third volume of his *Tour.* They are the themes of *Caledonia: A Poem in Honour of Scotland and the Scots Nation.* This poem was dedicated to the Duke of Queensberry, licensed by special act of the Privy Council in its meeting at Holyrood-House on December 3, 1706, and subscribed for by eighty-five of the principal noblemen and gentlemen of Scotland.

Three weeks earlier Defoe had apologized to Harley: "I am writing a poem in praise of Scotland. You will say that is an odd subject to bear a panegyric, but my end will be answered." Harley had never visited Scotland, and he saw it with the eyes of an English politician— not with the eyes of a traveler, merchant, projector, moralist, and poet. When Defoe wrote prose, he declared himself "contented to give an account of Scotland in the present state of it, and as it really is; leaving its misfortunes and want of being improved as it might be, and perhaps ought to have been, for those to consider of in whose power it is to mend it." When he wrote poetry about the northern nation, his central idea was always this:

Wake, Scotland, from thy long lethargic dream.[23]

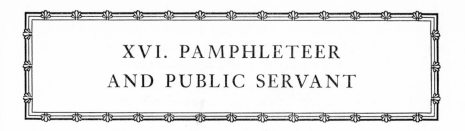

XVI. PAMPHLETEER
AND PUBLIC SERVANT

He is qualified for all sorts of employments in the state,
by a general knowledge of things and men.

Review, III, 7

EVEN BEFORE DEFOE'S TIME pamphlets had come to have an
immense influence on the public mind. A powerful tract might go far
toward ending a war or overturning a Ministry, and an able pamphlet-
writer was equally necessary to the government and to the Opposition. According to a story which was current in 1704, Cromwell's
secretary Thurloe was asked by Charles II, soon after the restoration
of the monarchy, how, when the Commonwealth party had both the
people and the power, it had lost both in a moment. Thurloe replied
that it was chiefly owing to the Cavalier pamphlets, which (though
far less numerous) had better wit and argument, so that the authority
of the government could not resist them.

The pamphleteers of the early eighteenth century had greater freedom than their predecessors. The Licensing Act had expired in 1695,
printers were free to issue anything which could not be suppressed as
seditious or libelous, and the increased reading public had set about
the business of deciding national and international matters for themselves. The upholsterer in Addison's *Tatler* essay, who "was much
more inquisitive to know what passed in Poland than in his own family, and was in greater pain and anxiety of mind for King Augustus's
welfare, than that of his nearest relations," was an exaggeration; but he
differed from many of his fellow Londoners only in degree.

For a public which liked to have its politics simplified, so that interest could be focused on one issue at a time, a hastily written and cheaply printed pamphlet of two or three dozen pages offered the ideal
medium of communication. Hawkers continued to retail new tracts on
the streets; pamphlet shops sprang into being; but the rapidly multi-

plying coffee and chocolate houses throughout London gathered about their crowded tables the largest available reading public. In a tract of 1711, the Lord of Hades is represented as asking a newly arrived ghost how the party wars of England are carried on:

Pluto. What sort of weapons do they use?
Belfagor. Pamphlets, Sir. You may go into a coffee-house and see a table of half an acre's length covered with nothing but tobacco-pipes and pamphlets, and all the seats full of mortals leaning on their elbows, licking in tobacco, lies and laced coffee, and studying for arguments to revile one another with.[1]

A fairly effective form of censorship, from which Defoe's *Review* suffered in its later years, arose when opponents carried off all copies of an opposition pamphlet or newspaper from these informal reading rooms.

Against writing as a profession, there was still a fashionable prejudice. A gentleman of fashion might toss off a prologue for a play, a lyric for a volume of miscellaneous poems, perhaps a lampoon for secret circulation in manuscript. But it was quite another thing to earn one's living by writing for the press; and the authors in lowest regard were often the political pamphleteers. Naturally the pay for writing such pamphlets was not high—perhaps two guineas for one of rather superior quality. Defoe sometimes reminded his readers that he made his living by engaging in business, not by writing. But he esteemed authorship too highly not to despise the wilful ignorance of genteel fools: "One of those wise, untaught gentlemen told me the other day he would not learn to write any more than just his surname, for fear the Devil should tempt him to turn author, and write politics."

It can hardly be supposed that Defoe ever "turned author." As a schoolboy at Morton's academy he was writing exercises on political subjects; a few months before his death he was editing the *Political State of Great-Britain*. Before his marriage he risked his standing among Whigs and Dissenters by refuting the notion that it would be better for Europe if the Turks seized Vienna from the Emperor. By the late summer of 1688 he had written two tracts to warn his fellow Dissenters against the craft of James II in offering religious freedom through an illegal extension of his arbitrary dispensing power.

But with the arrival of William of Orange he ceased to write as a solitary individualist. As early as April 9, 1689, shortly after the accession of William and Mary, a license was granted for the publication of his first tract in favor of the new regime: *Reflections upon the Late Great Revolution*. For more than forty-one years thereafter (with brief intervals of silence, and a few periods when he seemed uncertain about which of the contending factions represented the government or the interests of the nation), he was the ablest—and often the most prolific—pamphleteer for the Ministry.

This does not mean that he supported the Ministry of the day at all times and on all issues. From his own repeated use of the biblical phrase about "bowing in the House of Rimmon," it has sometimes been assumed that he acted with a servility which is disproved by his own writings. He remained unusually free despite the pressure which was exerted to influence all men in public life. A contemporary told of how Lord Stanhope was once in company, leaning on his arm and seeming to take no notice of his companions: "At last he started up, and in a kind of agony said, 'Well, I am now satisfied that a man cannot set his foot over the threshold of a Court but he must be as great a rogue as ever was hanged at Tyburn.'"[2] Defoe suffered in Newgate and in the pillory, and he sometimes ran the risk of Tyburn; but he never became such a rogue. The vehemence of the attacks on him, from 1683 until near his death, was due not to his subservience but to his independence. His personal tragedy in 1703 was first brought on by his defiance of the Ministry's attempt to curb the Dissenters. While he was supporting Harley in the winter and spring of 1710 and 1711 he still felt free to expose the government's tyrannical control of Scottish elections and to ridicule the reactionary October Club which soon came to dominate Harley's coalition.

Under William, Defoe remained a non-party man, as he would have preferred to be at all times. He held that "the only true fundamental maxim of politics that will ever make this nation happy is this—That the Government ought to be of *no party at all*." He observed that most issues of the day were actually decided for reasons of personal advantage, and that party principles had little significance in practice. He leaned toward the Whigs, because they professed to seek the ends he desired. When he accepted Harley's Tory administration during the last four years of Queen Anne, it was on the implied condition that it must continue to seek the same general objectives.

The Tories he hated were the Jacobites who were willing to plunge the country into civil war (particularly the men who had taken the oath of allegiance but were still in secret alliance with the Pretender), the extreme High Churchmen known as the High Fliers, and the spoilsmen. Bolingbroke seemed less concerned about the disastrous failure of his expedition against Canada than about his huge profit from supplying the troops with defective clothing. Nottingham was said to receive for himself and his close friends a total of £15,000 a year from the bounty of George I. Arthur Moore had risen from his low beginning as a footman, through stockjobbing and the purchase of an influential seat in Parliament and his later profiteering by means of court influence, until he was said to hold offices yielding an annual income of £13,000.

The Whigs he hated were the moneylenders and placemen who were willing to prolong a world war for personal profit or power, or the political clique who were eager to reject a favorable treaty of commerce in order to unseat their rivals in the government and who agreed to sacrifice their friends the Dissenters to win a temporary ally in the House of Lords.

It has often been remarked that political ethics was at a low ebb in the early eighteenth century. Prominent statesmen could hold high office under the English sovereign and yet pledge allegiance to the Pretender, Tories like Marlborough and Godolphin could ally themselves with the Whigs for temporary advantage, disappointed Whigs like Haversham could attach themselves to the Tories. It was a group of politicians who called themselves "the Patriots" that Walpole refused to bribe, as they desired and expected: "As to the revolters, I know the reasons and I know the price of every one of them."[3]

A modern historian has cited the judgment of a French observer that Bolingbroke had no objection to a Jacobite rising except that it would cause disagreement among the Tories: "Thus he shrank from provoking civil war over the Succession issue on which the Tories were divided, but, if we may believe d'Iberville, he welcomed the possibility that the Schism Bill might provoke civil war upon a sectarian issue on which the party could be united by appealing to its dislike of Dissenters." Defoe aroused bitterness among his fellow Dissenters by attempting to hold them in line under Harley, despite the Schism Bill and other betrayals of their cause.

His lifelong plea was that he "sought to allay the heats of faction." It was one of the many ironies of his career that he was engaged in more controversies than most other men have ever lived through and that his enemies persisted in regarding him as a firebrand. He was a Puritan and a Dissenter, but he never tired of expressing his esteem for the Church of England and his regret that he could not accept three of the Thirty-nine Articles and part of a fourth one. He was a Protestant to his fingertips, but he saw more worth in the Roman priesthood than did almost any of his Protestant contemporaries. He presented some deistic ideas so sympathetically in *Robert Drury's Journal* that one astute reader has questioned his authorship of that highly characteristic work. He saw all too clearly that Charles I had brought on his own overthrow, and he had profound respect for the abilities of Cromwell, but he denounced the illegality of Cromwell's regime. In middle life he assured his readers that his family had approved the restoration of the Stuarts and that one of their friends had suffered death for attempting to achieve it seven years before its ultimate success in 1660: "the author of this wears a mourning ring on his finger, given at the funeral of Mr. Christopher Love, a Presbyterian minister, beheaded *Anno* 1653, for the horrid fanatic plot contrived for the bringing in, as they then called him, Charles Stuart, and the restoring of monarchy." During his career Defoe engaged in five different kinds of political writing: (1) pamphleteering; (2) confidential reports to Ministers or other men in high position; (3) commentary on public affairs (as in the *Review*); (4) partial censorship of newspapers and tracts for the government by collaborating with the editors or authors; and (5) the writing or editing of such compendiums as *Mercurius Politicus, Mercurius Britannicus,* and certain parts of *The Annals of King George* and the *Political State of Great-Britain.*

He wrote pamphlets from 1683 until a short time before his death. There is no record of his reports to King William, as of those to Harley, Sunderland, Godolphin, and Stanhope, many of which are preserved in various repositories of manuscripts in England and published in G. H. Healey's edition of Defoe's correspondence. But we do know from later allusions that he made such reports; and on two occasions he assured Harley that he was repeating the same advice which he had already given King William. If the lost letters to William could be discovered, they might show a little less political acumen than Defoe afterward had, but perhaps they would be free from the caution he was sometimes obliged to use in stating unpalatable truths to ambitious and arrogant men of diverse personal and political interests. It is probable that he talked even more directly to William than he ever did to Harley.

According to the common practice of state officials in the reign of Queen Anne, Harley removed his correspondence as private property when he left office. But as the greatest collector of books and manuscripts in his day, he was likely to preserve what he carried off. Hence the Harley correspondence (incomplete as it is) gives us our fullest account of Defoe's life during the periods it covers, and it gives an altogether disproportionate emphasis to Defoe's relationship with Harley.

But Defoe spoke of possessing examples of the handwriting of four sovereigns. We know that he corresponded with Halifax, Godolphin, Sunderland, and Stanhope, and that for a time he received orders from Townshend. There is a virtual certainty that he worked for years in close co-operation with Walpole. In 1701 his contemporaries believed that he was intimately allied with Somers. A few of Defoe's letters to some of these men survive; others can be inferred from specific statements, as when Defoe told Harley of his correspondence with Halifax or when Godolphin told Harley of the letters he had received from Defoe through Mason.[4] Very rarely we can lay side by side the letters which Defoe wrote to different men at the same time.

From the examples of Defoe's correspondence which we do have, we can be sure of three things:

(1) His letters were not worked out with a view to publication; but they were extraordinarily interesting and often amusing to their receivers, so that they were frequently passed back and forth in the highest circles. At times Defoe expressed a fear that certain letters might pass through too many hands. Some of the most important reports to Harley have been lost because they were sent on to Godolphin and never returned.

(2) They offered better accounts of current events, and better analyses of current conditions, than any other letters of the age which have come down to us. The men who received his communications from Edinburgh had an insight into Scottish affairs which their rivals could only envy. It is not strange that Halifax sought to establish a correspondence with Defoe when he was working for Harley, or that Sunderland desired similar reports when Defoe was engaged for Godolphin.

(3) Except when he was in financial distress, Defoe gave little space to requests for self-advantage; but he found room for remarkably bold advice. He told Harley how to organize the secret service, how to conduct foreign correspondence, how to control the press, how to deal with the English Dissenters and the Scottish Presbyterians, how to establish a better South Sea project, how to improve the system of taxation, how to make an end of the Occasional Conformity bill, how to divide his opponents by placing some of them in

office, even how to become Prime Minister. We have certain proof that Harley not only received this advice and that he sometimes carefully labeled it as having been sent by Defoe, but that at times he even asked for more. The odd thing is not merely that Harley listened to Defoe's advice—for one of his great gifts as a politician was his knack of seeming to listen to contradictory advice from many different people—but that he acted on so much of it in his public career, whereas he was notorious for adopting few men's policies but his own.

As a commentator on public affairs, Defoe won high praise from many who had little interest in some of his other undertakings. His Tory and High Church opponents might attack the *Review* as a partisan periodical; later his former Whig allies might attack it as the exponent of the commercial articles in the Treaty of Utrecht or as the apologist for the cession of Spain to the grandson of Louis XIV. To a modern reader it seems remarkably free from partisan bias. Defoe attacks corrupt elections (not merely mob violence at the polls in Coventry), public immorality (not merely a country parson who got disgracefully drunk), and legal tyranny (not merely a magistrate who oppressed his neighbors). When he discusses larger issues, he always writes as a stateman and a liberal thinker.

It is true that he did not attempt to present systematic political theory in his writings. But as a modern historian has said, "short of originality of theory, Defoe contributed to political progress in every other direction. . . . It was Defoe who applied and popularized Locke, and drove home the philosopher's principles." He was widely read in controversial political writings. His *Jure Divino* was buttressed with footnotes to give an appearance of scholarly investigation to what was primarily a common-sense judgment. The moribund theory of the divine right of kings seemed to him silly in itself and insincerely held by the few who professed it. But his worst enemies could not honestly attack him as a republican or "a Commonwealth man." He was not interested in the assertion of republican theorists that the English constitution was inferior to that of Venice; and the oft-repeated claims for Greece and Rome as the models of freedom convinced him as little as they did Dr. Johnson.[5]

Defoe's political ideal was the constant adaptation of government to secure the welfare of the people as a whole. His ideal statesman was "the never enough to be praised" Marquis of Halifax—"a noble author who was an eminent Tory, though a friend to the constitution and to the Protestant interest (for such are consistent)," the same statesman whom the late Sir Walter Raleigh called "the man who was the practical genius of the English Revolution, and the acutest critical genius among English politicians."

It mattered little that Halifax was a nobleman, a Tory, an Anglican, and something of a worldly cynic, whereas Defoe was a commoner, a Whig, a Dissenter, and a Puritan idealist. Both men sought, above all things, to prevent party tyranny and the dissensions which might lead to civil war. Defoe had some searchings of heart when he recalled that Halifax had defeated the Exclusion Bill, which would have kept the tyrant James II from the throne; he declared that the defeat of that bill had brought on the Revolution and some of the foreign wars that followed it. But he probably thought Halifax had little choice in that matter if he wished to avoid an impending civil war. One of the most gratifying honors of his career must have come from the mistake through which his own youthful *Letter to a Dissenter from his Friend at the Hague* was included in the first issue of Halifax' *Miscellanies*. When he attempted to state his own political creed, he had only to refer to the creed of his master: "I remember a curious piece written on the character of a Trimmer, in which a Trimmer was justly proved to be much better than either Whig or Tory, since he was biased by nothing but the public good, and inclined either to the Whigs or to the Tories as they pursued that end."[6] For Defoe, "Trimmer" had none of its later suggestion of political dishonor. For him, as for Halifax, it meant one who sought to balance the ship of state, to keep it from tipping in midstream.

He honored King William as the great leader who carried the Revolution to success, and he accepted the Revolution as the best possible solution of a situation which had become intolerable. But he had only scorn for the crypto-Jacobites who swore allegiance to the new regime in order to hold office in church or state, or for the followers of James who deserted him only when he needed them. Among the High Churchmen, he preferred the Non-Jurors and confessed Jacobites, because they had not led James to commit acts of tyranny by promising absolute obedience which they refused to pay as soon as their own privileges were in danger.

Defoe held that political power was from the people, who had delegated it to the king and to Parliament, and that ordered government came through course of law when each of the three branches recognized its proper limitations and responsibilities. Only when king and Parliament failed did power "retreat to its original," the people as a whole. In case of an extreme abuse of power, the last resort was to popular violence:

> Mob's never useful but when tyrants reign.

One of his deepest objections to Sacheverell was that he appealed to the mob to support what he professed to regard as the interest of the Church:

> Of all the mobs with which this land is curst,
> Mobs for religion are the worst.

In lighter vein he ridiculed the most famous speech by Sacheverell as being like the ravings of an angry woman: "Will said, 'Pray God the Doctor han't been too free with my wife, for I find many sayings in that sermon so like hers in some of her tantrums that he never could have them from any other body.'"[7] He had much to say of the gross irregularities in representation in government by which a hamlet like East Loo sent four members to Parliament (as many as London), whereas the great community of Manchester (still called a village) had no magistrate higher than a constable. The bribery by which parliamentary seats were often obtained seemed to him the worst of national crimes, endangering the existence of Great Britain. A tyrannical government could clothe itself in the majesty of law by using national funds to buy perpetual power.

According to a recent writer, Defoe clearly saw the difficulty of regulating the relations between the king and the two houses of Parliament. His remedy was that the law should direct them. In the absence of law they should be guided by reason. "If for reason we may read convention, it may be suggested that Defoe knew all that could be known on this still vexed question."[8]

If we judged by their paid circulation alone, it would be easy to underrate the political influence of the *Review* and its successors. We have no way of making an accurate estimate of the thousands of citizens who read their newspapers and pamphlets in the coffeehouses. Many copies of pamphlets were distributed free by party managers (as was *Legion's Memorial*, of which a Tory journalist reported that thirty thousand copies had been disposed). The frequent references to Defoe by his rivals are sufficient proof that his writings were widely known.

At two periods, however, his influence seemed to wane. About 1712 and 1713 the more violent Whigs were demanding the overthrow of Harley, the demolition of Dunkirk after its surrender by

France, and the repeal of the commercial articles of the Treaty of Utrecht. The more violent Tories were hostile to Defoe's pleas for peace, unity, toleration, and the Protestant succession. At this time his opponents were as often Tories as Whigs, and he stood like a soldier in no man's land under fire from both sides. Later, during parts of Walpole's administration, Defoe's calm voice seemed to be drowned out by the strident cries for prosecution of the South Sea directors or by demands for the overthrow of Walpole on "Dunkirk Day." But the clamor of the vehement opposition journals is misleading as an indication of their sincerity or their effectiveness. Walpole bought off Thomas Gordon as soon as he chose to do so, and Bolingbroke went into a second exile after his ally Pulteney "plainly told him that 'his name and presence in England did hurt.' "[9]

No other one of Defoe's undertakings has aroused such disagreement as his collaboration with opposition editors to maintain a fairly effective censorship of the anti-ministerial press. As early as July 17, 1710, he was attempting to reach an understanding with John Dyer, author of the violent High-Flying *News Letter;* just after the death of Queen Anne he had a working agreement with Dyer by which he expected to be able to withhold the more objectionable statements. From August, 1714, until midsummer of 1715, he seemed to be writing as an independent observer of the changing political scene, giving qualified support to the new regime but suggesting a less partisan line of action than the Ministry chose to follow. He had no connection with any newspaper at this time. The main burden of his pamphlets was that the new sovereign, George I, was king of all his people, that his throne should be established in mercy as well as in justice, that certain members of the late Ministry had been received into the new government although their former colleagues were threatened with prosecution, and that the King's justice could not be carried out by the bloody triumph of a single faction.

But on July 12, 1715, three events occurred which made that day one of the most notable in Defoe's career. Robert Harley, Earl of Oxford, appeared before the bar of the House of Lords to receive the articles of impeachment against him, and he was ordered to be carried to the Tower four days later. After July 12, 1715, although Defoe repeatedly tried to aid him, Harley was never again Defoe's patron. On the same day, the Earl of Anglesey, who had been regarded by many as a Hanoverian Tory, betrayed his Jacobite leanings by a warm speech in which he declared "that it was to be feared these violent measures would make the scepter shake in the King's hands"; and although many of his fellow lords cried out "the Tower!" he was let off with an apology because the words had not been written down. On the very same day, in a humbler presence, Defoe was tried in the King's Bench Court on an old charge for which he had been arrested and released on bail on the previous August 28, when Attorney-General Northey expressed doubt that there was sufficient evidence against him. The charge was that in Hurt's *Flying Post* for August 19, 1714, a letter appeared which Defoe had edited; and although he had edited it to soften it down, the letter reflected on the Earl of Anglesey as a Jacobite.[10]

Chief Justice Parker must have been puzzled to see that Defoe was standing trial for allowing a newspaper to suggest that the Jacobite Anglesey was actually a Jacobite. Defoe was of course declared guilty —anything less would have been regarded as an acceptance of the insinuation against the noble Earl, who apparently still had friends in the Ministry. But Parker needed time for decision in such a delicate matter, and he deferred the sentence until the following term in November.

Meanwhile the government's public relations were steadily deteriorating. At court there were unpopular German ministers and mistresses; in many of the pulpits there were clergymen who professed Jacobite sympathies; in city streets there were rioters. By September open rebellion had begun in Scotland. Even after that rebellion had failed on the battlefield, a trusted correspondent was writing to the exiled Earl of Mar in France (April 7, 1716) that the High Fliers could be counted on to foment still another civil war: "The Bishop [Rochester] will do his part in animating the clergy, and warming the City of London from the pulpit the Sunday before the invasion is expected. Dr. Sacheverell, whose interest with the mob is as great as ever, has faithfully promised to obey orders and to lift up his voice like a trumpet when the word of command is given him." On June 12, 1716, the Lord Mayor and the Court of Aldermen of London were protesting that "great numbers of idle, vagrant, and disorderly persons do daily wander up and down the streets, fairs, and public markets of this City and the Liberties thereof, some of them singing ballads and vending papers and pamphlets highly reflecting upon his Majesty's person and government, corrupting the minds and alienating the affections of his subjects, causing animosities and stirring up seditions and riots."

For nearly a year after the death of Queen Anne the government had had no very effective popular writer in its service and no adequate means of combating the propaganda for a counter-revolution. Direct censorship had ended with the expiration of the licensing act in 1695. Suppression of printed books and papers through messengers of the press had become intensely unpopular as Bolingbroke had managed it during Harley's administration. An able writer for the government was desperately needed, as well as a new method of censorship which would not rouse more opposition than it silenced. In the late summer of 1715 both became suddenly available in one man.

Defoe has given us two accounts of his experience with Lord Chief Justice Parker and Secretary of State Townshend after his conviction in July. The first of these appears in a letter to Charles De la Faye of the secretary of state's office in 1718, the second two years later in a rhapsody called "A Vision of the Angelick World" appended to his *Serious Reflections of Robinson Crusoe*. And although the two statements are unlike in tone and purpose, they tend to confirm each other:

It was in the Ministry of my Lord Townshend when my Lord Chief Justice Parker, to whom I stand obliged for the favor, was pleased so far to state my case that notwithstanding the misrepresentations under which I had suffered, and notwithstanding some mistakes which I was the first to acknowledge, I was so happy as to be believed in the professions I made of a sincere attachment to the interest of the present Government, and, speaking with all possible humility, I hope I have not dishonored my Lord Parker's recommendation.

I know a man who . . . had a particular case befallen him, wherein he was under the displeasure of the Government and was prosecuted for a misdemeanor, and brought to a trial in the King's Bench Court where a verdict was brought against him, and he was cast; and times running very hard at that time against the party he was of, he was afraid to stand the hazard of a sentence and absconded, taking care to make due provision for his bail, and to pay them whatever they might suffer. In this circumstance he was in great distress, and no way presented unto him but to fly out of the kingdom, which, being to leave his family, children, and employment, was very bitter to him, and he knew not what to do; all his friends advising him not to put himself into the hands of the law, which, though the offence was not capital, yet in his circumstances seemed to threaten his utter ruin. In this extremity he felt one morning (just as he had awaked, and the thoughts of his misfortune began to return upon him), I say, he felt a strong impulse darting into his mind thus, *Write a letter to them.* It spoke so distinctly to him, and as it were forcibly, that as he has often said since, he can scarce persuade himself not to believe but that he heard it; but he grants that he did not really hear it, too.

However, it repeated the words daily and hourly to him, till at length walking about in his chamber where he was hidden, very pensive and sad, it jogged him again, and he answered aloud to it, as if it had been a voice, *Who shall I write to?* It returned immediately, *Write to the Judge.* This pursued him again for several days, till at length he took his pen, ink, and paper, and sat down to write, but knew not one word of what he should say, but *Dabitur in hac hora, he wanted not words*: It was immediately impressed on his mind, and the words flowed upon his pen in a manner, that even charmed himself, and filled him with expectations of success.

The letter was so strenuous in argument, so pathetic in its eloquence, and so moving and persuasive, that as soon as the Judge read it he sent him word he should be easy, for he would endeavor to make that matter light to him, and in a word never left till he obtained to stop prosecution and restore him to his liberty and to his family.[11]

For the second time in a dozen years the most independent political writer in England had been delivered into the hands of the Ministry—for no ostensible reason but publishing an inconvenient truth.

It is a pity that Defoe's letter to Parker has been lost. It not only "even charmed himself" but it roused the skeptical Parker to send "him word that he should be easy." Better still, it caused Parker to recommend him to Secretary of State Townshend. From August, 1715, it seems that Defoe was never again in active opposition to the government of the day except on special occasions (for which special reasons can be assigned), as when he held out against the vindictive prosecution of Harley, when for a time he defended Townshend and Walpole against their supplanters in the government, or when he opposed Sunderland's favorite peerage bill for limiting new creations as a blow at the future power of the Prince of Wales.

The best of Defoe's eighteenth-century biographers supposed that his political career ended in 1715, and that "the death of Anne and the accession of George I seem to have convinced De Foe of the vanity of party-writing." On the contrary, after the Earl of Mar unfurled the Pretender's standard on September 6, 1715, and set out to force his unwilling tenants into rebellion by fire and sword, Defoe plunged into the most active period of his political journalism. He poured out many scores of tracts on the Jacobite rising, the trials of the rebels, the Septennial Bill, the rights of English Dissenters and Scottish Presbyterians, the Bangorian controversy, the danger of a Swedish invasion, proposed legislation regarding manufactures and commerce, national credit, the South Sea Bubble, parliamentary elections, Wood's copper coinage in Ireland, and foreign affairs.

He carried on (or contributed to) numerous newspapers and other periodicals, and he wrote the semiofficial history of the military operations of the rebellion in *The Annals of King George, Year the Second*. For eleven months after the death of Abel Boyer in 1729, he took over the *Political State of Great-Britain* and transformed it from an anti-ministerial journal to a strong supporter of the government, until his own failing health must have compelled him to drop it. In the issue for October, 1730, his leading article was a discussion of the "mortality bills," or tabulated reports of the causes of deaths during each week or year. He announced that according to his calculations the annual bill "must be very much decreased this year from what it was last year, . . . as I shall more particularly explain in our next month."[12] But the journal ceased to be edited by the aging author, and the jibes against Walpole and Hanover in the next issue showed that the *Political State* had passed into the hands of the Opposition.

Defoe served the Hanoverian dynasty not only by his writings and his independent editorial work. His disguised censorship through collaboration with the Opposition editors began in 1716 and continued for at least ten years. He gave his account of this undertaking in a letter to Charles De la Faye in the secretary of state's office on April 26, 1718:

In considering after this which way I might be rendered most useful to the Government, it was proposed by my Lord Townshend that I should still appear as if I were, as before, under the displeasure of the Government and separated from the Whigs; and that I might be more serviceable in a kind of disguise than if I appeared openly. And upon this foot a weekly paper, which I was at first directed to write, in opposition to a scandalous paper called *The Shift Shifted*, was laid aside, and the first thing I engaged in was a monthly book called *Mercurius Politicus*, of which presently. In the interval of this, Dyer, the *News-Letter*-writer, having been dead, and Dormer, his successor, being unable by his troubles to carry on that work, I had an offer of a share in the property as well as in the management of that work.

I immediately acquainted my Lord Townshend of it, who, by Mr. Buckley, let me know it would be a very acceptable piece of service; for that letter was really very prejudicial to the public, and the most difficult to come at in a judicial way in case of offence given. My Lord was pleased to add, by Mr. Buckley, that he would consider my service in that case, as he afterwards did.

Upon this I engaged in it; and that so far that, though the property was not wholly my own, yet the Conduct and government of the style and news was so entirely in me that I ventured to assure his Lordship the sting of that mischievous paper should be entirely taken out, though it was granted that the style should continue Tory, as it was, that the party might be amused, and not set up another, which would have destroyed the design. And this part I therefore take entirely on myself still.

This went on for a year before my Lord Townshend went out of the office; and his Lordship, in consideration of this service, made me the appointment which Mr. Buckley knows of, with promise of a further allowance as service presented.

My Lord Sunderland, to whose goodness I had many years ago been obliged when I was in a secret commission sent to Scotland, was pleased to approve and continue this service and the appointment annexed; and, with his Lordship's approbation, I introduced myself, in the disguise of a translator of the foreign news, to be so far concerned in this weekly paper of Mist's as to be able to keep it within the circle of a secret management, also prevent the mischievous part of it. And yet neither Mist or any of those concerned with him have the least guess or suspicion by whose direction I do it.

But here it becomes necessary to acquaint my Lord (as I hinted to you, Sir) that this paper called the *Journal* [Mist's] is not in myself in property as the other, only in management; with this express difference, that if anything happens to be put in without my knowledge which may give offence, or if anything slips my observation which may be ill taken, his Lordship shall be sure always to know whether he has a servant to reprove or a stranger to correct.

Upon the whole, however, this is the consequence, that by this management the *Weekly Journal* and *Dormer's Letter*, as also the *Mercurius Politicus*, which is in the same nature of management as the *Journal*, will be always kept (mistakes excepted) to pass as Tory papers, and yet be disabled and enervated so as to do no mischief or give any offence to the Government.

To one biographer this secret censorship seemed a "happy reconciliation" whereby Defoe convinced the government of his patriotism and helped to prevent treasonable publications by intercepting them in advance, rather than by punishing the printers and publishers later. To another the plan was equally shameful to the government and its agent. To a third the arrangement has seemed unsportsmanlike.

But Defoe was not playing cricket. He was engaged in one of the deadliest of human struggles—a cold war; and he sought to keep this from spreading into open civil war as fervently as one of our contemporaries might seek to prevent a world war. In this undertaking his ethical standards (whether one regards them as right or wrong) were much the same as those implied in a chapter on "Spying and Scouting" by the founder of the Boy Scouts and the Girl Guides. In that chapter Lord Baden-Powell tells of a German spy who operated near Ypres as a cripple. The "cripple" was discovered to be a German agent, operating a "post box" to receive papers from German spies in the neighborhood. Lord Baden-Powell's closing remark is this: "He was tried and shot and I kept his placard as a memorial of a brave man."[13]

Defoe, too, was a brave man; more than once he recalled that in his service as a government agent he had run as much risk of his life as a grenadier upon a counterscarp. Sir John Clerk of Penicuik observed that he would have been torn to pieces by the mob in Edinburgh if he had been known to be serving as a spy. According to some of his later biographers, Defoe referred to a recent quarrel with his Tory colleague Nathaniel Mist in a letter which he published after he had ceased to write for Mist's *Journal:*

> My case concerns blood and life, and abundantly makes good that proverbial saying, *Save a thief from the gallows and he will cut your throat.* Take it at a distance thus: Suppose a man has an opportunity to save a gentleman from the utmost distress and the immediate danger of life, say it were from thieves or enemies or what you will; and suppose that very person (I may not call him gentleman any more) basely using, insulting, and provoking him, and at last drawing his sword upon his benefactor and using his utmost endeavor to destroy him. But his efforts failing, and being disarmed fairly at his weapon, you are to suppose then that his friend, however provoked, gave him his life, embraced him, sent for a surgeon to dress a wound he had in his own defence been obliged to give him, and after this showing him several acts of friendship and kindness: Suppose this man a second time obliged in a degree so extraordinary, yet upon all occasions returning abuses of the worst and grossest nature; I say suppose all this, and you reach a part of my case, though but a part.

Two biographers have expressed doubt that Mist was actually referred to here.[14] We only know that the story seems to fit Mist and that it seems applicable to no one else.

No secret agent is expected to register his name and occupation with the enemy, and in his work of censorship Defoe was often obliged to deny his employment. His editorial colleagues among the Tories were either ignorant of his politics or (knowing it) were glad to employ his expert services to increase the circulation of their journals. Tory readers did not lose by his efforts; he satisfied their prejudices by bantering the Whigs, and his *Mercurius Politicus* became so readable that for a time he felt obliged to run an opposition Whig journal, *Mercurius Britannicus*, to maintain a balance. These Tory readers might laugh the more merrily because of the ridiculous light in which the Whigs were sometimes presented in *Mercurius Politicus* or in the journals of Mist and Applebee. But they slept the more soundly if they took warning from the hints that Jacobite endeavors always failed, or if they read the long lists of Jacobite estates forfeited after the Earl of Mar's disastrous rebellion. The government certainly lost nothing from the small pension paid to Defoe; in spite of the treasonable efforts of Jacobites at home and abroad, there was no further invasion of England until long after his death.

The only losers were the rival journalists and the active Jacobites. Abel Boyer saw Defoe's monthly newsbook "rise upon the ruins of his own." The Pretender and his friends saw the Duke of Ormonde's expedition of 1719 fade out in a storm at sea and in a military fiasco in the Scottish Highlands (an attempted invasion in which the aging Harley was sufficiently interested to preserve among his papers a detailed account of the affair, which he—or one of his correspondents—must have received from an active rebel).

There is no doubt that Defoe believed he was acting as a friend to the Tory journalists whom he sought to keep out of the clutches of the law. He was present at the trial of the young printer John Matthews, Jr., who worked off the pamphlet *Vox Populi Vox Dei* and "was drawn in a sledge from Newgate to Tyburn, and there executed, according to the terms of the sentence for high treason"— "drawn, hanged and quartered, as is usual in cases of high treason." Young Matthews was the son and namesake of the Matthews who had published Defoe's *Review* until the Tories had frightened him out of his engagement, six years before his death in 1716. Abel Boyer, no sympathetic observer, added one brief remark in his account of the boy's execution: "He was about 18 years of age."[15]

The apparent omniscience of some of Defoe's pamphlets was due to the method by which they were supposedly written "Within Doors" by someone who had intimate knowledge of the government's plans. Certain others sought to reflect only the impressions of the man in the street—like *A Speech without Doors*, which was directed against Sacheverell in 1710. So in *The Talisman* of Sir Walter Scott, the Sultan professes to disbelieve in the existence of ice when he is disguised as an ignorant warrior; but when he reappears in his own person as Saladin, he serves sherbet to his guests in the desert.

Whether Defoe wrote "Within Doors" or "Without Doors," he was likely to maintain his assumed character. In *An Essay upon Loans* (1710) and *The Secret History of the White Staff* (1714) he was so clearly in possession of inside information that many readers attributed the tracts to Harley himself. But he took a very different attitude in *The Evident Approach of a War* (1727): "as I profess to be speaking as *without doors* only, I must content myself to ground all the reasonings and inferences which I shall make use of in this discourse from the public received reports of things; at least, such as are confirmed by repeated advices, are generally received for truth, and have not as yet been contradicted or disputed; without pretending, or indeed having any occasion to pretend, to secret intelligence, private information, or knowing any thing which should not be known." More amusingly, he sometimes chose the point of view of a supposed intimate observer of the scene—the French negotiator Monsieur Mesnager himself, or "the Right Hon. the Countess of ———" who related the secret history of the court of Queen Anne.

Defoe's defense of his political pamphleteering rested on his passionate conviction that he fought for essential justice, and that any pension he received was necessary to sustain him in his work—but never enough to sway his judgment: "He that defends Truth, and Truth only, cannot be mercenary; he that does nothing but what is his duty to do may be rewarded, but he cannot be bribed." In faraway Edinburgh, as early as 1707, he was writing for his *Review* what may be considered the code of public service which he believed, and which (as far as human frailty permitted) he sought to put into practice:

For my part, I value the instructing and informing one honest meaning ignorant Person, more than the detecting and confronting a thousand Knaves, and 'tis for the sake of these I write; for their Sakes I dwell upon a Subject sometimes longer that the Rules of Language allow, for their Sakes I repeat and repeat, and quote myself over and over; and can with Ease bear the foolish Banters of the envious Critick and Reproacher; I had rather say the same thing over twenty times, than once omit, what may this Way be useful.

I am, *without Vanity*, neither ignorant of the Rules of Writing, nor barren of Invention, that sometimes I repeat and quote what I have formerly said, which I know, those, *this Paper reaches*, never saw; 'tis for their Sakes I bear the Reproach of the scurrilous, who upbraid me with printing in this Paper, what I had in other Pieces printed before; thousands see this, that never saw the other, and what is it to them that it has been said before; do not our Ministers preach the same Sermons to different Auditories? if it does good here, 'tis not the worse for having been thought of before, let the Railers rail on.

The Design of this Paper to open the Eyes of the deluded People, and set them to rights in the things in which they are impos'd upon, shall, I hope, bear it out, in trespassing the common Rules of Authors; 'tis enough that it is confin'd by the Rules of Truth, and has never yet been detected in one Falsehood.

The unhappy People are deluded, are impos'd upon, are fermented, and their Spirits disorder'd, *and how?* By raising false Reports, affirming forg'd and barbarous Allegations, raising scandalous Surmises, and pushing about absurb, ridiculous and incongruous Whymsies, among the well meaning but ignorant People in both Nations.

These are the Things, I am to detect, these I make it my Business to inform; I am a Tool employ'd to do this, says some envious and malicious Haters of Peace—They are the Tools of the D——l employ'd to hinder and discourage any Man's laying himself out in common and publick Service, who would lessen any Man from being employ'd in a good Work.

If the Work be of GOD, to quiet the Minds of the impos'd upon abus'd People, to explain Truth to them, to detect Forgery and Lies, it would be an Honour to me to be employ'd in it.[16]

XVII. "THE MOVING FINGER
WRITES"

O but 'tis a scandalous employment, he writes for bread.

Review, IV, 351

In the spring of 1715 Defoe was momentarily at a loose end. The tradition that he was at the point of death from a stroke of apoplexy,[1] though confirmed by one of his publishers and accepted by many biographers, is belied by the continuing stream of his tracts at this time. Very likely he was physically ill, and he was certainly ill at ease; but he was continuing to write in spite of the uncertainties which beset him. As a political pamphleteer and agent, he had at this time no party and no active patron. As a journalist, he had outlived his own earlier periodicals and his earlier connections with the journals of other men; his new periodicals and new connections had not yet been established. He still maintained some connection with the English Dissenters and the Scottish Presbyterians, but even this was tenuous and doubtful at the moment. Many of these men were seeking favor for themselves or their churches at the court of George I, whereas Defoe was likely to be remembered as the defender of the late Ministry under Queen Anne. For the head men in that Ministry the penalty of death for alleged treason was being demanded from the pulpit by the redoubtable Bradbury.

It was at this moment, when he might have been so near despair, that Defoe brought out the book which was to make him, for the first time, not merely a political writer but a professional writer in other fields than that of current public affairs.

It is often impossible to be sure when a new book began to take shape in Defoe's mind. The sources frequently lay deep in his early thought and reading, or in his travels and experiences. The books were sometimes virtually finished long before they appeared in print. But the approximate date of publication can usually be known, and this date is likely to be significant.

Since 1710 Defoe had maintained some connection with Joseph Button of Newcastle. For a time they had collaborated on the *Newcastle Gazette*. Button had sent Defoe's spectacles on to him at Edinburgh after having them repaired at Newcastle. Button had printed the first edition of the startling political prophecies called *The British Visions*, which Defoe advertised so extensively in his *Review* when they were reprinted by J. Baker in London. Printing at Button's must have been very cheap, and Defoe knew from experience that it could be kept secret. It was to Joseph Button that he intrusted the manuscript of *The Family Instructor* and from whose printing house the unbound sheets of the printed book were sent down to London. On March 31, 1715, the book was published there by a man with established connections among Nonconformist readers, Emanuel Matthews.

Matthews knew from the first that the book must be sold, if at all, to buyers who would accept the pious precepts as readily as the admirable fiction. And so he called in one of the most popular of Dissenting clergymen, the Rev. Dr. Samuel Wright, to compose a letter of recommendation which would serve as a Preface. It has been supposed that Defoe sold the manuscript outright during his illness or convalescence, and that he was unable to read the proofs or to write the Preface. There is no indication that he had signed over the book completely to Matthews; even while Matthews was still publishing for him occasionally, the tenth edition of *The Family Instructor* was issued by N. L. and John Batley. No doubt the printing had been unusually bad. Defoe blamed this on the author's absence from the press; but Wright, in his prefatory Letter to the Publisher, blamed the provincial presswork: "The Printer has been faulty to a Degree, that I am afraid will render the Reader very uneasy; and I wish the Author had thought fit to communicate his Papers to you before they had fallen into such Hands."

Defoe had taken the risk of bad printing for the sake of the secrecy afforded by Newcastle. Whether he was critically ill or not, his relations with the Whigs and the Dissenters at this time were so precarious that he preferred to issue an anonymous book in far more obscurity than usual. The really significant facts (as Defoe explained in the Preface to the second edition on September 17) were that he had sought to conceal the authorship, some people had discovered who had written the book, and he feared that personal animosities would hinder its influence. He declared that the book would still remain anonymous as far as he was concerned, "leaving the discovery to go no farther than others think fit to carry it."

The discovery that Defoe was the author left Wright in a difficult position, and his interesting letter of recommendation had to be omitted after the first edition. But it had already served its main purpose. On March 31, 1715, Defoe was issuing a didactic treatise which had to find its chief sale among Dissenters and Low Churchmen, among whom the recommendation of so prominent a Presbyterian minister as Dr. Samuel Wright would be invaluable. By September 17 Defoe was re-established as the official propagandist for the government, with such influence that a few months later he was able to secure the release of his former publisher Keimer from the Gatehouse—solely by his personal intercession with Secretary of State Townshend.[2]

For the next fifteen years Defoe continued as a public servant—usually for the Ministry in office, occasionally (as for Walpole and Townshend in 1717) for statesmen in temporary eclipse. But never after 1715 was he engaged solely as a political journalist and agent; and after the appearance of *Robinson Crusoe* in 1719 his main attention was given to non-political considerations. This is the period of his most active work as a writer, when he earned the titles given him by one historian and one biographer, "Lonely Man of Letters" and "The Hermit of Stoke Newington."

In his Preface to the second edition of *The Family Instructor*, Defoe declared that he had designed it as a dramatic poem but was deterred because the subject was too solemn and the text too copious. For him this was one of the most fortunate of escapes. As a dramatic poem it would have been a pompous failure, whereas in his homely expository narratives interspersed with dialogues he produced the most popular book of domestic instruction in a century which took delight in didactic writings. It went through ten editions in his own lifetime, acquired a second volume in 1718 and a third (entitled *The New Family Instructor*) in 1727, and was the first of all Defoe's books to be reprinted in America. Because the royal copy has been preserved in the British Museum, some biographers have supposed that the children of George I were reared under its instructions. Whatever may be supposed for the families of the later Georges, this assumption is as unlikely as it is unkind; the Prince of Wales was thirty-one years old and George I had been divorced for more than twenty years when *The Family Instructor* was first published.

A modern biographer has written disparagingly of the tone of Defoe's religious dialogues, and it must be admitted that they were intended for the eighteenth century rather than for the twentieth. But that they were sincere and well intended no one who understands Defoe can doubt. That they were successful we have the testimony of many of his contemporaries and successors, including so good a judge as Benjamin Franklin.

In 1722 Defoe brought out *Religious Courtship*, and in 1727 the two parts of *The Family Instructor* were supplemented by *The New Family Instructor*. These books covered what seemed to Defoe the common difficulties between parents and children, masters and servants, husbands and wives, and young men and young women in matters of personal relationship, mutual conduct, and religious faith. In all or parts of certain other books, especially in *Conjugal Lewdness* (1727), he took up special aspects of some of these subjects.

Under the pseudonym of Andrew Moreton, Esq., he assumed for his imaginary author much of the individuality which he ordinarily reserved for his heroes or heroines, and five of his tracts attributed to that old gentleman were concerned with the welfare of the home and the community: *Every-Body's Business Is No-Body's Business* (1725), *The Protestant Monastery* (1726), *Parochial Tyranny* (1727), *Augusta Triumphans* (1728), and *Second Thoughts Are Best* (1728). One of his most elaborate didactic works was *The Great Law of Subordination Consider'd* (1724), directed at what seemed to conservative housekeepers the acute servant problem of the day.

In some of these writings Defoe was primarily the moralist, in some primarily the projector. *Augusta Triumphans* closed with a letter addressed to the newly elected Chamberlain of the City of London, demanding an accounting for the orphan's fund and an explanation of the continued tax to maintain the orphans. *Second Thoughts Are Best* was dedicated to George II, and copies of it were presented to the King, the Queen, and several members of both houses of Parliament.

The question has sometimes been raised, Why did Defoe leave at his death two unfinished and unpublished manuscripts, *The Compleat English Gentleman* and *Of Royall Educacion?* A year and a half before his death Defoe was returning the corrected proof for the first sheet of *The Compleat English Gentleman* to the printer John Watts, with copy for nearly three more sheets and a promise to supply the rest so that Watts would not be kept waiting. Perhaps Defoe found no time to continue the two treatises; perhaps he decided that his frank discussion of the education of royal children would be impossible. It is astonishing that he should have dared to begin the two treatises at all, for they seem to have grown out of a plan to approach the most dangerous subject in England at that time—the long and bitter quarrel between George I and the Prince of Wales over the care of the royal grandchildren.

During his last fifteen years Defoe continued to write didactic books, many of which were broadly utilitarian or factual rather than domestic, civic, moral, or religious. Some of these have to do with preventing street robberies, lessening the number of streetwalkers, providing seamen for the Royal Navy, maintaining or expanding English commerce, and sustaining public credit—especially during the crisis of the South Sea Bubble. Three which were meant to be most objective and factual are *An Essay upon Literature* (1726), *The History of the Principal Discoveries and Improvements, in the Several Arts and Sciences* (1727), and *Atlas Maritimus & Commercialis* (1728). In the great *Atlas* Defoe was able to make the first extensive approach to economic geography in the English language. Three other books fall in a borderland between entertainment and serious discussion, and between superstition and religion and psychology: *The Political History of the Devil* (1726), *A System of Magick* (1727), and *An Essay on the History and Reality of Apparitions* (1727).

With the possible exception of his long-popular works on the supernatural, the two of these miscellaneous didactic works which had the greatest sale and the most enduring appeal were *A Tour thro' the Whole Island of Great Britain* (1724–27) and *The Complete English Tradesman* (1725–27). In part this long-continued popularity may have been due to—in part it persisted in spite of—the mutilating revisions by which the publishers attempted to keep the books up-to-date after Defoe's death. The original *Tour* is Defoe very nearly at his best—the most enjoyable of all travel books about England and Wales and Scotland. *The Tradesman* has been praised as a *vade mecum* for young apprentices and damned as a loathsome expression of the purely mercantile point of view. Both are supreme examples of their own kind, beating all rivals out of their fields from the first.

In the ten years before 1724, John Macky's *Journey through England* was the most popular guidebook in the form of familiar letters. Thereafter (with its supplementary volume on Scotland), it was kept alive only by wholesale plagiarism from Defoe's *Tour*, in the effort to bring its conventional account of the countryside in line with Defoe's new emphasis on trade and the daily concerns of men.[3] The highest tribute to the *Tour* came from Sir Walter Scott, who owned a set of the first edition; for when Bailie Nicol Jarvie, in *Roy Roy*, boasts of the growth of his beloved Glasgow, he borrows the very language of Defoe.

The Tradesman has no such beauty as the *Tour*. But in its emphasis on good spoken and written English, on systematic industry, on the importance of sustaining one's credit, and on the integrity and the social value of an English merchant, it has its own moments of power.

*"You are a great traveler, and we honor you as such," said
a monk to Mr. Paton during a repast in the refectory; "but
the greatest traveler of your country we have heard of was
Robinson Crusoe of York, who met with many and
strange adventures, but at length, by the blessing of God,
returned to his native land."*

"Servia," *Quarterly Review*, CXVII (January, 1865),
195, quoting from Paton's *Danube and the Adriatic*[1]

THE MOST SIGNIFICANT DATE in Defoe's literary career
was April 25, 1719, when the first volume of *Robinson Crusoe* was
published. Before that there was no English novel worth the name,
and no book (except the Bible) widely accepted among all classes of
English and Scottish readers. *The Pilgrim's Progress* had many ele-
ments of great fiction; but it was intended as a work of religious instruction, it was meant for humble readers, and for a century it was
despised by literary critics.

The impact of *Robinson Crusoe* was greater, and in some ways
quite different. There were doubts about whether it was a genuine
travel book, a fraudulent travel book, or a legitimate work of fiction,
so that Defoe resorted to improvisations and equivocations to evade
questions about its truth to fact. But the esteem in which it was held
in the literary world is shown by the praise it received from Alexander Pope, by its immense influence on *Gulliver's Travels*, and by Dr.
Johnson's including it as one of the three books by mere man which
anyone would wish longer. Its popularity among the lowest classes
of readers was a source of jealousy which sought relief in a pretense
of scorn: "there is not an old woman that can go to the price of it,
but buys thy *Life and Adventures*, and leaves it as a legacy, with *The
Pilgrim's Progress*, *The Practice of Piety*, and *God's Revenge against
Murther*, to her posterity." For *Robinson Crusoe* not only created a
new literary form; it created a new reading public.

Because of its popularity among the semiliterate, there was a chance that it might sink to the level of the little chapbooks sold by itinerant peddlers. The Rev. James Woodforde purchased it with a life of a gypsy, *The Complete Fortune Teller*, and *Laugh and Grow Fat*, from "a traveling man and woman who sold all kinds of trifling books, &c." However, in 1806 the Rev. Mark Noble, hostile to Defoe as a Dissenter, admitted its almost universal acclaim: "I have never known but one person of sense who disliked it. Rousseau, and after him all France, applauded it."[2]

France was not alone in praising *Robinson Crusoe*. The story has shown the capacity to survive translation and sentimentalized adaptation and condensation and rewriting for children, preserving much of its potency in any garbled or truncated form. An Eskimo translation was published nearly a century ago in a newspaper in Greenland, illustrated with seven plates, one of which showed Friday prostrating himself before Crusoe to build a fire on the shore. Here, much as in the original, where the goatskins of Selkirk's cooler island were transferred to the tropics, we see Friday naked except for a scanty loincloth and Crusoe bundled tightly in furs as a true Eskimo, with a harpoon in the background and with waving palms and dense undergrowth on a low hill—the side of which is partly covered with snow. As in all great works of imagination, the inner vision has become more significant than external facts.

It has often been supposed that Crusoe was almost identical with Alexander Selkirk, but the influence of the Selkirk story on *Robinson Crusoe* has been greatly exaggerated. In all his writings Defoe had less to say about Selkirk's solitude in the Juan Fernández group west of Chile, on a real desert island 3,500 miles to the southwest of Crusoe's imaginary kingdom, than some other writers of the day. *A New Voyage Round the World* becomes more lively when Defoe's hero leaves the dull tasks of careening ship and catching goats on Selkirk's island to trade in Chile, and starts over the Andes on the exploration by which he hopes to prepare the way for his proposed English colony.

For Defoe at the beginning of 1719, the great fact was not that Selkirk had returned to England seven years before but that in the new war with Spain the South Sea Company's trade with Spanish America had come to an abrupt end. He had long been interested in Sir Walter Raleigh's attempts against Spain near the mouth of the Orinoco (where Crusoe was to be shipwrecked), and by the end of 1719 he was urging the South Sea Company, whose "charter begins at the River Oroonoque," to develop the neighboring mainland of Guiana—the cannibal coast from which the savages continued to endanger Crusoe on his island: "the author of these sheets is ready to lay before them a plan or chart of the rivers and shores, the depths of water, and all necessary instructions for the navigation, with a scheme of the undertaking, which he had the honor about thirty years ago to lay before King William, and to demonstrate how easy it would be to bring the attempt to perfection."[3] If the company declined this, he proposed that they give leave to a society of merchants (perhaps including himself) to undertake it for them.

Defoe had not yet established himself as the historian of the pirates. But as a journalist he had already written of the increase of pirates in the West Indies and of the appointment of Woodes Rogers in the previous year as captain-general, governor, and vice-admiral of the Bahama Islands to suppress them. If he wrote a novel in 1719, it would likely have something to say of the slave trade, of the jealousy between England and Spain, of pirates or mutineers (the rebellious sailors in *Robinson Crusoe* never got further than mutineering), and of an island near the mouth of the Orinoco River. No one could have foreseen how Defoe would develop his hero's solitary life on the island. That was apparently no part of his original plan for a narrative of wandering travels, but came as a "strange surprise" to Defoe himself—perhaps the most fortunate accident which ever befell any author in all literature.

Important as the public events of 1718 and early 1719 were for Defoe, the roots of *Robinson Crusoe* lie deeper in his life. From childhood he had been a traveler, he had camped out in Surrey in a hut as one of the boys who helped recover Sir Adam Brown's fish after they had been scattered by a flood, he had baked tobacco pipes in his kilns near Tilbury, he had long been interested in earthquakes. He regarded swimming as an indispensable accomplishment, he had engaged in building boats and ships, his brothers-in-law were both shipwrights, and when he wrote a historical account of the galleys of the ancients he sought advice from shipwrights about the possibility of operating three or four banks of oars. His own book on the Great Storm of 1703 was drawn on for Crusoe's two shipwrecks. His patron Sir Dalby Thomas had gone as governor of the African Company to the Guinea Coast, where Crusoe carried on his first commercial venture and toward which he was returning when he met with his great disaster. Defoe had a classmate at Morton's academy, Timothy Cruso or Crusoe, whose name (perhaps recalled by the island Curaçao [which Defoe spelled Curasoe] in the Caribbean) suggested the most famous name in all fiction. His early reading of Shakespeare suggested the method by which Governor Crusoe and his man Friday (like Prospero and Ariel in *The Tempest*) overcame their adversaries on the island.

It is possible that in failing to enter the ministry Defoe felt that he (like Crusoe) had disappointed his father. Certainly he gave his hero his own background as a Presbyterian who recalled the Shorter Westminster Catechism, read his Bible, and recorded his religious experience like any young Puritan. However skeptical we may be about interpreting the story as an allegory of Defoe's life, there are passages in which the memory of Defoe in Newgate certainly displaced the thought of Crusoe on his island: "How mercifully can our great Creator treat his creatures, even in those conditions in which they seem to be overwhelmed in destruction! How can he sweeten the bitterest providences, and give us cause to praise him for dungeons and prisons!"[4] It would be absurd to suppose that Defoe is identical with Crusoe; but no other author could have written this book.

In an article which Defoe wrote for Mist's *Weekly-Journal* of January 4, 1718, we find the hint for the otherwise incredible journey which Crusoe and Friday undertook from Lisbon to London in midwinter by way of the Pyrenees. Nothing would seem more unlikely than that the experienced traveler Crusoe would invite such unnecessary dangers and difficulties when he had returned so near to his home by the direct sea route. But in writing *Robinson Crusoe* a year later, Defoe could not resist the temptation to vary the adventures by using this earlier account of the danger of crossing the mountains in the snow, which he had ready at hand:

Our letters from Roussillon and the countries bordering upon the Pyrenean Mountains give an account that the snows have already fallen there in prodigious quantities, and that the ravenous beasts of those countries begin to come down in great numbers into the forests and waste grounds on the side of Languedoc; that a troop of wolves, with six bears among them, came down into a village near—and attacked the inhabitants in the very market-place; that several were wounded by them. But we do not hear of any quite devoured, the people having taken arms, and assisting one another attacked the cruel band of devourers, and killed fourteen of the wolves and two bears. Among the Wolves were some of a monstrous growth. The people of Languedoc have desired that one of the troops of hunters, established fifteen years ago by the King, may be allowed them, whose business it was, and for which they are paid equal to the horse of the Gens d'Arms, to hunt out and destroy wolves and other wild beasts. And we are told two troops will be ordered them, one into Languedoc and the other to Roussillon. And it is said the King of Spain has ordered six troops to be raised for the same purpose on the other side of the mountains, viz., in Catalonia, Arragon, and Navarre, where the same creatures make terrible havoc, and where a troop of wolves devoured five troopers, notwithstanding their firearms, and ate them all up, horses and all.

His favorable portrayal of a Roman Catholic priest in the second part of *Robinson Crusoe* was anticipated when his *Review* told of an Irish Catholic Jacobite who restored a purse to the rightful owner. Crusoe's method of balancing the advantages and disadvantages of his situation appeared in the *Review* in 1709. In *The Family Instructor* (1715) a white boy attempts to instruct the Negro slave Toby in religion, and Toby talks like Friday. A year and a half before Defoe sent his hero overland from China to Archangel, in the second part of *Robinson Crusoe,* he had told of Peter the Great's improvements in the land carriage between Muscovy and China. Later, in 1721, he described the thanksgiving procession of 280 Englishmen ransomed from slavery among Moorish pirates in Fez and Morocco—a scene like others he must have witnessed in London before he wrote of Crusoe's captivity at Sallee in Fez. In 1728 he referred to those who prayed to the Devil with "O,"[5] as Friday said the old men in his country prayed to Benamuckee in the mountains.

It is unnecessary to point out more of these numerous analogues. Defoe knew human life through experience and observation, as well as through his wide reading; and he had the artist's supreme gift of assimilating everything for his creative purpose.

A writer in *The Gentleman's Magazine* observes, "De Foe's life must itself have been singular. Whence came so able a geographer? Not only a geographer, but so well acquainted with the manners of savages, and with the productions, animal and vegetable, of America? Whence came he not only so knowing in trade, but so able a mechanic, and versed in so many trades? Admirably as Dr. Swift has contrived to conceive proportional ideas of giants and pigmies, and to form his calculations accordingly, he is superficial when compared with the details in *Robinson Crusoe.* The Doctor was an able satirist; De Foe might have founded a colony.

The last sentence suggests the profound difference between two great books. As one writer has stated it, Robinson Crusoe and Lemuel Gulliver "are unaccommodated man, poor, bare, and forked mankind stripped of its lendings. But the point is that Gulliver took off his clothes while Crusoe put them on."

The realism of *Robinson Crusoe* has been much admired, but perhaps overemphasized. It is true that some details to which objections have been raised—such as the northward drive of the Caribs (cannibals) across the continent of South America, their use of uninhabited Caribbean islands for occasional feasts on human flesh, and the dislike of the natives for salt—can be justified from sources familiar to Defoe. M. Louis Rhead, who made a detailed study of the island which he mistakenly regarded as Defoe's original, decided that Defoe's information is "wonderfully true as far as it goes." A more recent writer has pitched his claim for Defoe's realism even higher and has hailed *Robinson Crusoe* as "exactly classical" because it is based on the classical law that one should be romantic in action but realistic in thought.[6]

The wanderings of Crusoe in the first two parts, even more the moral essays of the third part, could be equaled or surpassed elsewhere. It is in the island episode, in which Crusoe comes face to face with the problems of mankind, that we have the supreme achievement. It was here that Defoe must have been led to recall the experiences of Robert Knox on Ceylon and of Alexander Selkirk on one of the Juan Fernández islands; but the story as he tells it is far superior to any other. In the end, it is the imagination that counts most in *Robinson Crusoe*. Coleridge was right in stressing what he called "the *desert island* feeling"; nowhere in all literature before Defoe could one anticipate the cry of the Ancient Mariner,

> Alone, alone, all, all alone,
> Alone on a wide, wide sea!

And Coleridge was equally right in pointing out how much would have been lost if Defoe's hero had been given unusual abilities. For then Crusoe would have ceased to be the universal representative, the person for whom every reader could substitute himself. But now nothing is done, thought, suffered, or desired, but what every man can imagine himself doing, thinking, feeling, or wishing for. Even so very easy a problem as that of finding a substitute for ink is with exquisite judgment made to baffle Crusoe's inventive faculties. And in what he does, he arrives at no excellence; he does not make basket work like Will Atkins; the carpentering, tailoring, pottery, &c., are all just what will answer his purposes, and those are confined to needs that all men have, and comforts that all men desire.

In modern life and modern literature, the Crusoe situation creeps in wherever man conquers his environment or adapts himself to adverse circumstances. When Sir Winston Churchill tells of his family life at Chartwell between two wars, we hear the familiar ring in the concrete details and sense the imaginative satisfaction that lies back of their recapitulation. In the humble society of *The Wind in the Willows*, Mole seeks food in his abandoned home to entertain Rat; and once again we recognize the authentic tone of *Robinson Crusoe:* "The result was not so very depressing after all, though of course it might have been better; a tin of sardines—a box of captain's biscuits, nearly full—and a German sausage encased in silver paper."[7] When Ralph Edwards made his dugout canoe in the Canadian Rockies, all he knew about such boat-building "was what he recalled from reading *Robinson Crusoe*." More than 130 years ago, an early explorer in the African hinterland east of Timbuktu told of his solitude during the rainy season at Kouka:

I had, indeed, already a little menagerie, which, if I would have allowed it, the sheikh would have added to daily, and I found in them great amusement—I might almost say much comfort. My collection consisted, besides my Loggun bird, of two monkeys, five parrots, a civet cat, a young ichneumon, and a still younger hyena: they had all become sociable with each other, and with me, and had their separate corners allotted them in the inclosure that surrounded my hut, except the parrots and the monkeys, who were at liberty; and while sitting in the midst of them of a morning, with my mess of rice and milk, I have often cast my thoughts to England, and reflected with deep interest on the singular chances of life by which I was placed in a situation so nearly resembling the adventurous hero of my youthful sympathies, Robinson Crusoe.

Amid all the changes that have taken place in South America and the neighboring islands of the Caribbean Sea, an island which has no location on modern maps still holds its own in the thoughts and affections of men:

For whatsoever one hath well said goeth forth with a voice that never dieth.[8]

XIX. POET AND WIT

*They say . . . that I am a bad poet, . . . That's true, and yet
they are liars, because they aver it in malice, not knowing
whether it be true or false.*

Review, IV, 347 (Defoe, quoting Samuel Colvil)

T HE IMMENSE POPULARITY of *Robinson Crusoe*, from its
first publication on April 25, 1719, had an indirect influence which
few people could have anticipated. It reawakened Defoe's youthful
ambition to be known as a poet, so that for the first time in five years
he brought out a new poem as his own. Exactly eleven months after
The Life and Strange Surprizing Adventures of Robinson Crusoe had
appeared, T. Warner published a rather handsomely printed quarto of
fifty-three pages entitled *"The Complete Art of Painting. A Poem
Translated from the French of M. de Fresnoy. By D. F. Gent."*

This was the only one of his books for which Defoe ever subscribed
himself as a "Gentleman," the last book which he publicly acknowledged as his own by signing his name or initials, and the last separate
poem—except for a street ballad or two—which he ever committed to
the press.

Not that he ever ceased altogether to write verses. But after the
failure of his ambitious English translation of the French translation of
Charles Du Fresnoy's *De Arte Graphica,* any new verses by Defoe
had to stand their chance of immortality by slipping unobtrusively
into his prose narratives or expository writings as illustrative passages
or as digressions.

It is perhaps strange that he should have chosen the translation of
Du Fresnoy as his most ambitious venture in the realm of non-political
verse. He was, of course, a professional translator from the French
for Mist's *Weekly-Journal,* and his interest in the art of painting was
active and intelligent. But this particular field was already well occupied by masters. John Dryden had translated Du Fresnoy, and as recently as 1716 the second edition of Dryden's translation had been

brought out with a prefatory poem by no less a celebrity than Alexander Pope.

In seeking to rival Dryden and Pope on their own established ground, Defoe aimed high. When he failed, he withdrew into comparative obscurity as a poet. But that should not be taken to mean that he ever ceased to like poetry—including that of his own composition.

In the world in which Defoe grew to manhood, any nobleman—even any merchant's clerk of superior gifts—might aspire to be a poet and a wit. He warned of "the wit turned tradesman"; but the allurement of literary fame attracted clever young men from all ranks of life. Among the "mob of gentlemen" who set the tone for the literature of the day, it was usually enough to write a single play for the stage, a lampoon for circulation in manuscript, a few epigrams to be quoted in the right circle. So eminent a statesman as the Earl of Halifax liked to be remembered as the youthful poet and the mature patron of literature. So unpoetic a soul as Robert Harley lamented his political downfall in doleful lines in imitation of Dryden. Defoe was often more proud of having written the most widely sold poem in the language up to that time[1] than of any other one of his hundreds of achievements.

His earliest poems were intended for his private devotions, and they were not published until 215 years after his death. In 1681 he transcribed from shorthand notes the sermons which John Collins had been preaching, and he followed these with seven "meditations" in verse. Imitative of Dryden, Cowley, and even Bunyan, irregular after the supposed manner of the Pindaric ode or regular after the pattern of the heroic couplet or the ballad stanza used in so much Puritan verse, these poems are earnest expressions of the thought and feeling of a young man groping his way through a deep religious experience. In this confessional, Defoe charges himself with none of the sins of the flesh which have sometimes been attributed to him but with the real sins of the spirit to which he knew that he was inclined: pride, self-righteousness, and outward zeal. Benjamin Franklin admitted that he could never acquire the virtue of humility;[2] the clear eyes of young Defoe recognized a like fault in himself.

For the next ten years we know little about Defoe the poet. He read omnivorously; and he came to know Butler, Dryden, and the leading Restoration playwrights so intimately that he could quote their works from memory as long as he lived, often modifying certain favorite lines to suit his purpose of the moment. His first known political poem was not published until 1691, but he was circulating satires in manuscript before then. In listing the merits of poets at the turn of the century, he assigned himself pre-eminence in the lampoon. Later he recalled how such satires had been widely current during the reigns of Charles II and James II, and he declared that if the freedom of the press was denied he might take his own share in issuing lampoons again.

For parts of his printed poems, there are indications of previous circulation in manuscript. Scraps of unacknowledged verse, some of them clearly Defoe's, appear in his later writings; fragments of unpublished *juvenilia* help to pad out *The Serious Reflections of Robinson Crusoe* and *The Political History of the Devil*. In his *Review* he inserted a poem on "Rebellion" which belonged to an earlier period, when he was under the spell of *Paradise Lost*. In *The Political History of the Devil* he offered a specimen of what seems to have been a youthful attempt to fill a gap "in the Devil's story . . . which Mr. Milton has taken little notice of."[3] If Defoe, in the confidence of his late teens or early twenties, did write a supplement to Milton's epic, the world has been spared further knowledge of it.

During the 1690's he was considerably influenced by suggestions from a son-in-law of Dr. Annesley, the original but increasingly eccentric printer and bookseller John Dunton. Defoe became an occasional contributor to Dunton's *Athenian Mercury*. It was for Dunton that he wrote an elegy on Dr. Annesley. It was Dunton who induced him to join a group which had some hope of establishing an English academy—until they realized that the support of a Richelieu was needed to promote "an enterprise which appeared too great for private hands to undertake." King William ignored Defoe's hint that he could eclipse Louis XIV by sponsoring the project.

It is hard to separate facts from chimerical fancies in anything undertaken by Dunton. But he does seem to have tried to draw an "Athenian Society" around him, with experts in different fields of knowledge to answer the questions sent in by readers, and even to interpret and popularize all the arts and sciences. Later Defoe ridiculed the pretense that, in a few associates like Richard Sault and Samuel Wesley, the *Athenian Mercury* had "a professor in all the heads." Dunton boasted of the nobleman who read his journal throughout; but what he really achieved was a significant development in journalism and in popular education.

Charles Gildon, whose *History of the Athenian Society* was such an extravagant mixture of flattery and banter that it could hardly have deceived anyone less vain than Dunton, asserted that England had the glory of giving rise to two of the noblest designs that the wit of man is capable of inventing—the Royal Society and the Athenian Society. He declared that Dunton's effort had exceeded the labors of Hercules, and that all the endeavors of all the great men of all nations and ages, from the beginning of learning to that time, had not contributed to the increase of knowledge so much as Dunton's institution of the Athenian Society.[4] To bolster the assertions of Gildon, contributions from several poets were added by way of further preface. Defoe celebrated the Athenian Society in an ode (1691) for which he was thanked by Dunton as one of "the chief wits of the age."

Some passages in the *Athenian Mercury* (later excerpted and reprinted by Dunton in the *Athenian Oracle*) are probably Defoe's. Among these are a scornful argument against a husband's fighting a duel with his wife's lover, a story from Knolles' *History of the Turks*, the discussion of an error made by a man in the wine trade, and the detailed account of a young merchant who has done business on a large scale and is desperate to know how to protect his wife and children as well as his creditors. Sometimes these passages show firsthand knowledge of Spain and the wine trade; sometimes they bear traces of Defoe's personal idiom.

Walter Wilson supposed that a wretchedly scrawled manuscript in the Bodleian Library represents a rough draft of an agreement between Dunton and Defoe in 1717 to issue a political journal called *The Hanover Spy*. But Lee was surely right in his judgment that this "was only one of the multifarious projects of Dunton's fertile brain; and probably Defoe never knew of its existence."[5]

Long after his connection with Dunton had ended, Defoe continued to believe in the value of academies if they could be maintained by adequate support. But he had less and less time for the life of a wit. In 1704 he did seek to increase the circulation of his *Review* by repeating some of the methods of the *Athenian Mercury*, such as questions and answers. He laid aside the pretense of infallibility which Dunton had assumed, and he soon admitted that he was no "Club" but a single individual with an occasional helper. But he brought on himself the anger of Dunton, who regarded the Athenian formula as his own property; and he soon tired of such discursive entertainment as being a distraction from the political purposes for which the *Review* was founded. In later years the *Review*'s leading articles left no space for such queries and answers.

From scattered passages in his writings it is clear that Defoe was acquainted with the coffeehouses—as with almost everything worth knowing in London. But his crowded life never allowed time for such leisurely evenings as Addison spent with the "little Senate" which surrounded him at Button's. The hours which most of his literary contemporaries gave to conversation, smoking, and deep drinking, Defoe devoted to travel, observation, and writing. So it was that their verses were published in thin sheaves, whereas Dunton could say of Defoe, "by his printing a poem every day, one would think he rhymed in his sleep."[6]

But a livelihood was not to be made by poetry. In the nine years after his bankruptcy in 1692, it seems that Defoe published no verse except the elegy in honor of Dr. Annesley and *The Pacificator* (1700), a contribution to the "War of the Wits" in which he presented the rival claims of the Men of Science and the Men of Wit, urging that each writer should strive for excellence in his own province.

It was Tutchin's attack on King William in *The Foreigners* (1700) which drew Defoe into national prominence as a poet. More hastily written replies, such as *The Reverse* and *The Natives*, appeared as early as August and September, 1700, and they were soon forgotten. Defoe seems to have bided his time. When his rebuttal, *The True-Born Englishman*, finally appeared in the next January, it went through ten editions in its first year, and it was pirated on a grand scale for distribution by hawkers in the streets.

Rising above its immediate purpose of defending William's character and his policies, this poem became the most famous of all attacks on the myth of racial superiority. Echoes of it are heard in the literature of the next two centuries, and even in the twentieth century it was reprinted in part by a Hindu for propaganda against domination by the English.

The outstanding merit of the poem is its statesmanship; in its general outlook it is as valid today as an attack on the 100 per cent American as it was in Defoe's time on the insular Briton. Next, one must admire its verve and its play of boisterous wit. One rival suggested that "this man in disguise has made his verses run lame, on purpose to dwell incognito." No doubt the lines could have been written more smoothly; but Dryden himself (if he had still been living) would not have needed to be ashamed of their vigor and their force. The success of *The True-Born Englishman* aroused jealousy among the conventionally educated writers of the day, as *Robinson Crusoe* was to do eighteen years later: how could a brick manufacturer who had attended Morton's academy write a poem which outsold the combined efforts of the collegians? There was also bitterness from the opponents of William, especially from the friends of the perennial candidate for the Lord Mayor's chair, Sir Charles Duncomb, whose flagrant vices came in for personal satire near the end of the poem. According to one contemporary, "Scandal is a never-failing vehicle for dulness. *The True-Born English Man* had died silently among the grocers and trunk-makers, if the libeler had not helped off the poet."[7]

But the poem did not die silently. In previous editions of the widely read collection called *Poems on Affairs of State* or *State-Poems*, Defoe had gone unnoticed. In 1703 he was recognized as the most popular poet of the day, and no less than ninety-two pages of the second volume were taken up by *The True-Born Englishman, The Mock-Mourners*, and *Reformation of Manners*. Tutchin had called his own poem Part I, but *The Foreigners* was dropped without a sequel. "True-Born Englishman," which had been a term of honor, suddenly became a term of derision—although one stubborn pamphleteer declared, "I am still in love with those words." As John Toland was widely supposed at first to be the author, Defoe was sometimes abused by mistake as a freethinker and as an Irishman.[8]

Tutchin was almost alone in attacking the central idea of Defoe's poem and in repeating his original claim that Englishmen were superior to foreigners. More often, critics pounced on some detail. Charles Leslie condemned a poor thing called *A Fable of the Beasts and Their King* by saying, "It looks like a piece of De Foe's poetry." Another pamphleteer declared: "If wit be a child of hell, our author is certainly a child of heaven; if those who have no manner of dealings with it deserve that name." The same writer ridiculed Defoe's list of Scottish heroes ("Her Gourdons, Hamiltons, and her Monroes") and dropped an insinuation in favor of the Pretender: "Our poetaster had paid ne'er the less deference to the invincible Nassau, had he placed his grandfather's family (*viz.* that of the Stewarts) which is the most ancient in Scotland, before that of Monroe, which I never heard was famous for any member of it, but one Mr. Monroe, who is a celebrated tobacconist."

Although Defoe's best advocates were the tens of thousands who purchased his poem, he was not without defenders in literary circles. One Churchman, writing on an entirely different subject, cited him with approval: "It is stuff to boast of a long series of ancestors where there is nothing else to recommend men: Surely this author never read the poem called *The True-Born Englishman*; for there is not an hostler, nor a pedler, but what is descended from a long series of ancestors of one kind or other. And so no less is every game-cock, race-horse, or setting-dog."⁹ By 1722 this idea was assured of applause in the theater, when it was presented by Sir Richard Steele in *The Conscious Lovers* (Act IV, scene ii).

After Defoe's *Good Advice to the Ladies* had raised a scandal in 1702 through being misunderstood as a dissuasive against marriage, Toland suggested (in a fictitious letter to a female friend) that its author might profit from blackmail. He credited Defoe with "an unlucky talent at writing merry ballads and waggish lampoons," and he expressed wonder "that the adventurous poet does not put all the timorous fair under contribution; which would be a surer way of enriching himself than by dabbling (as he does now) in politics, or by drudgery (as he did before) in trade."

In one of the English imitations of Boccalini's *Ragguagli di Parnaso*, the thirteenth "advertisement" tells how "Daniel de Foe petitions Apollo to be admitted into Parnassus, but is refused that honor." However, Defoe himself was not ready to accept any such judgment from his contemporaries. When the immense notoriety of *The Shortest Way with the Dissenters* was followed by his imprisonment, trial, and sentence, he wrote a *Hymn to the Pillory* to be sold on the streets, and he issued collections of his principal writings in which the pride of place was given to his poems. Even in his *Review* we find him theorizing about the harsh sound of *th*, imitating Boileau's ninth satire in a bantering account of his own difficulties as a wit, and apologizing for the lack of rhyme in a hasty poem of 128 lines written in three hours to celebrate Marlborough's latest victory: "I know some people will miss the jingle, and like the pack-horse that tires without his bells, be weary of the lines for want of the rhyme; but the subject has so much music in it, I doubt not it will make amends for the chime."¹⁰

Any serious discussion of Defoe's poems must allow for the fact that we can never be sure that we know them all. Some were written for circulation in manuscript, like the lampoon on Sir David Hamilton found on Defoe's person when he was arrested in 1703. Some were printed anonymously as folios or octavo half-sheets to be sold on the street. Even while Defoe was a prisoner in Newgate he published (October 2, 1703) *A Hymn to the Funeral Sermon*, a "Pindaric" poem of ninety-five lines attacking Paul Lorrain, the Ordinary of Newgate, for preaching a funeral sermon at St. James's, Clerkenwell, for Thomas Cook, a prize fighter who had been hanged at Tyburn on August 11 for murder. On October 9, in a savagely personal pamphlet entitled *Remarks on the Author of the Hymn to the Pillory: With an Answer to the Hymn to the Funeral Sermon*, Lorrain (or his apologist) replied to Defoe's accusation that

> *Pulpit-Praises* may be had
> According as the Man of *God* is paid

Whoever had the better of this satirical exchange, Lorrain continued to serve as Ordinary for the religious worship of the prison in which Defoe was still confined.

By far the most ambitious of Defoe's political poems was *Jure Divino* (1706), an attack on the theory of divine right which permitted a king to ignore the welfare of his subjects. This was his only poem in the classical pattern of twelve books, and it was provided with a motto from Juvenal—*Laudatur et alget* ("He is praised, yet not cherished"). *Jure Divino* had been written at intervals during a period of three years, and it was published by subscription at ten shillings in a handsome folio on "as good paper as could be bought for money." Although by his sentence of July 7, 1703, he was understood to be silenced for seven years, the title page announced it as "By the Author of The True-Born Englishman" and the Preface was signed "D. F." It was dedicated to Reason as the ultimate source of all legal authority; it devoted much of the twelfth book to praise of the political and military leaders of the hour (especially the Whigs); and it concluded with a personal tribute to Queen Anne.

A rival pamphleteer claimed that Defoe had offered two guineas for a prefatory Latin poem in his own honor because he could not write one for himself, and that publication of the poem had been delayed because his money had been refused.[11] In *Jure Divino* the author's work is eulogized in an introductory poem in English which is signed "A. O." The verse offered by this "Alpha Omega" reads wonderfully like Defoe's own.

Long as *Jure Divino* is, it represents less than half of Defoe's intention. He promised to supplement it by addenda "not yet finished," to be bound with the original sheets or to be read separately. But this promise was neglected during his repeated examinations before the commissioners of bankruptcy that summer and during his long stay in Edinburgh which began in early October. A second part was ready in manuscript, containing "some characters and some enlargements on particular transactions," which Defoe said he was prevented from publishing by "prudentials which I have not been over-apt to make use of in other cases." As this unpublished second part was actually written first, and as the greatest part of the whole poem was written in Newgate, the original manuscript must have had much to say of Nottingham and of Defoe's persecution in 1703. The Preface apologies for Defoe's failure to attack church tyranny as well as civil tyranny. But such an attack could not have been safely published in 1704, and after that Defoe was willing to pass such oppression by "as a lion slain."

Parts were in the press by October, 1705, and the Earl of Dalkeith (who died four months before the poem was published) is referred to as still alive. In some of Defoe's later quotations from *Jure Divino*, there are wide variations in language and in the arrangement of lines, as if he were recalling the poem as it was originally composed in prison.[12]

According to one Tory pamphleteer, Defoe had no intention of publishing any such poem, and the frequent delays were intended to bilk his subscribers. According to another, the doctrine of *Jure Divino* was the usual Whig cant of rebellion, and the author was the mouthpiece of his party. But if Defoe expected any very active support from the Whigs, he was doomed to disappointment. Although he asked for only a fourth of the book's price for each advance subscription, even that amount was obtained with great difficulty. John Fransham, who solicited for him in Norwich, wrote that "the greatest part of the city would have subscribed for the contrary subject." Some subscriptions were held back on the pretense that the book might never appear, some others were not reported by the agents who had received them. In the end, the eighteen agents through whom delivery was first announced shrank to eight, and several of these were new. According to one pamphleteer, the printer delayed the presswork for fear he would not be paid.[13]

Benjamin Bragg, who had been one of Defoe's principal publishers until he was refused a share in *Jure Divino*, announced that the book could be had from himself for five shillings, whereas the authorized edition cost ten shillings, or thirteen shillings bound with a picture of the author. Through a misreading of a statement in Defoe's *Review*, it has been supposed that Bragg claimed that his own pirated edition was published "for the sole benefit of the author." Actually, what he did claim was that, as the subscription edition paid a profit to the author, the pirated edition could be issued at less than half price "for the encouragement of trade." Defoe objected not only to the theft of his literary property, which occurred for no reason except his insistence on publishing independently without making terms with the booksellers; he also declared that Bragg had used the cheapest of paper, that his text had multitudinous errors, and that his picture of Defoe was a copy of a copy, "about as much like the author as Sir Roger L'Estrange was like the dog Towser."

With such competition from pirates, private publication of the poem was less remunerative than Defoe had expected; but his ten-shilling edition must still have had a fair number of subscribers, if we may judge from the excellent copies available today. The last separate English publication of the poem occurred in 1821, when the radical William Hone attacked the Holy Alliance by reprinting a condensed and revised version which he called *The Right Divine of Kings to Govern Wrong!* According to Hone's prefatory remarks on Defoe, "He was the ablest politician of the day, an energetic writer, and better than all, an honest man; but not much of a poet."[14]

During the three-year interval before *Jure Divino* was issued, Defoe touched on its basic ideas in several other writings; but we can follow his plans for the poem from its Preface and from advertisements in the *Review*. On September 26, 1704, it was announced in terms which showed that its approximate length was known. Further particulars were to appear in the next *Review*, but the subject was dropped at once. Defoe had already held back the poem while he remained in Newgate and, later, while Harley was overthrowing Nottingham and Rochester: "All those few and wiser Heads that had any respect for the Author, earnestly pressed me not to attempt it while the last Parliament was sitting, Measures having been taken, and the Party then powerful enough to blast it in its Birth, seize it in the Press, and suppress both it and me altogether, by the heavy Weight of Parliamentary Censure; and this laid it asleep a Year."

In the fall of 1704 he had to withhold it again while Harley was thwarting the third attempt to pass the Occasional bill. By February 13, 1705, it seemed that Defoe would be free to carry out his undertaking. He told an inquirer that the book had been stopped on an extraordinary occasion, but that it was now "perfecting for the press" and would be printed in March. He hoped to have it ready for delivery not later than the end of April. A few weeks later a like apology was given, with the addition that the sheets could be seen at the printer's. Those who had collected subscriptions were urged to report them, as copies would be printed only for subscribers. That summer Defoe was delayed for four months by a political journey, and in the next January he took two columns of his *Review* to refute the charge that he had broken faith with his subscribers. He guaranteed the poem's appearance, and he stated that certain benefactors had enabled him to go forward with the work. When the poem finally appeared, he would have printed the names of these benefactors, but they expressly forbade it.[15]

On May 24, 1706, Defoe informed John Fransham in Norwich that *Jure Divino* was finished, and awaited his order how many copies, bound or unbound, should be sent. On July 18, he advertised in the *Review* that subscribers could obtain it on Saturday (July 20) at any one of eight specified places in London and Westminster. On July 20 Bragg advertised in the *Observator* that the edition "for the sole benefit of the author" had been published in the country about a month since and in London on Tuesday last (July 16), but that his cut-price edition had been published on July 19. Since the authorized edition had been available in the country for so long, Bragg could easily have procured a copy a month in advance of his own date of publication. In the *Review* for July 20 and 27 and for August 3 Defoe attacked Bragg's dishonest procedure: "Whoever has a Mind to encourage such Robbery of other Men's Studies at their own Expense, may be furnished with the said Book, at Mr. Benjamin *Bragg's*, Publisher in ordinary to the Pyrates."

Jure Divino was Defoe's most ambitious literary speculation, one of the most characteristic statements of his political theories, and his longest poem. But here (as so often elsewhere) he was a cool judge of his own work: "As to the poetical part of it, where the argument lies strong, I have been very careless of censure that way, and have often sacrificed the poet to the reasoning style."[16]

In his other poems he used five principal patterns of verse for varying purposes. He considered blank verse suitable for a play or for the rough draft of a poem. If time permitted, the lines were to be polished into heroic couplets, which he regarded as the standard form of serious non-dramatic English verse. He admired *Paradise Lost* and knew it intimately, but his attempted supplement was written in heroic couplets. Although he was extremely fond of the octosyllabic couplets of Butler, he rarely used them except in paraphrasing *Hudibras*. For hasty political satires to be circulated in the streets, he used some variant of the ballad stanza. For the simple expression of personal experience, he employed the quatrains of a Nonconformist hymn. For poems which aimed at sublimity, he was likely to attempt something like a "Pindaric ode."

Critics down to our time have condemned Defoe's verse—except the best passages in his *Hymn to the Pillory* and in *The True-Born Englishman*, and they have often found high poetic quality in his best prose. But Defoe was loath to relinquish the medium of verse. He knew many of his poems by heart, and he continued to quote them— usually with the inexactness of familiar memory—as long as he lived. In so strange a context as his account of the commerce of Africa in his *Atlas Maritimus & Commercialis* (1728), he quoted a line against human slavery which had appeared in slightly different words in *Reformation of Manners* twenty-six years before:

They barter Baubles for the Souls of Men.

Less than a year before he died, and twenty-nine years after *The True-Born Englishman* had been published, quotations from it cropped out in the *Political State of Great-Britain*, which he was editing at that time. He continued to show personal interest in the poetry of the day, long after his critical judgment could have been of general interest. At times his estimates still seem acute, as when he anticipated Dr. Johnson in condemning Blackmore's *Prince Arthur, Job*, and *Eliza* while giving high praise to his *Creation*. Defoe's strictures on Pope's *Homer* probably helped to win the place in the *The Dunciad* which was otherwise so uncalled for.[17]

Regarding translation, Defoe had his own theories. Perhaps it was altogether in jest, but it was certainly not out of character that in 1707 he sought to ingratiate himself with the Scottish Presbyterians by proposing to translate or versify the Psalms: "I treat with the Commission to make them a new version of the Psalms, and that I'll lock myself in the College two years for the performance."

In the long years which followed the triumph of *The True-Born Englishman*, Defoe's vogue as a poet never subsided among the common readers quite as completely as it did among the wits. Perhaps, as he tells us more than once, many of his readers expected him to brighten the pages of his *Review* with lyrical effusions. After the victory of Oudenarde in 1708, the "Madman" who was introduced to bear a part in the dialogues of the *Review* rebuked him for not fulfilling these expectations: "the world has been expecting another Hymn to Victory upon the occasion, and a new court to the D. of Marlborough." Defoe could only answer—from his cool head, if not from his sanguine breast—"my harps are long since hung on the willows, my brains have done crowing."[18]

> *...to be reduced to necessity is to be wicked; for necessity*
> *is not only the temptation, but it is such a temptation as*
> *human nature is not empowered to resist.*
>
> *Colonel Jack* (Tegg ed.), p. 175

B E F O R E January 27, 1722, there was perhaps no considerable literary work in the world which was based on an intelligent and sympathetic understanding of the misfortunes of an unprotected woman in
contemporary society. Certain Renaissance painters had caught something of this understanding and sympathy from the teachings of Jesus.
But the common attitude of writers before Defoe was a scornful presentation of the criminal or the fallen, or a jesting presentation of sul-
lied humanity as a subject for mirth.

To Defoe, always seeing human experience with the eyes of a social
historian, vice and crime were subjects not for scorn or mirth but for
sympathetic concern. All too often it was society itself which caused
the original crime, even in the attempt to correct other wrongs. Moll
Flanders, born in Newgate, is allowed to speak for the author who
created her: "there are more thieves and rogues made by that one
prison of Newgate, than by all the clubs and societies of villains in the
nation."

As early as July, 1720, Defoe had written a letter from "Moll of
Rag-Fair," an expert pickpocket, but—like her more famous namesake—caught in the act when she attempted to rob a shop. This earlier
Moll had returned to England before the end of her sentence of transportation to the colonies, so that she was in constant fear of being
discovered or hanged; and she was being blackmailed by an acquaintance who threatened to inform on her.

As late as December of 1730, in his last tract, published about four
months before his death, Defoe mentioned another Moll in his account of the "night-houses" which served as training schools and as

houses of refuge for the young criminals of London: "there are other sinks of Wickedness which want cleansing, besides there is the Dominion of MOLL HARVEY; tho' she was rampant enough, and has not many equals, yet there are other Ladies of Fame, whose Stock of Assurance has carried them great Lengths, in Defiance of the Laws, and of the Magistrate; and till these are attack'd, and that with the same Vigor and Resolution, our Reformation will never merit the Title of UNIVERSAL."

A more immediate source for the criminal career of Moll Flanders is to be traced in a news story which Defoe wrote for Mist's *Weekly-Journal*. This was not published until nearly eight months after the novel appeared, but it told of a female criminal whose record must have been long familiar to Defoe: "Moll King, a most notorious Offender, famous for stealing Gold Watches from the Ladies' Sides in the Churches, for which she has been several times convicted, being lately return'd from Transportation, has been taken, and is committed to Newgate."[1]

The great innovation in Defoe's first social novel was not in his vivid portrayal of the expert pickpocket and the accomplished prostitute, remarkable as this is in its way. It was not even in his account of the new life that beckoned in a new land—although no other writer of the age gave so encouraging and yet so realistic an account of the advantages a transported felon might have if he thought of himself as a colonist who might acquire a stake in the land of his enforced adoption. So far this would be the Crusoe story in another guise, with transportation serving instead of shipwreck, and with a thinly settled colony replacing the desert island.

Defoe's originality appeared more clearly in his going back to the beautiful little girl long before she acquired the notorious name of Moll Flanders—the innocent but sensuous Betty, born in Newgate to a mother who escaped hanging only because of the expected birth of her child. The crime for which Betty's mother was convicted, and which shaped little Betty's future life, was the stealing of three pieces of holland from a mercer in Cheapside—"a petty theft, scarce worth naming." Perhaps it was as well for Betty that her mother was transported, so that the infant daughter lived for a little while among her mother's relatives. Perhaps it was well that, after being carried about by gypsies for a brief time, Betty hid herself at Colchester and refused to go away with them, so that she was taken up by the parish officers and put in charge of a poor woman who kept a little school.

In her old age Moll regretted that she had not been treated like the destitute children of criminals in France, who "are immediately taken into the care of the government, and put into an hospital called the House of Orphans, where they are bred up, clothed, fed, taught, and when fit to go out, are placed to trades, or to services, so as to be well able to provide for themselves by an honest industrious behaviour. Had this been the custom in our country, I had not been left a poor desolate girl without friends." Betty became the favorite of the poor woman who served as her nurse and teacher, and equally so with the women and girls of Colchester who made her acquaintance. But she grew up with no money to assure her marriage, and with a love of fine clothes, a dislike of hard work, and a desire to be regarded as a gentlewoman. The hopelessness of her situation is brought out in an early dialogue with her nurse and teacher:

Why, what, said she, is the girl mad? what would you be a gentlewoman? Yes, says I, and cried heartily till I roared out again.

This set the old gentlewoman a laughing at me, as you may be sure it would. Well madam, forsooth, says she, gibing at me; you would be a gentlewoman, and how will you come to be a gentlewoman? What will you do it by your finger's ends?

Yes, says I again, very innocently.

Why, what can you earn, says she: what can you get a-day at your work?

Three-pence, said I, when I spin, and four-pence when I work plain work.

Alas! poor gentlewoman, said she again, laughing, what will that do for thee?

With such a beginning in life, things never went well with Betty for long at a time. Until she reached a passive state in old age, the apparent advantage of the moment brought on the catastrophe which always followed. At Colchester she was taken into the home of some of her female admirers. Here, as the daughters of the family had private masters to teach them, Betty learned, by imitation and inquiry, to dance, to speak French, to write, and to sing, and later to play on the harpsichord and spinet. The daughters of the family still had the wealth and the social position, but Betty was all too conscious of her superior abilities and her beauty.

In the family there were two sons—the heir, who was unwilling to marry until he was sure of the inheritance, and the younger brother, who was willing to sacrifice self-advantage for love. But the older brother spoke first, and Betty became his mistress before she was old enough to be her own. In less than half a year the younger brother was urgent to marry her; and the elder brother (whom she still loved) cleared himself of responsibility by insisting on her acceptance of the offer.

Her varied catastrophes have been made famous by the title page: "The Fortunes and Misfortunes of the Famous Moll Flanders, &c Who was Born in Newgate, and during a Life of continued Variety for Three-score Years, besides her Childhood, was Twelve Year a Whore, five times a Wife (whereof once to her own Brother) Twelve Year a Thief, Eight Year a Transported Felon in Virginia, at last grew Rich, liv'd Honest, and died a Penitent Written from her own Memorandums." The list seems incredible in itself; but her adventures follow each other in natural sequence. Betty is soon a widow, and she makes an unfortunate marriage with a gentleman tradesman who goes bankrupt and flies to France. To escape arrest for his debts, she takes refuge in Southwark in the privileged region known as the Mint. Here, for the first time, she assumes the name of Mrs. Flanders.

After this, she continues to snatch at apparent advantages, only to have them involve her in new difficulties. She marries her half-brother in Virginia only because she does not know her mother. The dashing young fellow in Lancashire whom she mistakes for a man of fortune goes on the highway when he finds that she is almost as penniless as he; and they are happily reunited only when they accept transportation to Maryland together.

In all her misfortunes, Moll never learns economy. Even the caution which leads her to hold back part of her possessions provides for further luxuries rather than for future subsistence. The hard and calculating Roxana, Moll's opposite number in Defoe's gallery of women, could say of herself, "having large sums to do with, I became as expert in it as any she-merchant of them all."[2] Poor Moll could not thrive until she was on a remote plantation where there were no luxuries to buy.

Her virtues are as apparent as her faults. She is brave, generous, affectionate, and gentle even in her acts of crime. The very children whom she robs are drawn to her. Unwilling as she is to engage in hard work, she is active and alert to an unusual degree. Like a character in one of Wilde's comedies, she can resist anything except temptation. But against that—with her background—she has little chance.

Eleven months later Defoe published the second of his social novels, one which served in part as a foil to *Moll Flanders*. In *Colonel Jack* certain roads to success, which were forever closed to Moll Flanders, opened naturally to a young man soon after he had acquired the will to reform and to succeed in life. Moll's forlorn hope of living as a gentlewoman was the primary cause of her shame; for Jack, the dream of becoming a gentleman was the source of his ultimate salvation.

Jack's dream of becoming a gentleman was perhaps grounded on a passage in a book which Defoe knew well, possibly in the French original published in 1687, certainly in the popular English translation which reached a third edition as early as 1705. *The Memoirs of the Count de Rochefort* was written by Courtilz de Sandras, who also created the original of the hero of *The Three Musketeers*. Perhaps the author who exerted such influence on Defoe and Dumas does not deserve the oblivion to which literary historians have consigned him.

More than once Defoe cited the *Memoirs of the Count de Rochefort* as a book which he knew familiarly and which he expected his readers to know. On page 14 of the third edition of the English translation, the curate fails in his appeal to the young hero's hard-hearted uncle, and then he bids the youth an affectionate farewell:

> The Curate seeing him so unnatural, could not forbear weeping, and taking me in his arms, entreated me once more to have a little patience; but finding it impossible to shake my resolution, he pull'd out of his Pocket two Crowns and gave them to me, telling me he was sensible that I should want them, and was sorry he was not in a condition to assist me better; so praying God to bless me, told me I was always to remember that I was born a Gentleman, which oblig'd me to suffer a thousand deaths rather than to do a base action, or anything unworthy of my quality.

In Defoe's narrative, Jack's gradual break with his instructor in crime begins in a disagreement on the meaning of the life of a gentleman:

> Why, says he, we will take the highway like gentlemen, and then we shall get a great deal of money indeed. Well, says I, what then? Why then, says he, we shall live like gentlemen. . . . Why, says I, was it like a gentleman for me to take that 22s. from a poor ancient woman, when she begged of me upon her knees not to take it, and told me it was all she had in the world to buy her bread for herself and a sick child which she had at home? Do you think I could be so cruel, if you had not stood by and made me do it? Why I cried at doing it as much as the poor woman did, though I did not let you see me.[3]

For stories dealing so largely with the underworld, *Moll Flanders* and *Colonel Jack* are remarkably free from the exploitation of an interest in vice. In his social tracts Defoe makes it clear that he regards the houses of prostitution called "night-houses" as the schools of young criminals; but we hear relatively little of such places in either novel. Moll's childhood governess is a kindly instructor who has no thought of attempting to trade on her virtue. Colonel Jack's widowed nurse does her best to provide a decent home for him and his two comrades, until her death launches all three boys unprovided into the world.

Both Moll and Jack were illegitimate children; but whereas Moll's mother was a condemned thief in Newgate, Jack was told from infancy that he "was a gentleman." The hardships of his childhood are movingly told, but it is clear from the first that he will escape from his environment when the chance arises. His great opportunity came to him in three ways. He was led to intrust his first considerable gains from theft to a friendly man of business; and although this ill-gotten money was spent for supplies for his Maryland plantation which were mostly lost at sea, he had acquired the habit of thrift. Secondly, he soon realized the handicap of his illiteracy and seized opportunities to put himself under instruction—first in Edinburgh, where he learned to write and to keep accounts; later in Maryland, where he followed, under a tutor, the ideal course of study which Defoe later outlined in *The Compleat English Gentleman.*[4] Most of all, Jack was struck by his own cruelty in robbing the poor old woman of her all, and he returned later to repay what she had lost. From that time, Jack might continue to harbor with thieves and even to share part of their loot; but he never committed another theft, and he gradually became one of the most honest of men.

Like Sir Walter Scott, Defoe would frequently allow a favorite character or situation or idea to run away with his pen, so that the parts of some of his novels are better than the wholes. Unity and concentration came more or less fortuitously. More often, and more characteristically, we have a succession of episodes, some of which (like the narrative of Jack as a young thief) rise to the height of the greatest fiction.

Many of the strands of *Colonel Jack* are to be found elsewhere in Defoe's writings, or even in his personal life. One situation had been touched on by Defoe thirty years earlier in Dunton's *Athenian Gazette,* and it was repeated in Applebee's *Journal* almost two years before the novel was published—that of the meek husband whose unfaithful wife seeks to provoke him into a duel with her paramour. Another idea had been sketched out nine years before in *A General*

History of Trade, when he wrote of the multitudinous creeks of the Chesapeake as affording water carriage for transporting tobacco to Europe. The theme of the interloping English merchant who braves the tyrannical restrictions of the Spanish rulers in America to trade with the planters had appeared two years before in *Captain Singleton,* and it was to recur three years later in *A New Voyage Round the World.* The horse which Jack's companion steals at Puckeridge, and which Jack restores to the rightful owner, recalls the false accusation that Defoe had stolen the Coventry horse which he borrowed for his traveling companion but was unable to return until much later. Colonel Jack's feverish dreams of his capture by the constable are variants of Defoe's own dreams of his capture by the Queen's messengers in the fateful month of May, 1703. The glasshouses, in the warmth of whose ash holes and annealing arches Jack and his companions find shelter at night, had been foreshadowed in a letter to Harley from Edinburgh (November 26, 1706) mentioning the report that Defoe would go into partnership with a member of the Scottish Parliament in a glasshouse; and they were to reappear in his last tract, where he tells how young boys are sent out from night-houses to learn the arts of crime: "At first, and while they are very young, they lie abroad in the Streets, and upon Bulks, or in the Glass-houses, under the very Furnaces and in the warm Ashes, and go abroad a thieving in the Day."[5]

Of the military career in Europe, which figured so largely in *Memoirs of a Cavalier* and was later to be the staple of *Captain Carleton,* Colonel Jack soon gets more than enough. Defoe chose to ignore the promise of the title page that his hero "went into the wars, behaved bravely, got preferment, was made a colonel of a regiment, and fled with the Chevalier, is still abroad completing a life of wonders, and resolves to die a general."

The marked discrepancy between the title page and the narrative is explained by the political situation in 1722. When Defoe began the story, the last Jacobite uprising lay three years behind him, and he felt free to present an adherent of the Pretender as a romantic and successful figure. But in the late summer of 1722 a new conspiracy against the government was exposed. On August 24 the Bishop of Rochester was arrested, and he was still in the Tower awaiting trial when Defoe's novel was published on December 20. Counsellor Layer had been sentenced for high treason, but had been reprieved until January 19.

In the novel as it was published, Colonel Jack was no longer a flamboyant rebel, serving under the Chevalier and resolving to die a general, but a peaceful English planter near Chesapeake Bay. He had hoped to conceal his one brief and foolish appearance with the rebels in England in 1715 by swimming a river, hiding in a forest, shooting his horse and covering the carcass in a gravel pit, and then returning secretly to his terrified family. But after he had crossed the Atlantic to his tobacco plantations, he was thrown into a panic by the unexpected appearance of some of the Scottish rebels who had served with him at Preston and who had been transported instead of being hanged. Colonel Jack screened himself from possible recognition by his old comrades, but he did not feel secure until word came from England that "the king had signed an act of grace, that is to say, a general free pardon."

For a page and a half the repentant Colonel Jack pours out his gratitude to the benevolence of George I, saying that the pardoned rebel who revolts again "deserves no pardon after it, either from God or man." Colonel Jack admits that "all this is a digression."[6] But in a London excited over the latest conspiracy of the Jacobites, Defoe was glad of an opportunity to point out that the rebels who had come off safely in 1715–16 were ungrateful to plot another rebellion in 1722.

The most moving parts of the story—as of every other story by Defoe—are the Crusoe-like passages in which the author thought himself into the role of the main character and let the narrative work itself out naturally. What would a young thief do when he had stolen money for the first time? What emotion would a ragged and half-starving boy have when he bought his first warm stockings? How would it feel to sleep in the warm ashes of a glasshouse, and to be awakened "in the dead of the night" by the constable and his watch? How would it affect one to stand by while his comrade was lashed at Bridewell?

Roxana, like *Moll Flanders*, deals with the economic insecurity of an unprotected woman. But here the heroine is no innocent little girl who is thrown into a life of vice and crime against her will, but a calculating adventuress who finds that she can secure a life of luxury by trading on her personal charms.

One of Defoe's originals for her character was the notorious Mrs. Mary Butler, the former mistress of the second Duke of Buckingham, who was convicted of forging bonds for very large amounts in the name of Sir Robert Clayton, the trustee of Buckingham's estate. The printed account of Mrs. Butler's trial was in Defoe's library, and he made use of it in his portrayal of Roxana and her financial adviser, "good Sir Robert, . . . the same faithful friend."

A second original was Mademoiselle Bardou, an ugly but graceful Frenchwoman who amused the court of Charles II with her dancing until the King grew weary of her and banished her from the royal circle on a small pension. The name Roxalana or (in its shortened form) Roxana had an intricate history on the English stage and in the intrigues of the court of Charles II, tracing back through the sultry oriental queens in Davenant's *The Siege of Rhodes* and Lee's *The Rival Queens* to its originals in the seraglio of the Turkish Empire.

The Roxana who retains a cynical detachment toward those who love her, who debases her faithful maid so that she will not be annoyed by her reproaches, and who is willing for her own daughter to be murdered if that is necessary to silence inconvenient inquiries is of a colder and harder and baser nature than the well-meaning Moll Flanders, who retains a kindly feeling toward those who have wronged her most. In spite of the strange anachronism by which Roxana, who was an infant in 1683, becomes the mistress of Charles II, who died in 1685, the novel is close-knit in its narrative development. Unfortunately, it is usually marred by the inclusion of the mediocre supplement which was added fourteen years after Defoe's death, in which the retribution at which Defoe only hinted is spun out interminably.

One of the strangest misconceptions about Defoe's writings is that he padded out his books in this fashion, and that the multiplicity of interests in some of his novels resulted from a desire to swell out his volumes. The first half of this charge was stated by one of the most verbose writers in the English language (if Samuel Richardson was the author of the Preface to the 1738 edition of *The Complete English Tradesman*): " 'Tis well known that he was obliged to make a trade of writing, and rated his labors according to the number of sheets which composed the book he undertook, so he suffered himself to run into this luxuriancy, very probably, more in compliance with his circumstances than according to his judgment."[7] Strange words these, if they really came from the author of *Sir Charles Grandison*.

As Defoe explained, he often used repetition and restatement to hold the attention of simple readers; but for the eighteenth century he was a remarkably concise writer. The exiled Jacobite leader Lord George Murray might complain bitterly of a French author who proposed coming to his subject "only in the ninth volume," or of another who spun out to six volumes in thick octavo a history which would have been more valuable in two. Almost any pamphlet by Defoe is half the length of the corresponding tracts by his opponents; the typical Defoe pamphlet was meant to be brief and easily read, and to sell at a price which made wide distribution possible. His novels are among the shortest of their kind; he rarely worked out any subject for all he could make of it. The most fertile theme in fiction—Crusoe's solitary life on the island—was completed in sixty-five thousand words, a compression few other writers would have dreamed of. On page 7 Crusoe meets with his first shipwreck; on page 6 of another story the Cavalier goes abroad for his adventures; on page 10 Colonel Jack has his first alarm from a constable; and on page 10 (from the masthead of the sinking *Degrave*) Robert Drury sees land on Madagascar.

Defoe recognized that his trouble was not wordiness but impatience. To a head teeming with ideas, the problem was rarely how to find enough material. In the frantic attempts to supply continuations for *Robinson Crusoe*, the hastily compiled third part fell short of the publisher's requirement, and the irrelevant and separately paged *View of the Angelick World* was tacked on to make up the completed book for sale. But this was a rare exception. Defoe's usual practice is best explained by himself:

> I am quick to conceive, I am eager to have done, unwilling to overwork the subject. I had rather leave part to the conception of the readers than to tire them or myself with protracting a theme, as if like a Chancery man or a hackney author I wrote by the sheet for hire. So let us have done with this topic and proceed to another.

> I must beg the reader's indulgence, being the most immethodical writer imaginable; 'tis true, I lay down a scheme, but fancy is so fertile I often start fresh hints, and cannot but pursue them.[8]

This was the favorite method of Defoe as of Scott; and although it has obvious defects, it often shows "strange surprising" virtues.

In *Captain Singleton* the germinal idea is to be found in the frequent newspaper notices of kidnappings by gypsies or other vagrants, such as one Defoe may have read in the *London Gazette* when he was an impressionable boy of eleven. One of Colonel Jack's early associates was a kidnapper of children, and Moll Flanders during her infancy was carried off by gypsies. *Captain Singleton* began with a child carried off by a professional kidnapper, sold to a beggar "to set off her trade," and after that, sold to a gypsy. But where was Defoe to go from there?

At the transitional points the story veers uncertainly, like a sailing vessel about to change its course. But it moves off swiftly after Defoe has once determined on a new direction. The marooned mutineers blunder along until they cross from Madagascar to the mainland, and the author recalls a story about how an Englishman named Freeman had met a party of Portuguese who had ventured on an overland journey across Africa.[9] The vicious Portuguese sailors, would-be murderers and the dregs of a nation which had previously been condemned as "the most perfidious and debauched, the most insolent and cruel, of any that pretend to call themselves Christians in the world," become loyal comrades in arms; and the irresponsible boy Bob Singleton shows himself suddenly a born leader of men.

In the second part, after the gold from the Guinea Coast has been squandered in London, the now aimless Singleton is drawn into a plot to steal a ship in the Groyne (as the famous pirate Avery had done), and he is launched on a piratical career which the real Avery might have envied. However, the story must be wound up in some way, and the already conventional ending of a successful pirate establishment on Madagascar had been overlooked. Singleton must get back to England; and (as both statesmen and journalists in England had been suggesting for twenty years before Defoe wrote this book) the piratical treasure must be brought back too. The only feature of the accepted plan that was missing here was a division of the pirate's loot with a benevolent government in exchange for a pardon. But as Singleton preferred secrecy to a public pardon, it would be unreasonable to expect him to share his treasure with anyone but his new wife and his brother-in-law, the ever faithful Quaker William.

The fault of *Captain Singleton* is not padding, but frequent irrelevance. When Defoe was uncertain what story he meant to tell, he could make sad work of it. Once he had decided on a course for his hero, he knew how to follow it. Four stories in *Captain Singleton*, yes; and each not without merit. But here the parts remain greater than the whole.

With his unparalleled knowledge of human experience, and with his wide and deep sympathy for men and women, Defoe becomes one of the immortal novelists when he shares the solitude of the desert island, or begins the long trek across the unexplored interior of Africa, or lands on the hostile shore of Madagascar, or stands within the walls of Newgate Prison in the hourly expectation of being hanged. This is nowhere so well stated as in a profound and beautiful paragraph by Walter de la Mare:

But more hauntingly yet descends silence and solitude upon the reader in *The Journal of the Plague Year*. Defoe's masterly English, compounded of the Bible and the raciest vernacular, is nowhere else so impressive. The "saddler's" narrative enslaves the mind and seems to shut off all retreat—the first gossip and stir of distrust and foreboding, the cumulative innuendo, the facts and figures that take in their nakedness as sinister a bearing as the far-off waft across the water of a pirate's ancient itself; the thronging, mocking, terror-stricken crowds; the quacks and seers and occultists; the deepening hush broken ever and again by a piercing cry; and then at last the deserted, grass-grown streets, the barred doors, the watchmen and the bell; and the gathering, drifting mist of death settling thickly upon all. A shadowy form seems to stoop over the writer's shoulder, compelling him, though intent only on the bare facts and on his own shadow wandering through the London of his childhood, to record its mysterious presence in his sharp deliberate prose.

But almost as remarkable as his power of evoking solitude is the unflagging verve with which Defoe comes again and again to confront the environing world. One of the best-known modern novelists has said that he recognized only two kinds of novels—those that had life and those that lacked it. Defoe had this exalted attribute—that of life—in his books and in his private undertakings, as few men and fewer authors have ever had it. In the words of Sir Walter Besant, "The same Defoe writes *The Shortest Way with the Dissenters* and *Moll Flanders*. It is not an old gladiator worn out by many fights, many wounds, and the touch of time. It is the same man, strong and resolute; . . . his step is as firm, his carriage as erect, his arm as strong, as when he first began, forty years before."[10]

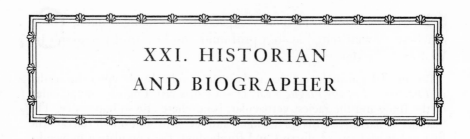

XXI. HISTORIAN
AND BIOGRAPHER

... a historian should write in temper, even of those actions which were not perform'd in temper, and treat all sides with an impartial respect.

The Impartial History of the Life and Actions
of Peter Alexowitz, The Present Czar
of Russia (1723), p. 111

THE NOVELS OF DEFOE are incidental in his career. His more serious concern was in the field of history. By the time he was twenty-two he had compiled a manuscript called *Historical Collections*, containing passages excerpted from several authors and prepared for the press. This was never published, and it has not been located since the eighteenth century. By the time he was forty he was able to declare, "truly I have read all the histories of Europe, that are extant in our language, and some in other languages." His constant sense of the historical background distinguished his early political writings from those of many of his rivals. His references to current events drew strength from his knowledge of what had happened before, and he was often enabled to make shrewd guesses of what was likely to happen again. But it was not until he was about forty-nine years old that he published his first considerable work as a historian.

As early as January 27, 1707, he wrote to Harley, in a jesting account of his supposed activities in Scotland: "Now I give out, I am going to write the history of the Union in folio, and have got warrants to search the Registers and Parliament books, and have begun a subscription for it." In sober earnest he was advertising in his *Review* two months later: "Preparing for the Press, and a great Part of it finished, A *Compleat* HISTORY OF THE UNION. *The Work will contain about* 250 *Sheets in* Folio, *to be finish'd in six Months from the* UNION: ... *By the Author of the True-Born* Englishman."[1] But unexpected delays kept the book from appearing in Edinburgh until 1709.

As author of the *History* Defoe had several different motives. The book was meant to be sold, like almost everything else that he wrote. It was meant to do honor to the Queen and to the men who had carried the Union through to success. And it was intended as a record of the aims and methods of those who had secured the Union, so that there need be no breach of faith and no misunderstanding in the future. In the spring of 1712, when it was thought that Parliament might violate some of the conditions of the Union, Defoe had sheets of the Edinburgh edition brought to London to be published there for the first time.

His advantages as author of the book were many. He was dealing with the greatest political achievement of the reign of Queen Anne, he had free access to the relevant documents, he had attended the meetings in Edinburgh and had served on important committees with some of the principals there, and he understood better than anyone else the issues at stake in such a Union.

But he had difficulties as well. His habitual irony and his bantering style of writing were ruled out from the first, his personal relationships had to be kept out of sight even more than usual, he was an object of suspicion in Scotland as an Englishman and an English Presbyterian, he had to make every possible allowance for national prejudices and irritated sensibilities, and—in his extreme care to preserve the official records—he was in danger of giving his readers little more than the minutes of Parliament and detailed notes on committee meetings. Competent historians have regarded *The History of the Union* as invaluable in its field; but some lovers of Defoe have found it the nearest to a dull book that he ever wrote.

Two years later appeared Defoe's first venture as a biographer: *A Short Narrative of the Life and Actions of His Grace John, D. of Marlborough*. This is more of a controversial tract than a direct narrative; but it gives an outline of the principal events in Marlborough's military career, and it introduces what became one of Defoe's favorite devices in biographical writing. It is ostensibly written "By an Old Officer in the Army"; and although this supposed author nowhere gives his name or rank, the partial identification enables Defoe to explain the military career of Marlborough, to refute the tradition that the betrayal of William's plans by Lady Marlborough prevented the capture of Dunkirk, and to ridicule those coffeehouse critics "whose mouths go off smartly with a whiff of tobacco, and fight battles, and take towns over a dish of coffee."

The attribution of authorship to "an Old Officer in the Army" served Defoe in several ways. It enabled him (without detection by Harley or others) to defend Marlborough at the time when several members of the Ministry were planning his impeachment. It solved one of Defoe's most persistent problems as a writer on political subjects: How was he, who drew so largely on information not accessible to the public, to justify his frequent practice of writing "Within Doors"? When he wrote as Defoe, the former confidant of King William, he could indulge in an occasional allusion to something he had heard from the King's own lips. But how, in an anonymous tract like this, could he be supposed to understand the secret reasons for William's distrust of Marlborough or his subsequent confidence in him? It was here that "an Old Officer" was most useful; the general reader would expect him to know what happened in the army or in the court.

There was still another, and a wider, advantage in the introduction of such a fictitious author. It gave Defoe a literary freedom which he needed in his finest writing. As Daniel Defoe he might be attacked for tautology or for loose grammatical constructions or for meanness of style; even when he professed to despise such criticism, it is evident that he felt hampered by it. Furthermore, without being a playwright he often expressed himself most freely through his *dramatis personae* and in the scenes and situations in which his characters were placed.

His controversial tracts were written against a background of history, and frequently they assumed something of its form, as in *The Secret History of the October Club* (1711), *An Essay on the History of Parties* (1711), and *The History of the Jacobite Clubs* (1712). A monthly undertaken to justify the commercial articles of the Treaty of Utrecht by a wider view of economic principles was called *A General History of Trade* (1713).

After the accession of George I, Defoe attempted to defend Harley by dissociating him from Bolingbroke's wing of the Tories through a series of "secret histories" and "memoirs." But this was a difficult line to maintain. Bolingbroke was still most unwilling to be singled out as the leader of the Jacobite faction in the late Ministry; Harley winced under the common suspicion that he had written or inspired *The Secret History of the White Staff*. When Harley objected to the defense which had been offered, Defoe issued *The Secret History of the Secret History of the Staff, Purse and Mitre* (1715) to relieve him from any responsibility for previous efforts in his behalf.

More significant than these ephemeral tracts is *An Appeal to Honour and Justice*, an autobiographical sketch published in Defoe's own name on February 24, 1715, as a defense of his public services under King William and under the last three Ministries of Queen Anne. The dominant tone of this moving apology is one of bewilderment. After twenty-five years devoted largely to the government, Defoe did not know where he stood. The new King was a foreigner; most of his advisers seemed more interested in self-advantage or in party revenge than in an enlightened national policy; and the old Ministry had not only fallen from power but had divided into hostile factions (although a few of its most prominent members had succeeded in attaching themselves to the new sovereign).

The stroke of apoplexy which "the publisher" gave as excuse for the author's abrupt conclusion was exaggerated, but it was probably not fictitious. As early as February 2, 1707, Defoe had urged Harley to take care of his health, citing his own experience as evidence.[2] After 1710 his allusions to his ailments become more frequent. It is hard to think of Defoe as ever being ill, but it is clear that (especially after he was past fifty) he sometimes endured physical infirmities like other men.

An Appeal to Honour and Justice was written hurriedly and without notes; but it seems substantially reliable if one allows for the fact that it was intended not for posterity but for certain ruthless contemporaries, "His Worst Enemies," the powerful leaders of the Whigs. Some of these men knew much about his acquaintance with King William, but they wished to forget that; some of them knew how deeply Defoe had suffered to protect them in 1703, but they wished to forget that too; all of them surmised much regarding his close association with Harley in more recent years, and it was important to tell them no more about this than they already knew.

A few months later, perhaps in August of 1715, after Parker had recommended Defoe to Townshend, his course was clear. Bolingbroke had condemned himself forever by his flight and voluntary exile, Harley had gone manfully to the Tower to await his long-deferred trial, and Defoe had been accepted once more as the official propagandist for the government. This was a far less lucrative and honorable post than it has since become, but it was as important then as now. Again he had come through great personal danger without betraying the fallen Ministry under which he had served, and he could prove as useful to Townshend as he had been to Townshend's predecessors.

But on July 6, 1715, a few weeks before his final reconciliation with the Whigs, he published his second considerable history. As this was a favorable account of the wars of Charles XII of Sweden, the archenemy of George I in his Hanoverian domains, it is necessary to inquire why Defoe wrote a book with such dangerous political implications and why he published it just then.

He had always been interested in Charles, but he continued to regard him in two very different lights. As the last of the great Swedish kings, the military hero and the champion of Protestantism, Charles was sometimes named as the third man in Defoe's ideal company of soldier-kings, together with Gustavus Adolphus and William III. In reporting his death a few years later, Defoe actually adapted for him the same praise which he had borrowed for William from a tribute to Gustavus in the *Swedish Intelligencer:*

Their *Sons, Sons, Sons,* shall ask what *Gyant's That?*

Probably Defoe did not blame Charles for the repeated remonstrances which the Swedish ambassador Liencroon made against his critical remarks about Swedish affairs in the *Review,* even though he was questioned by the Ministry on account of them. But Charles had accepted the aid of William with the understanding that he would soon join the Allies against France, and after the accession of Anne he had broken faith. When he had repelled the enemies of Sweden, he had refused all offers of peace and had become the aggressor. He had violated international law by demanding the surrender of Count Patkul for torture and death. When his army lay idle in Saxony and he could have brought Europe to a just peace by his preponderating influence, he chose to march eastward for his own selfish ends. He had laid waste his former territories, and he had allowed Czar Peter to carry off his undefended subjects in the rear of his army while he advanced for further conquests. And after his daring escape from Turkey in 1714, he had turned his thoughts to revenge on George I, not only by threats against the Hanoverian domains, but by hostilities toward British ships in the Baltic and by plans for invading Scotland to establish the Pretender on the throne of Great Britain.[3]

But however deeply Defoe had thought about the career of Charles, *The History of the Wars, Of his present Majesty Charles XII* (1715) does not rise above the level of hack work. Hastily and carelessly thrown together for the booksellers, at a time when Defoe was greatly in need of money, and after the unexpected return of Charles from virtual captivity in Turkey had made him again the most talked-of sovereign in Europe, it is largely based on printed material easily accessible in England. Even the gross error of fact with which it concludes was only partly corrected in the supplement added in the second edition five years later.

In 1717, in *A Short View of the Conduct of the King of Sweden*, Defoe used the current English fear of Charles as a pretext for reworking *The History of the Wars* in a very skilful piece of feature-writing. In the same year had appeared *Minutes of the Negotiations of Monsr. Mesnager*, with a mystifying passage about Defoe's relations with Sweden. In this the French negotiator explained how the Swedish resident in London (the same Ambassador Liencroon who had protested against Defoe several times before) had recommended a certain pamphleteer to him as the author of a tract which (as we now know) Defoe had published in 1711. Mesnager was so pleased with the tract that he sent the author a hundred pistoles; but he learned that the author was in the service of the Secretary of State (Harley) and that he had told the Queen of the hundred pistoles.[4] The mystification was continued in the second edition of *The History of the Wars* in 1720, when the "Scots Gentleman in the Swedish Service" rejoiced that his earlier edition had met with "the bounty and goodness of his Swedish Majesty to an author unknown and remote."

Whether or not Defoe received any financial reward from Charles (which in all other respects seems unlikely enough), his views remained unchanged for more than twenty years: he admired the military hero, but he condemned the selfish tyrant and the incompetent statesman.

The three lives of Charles XII must have been profitable, for in 1723 an entirely different group of publishers brought out Defoe's history of Peter the Great, "written by a British Officer in the Service of the Czar." The literary techniques of *Peter* are almost identical with those employed in the two editions of *The History of the Wars*. In a great number of passages it is certain that exactly the same source material is being used, with a reversal of the point of view. *Peter* ends abruptly after the death of the Swedish king, with a lame apology that the book had become too long. The real reason for the abrupt close was probably that Defoe's material was mostly concerned with Charles, and that he had little to add after that had been employed.

So far we have found Defoe excelling rival historians only because, even in his hack work, he wrote with a more lively style; or because he knew more of the geography and the historical background of the countries concerned; or because he was better informed about current events and more alert to the policies which lay behind those events. But on May 24, 1720, appeared a book which in many respects justified his being regarded as a real historian.

The publishers of *Memoirs of a Cavalier* were almost the same as those for the second edition of *The History of the Wars*, but the superiority of the author's workmanship is almost beyond belief. The Cavalier who tells the story is no nonentity like the "Scots Gentleman," introduced only to give a bald account of the actions of his betters. He is the second son of his father, born in Shropshire and a student for three years at Oxford, where his chief reading (like Defoe's) was "history and geography." As his father's favorite son, he was offered an advantageous marriage. But he was allowed to follow his inclination to travel on the Continent; and from the day of his arrival at Calais, "on the 22nd of April, 1630," he is almost as real a man as Robinson Crusoe. The editor of a later edition found a name and a father for him—Andrew Newport, Esq., second son to Richard Newport, Esq., a young man who knew the countryside and the byroads because he "had traveled over the way he describes." (What man before Defoe had ever know them so well?) In a still later edition the Cavalier became the author in his own right as "the Honourable Col. Andrew Newport, a Shropshire Gentleman," and his modest personal narrative was furnished with a careful index to enable the student of military history to analyze his adventures.

Memoirs of a Cavalier was surely one of Defoe's own favorites. Here, as nowhere else, he could make full use of the manuscripts he mentioned many times, some of which must have been written by the Scottish soldiers of Gustavus; here he could express freely his own interpretation of English history during the civil war period; here he could throw a light on the chaos of war by his observations on social and economic conditions; here he could describe the battles (in England as well as in Germany) to which he could only allude in his other writings; here he could introduce his first hero and show Gustavus Adolphus as he liked to show his heroes—smiling.

The Cavalier's travels lay over roads which Defoe had traversed in person; the historical events had been familiar to him from childhood, in books and in the talk of the veterans he had known. There are discrepancies, as in most things written by such hasty writers as

Shakespeare and Defoe and Scott. The details of some battles or campaigns are confused; and although the Cavalier's manuscript is said to have been secured as plunder at or after the battle of Worcester (1651), it refers to the restoration of Charles II (1660). But soldiers have remarked on the accuracy of the military details, and historians have observed that the spirit of the English civil war is nowhere else so vividly presented. A master of historical narration in our own time has repeatedly declared that he has sought in his own writing to follow the method of Defoe's *Memoirs of a Cavalier*.[5]

Defoe could hardly have improved on the book, although he continued to make use of loose ends which he had omitted. Four years later, in the first volume of the *Tour*, he devoted twenty-three pages and a folding map to a diary of the siege of Colchester in 1648—a fascinating thing in itself, but quite out of scale where it appeared. Anywhere else in his writings he could call up anecdotes of a Cromwellian officer, or of the battle of Leipzig, or of the gallant Scots who fought in the Swedish army, or of Gustavus' system of supporting his horse by placing infantrymen in the gaps.

Eight years later Defoe tried to repeat this success with a military memoir laid mostly in Spain during the War of the Spanish Succession. Here again we catch echoes of long memories, as when Defoe allows his hero to refer (p. 5) to a painting in the house of the Earl of Mulgrave (the same nobleman who, as Duke of Buckinghamshire and Normanby holding the office of Lord Privy Seal, went with Nottingham in July, 1703, to badger Defoe in Newgate). The book was written, in part, as a humorous glorification of the vain old Earl of Peterborough, and it did make use of the name of an obscure veteran of the war. But for a modern reader it is most intelligible as an imitation of *Memoirs of a Cavalier* which did not equal its model.

The Memoirs of an English Officer (almost immediately renamed *The Military Memoirs of Capt. George Carleton*) found few purchasers, so that the reappearance of the unsold sheets with frequent changes of the title page or of some details of the dedication or the preface is one of the minor perplexities of Defoe bibliography. Even Dr. Johnson had never heard of it until late in life; but he sat up all night when a friend sent him a copy, and he "found in it such an air of truth, that he could not doubt of its authenticity."

The last issue of the book in the eighteenth century, a final attempt to work off the unsold sheets in 1743, was prompted by the War of the Austrian Succession, and the new title page acclaimed Carleton as "an English officer who served in the two last engagements against France and Spain." Sixty-six years later, when there was a renewed interest in Peninsular campaigns, the book was rediscovered by Walter Scott, who persuaded Constable to issue a handsome edition of it in 1809.

Since that time historians have been unable to let *Captain Carleton* alone. Sometimes, like Lord Mahon (later Lord Stanhope), they condemn Defoe scornfully, but give high praise to "Captain George Carleton, who has left us a plain, soldier-like narrative of what he saw and heard,—the most valuable, perhaps, because the most undoubtedly faithful and impartial, of all our materials for this war." Sometimes they reject *Captain Carleton* as an authority or pretend never to have heard of such a book; but they soon let the Captain slip in by the back door as "an English officer of those days" or as "an eye witness." Stebbing, after declaring that "it is too hazardous to cite Carleton's Memoirs as sober history," went on to base much of his life of Peterborough on him and even to cite him by name at least eight times.

It seems virtually impossible to write a history of the war in Spain in Queen Anne's time without drawing on the book, willingly or unwillingly, consciously or unconsciously. In a recent work professedly based on deep research in the great libraries and record offices, the Duchess of Popoli suddenly comes running out of Barcelona with her hair flowing down her back, to seek the protection of the gallant Earl of Peterborough—and the reader knows all too well that the modern historian (like his predecessors) is breathing the heady air of the *Memoirs of Captain Carleton*.[6]

The book has many of the high virtues of *Memoirs of a Cavalier*, but it is still an inferior production. Local guerrilla fighters such as the Miquelets were no equals for the gallant Scots in foreign service, and the erratic and amorous Earl of Peterborough was a grotesque substitute for the great Gustavus. A distant war to decide which of two men of straw would be made King of Spain had no such significance for Defoe's readers as wars for religious or political freedom in the Empire and in England. The hero himself is an old professional soldier, not a generous young volunteer; and even when he is more than a shadow, he is an anachronistic impossibility. The last of his fighting is over long before we reach the end of the book, and the later pages are padded with such extraneous matter as a singular mine explosion, an account of Spanish customs regarding convent life and religious worship, a surprising flight of eagles, bull feasts, a description of Madrid, and a narrow escape from being drowned.

The sudden change of title from *The Memoirs of an English Officer*, only eleven days after the book was published, could hardly be expected to increase its sale; more likely it was due to the vanity of Captain George Carleton himself. Some of the irrelevant digressions show the author's reliance on *The Ingenious and Diverting Letters of the Lady——'s Travels into Spain* (London, 1708), a translation of a French work by the Countess d'Aulnoy. But the worst digressions were due to the existence of an actual Captain George Carleton, who was not satisfied with giving his name to a book by Defoe but insisted on attempting to condense and to amplify Defoe's work while it was going through the press.

This explanation of Captain Carleton's intrusion would be mere guesswork if it were not confirmed in detail by marginal notes in a copy of the first edition owned by Sir Harold Williams. These contemporary notes were entered by someone who had compared the manuscript with the printed copy—someone who knew Peterborough and Carleton, but whose handwriting was unlike Defoe's. This annotator pointed out, near the top of page 76 (where an abrupt break occurs), "2 sheets wanting." As the book was printed in octavo, this may mean an omission of no less than 32 pages, not merely two pages of manuscript. Near the top of page 322, where there is another abrupt transition, the annotator remarked, "Here is much omitted that Lord Peterbor had approved." The notes indicate arbitrary insertions as well as omissions. The unnecessary list of names at the bottom of page 77 was labeled "ffoist." The four wildly irrelevant concluding paragraphs were dismissed by a note on page 351: "This Carleton foisted in to ye End as well as some few oth^r passages: which on reading may be distinguish[ed] to be his own."

Defoe had obviously intended to end the book with the highly characteristic sentence in which he gives the supposed reflection of the old soldier when he finds how English political parties disagree over the Treaty of Utrecht—a statement of Defoe's own political creed, which could be matched many times in his writings: "But *Whig* and *Tory* are, in my Mind, the compleatest Paradox in Nature; and yet like other Paradoxes, old as I am, I live in Hope to see, before I die, those seeming Contraries perfectly reconcil'd, and reduc'd into one happy Certainty, the Publick Good." Just after this, thanks to the annotator, we can be certain of the interference of the maundering veteran whose name Defoe had been obliged to employ, however little use he made of his confused reminiscences.

A page and three-fourths remained blank on the last leaf of Signature Z——, and Captain Carleton was still hanging around the printer's shop to see that this space was filled to his own satisfaction. One can trace the association of ideas by which Carleton was led to think of the four concluding paragraphs in their bewildering order. First he wished to insert one more statement about himself, and that led to a paragraph about his visiting General Mahoni at Madrid. The second paragraph was prompted by what Mahoni had told him about the battle of Saragoza (Saragossa). That in turn led him to insert a typical guidebook account of Saragoza, with special mention of its very numerous churches and convents. And that brought the old soldier to think of ending the narrative with a Roman Catholic prayer—perhaps a pious and natural conclusion for Carleton himself, but utterly incredible for Defoe. As a result, the four final paragraphs serve as an anticlimax to an already finished book, and of these four the two concluding ones give perhaps the strangest and most disconnected ending in existence for a book of military annals:

Saragoza, or Caesar Augusta, lies upon the River Ebro, being the Capital of Arragon; 'tis a very ancient City, and contains fourteen great Churches, and twelve Convents. The Church of the Lady of the Pillar is frequented by Pilgrims, almost from all Countries; 'twas anciently a Roman Colony.

Tibi laus, tibi honor, tibi sit gloria, O gloriosa Trinitas, quia tu dedisti mihi hanc opportunitatem, omnes has res gestas recordandi. Nomen tuum sit benedictum, per saecula saeculorum. Amen.[7]

In the same year which saw the publication of Memoirs of a Cavalier, Defoe embarked on his career as the official historian of pirates, highwaymen, and their fellows. The undertaking opened a new area for him, but his interest in the subject was already an old one. In his boyhood and early manhood the London Gazette had hundreds of notices of the Moorish pirates in northwestern Africa and (rather later) of the European pirates in the West Indies and Madagascar. In fact, it would have been hard to avoid some interest in piracy in the England in which Defoe grew up. Sir Robert Holmes, James II's "Sole Commissioner for Suppressing of Pirates," advertised a great reward for the apprehension of agents of the American pirates who appeared in England or in the plantations or other Dominions "with intent to seduce others of His Majesty's Subjects." Henry Morgan, who had returned from his exploits rich enough to buy a knighthood and to triumph in the King's Court Bench against his defamers, was awarded £200 damages from a publisher who had risked telling inconvenient truths about his career.

Defoe himself had been taken by Algerian pirates between Harwich and Holland. His friend John Dunton was terrified fifty leagues off the Lizard by the approach of a Virginia merchant vessel mistaken for a pirate from Sallee (the seaport on the northwest coast of Morocco). In a political pamphlet of 1697 Defoe remarked that "there is a difference in slavery, Algiers is better than Sally."[8] But it was in Sallee, the worst of Moorish cities, that Robinson Crusoe was held as a slave by a pirate; and the castle fort in the outer harbor which he had to pass as he escaped in an open boat with Xury is clearly depicted in the large plate of "Salee" opposite page 178 in John Ogilby's *Africa*, of which Defoe owned a copy.

Late seventeenth- and early eighteenth-century travelers, whose works Defoe knew so well and some of whom he knew in person—Bartholomew Sharp and Lionel Wafer and Thomas Phillips, William Dampier and Edward Cooke and Woodes Rogers—were sometimes pirates themselves, and all of them had been obliged to associate freely with pirates. During the 1690's England echoed with reports of Captain Avery, a pirate in four continents whose men kept drifting back to Ireland or England to be hanged. The significance for Defoe of the pirates (and to a less extent of the highwaymen and other criminals) may be sketched under six different heads.

Highwaymen were never thought of primarily as a source of military power. Although condemned robbers were often allowed to escape the gallows by serving abroad in the army, and notorious highwaymen often dignified their profession by declaring Jacobite sympathies, no one regarded them as a factor in international affairs. But after one unsuccessful attack on Algiers by Charles V of Spain in 1541, no nation seriously challenged the supremacy of the Moorish pirates in their favorite haunts before the nineteenth century. The greatest of European monarchs preferred to wage only local wars against them, or even to make temporary alliances to secure aid against their own European rivals or to purchase immunity for their own citizens.

The European pirates in America, Africa, or Asia had no such pretense of national existence. But they often had considerable fleets, and their amphibious forces in the West Indies sometimes sacked a fortified town. It was no longer likely that sea rovers would return from

the Spanish Main to defend England from an Armada, but Whitehall
approved of plans of West Indian conquest which presupposed co-
operation with buccaneers. The Captain Vaughan who served the
exiled James II at sea was tried at Justice Hall with some of Avery's
men; and although the charge against him was the nobler one of high
treason, he was hanged, like the pirates, at Execution Dock.

According to a romantic tale which Voltaire told as true and which
later found its way from his history of Charles XII to the immense
and learned critical record of Madagascar by the Grandidiers, about
1716 the Marquis de Langallerie and the pretended Landgrave de
Linange made a serious proposal to enlist the Madagascar pirates as
allies of Sweden and to employ Avery's fleet to aid Charles's invasion
of Scotland on behalf of the Pretender. Possibly Voltaire picked up
this story at Lausanne (where one of the principal streets still bears
the name of Langallerie, with a historical plaque in his honor). In
1721–22 sailors and ships of the Swedish Madagascar Company (by
no means hostile to the Madagascar pirates) were pressed into temporary service for the Pretender under the Duke of Ormonde in
Spain.[9]

A second source of public interest in the pirates, even more appealing than their supposed naval power, was their supposed wealth. One
of the unluckiest ventures of William III was his granting a charter to
Somers, Orford, Romney, and Shrewsbury which entitled them to fit
out a ship to prey upon the pirates. Although the great Whig lords
escaped from the prosecution intended by a Tory House of Commons,
their employment of Captain William Kidd as their agent led to his
hanging in chains at Execution Dock as one of the most famous but
least successful of pirates. In fact, there was little evidence to convict
him of piracy, and the prosecution had to rest its case primarily on his
killing of the gunner Moore. If the brutish but loyal Kidd could have
been persuaded to testify against his employers, he could have gone
free, and the course of English history might have been considerably
altered by the loss of four such eminent party leaders.

During the War of the Spanish Succession which followed, national
expenses continued to mount high above anticipated revenues. It was
fascinating (in the House of Commons or in the public press) to
reckon the vast sums which would be brought into the Exchequer if
the Madagascar pirates were allowed to purchase immunity. In 1703 a
detailed account of the finances of the Madagascar pirates was submitted, according to which, if they paid only a fourth of their esti-

mated wealth for pardon and immunity, the government would gain over six millions sterling—at that time far more than enough to wipe out the national debt. Four years later Peregrine, Marquis of Carmarthen, was offering a proposal to the House of Commons to explain why he (through whose zeal and industry a proposal for suppressing the Madagascar pirates had come to the Queen's attention) should be given command of an expedition of at least six men of war, "to protect the very great treasure that will be seized as well as that which the repentant pirates bring with them." The repentant pirates would presumably be allowed to bring back three-quarters of their estimated wealth for their own use, or about £18,000,000.

If such a proposal could make a sensation in Defoe's London, it was far more welcome in Edinburgh during the anguished years which followed the collapse of national hopes for a trading colony in Panama. In June, 1705, William Greg wrote repeatedly to Harley to tell him of the profound impression made on several of the grandees by two "Deputies from Madagascar," who talked of bringing five millions sterling and fifty ships from the pirates "to have themselves and their worthy fraternity enfranchised here." Although the senior delegate, Captain Bryholt, soon scaled down his estimate of the pirates' strength to ten ships and a thousand men, and his financial project to a plan for slave-trading from Madagascar to Brazil, he still got an enthusiastic reception from the African and Indian Company of Scotland.

A third source of Defoe's interest in piracy concerned the obstruction to trade. The exploits attributed to Avery and Kidd aroused such animosity in Asia as to endanger the existence of the East India Company. Traffic to and from the West Indies or Virginia was almost cut off at times by their successors on the high sea. Defoe was always alert to any menace to commerce; and in one of his last books he devoted a chapter to an earnest proposal for rooting out the pirates of Tunis, Tripoli, Algiers, and Sallee, in order to restore trade on the north and northwest coasts of Africa.[10]

Fourthly, as the first social historian, and himself a man intimately acquainted with Newgate, Defoe was deeply concerned about the conditions which were so largely responsible for the development of social outcasts and criminals. He had much to say of the economic struggle of an unprotected woman in London, of the fate of boys who grew up as foundlings, of the poverty of the west coast of Africa which gave rise to the trans-Atlantic slave trade, and of the unemployment of seamen after the Treaty of Utrecht which led so many of them to become pirates.

Still further, he had a romantic interest in the adventures of high-waymen and pirates. To one so fond of geography and travel, there was a fascination in the exploits of Captain Singleton in so many parts of the world, culminating at last in his return to England with all his wealth (repentant, no doubt, but under no obligation to give a fourth to the government, according to the old plan).

Finally, there was in the last years of Defoe's life a ready sale for lives of criminals. With the rapid increase of a semiliterate reading public, an exciting life of a really interesting criminal had a more immediate sale than any other book of the day. The greatest best-seller of modern times, *Robinson Crusoe*, required three months and twelve days to reach its fourth edition; five years later Defoe's *Narrative of all the Robberies, Escapes, etc. of John Sheppard* reached its eighth edition in four months. Once Defoe had decided to enter the field, he soon established himself as the biographer of pirates and (to a less extent) of other criminals of adventurous lives.

By the established custom of Newgate and Tyburn, the two officials who served the condemned man at the scaffold could lay claim to certain perquisites. The hangman was entitled to the clothes and the immediate personal possessions of those he executed, and the prison clergyman who rode with criminals on the cart to Tyburn (the Ordinary of Newgate) was authorized to sell their "dying speeches." Dying speeches might be works of political significance or of literary merit, if a Gilbert Burnet collaborated with a man like Lord Russell. More often, under the conventional guidance or authorship of an Ordinary like Paul Lorrain, they followed the baldest of patterns— details of crime to satisfy the mob, with the moralistic confession prompted (or composed) by the Ordinary, which so often made the condemned man meet death as "an unworthy son of the Church of England."

In 1714 some hack (or group of hacks), writing lives of highway-men and other criminals under the pseudonym of "Captain Alexander Smith," began to emphasize ribaldry and (through wholesale plagiar-ism from writers from Boccaccio to the authors of *The English Rogue*) to give a spurious literary tone to their narrative. A rival did not greatly overstate the case against "Smith" when he wrote:

What an object of contempt and ridicule is Captain Alexander Smith, *alias* Will. Hawkins, *alias* B——ge, *alias*, &c. His works are a confused lump of absurd lies, gross obscenity, awkward cant, and dull profaneness. If you find a story, or but one sentence, in all his scribbling that is even tolerable, depend upon it he stole it; he has the most unlucky talent at invention of any man breathing, for he's as great a stranger to fable as to truth. He's so far from writing probabilities (without which even a romance would be monstrous) that he tells you of things that are entirely impossible; lies that Sir John Mandeville would have been ashamed of. And yet the fool diverts the populace—and so does a monkey, but much more agreeably.[11]

In his earlier writings Defoe had much to say about pirates and highwaymen. Even in the first two parts of *Robinson Crusoe* there had been a good deal about mutineering and piracy. Later in the same year, in *The King of the Pirates*, he had written only to ridicule the exaggerated stories of Avery's wealth and power. But on June 25, 1720, he became a staff writer for John Applebee, a publisher who specialized in the lives of criminals.

After Paul Lorrain died in October, 1719, some financial arrangement must have been made by Applebee to satisfy the claim of the new Ordinary of Newgate. Even the unfortunate criminals expected to receive compensation for the publication of their shame. About the time Defoe abandoned the field, it appears that some of the criminals had learned the trick of selling exclusive rights to their lives to more than one publisher. But in the bantering letter which Jack Sheppard supposedly wrote after his temporary escape from prison, he added a postscript: "Pray, my services to Mr Or——di——y and to Mr App——ee" (the new Ordinary of Newgate and Daniel Defoe).

Between 1720 and 1726 Defoe seems to have made public appearances as "Mr. Applebee" or as "Mr. Applebee's man" and to have received from criminals in their cells or at the scaffold the manuscripts which he had previously furnished them and which were to be published immediately as their authentic lives. To the thousands who watched an execution, it must have been a very effective advertisement for a forthcoming "life" to see it handed by the criminal to his official biographer. Defoe produced biographies or other narratives of many criminals, with two each for the notables Jack Sheppard and Jonathan Wild. A few of these were written for other publishers than Applebee; and one was laid in France, telling of the Cartoucheans who murdered the English gentlemen near Calais.

But Defoe was far less interested in the sordid lives of pickpockets or housebreakers, important only on the day when they stood before the public to be hanged, than in the vast and complex subject of piracy. There had been a Dutch work on the buccaneers of the West

Indies, and occasional biographies or narratives of English pirates by a few other writers, before the first volume of *A General History of the Pyrates* appeared in 1724. But in that book, and in its second volume which was published in 1728, Defoe established himself as the supreme authority in the field.

This book has not only been a favorite of literary men, from Walter Scott and Stevenson to Conan Doyle and Herbert Ravenel Sass; according to the bibliographer Sabin, it has been indispensable for the study of certain aspects of American colonial history. But most of all it was a favorite with Defoe himself. In Mist's *Weekly-Journal* for May 9, 1724, the first volume of "Captain Charles Johnson's" *History of the Pyrates* was advertised to appear on the next Monday (May 11). In the *Weekly-Journal* for the following Saturday (May 16) the book was announced as published, and it was advertised again in many subsequent issues. In three numbers of the *Weekly-Journal* (May 23, June 6, and August 29) Defoe used his leader essays to review it and to promote its sale. Here, as nowhere else in his writings, we find Defoe appearing almost in his own person to show his unique mastery of a long and complicated book of his own which had just come off the press. The first of these essays ends on a note of high praise: "We received the same Kind of Pleasure from a Book of this Kind, as a Man does in travelling thro' a pleasant Country newly discovered, where every Thing he meets gives him an agreeable Surprize."[12]

Defoe was now fully established as the professional writer. We have an account of him as he was seen by his future son-in-law in this same year of 1724, at his suburban home at Stoke Newington, when he "amused his time, either in the cultivation of a large and pleasant garden, or in the pursuit of his studies, which he found means of making very profitable. He was now at least sixty years of age, afflicted with the gout and stone, but retained all his mental faculties entire." "All his mental faculties" had become "very profitable." The boy's delight was now the profession of the elderly man. In 1726 Defoe wrote, "now I study books, as I formerly did men."

In the last dozen years of his life he might write on a wide range of subjects—literature, magic, apparitions, the Devil, political controversies, the principal discoveries and improvements in the several arts and sciences, his friend the late Dr. Daniel Williams, one of his early heroes Sir Walter Raleigh, a bookseller's preface to the poems of Sedley, a tongue-in-cheek puff for a fortuneteller, the British woolen manufacture, or the unreasonableness and ill consequences of imprisoning the body for debt. Always he retained his keen sense of the human experience which lay in the years or the centuries which had passed. Of all his observations he could say, as he said of his own *History of the Pyrates*, "I am most entertained by those actions which give me a light into the nature of man."

Behind him lay his own wide range of experience, his vast reading, and his carefully collected notes. Now that most of his work for the government could be done in his own study, there was, at last, time to write. Much of this writing was devoted to his unremitting attack on the Pretender's claim to the British throne, which he regarded as a snake scotched but not killed. He not only gave accounts of the overt acts of the Jacobites, such as street riots and rebellion in arms. Following the tradition of the Greek historian Thucydides (and perhaps even more closely the pattern of the Infernal Council in Milton's *Paradise Lost*), he undertook to tell what went on in the secret meetings of the rebels or conspirators. This last device gave him a chance to use his favorite method of writing "Within Doors," and thus to show the hopelessness of the Jacobite cause as seen from the inside.[13]

A notable example of this method appeared early in 1710 in one of his favorite tracts, which he never tired of quoting as "the Doway letter"—*A Letter from a Gentleman at the Court of St. Germains*. By 1714 it had become his standard practice. *A True Account of the Proceedings at Perth* (1716) is so effective in this way that it has been widely accepted as a primary source for the history of the rebellion, and a modern historian has singled out its "councils" for particular notice: "Gives a full account of the Councils held at Perth on January 28, 1716, and following days, at which the retreat was resolved upon." So essentially true to fact were Defoe's "councils," and so lifelike in their narrative style, that in the *Miscellany* of the Spottiswoode Society *A True Account* was assigned to the Master of Sinclair. At least one Jacobite owner of the original tract scratched out the title-page ascription to "a Rebel" and wrote in his own attribution to "an old Royalist."

An even more daring variation of the method was Defoe's use of the so-called *Journal of the Earl of Marr's Proceedings* (1716), which he republished in England with a long Preface of his own in which he welcomed the *Journal* of the Pretender's Secretary of State as an exposure of the futility of all Jacobite schemes.

One should not suppose that Defoe had no imitators. A rival biography of Shrewsbury appeared entitled *The Life and Character of*

Charles Duke of Shrewsbury. In a Letter to a Noble Lord. By a Gentleman that was Privy to the most material Passages (1718). This was speedily and deservedly forgotten. But even today Defoe's *Memoirs of Publick Transactions in the Life and Ministry of his Grace the D. of Shrewsbury* (1718) is almost inescapable for an understanding of Shrewsbury. Nicholson and Turberville cite it at least eight times in the footnotes to their authoritative life of Shrewsbury, and they follow it much oftener than they cite it.

One special student of the art of biography (scornful of Defoe's biographies wherever he knew their author) saw in *The Memoirs of Majr. A. Ramkins, A Highland Officer, Now a Prisoner at Avignon* (1719, but actually 1718) a superlative example of what he took to be genuine autobiographical writing. He apologized for one long quotation by saying: "This is his account of the Battle of the Boyne, which is quoted at length because it shows vividly the difference between the autobiographer, who risks his neck, and the omniscient historian, who risks only his opinion."[14] But a student of Defoe recognizes the *Memoirs* as an example of his writing "Within Doors." "The Highland Officer" is not meant primarily to tell of his actions but to afford still another revelation of the futility of the Jacobite cause.

On the whole, Defoe's historical writing is remarkably accurate, especially in its portrayal of characters and motives, in its geographical and historical background. But any man who writes rapidly or who relies so often on his memory will make some mistakes in details. Defoe, like Scott, was rather careless about dates and numbers, and he was a notable historian only when he wrote of character and action and the significance of events. Sometimes, when he speaks of his own life, such slips seem strange indeed, as when he refers to the sixteen months between the death of King William and his own confinement in Newgate as six months, or to the twenty-six years between two of his books as "almost forty years." In some of the parallel lists of historical events, of which he was so fond, he admits great confusion. In a few other passages, there are obvious errors which must be regarded as slips of the pen, as when he attributes Mark Antony's speech over Julius Caesar to Octavius.

In his *Tour* Defoe made a deliberate attempt to shut out antiquarian research as foreign to his purpose. But he soon felt drawn to "the delightful view of antiquity," so that it was a matter of regret that he had begun by excluding his observations of ruins and monuments:

Though the earth . . . has defaced the surface, the figures and inscriptions upon most of these things, yet they are beautiful, even in their decay, and the venerable face of antiquity has something so pleasing, so surprising, so satisfactory in it, especially to those who have with any attention read the histories of past ages, that I know nothing renders traveling more pleasant and more agreeable.

But I condemned myself (unhappily) to silence upon this head, and therefore, resolving however to pay this homage to the dust of gallant men and glorious nations, I say therefore, I must submit and go on; and I resolve once more to travel through all these northern countries upon this very errand, and to please, nay, satiate myself with a strict search into everything that is curious in nature and antiquity. I mortify myself now with the more ease, in hopes of letting the world see, sometime or other, that I have not spent those hours in a vain and barren search, or come back without a sufficient reward to all the labours of a diligent enquirer.

His real objection to his predecessors' emphasis on antiquity was that it shut out all concern for the social and economic history in which he was the pioneer. He condemned the more famous books of travel on this very ground:

I observe that several of the authors I have just mentioned have written largely of the ancient families of the nobility and gentry of Great Britain; their originals, names, arms, and sometimes the history of particular men among them, who have made themselves famous in the world, of which the gentry of England have produced many.

But I have met with very few that take notice of the common people; how they live, what their general employment is, and what the particular employment of them is in the several counties respectively, and yet I found this an inquiry very full of useful observations.[15]

As a Puritan, Defoe felt constrained to say that "usefulness is, or ought to be, the principal aim of historians." But like the other creative artists who refused to divorce morals from art—Rembrandt, Milton, and Bach—he also stressed the sense of enjoyment, as when he declared that, of all subjects of reading and study, history is "the most delightful, as well as instructive."

The pessimism which falls upon so many elderly writers never clouded his vision as a historian, even amid the personal insecurities of his last days. But at times he wrote whimsically of the transitoriness of fame, by which the record of human achievement fades into a poem, or into a dimly remembered dream: "the Siege of Troy, were it unsung by Homer, what should we have known of it? And even now we scarce know whether it is a history, or that ballad-maker's fable to get a penny."[16]

XXII. TRAVELER

I ... was always too curious to look into every nook of the world wherever I came.

Robinson Crusoe (Tegg ed.), II, 201

THERE APPEARED on May 21, 1724, the first of the three volumes of what is perhaps the most characteristic book Defoe ever wrote. No other author of his time could have written *A Tour Thro' the whole Island of Great Britain,* but most of Defoe's life was an unconscious preparation for writing it.

No doubt, as novelist and historian, he made much use of conventional literary source materials. His working collection of books, manuscripts, and maps was (for his special interests) one of the most remarkable ever owned by an English author. But we would misunderstand his literary art, as well as much of his personal life, if we allowed ourselves to think of him primarily as having grown up in a library.

In the early eighteenth century most English literary men rarely stirred from London, and their slight knowledge of the outside world usually came from hearsay or from books. The excitement which the Earl of Peterborough aroused wherever he went was largely due to the fact that he had actually traveled. Pope was never out of the southern part of the island of Great Britain. Addison's one tour on the Continent was as conventional as his published account of it. Swift went back and forth on his unhappy trips to and from Ireland, fuming at a week's delay in Wales on account of adverse winds. Half a century later Dr. Johnson's visit to the Hebrides was thought to justify two major books and the astonishment of the world of letters. It is true that Johnson was a great reader of travels, and he spoke enthusiastically of the man who would visit the Great Wall of China. In his mind, at least, Johnson was willing to "Survey mankind, from China to Peru."

Steele arranged materials for the *Tatler* as reports from his own apartment and from three coffeehouses and a chocolate house in London and Westminster, and it was not long before the essays from his apartment began to crowd out the others; but Defoe's *Review* shows an unflagging interest in whatever was happening in western Europe. If we think of his contemporaries in velvet coats, smoking churchwarden pipes at their ease, we must picture Defoe in a rough weatherproof coat, on horseback or on foot, forever traveling and forever observing. Biographers have sometimes regretted that he missed the social life of the London coffeehouses; but his loss as a clubman was his gain as a citizen of the world. His firsthand knowledge of places and events, of the speech and manners and appearance and character of his fellow men, lies back of all his thought and all his writing.

Among literary men of the century his only rival as a traveler was John Wesley; but Wesley's journeyings were circumscribed by his work as an itinerant preacher. Defoe went to Bath, Epsom, Tunbridge Wells, and Derbyshire for his health; to Newmarket and Nottingham and Doncaster for the races; to Somerset for Monmouth's rebellion; to Portugal and Spain and France as a merchant; to Edinburgh to promote the Union between England and Scotland and to maintain good relations between the sister countries; to the Scottish Highlands to sound out a Jacobite chieftain. Often he was a news reporter, often a government spy.

On some pretext, or without any, he saw almost every nook of England, Wales, and Scotland, besides many regions on the Continent south of Denmark and west of Poland, Bohemia, and the Adriatic. He had exceptional information about some parts of Russia, probably at second hand. Once when he referred to "the grand seignior's terrace in the outer court of the Seraglio, next the sea," he apologized because he knew Constantinople only through his reading. If he could have shared the experiences of Crusoe, perhaps he would have liked best the long voyage round the world. He had what Crusoe called "the wandering disposition . . . born in my very blood."[1]

The untraveled Swift could ridicule the scanty knowledge of remote countries:

> So Geographers in Afric-Maps
> With Savage-Pictures fill their Gaps;
> And o'er unhabitable Downs
> Place Elephants for want of Towns.

Defoe had no opportunity to visit the interior of Africa. But long after it was opened to exploration by others, his account of the country in *Captain Singleton* (based largely on what he had learned from the narrative of the former Guinea trader Mr. Freeman[2] and from the reports of such friends as Governor Dalby Thomas, the ship's surgeon John Atkins, and others) was still considered a marvel.

Unknown regions shrank rapidly as the modern world was being outlined by travelers. But more important for Europeans than the gold and the ivory, the medicines and the furs, were the ideas brought back from abroad. Travelers made observations of the measurement of the earth's circumference, of eclipses and winds and ocean currents and tides. Theories of government, of human nature, of social relationships, of religion, were re-examined in the light of what could be learned about other peoples. A philosopher like John Locke need not surprise us when he refers to the practice of a tribe in the interior of Brazil. A young physician who had made a trip to Jamaica became a student of foreign plants and animals and a correspondent of inquirers everywhere. The studies of Dr. Hans Sloane were an easy mark for Tory ex-collegians and idle wits, to whom any learning not derived from classical literature might seem ridiculous. But Sloane continued to make his great collection, so largely based on the travels of himself and others, which later became the nucleus of the British Museum. We cannot be sure that Sloane and Defoe ever met; but the sale catalogue of Defoe's library in the British Museum is Sloane's own copy, and it is certain that Defoe used (and perhaps at one time owned) a long and important manuscript of travel now preserved in the Sloane Collection.[3]

Except to illustrate some statement of fact or some general proposition, Defoe rarely mentions his travels. He speaks of his capture by pirates as an example of the hazards of shipping in the Channel and the North Sea during the last years of Charles II. He tells of one of his earliest trips to France to describe the method of running past the customhouse, or what seems to have been his last trip to Paris to picture France at the time of the Mississippi Bubble in 1720. He repeats himself, as any rapid writer will do; but he rarely fails to confirm what he has stated before. When he tells how Verrio's paintings in St. George's Hall (Windsor Castle) were altered while he was abroad for several years, we can be confident that he is right. When he tells of the great bullocks he saw in Sussex in 1697, his second account will confirm his first in minute detail, although it was written thirteen years later, when his host had been dead for twenty-three years and no one could be expected to recall his previous statement.[4]

His first considerable trip from London was made in the winter when he was seven or eight years old. The last of the great Dutch wars had not yet begun, and the coal ships from Newcastle had been enjoying a flourishing business. This was near the time when his mother died, and the little boy seems to have been taken from his London home to stay with relatives. He went by way of Harwich on the North Sea, and then twelve miles on the inland waterway to Ipswich, which lay like a half-moon on the bank of the river. He must have found the ways of these seafarers wintering on land as interesting as David Copperfield did the life in Mr. Dan Peggotty's house. Long afterward he told of his boyhood impressions of Ipswich, when its prosperous shipmasters had moored their two hundred colliers along the riverside and had retired to the comforts of their homes. On this coast, some forty-five miles north of Harwich, Robinson Crusoe met with his first shipwreck.

About 1670 Defoe first drank the waters at Bath, and in that year or the next he was attending James Fisher's school at Dorking. Around 1676, on the course at Banstead Downs not far from Dorking, he became well acquainted with the sport of horse racing. More than forty-five years later he could still write of the Downs in a spirit of rapture: "When on the public race days they are covered with coaches and ladies, and an innumerable company of horsemen, as well gentlemen as citizens, attending the sport; and then adding to the beauty of the sight, the racers flying over the course, as if they touched it not, or felt the ground they run upon; I think no sight, except that of a victorious army, under the command of a Protestant King of Great Britain could exceed it." And "about four miles, over those delicious Downs," brings us to a health resort where he spent some of the few carefree hours of his life, seeing "nothing of business in the whole conversation of Epsom."[5] Later he recalled the observations he had made there in the late afternoons, after the company had reposed two or three hours in the heat of the day:

The ladies come to the shady seats, at their doors, and to the benches in the groves, and covered walks; . . . Here they refresh with cooling liquors, agreeable conversation, and innocent mirth.

Those that have coaches, or horses (as soon as the sun declines) take the air on the Downs, and those that have not, content themselves with staying a little later, and when the air grows cool, and the sun low, they walk out under the shade of the hedges and trees, as they find it for their diversion: In the mean time, towards evening the Bowling-green begins to fill, the music strikes up in the Great Room, and Company draws together a-pace: the gentlemen bowl, the ladies dance, others raffle, and some rattle; conversation is the general pleasure of the place, till it grows late, and then the company draws off; and, generally speaking, they are pretty well as to keeping good hours; so that by eleven a clock the dancing generally ends, and the day closes with good wishes, and appointments to meet the next morning at the Wells, or somewhere else.

But in 1676 the countryside was not devoted entirely to innocent mirth. Defoe's keen interest in highwaymen was already aroused by the most famous of English highway robberies, which was committed in the neighboring county of Kent by "Swift Nicks" Nevison at four o'clock one morning. Nevison crossed the Thames on a ferry and rode his bay mare to York, where he established an alibi by changing clothes and laying a bet with the Lord Mayor on the bowling green about eight o'clock on the same day.[6] This almost incredible exploit was long afterward dressed up in fictional form and transferred to an insignificant highwayman named Dick Turpin.

Before the death of Charles II (1685) Defoe had made many trips in England, and he had visited the Continent. In 1680 he was at Liverpool, apparently on business. In 1685 he was in Somerset with Monmouth's army. Within the next few years he had made at least two other trips abroad. He came to know the language and customs of Holland. It was probably in Flanders that he saw a painting of Solomon turning his back on the house of God and going in procession to sacrifice to the Devil. In a Flemish city conquered by Louis XIV he heard a public oration at the College of St. Omer, in which a Jesuit declared that the graduates of Oxford and Cambridge perjured themselves by the oaths they treated as trifles. He spoke contemptuously of news writers who blundered in geography because they "never went up the Rhine into Germany." He mentioned the baths he had seen at Aix-la-Chapelle, and he recalled the chamber of rarities he had visited in Munich. He referred familiarly to Hamburg, Amsterdam, and Paris, and he compared the long bridges at York and Ayr with the Rialto of Venice. He knew Florence, Rome, Abruzzo, and the towns of southern Italy. He remembered the details of a painting he saw in Naples.[7]

When he strayed into telling of "a wonderful passage cut through a mountain near Briançon, on the frontiers of Dauphiné," he brought himself up with the apology, "But this is a digression." In his many comparisons of Wales with the Alpine regions, he is speaking from long memories. In Wales, except for the language of the people, he could have imagined that he was passing from Grenoble to Susa, or through the country of the Grisons. The numerous Welsh lakes and even the popular fables about them reminded him of what he had seen among the Switzers. He went on: "I must confess, I that have seen the Alps, on so many occasions, have gone under so many of the most frightful passes in the country of the Grisons, and in the mountains of Tirol, never believed there was anything in this island of Britain that came near, much less exceeded these hills, in the terror of their aspect, or in the difficulty of access to them."[8]

The harbor of Marseilles, the canal of Languedoc, the palaces and the homes of the nobility near Paris and on the Loire and the Loing, were sources of endless interest to him. He objected to many things on the Continent, such as the wealth of the clergy and the poverty of the common people; but his nationalism did not obscure his vision: "Far be this from a True-born English temper in me, of being vain of my own country. I am none of them. I know too much of other parts of the world, which in comfortable climates, delicious fruits, charming, healthy, and pleasant weather, and some other things too, out-do us very much." Sometimes he liked to think of the possibility of escaping from the party tyrannies of England: "I assure you, gentlemen, strangers use us better abroad."[9]

In 1688 he rode as far as Henley to welcome William in his triumphal march to London. He was at Ipswich in 1689, and in 1690 he returned to Liverpool. After 1695 he traveled widely in England as an agent for William, and he rode through the Highlands to the northern extremity of Scotland. In his *Review* for February 22, 1711, he could say freely (although his recent tours for Harley were still kept secret as far as possible):

I have, within these twenty years past, traveled, I think I may say, to every nook and corner of that part of the island called England, either upon public affairs, when I had the honor to serve his late Majesty King William of Glorious (though forgotten) Memory—or upon my private affairs; I have been in every county, one excepted, and in every considerable town in every county, with very few exceptions. I have not, I hope, been an idle spectator or a careless unobserving passenger in any place; and I believe I can give some account of my travels if need were.

One writer has suggested that "Defoe was already a traveler when Harley became his patron; his knowledge of England was in all probability one reason why the minister employed him."[10] In 1722 he was still journeying in England to check doubtful passages in his forth-coming *Tour*.

Wherever he traveled, Defoe was the poet, the novelist, the histo-rian, and the social philosopher, as well as the commission merchant, the political agent, or the accountant to the commissioners of the Glass Duty. He expressed regret that he failed to arrive in Hertford-shire to see a maid possessed by the Devil. He lingered on his travels to see the bottom of the roads dug up. In bursts of poetic feeling, when he reached each extremity of the island, east or south or west or north, he went beyond the farthest inch of dry ground and set his foot or his horse's feet into the sea. Sometimes he traveled on horse-back or by stagecoach; sometimes he walked. After the favorite com-rade of his journeys had settled in Scotland, he inserted an advertise-ment in his *Review:* "A person about 50, who designs for his diver-sion only to travel into several parts of the West, would be glad of a suitable companion in his foot perigrinations. He may be heard of at Mr. Salkeld's, a Bookseller in Cornhill."[11] Nine days later he changed the advertisement to read "An elderly person"—but that description could not have seemed suitable for Defoe.

His movements may seem to us painfully slow; but we have lost as much as we have gained by speed. He saw and heard, and did not merely fly over. During a political crisis he wrote: "I have traveled near 300 miles, through the tumultuous crowds of the poor distracted people. I have discoursed with them, and I have found them verily persuaded to believe these things." When he was in Tunbridge Wells for his health, he studied his fellows on the walks, "where fools and wise men often talk together for mutual edification." At Plymouth, on his second mission for Harley, he saw a great storm in the Channel, with the loss of nearly all of a fleet of fourteen ships, and here again *Robinson Crusoe* was slowly coming to birth. Parts of *Moll Flanders* reverse the travels he later outlined in his *Tour*. The publisher of the second edition of his *Memoirs of a Cavalier* was convinced by the expert knowledge of the terrain that the author must have been the Cavalier himself.[12]

When Defoe was moving about Spain as a commission merchant, he was acquiring his store of Spanish proverbs, the knowledge of the country which reappeared in *Captain Carleton*, and the insight into trade with South America and the West Indies which underlies his proposals for an English settlement in Chile or the Argentine, for the conquest of the West Indies, or for the development of the South Sea trade. He admitted that the extreme fondness of the Scots for foreign travel interfered with labor at home; but he remarked on the liberal education of the Scottish gentlemen who had gained reputation abroad, whereas the English gentry often stagnated in their own country.[13]

He declared that a student could learn from the dead by reading, but he could learn from the living by travel:

> The desire of travel is a happy curiosity to him who has a genius to improve it; . . . If I were asked what countries I would have him visit, I should name Spain, France, Germany, Muscovy; but, above all, Italy. Here he should make his longest stay; here he will meet with many remains of the grandeur of the greatest people in the world; he will observe the boldness and skill of modern architecture in their churches and palaces; he will meet with every thing that's rare and wonderful in gardens, terraces, fruits, pictures, statues, and libraries; he will have an opportunity of looking into the wisdom and policy of its several commonwealths; of observing the general good sense of its inhabitants; and, above all, the politeness and delicate wit of its men of letters.

But he was quick to admit that travel could be supplemented by reading: "I have sometimes after supper traveled throughout two or three provinces of the Persian Empire without the least fatigue, and rise fresh the next morning to pursue my journey. I have perhaps that day gone over a great part of the Mogul's dominions, and visited China, and could give a better account of the laws, policies, trade, and manufactures of those several countries than any of our East-India captains."[14]

Before the publication of his *Tour*, books of travel and topography too rarely came home to "men's business, and bosoms." Camden's *Britannia* told more of Anglo-Saxon etymologies or Norman charters or ecclesiastical foundations than of the modern England in which men lived. Adams' *Index Villaris* emphasized the noblemen and gentry residing in each town and the Deanery in which a parish was located, so that a reader could tell whether any town had a baronet or three gentlemen living in it, or whether the nobleman of the neighborhood had received the Garter. Defoe's *Tour* is summarized in part by a modern historian (who does not take the trouble to tell that his statement is based on Defoe): "London drew provisions and necessaries from all over the country, coals by sea from Newcastle, cheeses from Cheshire, droves of geese and turkeys waddling from Norfolk, timber from Sussex and black cattle from Wales, fresh salmon from the Severn and Trent and even from the Tweed."

Defoe's writings have influenced the travels of his successors all over the world, whether those successors have gone only to Walden Pond at the edge of a New England village or as far away as Vailima in the Samoan Islands of the Southern Sea. When René Caillié came back to France in 1828 to win the national prize for exploration (as the first white man to tell of reaching the mysterious city of Timbuktu, and opening a vast region of the Dark Continent to Europeans), he spoke of the meager education which had shaped his poverty-stricken youth: "The History of Robinson Crusoe, in particular, inflamed my young imagination: I was impatient to encounter adventures like him; nay, I already felt an ambition to signalize myself by some important discovery springing up in my heart."[15]

XXIII. PROJECTOR

I who am originally a projector.

The Political History of the Devil (Tegg ed.), p. 272

THE FIRST PUBLISHED BOOK to which Defoe ever signed his initials as the author was *An Essay upon Projects* (1697). His last tract issued during his lifetime was *An Effectual Scheme for the immediate Preventing of Street Robberies, and suppressing all other Disorders of the Night*, published on December 15, 1730, only four months and nine days before his death. Neither work ranks near the top of his literary achievements, but both are highly characteristic of Defoe's way of thinking. It was *An Essay upon Projects* which Benjamin Franklin recognized as having influenced his life; it was *An Effectual Scheme* which anticipated by two centuries the problems of modern lie-detection procedures.

From boyhood his most cherished belief was that most of mankind's problems could be solved by the ingenuity of man. Classical scholars often maintained that the golden age lay in the past; Defoe was always an advocate of progress. What interested him most in ancient history was the record of how men made their inventions and achieved their discoveries. Like Robinson Crusoe, he could have said of himself, "My unlucky head . . . was . . . filled with projects and designs."

The age in which he grew up had special need of projectors. The Fire of London had called for the rebuilding of the city. After that came the development of stock companies, the improvement of highways, the gradual substitution of machinery for manual labor, the expansion of overseas trade, the growing interest in natural science, and the long-continued wars with France which demanded an immensely increased national revenue.

The poverty of many of the aristocracy and gentry, who had some inherited capital but no productive employment, led them to promote highly speculative enterprises at home and abroad. In 1687 Phipps recovered for his aristocratic patrons £300,000 from a West Indian wreck, and this dazzling success stimulated attempts to recover coin or bullion in many parts of the world. In May, 1691, an experiment was made on a wreck in Scotland with "a new engine" in the form of a diver's bell with air supplied by barrels. On October 17 of the same year a Cornishman named Joseph Williams patented a diving engine.

Defoe made his first venture as a projector when he invested £200 for ten shares in the company formed to exploit Williams' invention. Because of his energy and his skill in bookkeeping, he was made secretary-treasurer, without salary and against his desire. To provide working capital, ten shillings was levied on each share; and the secretary-treasurer was required to collect the assessment. Williams had invested no money in the company but had received four hundred shares for his engine; and now that a cash assessment was levied on his stock, he gave Defoe part payment in money and part in notes. But on February 3, 1693, he was suing Defoe and the goldsmith who had cashed the notes. The goldsmith replied that he had received them from Defoe in the regular course of business; Defoe stated that he had sought only to recover the amount he had advanced on them to meet Williams' own assessment. As some of the notes proved worthless, Defoe lost not only the £200 he had invested in the company but part of his loan to Williams.

We do not know whether Williams won or lost his suit, but it is clear that he had received £2,360 in shares for his invention of an unsuccessful diving engine. Later Defoe referred philosophically to his own misfortune as a warning to other investors: "I could give a very diverting history of a patent-monger, whose cully was nobody by myself."

So ardent a projector as Defoe was not to be discouraged by the failure of one diving engine. Twenty years later his brother-in-law Robert Davis wrote to Robert Harley, then Earl of Oxford and Lord High Treasurer, to offer for sale a better one of his own construction, inclosing the following certificate which had been signed nine years earlier:

We whose names are hereunto set, inhabitants of the Lizard parish, in the county of Cornwall, do certify that Mr. Robert Davis did, in his diving engine, go down in the sea several fathoms under water, at a place called Purpeare [Polpeor?] Cove, and did sing the hundredth Psalm under water, and afterwards go several times under water in his said engine at the Bumble Rocks, where were taken up several bars or pigs of silver, some years ago. We do further declare that there have been several persons with divers sorts of diving engines in order to go under water at the silver wreck aforesaid; but none of them could ever go down to that depth the said Davis did; nor were their engines so completely contrived for going under water as the said Mr. Davis's is. To the truth of the premises we have set our hands this five and twentieth day of September, 1704.[1]

But even this perfected engine of Robert Davis was being offered for sale at a fraction of its original cost. Again Defoe appears as the unlucky projector—for he must have prompted the letter. Davis himself was settled as a shipbuilder in Scotland, where he was unlikely to hear that the son of Defoe's patron in London had received a patent for salvaging wrecks. It is hardly credible that Davis would have risked such an offer to the man who was virtually Prime Minister, or that he would have dared to identify himself as the agent of Defoe without the approval of his brother-in-law.

In the next year after Defoe had bought shares in the company formed to promote Williams' diving engine, he invested in another equally unsuccessful speculation. But this one might have been highly profitable if his impending bankruptcy had not brought it to an untimely end.

Fourteen years later the eminent scientist Nehemiah Grew advocated the raising of civet cats in England for the sake of their glandular secretion, a basic commodity in the manufacture of perfume, which had become a monopoly of the Dutch. In this field, as so often elsewhere, Defoe was in advance of his contemporaries, and he suffered a personal loss through his foresight and his daring.

In 1692 he owned sixty-nine or seventy civet cats. But in less than one year he had been obliged to abandon this establishment to men who first stripped him of his property and then sued him for his alleged failure to meet his obligations to them. In the collapse of his affairs during that long year of bankruptcy, most of the outsiders who had a hand in his affairs were able to profit by his misfortunes. In his attempt to pay for the civet cats and then to sell them, Defoe lost his down payment of £200, his notes for £300, and nearly £800 of his mother-in-law's money.[2]

Defoe was struggling in the toils of complete bankruptcy, with neither time nor capital to make a success of any enterprise. His attempt to raise civet cats was perhaps a desperate venture, undertaken by a desperate man to save his estate from ruin. But the venture itself was no absurdity.

A third project of Defoe was highly successful for a time, and he might well have become a rich man if political persecution had not put an end to it in the summer of 1703. At some time after 1694 he developed a brick and tile factory on marsh lands near Tilbury, which he had owned since about 1690. On March 6, 1697, Daniel Foe, brickmaker, was paid £20 for bricks used in building the Greenwich Hospital. A little over six years later a legal claim was made for drink allegedly provided to his workmen, and Defoe answered this from Newgate four days before he was sentenced to the pillory. Even if we suppose that the claim was a just one, there is no evidence that he did not pay his bills while he was solvent, or that his brick and tile works fell into difficulty until the Tory government drove him into hiding.

The clearest explanation of his operations near Tilbury appears in a letter to Harley:

All my prospects were built on a manufacture I had erected in Essex, all the late King's bounty to me was expended there. I employed a hundred poor families at work, and it began to pay me very well. I generally made six hundred pounds profit per annum. I began to live, took a good house, bought me a coach and horses a second time, I paid large debts gradually, small ones wholly, and many a creditor after composition whom I found poor and decayed, I sent for and paid the remainder to, though actually discharged.

But I was ruined *the shortest way*.[3]

In the same letter Defoe tells Harley that his loss through the closing of the brick and tile works was above £2,500, and later he put this at £3,000 or £3,500—no real discrepancy when we recall that claims and interest on the claims were mounting steadily.

Elsewhere Defoe makes several references to the few years of happiness he enjoyed in his house on the Thames near the river's edge: to his small pleasure boat rowed by two servants, to his coach and horses, and to the view he had from the shore. A French biographer has sought to complete Defoe's felicity during his interval of prosperity by giving him an acknowledged mistress at Tilbury.[4] The only evidence is that such a charge appeared in *The True-Born Hugonot*, a doggerel poem expressing the attitude of extremists who hated the reformation of manners as much as they hated political freedom and religious toleration. The poem's added charge that Defoe's coachman did not know where his master went at night meant only that the secret adviser of King William did not make a confidant of his coachman.

The totally unconfirmed statement that Defoe kept a mistress near his home and his place of business did even less justice to his intelligence than to his character. Such a falsehood would be absurd if laid in London—but a credulous reader in London might believe anything discreditable to a man he disliked if it were laid out of the city in an obscure place like Tilbury. This technique of what the wise Dr. Arbuthnot called "the art of political lying" was used later many times against Defoe. Attention could be distracted from the justice of his cause and the success of his political missions by an account of an imaginary happening hundreds of miles away—an alleged prosecution for reflections on a public official, an alleged flight from creditors, an alleged theft of a horse in Coventry. As soon as one falsehood was exposed, it could be replaced by another laid in a more distant place. But it is inexcusable that this long-forgotten lie about a mistress at Tilbury should have been repeated two and a half centuries later as an accepted fact.

Defoe was justly proud of having "employed 100 poor people in making pan-tiles in England, a manufacture always brought from Holland," and his brick and tile works were admirably located with water carriage for the London market. But original projectors rarely accumulate fortunes. A few weeks after he was discharged from Newgate Prison, the Great Storm swept over England, stripping roofs in London and creating an undreamed-of demand for new pantiles. But Defoe no longer had any tiles to sell, or any kilns to bake them.

It is Defoe's ideas which are significant for the world today, not his business undertakings. When Benjamin Franklin told of his father's little library, he wrote: "There was also a book of Defoe's called an *Essay on Projects* and another of Dr. Mather's *Essays to do Good,* which perhaps gave me a turn of thinking that had an influence on some of the principal events of my life."[5] This reference is significant for Defoe alone. Either Franklin had forgotten everything about Mather's feeble and verbose little volume except its misleading title or (as elsewhere) he went out of his way to flatter Boston and the descendants of Mather.

The Preface of *An Essay upon Projects* was directed to "Dalby Thomas, Esq., One of the Commissioners for Managing His Majesty's Duties on Glass, &c." Defoe addressed him here not as the commissioner under whom he served, nor as his friend, but as the best judge of the subjects discussed in the book. He reminded his friend that one of his plans had been contrived long before; but he acknowledged his indebtedness to Thomas for some ideas about county banks, warehouses, and friendly societies.

Dalby Thomas was a man of more energy and daring than sound judgment. In 1687 he was associated with others in procuring a monopoly for the sale of commodities from the West Indian plantations; but this was opposed by the West Indian merchants in London, and it was dropped after the Revolution. In the 1690's he was associated with Thomas Neale in proposing taxes of the wildest sort, such as two shillings a week on beds to yield £8,000,000 a year, and a tax on pictures and graven images to yield another fabulous sum (with the added advantage that pictures and graven images were condemned by Holy Scripture). Thomas joined Dr. Hugh Chamberlen in a project to finance a "General Fishery" by issuing paper money secured by lands, on the assumption that the annual income from the lands for one hundred years could be anticipated without detracting from their value. Such schemes were based on two great fallacies: that immense new levies could be laid with no additional burden on citizens already paying the established taxes, and that wealth could be doubled by retaining capital and floating its equivalent in paper currency.[6]

Defoe avoided Thomas' financial panaceas; he profited by his sounder ideas, his friendship, and his political influence. In April, 1694, Thomas was made one of the managers of the Million Pound Lottery; and in September, 1695, he was made one of the three commissioners for managing the new Glass Duty (a tax on windows). Defoe was soon made accountant for the commissioners, and he held the office until the Glass Duty was repealed in 1699. He was also named as a manager-trustee for the royal lotteries in October, 1695, and again in March, 1696. Nineteen years later he explained his first appointment under Thomas: "Providence . . . made me refuse the best offers of that kind [such as an appointment at Cadiz in 1694 as a commission merchant], to be concerned with some eminent people at home [Dalby Thomas and others] in proposing ways and means to the government, for raising money to supply the occasions of the war then newly begun. Some time after this I was, without the least application of mine, and being then seventy miles from London, sent for to be accountant to the commissioners of the glass duty, in which service I continued to the determination of their commission." Eleven years after that, he still recalled that he had known when punctual bookkeeping "has recommended a tradesman so much to his creditors, that after the ruin of his fortunes, some or other of them have taken him into business, as into partnership, or into employment, only because they knew him qualified for business, and for keeping books in particular."⁷ It is quite likely that Thomas was one of Defoe's many creditors, but there is no other evidence for it than this passage.

In September, 1703, Thomas (now Sir Dalby Thomas) was made governor and general of the African Company's settlement in Guinea; and he sailed from Portsmouth with two frigates and four companies of soldiers, facing the prospect that he would soon be carried off by fever. Defoe kept in touch with him, perhaps by personal correspondence, certainly by interviewing travelers and by reading the governor's reports to the African Company in London. At late as 1728 he was arguing in favor of tea-planting in Guinea, on evidence from the garden of the late governor.

Perhaps it was his friendship for Sir Dalby Thomas which led Defoe to dabble a little in stock of the African Company, giving £800 for two shares which fell so in price that he got less than £100 for them. By June, 1710, he had no investment in the company. In the long struggle in Parliament between the company and its unchartered rivals, he supported the company's right to a fair return on its outlay and the importance of the African trade (which he said could not be maintained by the Separate Traders). But he was not forgetful of the bad management of some later governors. And he saw the folly of delegating all trade to vast organizations, which often substituted stockjobbing and committee direction for effective personal management: "we are so fond of companies, it is a wonder we have not our very shoes blacked by one, and a set of directors made rich at the expense of our very black-guards."⁸

His views on human slavery (the main reason for the African Company's existence) are not basically inconsistent. He pointed out that the slave trade was profitable, and that without slaves there was no way of getting sugar from Barbados or sustaining the West Indian colonies. But when he spoke of the moral wrong, he was more than a century in advance of his fellow countrymen.

Sometimes he spoke of the helpless Africans with pity, as wretches who were treated "as a poor heap of useless creatures, fit to be bubbled, and made slaves of to the rest of the world." Sometimes he blamed the evil on the undeveloped commerce of western Africa; the natives, among whom slavery had been established for many centuries as the basis of the economic order, having nothing else to offer to the world, sold each other. Elsewhere, while admitting the economic advantage of slavery, he regretted that things were as they were:

The work of the islands, which is the planting canes and making sugar, whether in the field or in the sugar-works, is of that nature, the labor is so severe, the climate so hot, the food so coarse, that no Europeans were ever yet found could go through it—at least not to the profit of the planter. They must have people used to the extremities of the weather, entirely subjected to the government and correction of the cruelest masters, that they may be whipped forward like horses, that can live on what is next to the offal of food, like beasts, and never knew better; that have the strength of the ox and know no more of liberty; and that suffer everything the horse suffers, but being flayed when they are dead, which would be done too, if they could get 6d. for the hide—These they get their wealth from—And these, I doubt, they have much to answer about, as to cruelties and barbarities; which it is not my present work to inquire into.

In his works of fiction he showed unusual interest in the moral welfare of people usually regarded as slaves rather than as human beings. But in his *Reformation of Manners,* where he was free to speak as a social satirist without consideration of economic problems, he wrote one of the earliest and most powerful attacks on the institution of slavery:

> The harmless natives basely they trepan,
> And barter baubles for the souls of men;
> The wretches they to Christian climes bring o'er,
> To serve worse heathens than they did before.

Twenty-four years later, in the midst of his discussion of the economic outlook in Africa in his *Atlas Maritimus & Commercialis,* he quoted (inexactly, from familiar memory) the second line of the same passage from his *Reformation of Manners.*[9]

Defoe favored or opposed the plans of three projectors more famous than Sir Dalby Thomas. These were William Paterson, John Law, and Charles Montagu (better known as Baron, later Earl, of Halifax). It has been assumed that Defoe acted as adviser in the 1690's when Halifax was carrying out his daring financial measures to restore national credit—such as the founding of the Bank of England and of the New East India Company, the floating of exchequer bills bearing interest until redemption, and the recoinage of the nation's unmilled and badly clipped silver money.

Defoe praised Halifax' device for anticipating the revenue with interest-bearing notes. When Halifax secured the passage of "An Act for giving like Remedy upon Promissory Notes as is now used upon Bills of Exchange, and for the better Payment of Inland Bills of Exchange," Defoe wrote to express approval (ostensibly without knowing that Halifax had written the bill) and to ask for more explicit instructions about what he should write on the subject. Later he indorsed the principle of paper credit for the inland trade.

We know of only four letters from Defoe to Halifax, of which three survive. In April, 1705, he thanked Halifax for mentioning him to Lord Treasurer Godolphin and hinted that he had kept Halifax' secrets when he passed through Nottingham's inquisition. That summer he wrote two letters thanking Halifax and his friends for a subsidy to the *Review* and sent copies of a new pamphlet in which he had replied to Dr. Drake's attack on the Ministry. In November of the next year he informed Harley that Halifax had asked him for reports on Scotland, adding that he would not send further reports without Harley's approval.[10]

In the last book of *Jure Divino* he devoted eighty-eight lines to the praise of Halifax—more than to Marlborough, far more than to any other nobleman. He spoke of Halifax' skill as orator and poet, as statesman and "man of conduct"; but he rejoiced chiefly in his triumph against the attempted prosecution by the Tories in 1704. The long passage on Halifax was probably completed when *Jure Divino* was first announced for publication in the autumn of that year. When this vindication of Whig doctrine was finally published, the folio edition was offered to subscribers at the unusually high price of ten shillings. Halifax was a very wealthy man; perhaps he was one of the principal subscribers.

Halifax and Defoe acted toward each other with extreme discretion, for they both knew what it meant to be imprisoned for political acts or opinions. Every new step was taken by Halifax. Not a scrap of his letters to Defoe can be found, and his most important communication was expressed cryptically and was transmitted orally through Defoe's brother-in-law, who apparently did not understand the message he carried. Defoe was almost equally cautious in his dealings with Halifax; he never knew how far he could safely go with a powerful nobleman who was more politician than projector.

William Paterson appeared in Defoe's life several times: first as a fellow servant under William III, when Paterson resided at Hampton

Court and was sometimes consulted by the King on economic matters and on the affairs of Scotland; next as Defoe's intermediary with Harley, and later as a fellow agent under Harley; last as a querulous and greedy rival, whose paper calculations showed such indifference to the rights of the nation's creditors that Defoe called him "that infamous projector."

John Law had won notoriety in Scotland and in London early in life, before his escape to France after killing a man in a duel. But in July, 1719, Defore did not know his real name or nationality, referring to him as "an English gentleman, whose name is Laws." Later that year Defoe had come to regard him with amazement and suspicion. During most of 1720 he watched Law's projects with increasing contempt, especially when the rapid development of the South Sea Bubble made it appear that England would suffer from a financial mania like that of the Mississippi Company in France. In August he told an amusing narrative of his recent trip "upon some extraordinary business over to France," describing the French shopkeepers' eagerness for English gold on his arrival and their unwillingness to accept the legalized paper he was supposed to be bringing back from Paris on his return. Near the end of 1720, when Law boasted that he could shake the finances of England by manipulating the stock market, and in 1721, when Law sought to re-establish himself in London, Defoe opposed him openly. In the years of Law's subsequent exile and poverty he referred to him with pity, as a victim of the extravagance and dishonesty of the French regent.

Defoe recognized Law's achievement in funding the French national debt and eliminating the huge profits made by farmers of the revenue; but he was one of the first to foresee the collapse of Law's system when it had been blown into a bubble. Furthermore, he thought about the significance of such success and such failure. So enlightened a man as the ambassador to France, the Earl of Stair, thought of Law primarily according to his own concerns. Stair actually introduced Law in Paris, and sought at first to recoup his own finances. His later denunciation of Law to the British Secretary of State was tinged by his personal disappointment. Defoe's own estimate was quite objective:

> The case is plain, you must put on a sword, kill a beau or two, get into Newgate, be condemned to be hanged, break prison, IF YOU CAN,—remember that by the way,—get over to some strange country, turn stock-jobber, set

up a Mississippi Stock, bubble a nation, and you may soon be a great man; if you have good luck, according to an old English maxim:—

> Dare once to be a rogue upon record,
> And you may quickly hope to be a Lord.[11]

A few months after the rise and fall of the Mississippi Bubble in France came the rise and fall of the South Sea Bubble in England. This was the wildest of the projects in Defoe's England, and he has sometimes been mistakenly held to blame for it.

But Defoe was concerned with the long-range possibilities of English commerce and English colonization. The politician Harley thought very little about the future prospects of English trade; his organization of a South Sea Company in 1711 which would appeal to speculative investors gave him an opportunity to save his Ministry by allowing the company to assume responsibility for increasingly burdensome floating debts. To the Hanoverian court circle, to many politicians and capitalists, and to the general public in 1720, six years after Harley's company had passed to the control of his Whig successors, South Sea stock offered a road to immense wealth by quick purchase and resale in a bull market.

Defoe was bitterly opposed to the frantic or dishonest speculations of 1720, and he had given only cautious and grudging support to Harley's rather dubious project of 1711. It was the opportunity for expanding commerce and for permanent colonization that aroused his enthusiasm.

As a lifelong admirer of Sir Walter Raleigh, he was always interested in projects for English expansion in South America. Perhaps he admired Raleigh primarily because he was a projector, a patriot who believed that the future of England lay in maritime and colonial development. He not only knew Raleigh's printed works; he owned some of his manuscripts and charts as well. In his youth, too, he heard how it had been proposed under Cromwell to establish a colony between Spanish North and South America. That plan was set aside for an unsuccessful attack on Hispaniola, but the failure was offset in part by the capture of Jamaica. Even after the middle of the eighteenth century, a distinguished French visitor in England recorded the current belief that only the death of Cromwell prevented his conquest of the New World.

But it was as a young merchant in Spain that Defoe learned of the enormous profits which Spain derived from its colonies. In a Europe impoverished by the scarcity of gold and silver, the most exciting reading of the year was found in the reports of the galleons from Mexico and South America, with many millions of pounds worth of bullion, besides vast quantities of jewels and silks and spices and dye-wood. There was an immense amount of smuggling, even on the royal galleons; but the King of Spain's "royal fifth" of all precious metals mined in the colonies and his import tax on all goods brought into Spain had become the principal sources of his revenue, without which he could not wage war or maintain his civil government. Delay of the great flota or even of the smaller flotilla threatened national catastrophe. When the English fleet attacked the galleons which had run into Vigo Bay (1702), the Spanish government seized most of what had escaped the English, because it had anticipated the revenue expected from these ships.[12]

Defoe knew how badly the trade was managed and how easily it could be expanded. For thirty-five years he kept coming back to the subject. The special appeal of the South Sea trade was that it offered the prospect of an expanding commerce. Most markets were glutted with goods, or they were difficult to reach because of natural barriers or artificial governmental regulations. Established trade with Old Spain was the most important part of England's foreign commerce, and this was not to be lightly sacrificed by provoking national ill will. But the future lay in the West Indies, in Mexico and Central America, most of all in South America.

Spain not only controlled the trade of its American empire from the eastern harbors in Mexico and Central America; from Acapulco on the west coast of Mexico its ships had an avenue to the Orient. The notion that a like success was possible to outsiders lay behind the Scottish attempt to combine an East India Company with a trading colony on the Isthmus of Panama.

To Defoe the Orient was of secondary importance. The West Indies and South America offered the most promising markets in the world—by trade to Spaniards, or to the aboriginal peoples, or to the settlers in new English colonies. The only serious barriers were the monopoly built up by the French while they held Spain as a conquered province and the jealousy of the Spaniards themselves, who (incapable of managing their overseas trade) were unwilling to admit rivals. French competition could be overcome by Marlborough's success in war, by control of the sea, or by superior commercial management. Spanish jealousy would have to be overcome by conquest, placated by treaty, or circumvented by trading through newly established English colonies. In the early years of the War of the Spanish Succession, while Archduke Charles was a needy claimant to the Spanish throne and a dependent of Queen Anne, concessions to the English could be won from him; but it was understood that if he ever became the real King of Spain, he might have to revoke these concessions or lose his new throne.

For thirty-five years, whenever there was a prospect of war with Spain, Defoe recurred to the project of seizing Havana or the nearby Bay of Honda and thereby getting control of the trade routes, making England master of the sources of Spanish wealth. At a time when William could not risk war, pressure from Spain and the two East India companies at home forced him to discountenance the Scottish colony at Darien (1698). But the King was attracted by the idea of conquest in the West Indies, and the terms of his Grand Alliance (1701) provided that England was to retain whatever possessions it acquired in that way.

In a previous chapter we have seen how Defoe drew up plans for William's proposed West Indian expedition. Later he referred to the failures to put this project into effect: the unsuccessful voyage of Admiral Benbow in 1701; the bill authorizing a more vigorous prosecution of the war in the West Indies, which was lost in a parliamentary wrangle in February, 1703; and the abandonment of the Earl of Peterborough's expedition in the spring of 1703.[13] Thereafter, any threat of hostilities with Spain might prompt Defoe to write a new tract.

Near the end of the reign of William, Defoe submitted to him and to the Earl of Portland a plan for an English colony in Chile, to be supported by a sister colony on the Atlantic coast in what is now Argentina. Communication between the two would be maintained by river and across the mountains, as well as by the long ocean route southward through the Strait of Magellan. The natives would be friendly, and the soil and climate would be favorable—as they had not been for the Scottish colony at Darien.

In July, 1711, Defoe sent a draft of this proposal to Harley (recently made Earl of Oxford), assuring him that no one had known of it but King William and the Earl of Portland, and that he had destroyed the original to keep it out of Nottingham's hands. William had approved it, and he would have put it into effect if he had not died suddenly. Defoe recognized that full consent of the Spaniards was not to be hoped for; but even if they refused to trade, the English colonies would have all that was needed for inhabiting, planting, and commerce.

In 1716 Defore was interested in a plan by which the South Sea Company was to be allowed a settlement not far from Buenos Aires, and he expressed a willingness to exchange Gibraltar and Minorca (which cost £100,000 a year to maintain) for the entire possession of the Spanish colony at Buenos Aires.

At the close of 1719 he reported, among new projects for economic expansion, that "Another [sort of cunning men] are preparing a scheme for pursuing the ancient and famous design of Sir Walter Raleigh, for planting a large British colony in the country of Guiana and the great river of Ooronoko in America so well attempted (but betrayed) by the great man Sir Walter. . . . Another sort, we hear, are proposing the like settlement in the South part of America, in the latitude of 45, as well on the east as the west side of the continent." The second plan was the same one he had proposed to Harley eight years before. He outlined it again in *A New Voyage Round the World*, sending a party of travelers over the mountains from Valdivia in Chile by the rivers to the Atlantic Ocean to show just how it could be done. In 1727 he was again pointing out how England, by securing the Gulf of Honda west of Havana or by blocking Porto Bello from the sea, could control trade with the Spanish colonies without military conquest of the land.[14]

If such projects meant only imperialistic expansion, Defoe would have to be regarded as a jingoist. But to him, as to Sir John Narborough before him, the Spanish colonies were artificial institutions, incapable of developing the regions or of affording adequate trade for the natives and for the Spanish settlements scattered so thinly along the coastline of a great continent. He held that a colonist was worth ten times as much to the national trade as a citizen who stayed at home, and he urged that the land below Buenos Aires was rich in pasturage and could produce wheat abundantly. For those who considered national pretensions sacred, he cited the fact that Sir John Narborough had erected a cross of wood and had claimed the country for Charles II: "This I mention (not that I think anybody has a right to dispossess the natives of a country) to intimate that at least the English have as good a title to it as any other nation whatsoever." Chile was so remote from the main settlements that Spain had made no serious effort to colonize it, and would be unable to attack an English colony there. The Spaniards had never deserved their good fortune in South America: "it is the opinion of some, that ten thousand men, of regular troops, from hence, might, at any time, take their whole American Empire from them, with all its mountains, and millions of gold and silver; nor was so large a dominion, and so rich, as that of America, ever known in the world to be enjoyed under so weak a defence, so small a guard, and that guard of such unsoldierly, cowardly, and wretched people, as have always been placed there, and are there even to this day."

While England was at peace with Spain, Defoe never ceased to point out the illegality of trading with the Spanish colonists except through the established monopoly of the Chamber of Seville. In fact, as this trade was largely carried on with English capital, and even by English merchants in Cadiz who had adopted Spanish names, any attack on the authorized system was an attack on English commerce. But when he wrote with imaginative sympathy about a homeless wanderer like Robinson Crusoe, or a pirate like Captain Singleton, or merchant adventurers like Colonel Jack and the narrator of *A New Voyage Round the World*, he showed the clandestine trade of the English in Spanish America in its most favorable light. Crusoe met with his final shipwreck in an illegal expedition to the Guinea Coast to bring slaves to the Brazilian planters, so as to avoid the high prices charged by the licensed Portuguese slave-traders. In its contempt for the freedom of trade and for the rights of traders, Spain (like Portugal) opposed the economic basis of society.[15]

In May, 1711, the South Sea Company was established by Harley, ostensibly as a company to promote trade with the West Indies and South America, but primarily to serve as a financial holding company to absorb the immense floating debt of the nation—and thereby save Harley's administration. There is no evidence that the undertaking was suggested or fully approved by Defoe. At this time the two men were not in close agreement on public affairs, and they were almost completely out of touch. In the spring and early summer of 1711, when the fate of Harley's regime depended on the success or failure of his South Sea project, the most daring pamphleteer of the age, editor of a political journal which appeared three times a week, hesitated two and a half months before throwing his weight in favor of it. The Scots were inclined to regard William Paterson as the real father of the scheme; certainly Defoe neither deserved nor wanted any such credit.

Nine years later, during the South Sea crisis of 1720, Defoe sought to prevent a panic. The Earl of Sunderland's Ministry was intensely vulnerable to attack because it was held responsible for the manipulation of South Sea stock. But the company had assumed so much of the national debt that its failure would have discredited the nation's finances. Perhaps the Hanoverian dynasty came nearer to complete overthrow in Exchange Alley than it ever did on any battlefield.

Defoe held that the Pretender was not to be let in through a collapse of confidence in the government; stocks were not to be sold so cheaply that foreigners could buy the nation's indebtedness for a song; the directors—if guilty—were to be punished, but their guilt required legal proof, and national security was even more important than deserved punishment. Thereafter he supported the national credit and condemned stockjobbing and the South Sea directors. But when the stock could be secured for a fair price, he bought eight shares as an investment for his daughter Hannah.

After the *Asiento* (the license for selling slaves in Spanish America) had been surrendered to Spain for £100,000, the company devoted itself to the payment of annuities. In 1854 its last stock was paid off or converted into other securities. In the words of Viscount Erleigh, "It is to be hoped that few worthy Victorians detected the wild South Sea strain in their sober-sided Consols."

But Defoe knew that his own South Sea plan had not failed, for it had never been tried. In the dream-fulfilment of *A New Voyage Round the World*, he allowed his narrator to visit Chile and to send an exploring party over the Andes and down the rivers to the sea. From the account of the interior which these travelers gave when they were picked up on the Atlantic coast of what is now Argentina, Defoe's merchant-explorer assured his readers: "I take the liberty to recommend that part of America as the best and most advantageous part of the whole globe for an English colony; the climate, the soil, and, above all, the easy communication with the mountains of Chili, recommending it beyond any place that ever I saw or read of." Only two years before his death, when there was a prospect of war with Spain, Defoe was prepared to offer his favorite project once more: "How easy would it be for the English to dispossess the Spaniards of the whole kingdom of Chili? the richest in gold, the weakest in strength, and capable of being improved, even to prodigy, far beyond any of the other dominions of the Spaniards in America, of which I could give unanswerable proof if that were any part of my present work."[16]

He continued to dream his great dream of a joint settlement in Chile and the Argentine, each colony supporting the other by communication across the mountains. An English settlement south of Buenos

Aires was approved by treaty with Spain in 1716, but it was never founded. Still, in our own time, when the nations of Europe find it increasingly difficult to feed their citizens, what he called "the Whole Island of Great Britain" derives much of its grain and most of its meat from the fertile plains of the Argentine, where Defoe planned to establish an English colony more than two and a half centuries ago.

A common subject of remark among eighteenth-century travelers was the relative absence of trees in Scotland. One modern historian says that the saplings were eaten off by the cattle or deliberately broken by peasants for fear they would harbor birds to destroy the corn. One of Defoe's contemporaries wrote that the Scottish gentlemen attempted to cultivate plantations, but the country people destroyed them secretly so that the trees would not spoil the ground and "eat the heart out of it." To Defoe, the main difficulty was bad planting; gentlemen lost their young trees because they provided no support against the wind. He was ready with a plan for a triangular frame of three stakes, to prevent the saplings from being blown far enough to shake the roots—a method which will be indorsed by anyone who has raised young trees in a windy region.

He had a keen eye for the annual harvest, and he rejoiced when he could report from Scotland, "they have had more corn this year, and a better season for curing and getting it in also, than they have had both the preceding years." But he knew that the occasional year of good harvest was no answer to problems raised by bad methods of farming. He declared that Scotland was inferior to England only in its lack of development, and he offered proposals for improving the land. Two generations before Coke of Norfolk had transformed the English county of which it had been said, "all you will see will be one blade of grass and two rabbits fighting for that," Defoe had anticipated some of the methods of Coke (and of Louis Bromfield) by urging inclosures to manure the land and the storing of winter provisions to sustain the cattle during the cold weather.[17]

All Europe knew the Scots as soldiers, but even the Scottish patriot Fletcher of Saltoun is said to have declared that his countrymen had no capacity as tradesmen. In the *Review, Caledonia, A Scots Poem,* the *History of the Union,* and the *Tour,* as well as in several tracts, Defoe was the pioneer who marked out many of the lines of commercial and industrial activity by which the Scots soon rose to fame among the merchants, the bankers, and the engineers of the world.

One of the happiest intervals in his life came when he laid aside his political mission in Edinburgh and went down to visit the Lord High Commissioner, the Duke of Queensberry, at his country estate in Dumfriesshire. Queensberry showed personal letters he had received from King William and Queen Anne; apparently he told at least one important anecdote about William which Defoe used in his later writings. But the Duke was too shrewd a judge of men to allow so eminent a projector to leave without securing his advice:

While I was at Drumlanrig, being desired by the late Duke to make some observations on his Grace's estate there, which is very great, in order to some English improvement, I, in particular, viewed some of the hills to the north of the Castle, and having a Derbyshire gentleman with us, who was thoroughly acquainted with those things, we discovered in several places evident tokens of lead mines, such as in Derbyshire and in Somersetshire are said never to fail; and to confirm our opinions of it, we took up several small pieces of ore in the gulls and holes, which the rain had made in the sides of the mountains, and also of a plain spar, such as is not found anywhere without the ore. But the Duke's death put an end to these inquiries, as also to several other improvements then in view.

Defoe's employment as a prospector for mines came to an end with the death of Queensberry. But even now, a few miles above Drumlanrig at Wanlockhead and at Leadhills, lead is still produced from "some of the hills to the north of the Castle." And when an American botanist visited Edinburgh in the summer of 1939 to attend a scientific convention, he observed the finest wheat where Defoe had hoped that it would be grown—in the fields of East Lothian.

Defoe had seen herrings in the firth near Edinburgh so thick that boys tossed them into boats with their bare hands. But the Scots had lost the fishing on their own coasts to the Dutch, partly through stupid insistence on bringing the fish ashore before they were sold, partly through lack of capital and organization to carry on the trade. Capital could be supplied from England, but the English opposed anything which would strengthen Scotland. Sir Richard Steele's fish-pool project seem to Defoe a stockjobbing fraud; the regular fishing smacks could achieve whatever was needed if they were sufficiently maintained.[18]

When it was feared that England might lose the Newfoundland fishery by the Treaty of Utrecht, Defoe suggested that the British should remove their Newfoundland trade to the northwest of Scotland. He urged the Scots to develop their coal trade, he started a manufacture of linen and acted as a broker for Scottish salt, and (through his brother-in-law) he made a start in the building of ships at Leith. It was not a baseless report which he encouraged among the Glasgow men that he was to be a fish merchant. Ten years later he wrote a detailed account of the herring fishery, suggesting that the South Sea Company could use its idle capital there.

However, his projects were always subject to correction by experience. At his own cost he found that fish could be loaded at Newfoundland in one-fifth the time required on the Scottish coast, and he came to realize that the Dutch had economic advantages which were not easily overcome. The chief markets for white herring were Danzig and Königsberg in the Baltic, where the Dutch had a favorable rate of exchange and from which (because their nation imported so large a share of its food) their herring vessels did not return empty but came back loaded with corn.[19]

In an age when intervals of peace were followed by long wars, fishing smacks had great value as auxiliary naval vessels. Besides, the fishing trade lowered the price of provisions and employed a great number of the poor. The rapid alternation between the demand for seamen in wartime and their partial employment in times of peace caused much of the piracy which reached its height after the Peace of Utrecht. Defoe remarked, "during the long peace I have not so much as heard of a Dutch pirate. . . . When the Dutch ships are laid up, they have a fishery where their seamen find immediate business and as comfortable bread as they had before."

In wartime, national survival depended on the ability of the naval officers to man their ships. It was estimated that more than fifty thousand English seamen were lost "by battle, disease, and disaster" during the wars with France in the reigns of William and Anne.[20] Competition for seamen resulted in excessively high pay, in brutal pressing and kidnapping, and in the delays which often sent English ships limping out long after their enemies were in the Channel.

Defoe sought not only to remedy the wrongs of sailors by putting an end to press gangs and kidnappers, by insurance against injury or death at sea, and by safeguarding wages; he also proposed a registration office, with courts in every English seaport, to provide seamen. These men would never be out of employment, no man would dare to desert, no unemployed sailor would be tempted to turn in desperation to piracy, the nation would never lack men for its navy. Such a system would strengthen the fisheries, maintain the seaborne trade, and restore England's naval power.

Some variant of this proposal was outlined in *An Essay upon Projects* (1697). It was suggested again in the *Review* (January 13 and 16, 1705), arousing such interest in the House of Lords that Defoe was called on to submit his plan to a select committee. In the *Manuscripts of the House of Lords* one can read Defoe's proposal and can trace the stages by which he was called on by the select committee to make it good; how he was asked to lay his plan before Prince George, the Lord High Admiral (February 10, 1705); and how (March 3) he was given time until the next session to prepare a statement of his project. But it was never adopted—partly because of the death of Prince George, who had favored it; partly because of the strange English fear of selective service, even in an age which tolerated press gangs and kidnapping. Three years before his own death, Defoe offered the plan in a new tract. To anyone who still doubts the accuracy of Defoe's factual statements, it should be a revelation to see how the tract of 1728 is confirmed by the secret records of the select committee of the House of Lords, written out by their secretary in 1705 and never published until 1912.[21]

Defoe gave his support to a project for making navigable the River Dun (Don) in Yorkshire. In his *Tour* he did remark that the uncontrolled river, because of its source in the mountains, was subject to violent floods. But this fact was no argument against control of the river for navigation, and it was misrepresented and grossly exaggerated by the neighboring gentry and by merchants in rival communities as a pretext for their selfish opposition. Defoe defended the projectors in his newspaper, the *Daily Post*, in a vigorous letter which declared that "all that is said of this kind is as mere romance as the *Life of Robinson Crusoe*." Because of the objections, the river was made navigable only to the village of Tinsley instead of to Sheffield; but the act authorizing the improvement finally received the royal assent on May 24, 1726. Shares of the navigation company sold at £100 each; but in the next century, when the company was absorbed into the Manchester, Sheffield, and Lincolnshire Railway, they had risen to £3,000.[22]

A complete analysis of Defoe's projects would give us something like a history of his age. But two of his interests are so characteristic that they should be considered here.

From the time of Queen Elizabeth statesmen had sought to prevent unemployment by two steps: first by developing and encouraging English manufacture, afterward by punishing sturdy beggars and requiring the unemployed to find the work that was available.

As a manufacturer of brick and tile, Defoe had encountered the dissolute worker (who spent his wages for drink and left his family unprovided for) and the idle worker (who refused any employment). In one of his tracts, and again in his *Review*, Defoe told an anecdote of his experience: "I affirm of my own knowledge, when I have wanted a man for laboring work, and offered 9s. per week to strolling fellows at my door, they have frequently told me to my face they could get more a-begging, and I once put a lusty fellow in the stocks for making the experiment."[23]

Defoe's long controversy with Lord Haversham grew partly out of Haversham's attempt to erect government-subsidized workhouses, employing workmen at national expense in direct competition with industries which supported the nation's economic system. Defoe approved of hospitals and pensions for the aged, the crippled, and the infirm; but he did not wish to destroy private industry by subsidized competition or to encourage the drone at the expense of the worker.

Some of the worst social evils of the age grew out of the system of parish relief, by which each parish sought to throw the burden of its poor upon its neighbors. A favorite economic doctrine held that the wealth of a nation depended on the number of its inhabitants; but that theory and the whole system of relief came to a severe test in the summer of 1709. Ten thousand refugees from the Rhenish Palatinate came to England to escape the miseries of war and the oppression of their own Elector. In their temporary quarters on the outskirts of London, they aroused deep resentment as foreigners in nationality and language and religion, who had come in a year of bad harvest to eat the bread of the English poor.

The unhappy strangers continued for a time to be sheltered in huts on the heaths near London. Queen Anne contributed heavily toward their relief, and the congregations of many churches gave donations. Some of them ("the Pennsylvania Dutch") were drawn to America; others attempted a settlement in Ireland or wandered about until they drifted back to Germany.

Aside from the settlement in Pennsylvania, the only rational plan for their care was that which Defoe proposed to Godolphin in 1709, sketched in his *Review* in the same year, restated with an outline map and elaborate calculations in his *Tour* (1724), and repeated in a different form in *A Plan of the English Commerce* (1728). The first plan was intended to provide for the needy immigrants; the last was ostensibly a method by which three lords of neighboring manors were to improve their property by developing a town in an unpeopled countryside. The first was laid in "the several forests and wastes of England"—especially in the New Forest of Hampshire; the last was said to be in "the south parts of England"—in much the same region.

Defoe assumed that the tenants would be willing to work and that each could make some contribution to the community. Provision was made for the sick and the poor, not for the idle. The land was to be parceled out in farms. The co-operative efforts of the community were to lead to a church and a school and shops, to handicrafts and medical services and the like. Tenants were to receive a capital loan and the encouragement of low rent or taxes; in twenty years' time the community would be so profitable that there would be no further question of its maintenance.

But the project, so carefully thought out, was never attempted. In the late autumn of 1709 Englishmen were more interested in futile religious and political controversies, aroused in part by the notorious Dr. Sacheverell, than in solving a social and economic problem. By August of the next year the Lord High Treasurer to whom Defoe had submitted his first plan had fallen from power. As Defoe declared afterward: "More money than would have done this was expended, or rather thrown away upon them here, to keep them in suspense, and afterwards to starve them; sending them begging all over the nation, and shipping them off to perish in other countries. Where the mistake lies is none of my business to enquire."[24]

In *An Essay upon Projects* Defoe told of a successful fire engine prompted by the Fire of London. He devoted several chapters to proposals for pensions and insurance (but not life insurance, against which there was still strong religious prejudice). As we have seen, his bankruptcy was due primarily to his engaging in wartime marine insurance without government support to meet the immense and unpredictable losses. He had set his second son up in business for himself; and in 1719 this Daniel, Jr., became answerable for £1,000 for a marine insurance company, the Ram & Colebrook Society, which soon developed into the London Assurance. In 1720 Daniel, Jr., made a series of transactions in the company's stock. In 1721 the marine charter was implemented by the grant of another, which allowed the company to undertake fire and life business. On August 2, 1721, Daniel, Jr., took out fire insurance policies in the London Assurance (Nos. 319 and 323). On November 18 Defoe himself secured Policy No. 776. The son allowed his policies to lapse after the first year, but the father's were in force at least as late as 1725.

In his satirical account of his own imaginary periodical to be called *The Projector,* Defoe alluded to some unwise investments made for the insurance companies: "In No. III I shall demonstrate that the Saddlers' Hall Directors are as good mathematicians as the gentlemen of the Sun-Fire, though the former wisely laid out part of their capital in South Sea at 750, as the latter entrusted their whole Darby in the hands of a brace of bankrupts." But he never lost faith in the future development of insurance. According to the records of the Sun Fire Insurance Office Limited ("Founded in the Year 1710"), he was insuring his home with that company as late as January 7, 1728 (1729). On that date he paid a premium of fourteen shillings on Policy No. 46589: "Daniel De Foe of Stoke Newington, Gent. on his Dwelling house only brick, situate as aforesaid exclusive of all manner of outhouses or adjoining Buildings, not exceeding seven hundred pounds. . . . £700."[25]

As an insurer of other men's property, Defoe had met with "the slings and arrows of outrageous fortune." But in his own contribution to the theory and the practice of insurance he served a purpose not unlike that of the coral. The wreck of his personal fortunes lies near the base of one of the most stable business undertakings in the modern world.

XXIV. ECONOMIST

I entered upon my beloved subject of Trade.

Review, [IX], 115

I T WAS DEFOE'S HIGHEST MERIT as an economist that he was
the first prominent English writer to see national concerns with the
eyes of a social historian. He had his own share of interest in constitutional government, in the history of the church, even more in the military annals of many lands. He knew as well as others the splendor of
national prowess in the conquest of France under Edward III, but he
asked how the common people fared in the midst of such splendor:

These glorious things gutted England of its wealth, made the monarch
powerful and his people poor.

In all his Parliaments we see not one act for the encouragement of trade,
for enlarging commerce, for employment of the poor, for setting up manufactures. To speak the truth, I question if the word manufacture or manufacturer were known in the country; and, for aught I see, as the tailors were
the only merchants, so the shoemakers were the greatest manufacturers
in the kingdom.

All this while England lay neglected to the last degree; her sons knock-
ing their heads against stone walls, and ranging the field of war in foreign
countries, pursued their own poverty, and sought misery, for the glory of
their monarch.

But at home it was all a miscellany of sorrow: villainage and vassalage
comprised the poor; knighthood and esquireship took up the middle gentry;
and glory dwelt only among the barons and princes.

Henry VII was most often remembered as a despotic and a penurious
king; to Defoe he was a great sovereign because he encouraged English manufactures.[1]

Sometimes Defoe's opponents sought to belittle his discourses on
trade, as they sought to belittle everything else that he did; sometimes
they attacked him because their own party politics required them to
oppose his commercial policies. But whenever they wrote without
personal or political bias, they were likely to show their high regard

for his economic writings. Often they did this unconsciously, as when they attributed his *Essay upon Credit* and his *Essay upon Loans* to Robert Harley himself; occasionally they did it directly, as when the High Church propagandist Dr. Joseph Browne admitted that Defoe the economist was a far more significant man than Defoe the Dissenter:

To give my opinion of this author and to do him justice, he writes with a great deal of clearness and perspicuity when he meddles with business he understands; . . . I acknowledge he has treated the affairs of the nation in relation to trade and commerce, particularly in his late *Review* about bankrupts, with a great deal of compassion towards the unfortunate, and with many home arguments to such unmerciful creditors as would treat their debtors worse than Turks use their dogs, though they are not assured but that the same case they are prosecuting with such severity may be their own in a few days.[2]

But their more usual attitude was one of contempt for commercial interests. The first issue of the *Examiner* (August 3, 1710) dismissed such matters as unworthy of its consideration: "I shall leave the African Company and the coals to the *Review*." After Swift joined forces with the *Examiner*, its attitude toward trade changed from dislike to scorn; and on December 28 of the same year we find Swift suggesting that trade is too contemptible a thing to be regarded seriously by statesmen: "But these men come with the spirit of shop-keepers to frame rules for the administration of kingdoms; as if they thought the whole art of government consisted in the importation of nutmegs and the curing of herrings."

Defoe not only knew how important commercial interests are in the government of a nation; his knowledge of the subject came from personal experience. The most famous economist of the eighteenth century read lectures on political economy in a cloistered college and wrote his *Wealth of Nations* in the retirement of a provincial Scottish town; later he was made commissioner of customs, but at no time was he actively engaged in trade. Defoe was a citizen of the world of trade, from infancy to old age. He was born, he lived, and he died in the greatest of trading cities, and he engaged in trade almost everywhere he went on his travels. His father was a tallow-chandler who apparently became a butcher. Defoe himself was established as an independent merchant by the time he was twenty-three. The last of his works published in his lifetime was an expanded edition of *A Plan of the English Commerce*, on January 13, 1731.

His acquaintance with trade came long before his theory on the subject; and when he was first called on to express his views, it was as a man of mercantile experience. By the time he was twenty-six he "had the honor to see a calculation made to the Privy Council," by which "it appeared that we paid to France for our imports from thence, over and above what goods they received from us, above £850,000 sterling per annum." At the beginning of William's reign he saw that the trade favored France; but when the balance of trade shifted, his opinion shifted with it. Before the death of Queen Mary in 1694 he had testified before the Privy Council and both houses of Parliament in favor of England's trading with France (even in wartime) instead of abandoning that profitable commerce to the ever alert Dutch.

We can get some idea of the extent of Defoe's experience with taxation from a statement made by his rival as an economist, the High Tory Dr. Charles Davenant. While Defoe was accountant to the commissioners of the Glass Duty, who collected the tax on windows, Davenant complained that he could not perfect his own accounts because Defoe would not let him see the ledgers: "the books of the principal offices have been in a manner shut up against any inquiry he desired to make." But Davenant estimated with confidence that the total glass duty from September 29, 1695, to August 17, 1697 (about half the period of Defoe's term of office), amounted to approximately £25,000.[3]

In *An Essay upon Projects* (1697) Defoe was more concerned with practical suggestions than with any theory of political economy. Here, for almost the last time in his life, he was free to revise his manuscript at leisure for several years, with little thought of discussing affairs of the moment. Thereafter, nearly all his economic writings need to be read in connection with the newspapers, the journals of the two houses of Parliament, and his own correspondence with the ministers of state. All too rarely was he free to speak of trade in general. Far more often he was obliged to write of the East India Company as it influenced the elections of 1706, of the proposal of Sir Humphrey Mackworth in 1704 to employ workhouse labor to compete in the woolen trade, of the bill for the relief of insolvent debtors in 1706, of the economic consequences of the Union with Scotland in 1707, of the effect on public credit of the overthrow of the Whigs in 1710, of Harley's South Sea project in 1711, of the proposed opening of the trade with France in 1713, of the difficulties of the African

Company, of the unrest of the weavers, of the lowering of interest on the national debt, of the crash of 1720, and so on through the long list.

This constant pressure of immediate concerns obliged Defoe to write more often as a journalist than as an economist. Again and again he would be ready to "launch out into this vast ocean of trade," only to be called abruptly back to the present moment. In his *Review* for July 8, 1710, he felt encouraged to announce:

The Author of this paper having received many importunate letters a long time, pressing him to go on with his so often promised discourses upon trade—gives this notice,

That having often essayed to carry on a continued discourse of trade in this paper, but being unavoidably prevented by the fury of the times, an unhappiness the Author did not foresee when this work was undertaken—And finding it impossible to have his essays upon trade pursued in this paper, in such an uninterrupted manner as a subject of that consequence requires; some gentlemen, who desire that work to be carried on, have made a proposal for the writing of a REVIEW to be entirely taken up upon the subject of trade, with a miscellany, or a part reserved to handle particular cases in trade—And expressly conditioned not to meddle with matters of state, divisions of parties, or anything relating to the affairs of government, civil or ecclesiastic.

This work is proposed to be subscribed by such gentlemen as think fit to encourage it, till it may be able to support itself; in which the Author hopes he may please you all, and may have an opportunity to lay down the unpleasant subject of the nation's divisions; a thing he has long desired to do.

But five days later he was once more engulfed in discussions of the impending change of the Ministry and in the clamor over the triumphal western journey of the factious Dr. Sacheverell. In his hurried thinking and writing, general ideas had to tumble in when he could find time to admit them. But the very immediacy of his interests kept him close to the facts, so that his economic thinking never lost touch with reality: "My text shall be taken out of no book, no not the Bible, but in the foot of the account, or as the merchants call it, the net produce of the present state of the world.[4]

Sometimes his enemies charged that he wrote on behalf of the African Company, or in support of the commercial articles of the Tory peace with France, or in favor of the keelmen who operated the coal barges at Newcastle. But an impartial reader can only marvel that he remained so nearly consistent in his economic views over so long a period of time, regardless of whatever party might be in office at the time. For nearly thirty years, far longer than anyone has ever supposed that he was employed by the African Company, he was saying exactly the same things about the slave trade. For nearly forty years he favored reciprocal trade with France—as long as that trade could be made profitable to England and without regard to the claims of Dutch merchants, or of Whig politicians who were willing to betray the commercial interests of England to gain Dutch support for their attack on Harley's administration. It is difficult to see how he could be supposed to seek any personal advantage by defending the poor keelmen against the exactions of their employers and of the City Corporation of Newcastle; for here, as in his attacks on the men who ground the faces of the poor by fixing exorbitant prices on bread and candles and coal, he was supporting defenseless individuals against a powerful monopoly.

Sometimes he may have had a personal stake in presenting private interests—as perhaps when he wrote for the wine importers Brook and Hellier, the brass manufacturers who offered Harley a superior coinage, his brother-in-law with his project for shipbuilding in Scotland, and the men who sought to improve navigation on the Don. In several such matters Defoe was not entirely disinterested; but this does not mean that he was dishonest, or even that his recommendations were unwise. Most of these projects seemed likely to succeed with a fair trial; and the shares of the Don River navigation company were called in at thirty times their par value a century after Defoe's death.

But it is not in his theoretical or controversial or journalistic writings alone that Defoe looks at the world as a social and economic historian. The same wide outlook is evident in such a poem as *Caledonia*, such a travel book as the *Tour*, such a manual as *The Compleat English Tradesman*, and such works of fiction as *Moll Flanders*, *Colonel Jack*, and *Robert Drury's Journal*. At times Robinson Crusoe has been held up by university lecturers as the exemplar of our fundamental economic problems. Shelter and clothing and food, social life and the division of labor, manufactures and agriculture and transportation—all have been brought home in the classroom by references to Crusoe's cave and to his stockade and to his country house; to the shirts and ship biscuits that he brought off the wreck, and to the umbrella that he made to ward off the sun; to the little family that he trained up around him, and to Friday, who shared his toils; to his awkwardly made pottery, to the grains of rice that he scattered, and to the boats that he built so laboriously in his effort to escape from the island.

Next in importance to this social and economic outlook was Defoe's passion for statistics, by the use of which he anticipated the modern scientific study of facts which has displaced the older theorizing about "natural laws" of commerce and the attributes of "the economic man." In his time the imperfectly kept parish registers were for many communities the only available bases for statistics. The land area of England had never been accurately computed, there was no reliable way of determining the population, statistics of health and trade and employment were rudimentary at best. The main reason for the preference for taxes on chimneys and windows was that chimneys and windows could be easily counted. Even the basic land tax was levied on the wildest variations of assessed valuation. Most of the detailed information recorded in a modern census was not even sought for, and such modern governmental devices as selective military service and the graduated income tax would have been impossible to administer.

Dr. Davenant quoted with high approval the estimates of Gregory King, such as the conjecture that England's population would double in six hundred years, so that it would amount to about 11,000,000 by the year 2300. Such calculated guesswork had become fashionable under the name of "political arithmetic," and for this Defoe had little respect. But wherever statistics were available, Defoe was likely to gain access to them. In 1706 the committees of the Scottish Parliament relied on him to supply minute details regarding trade and excises and equivalents and drawbacks under the proposed Union. In his *Mercator* he had (by his own account) the help of "original papers, documents, and authorities to speak from," and (according to his opponents) "the command of all public papers in the Custom-House."[5]

Defoe could not write a history of the pirates without seeking special information regarding the tonnage and class of the ships, the number of guns which each carried and the additional number which could be mounted if the decks were altered, the size of the crews, and (wherever possible) the course sailed on each voyage. Ten years before he published his two books on the Great Plague, he was collecting bills of mortality for the plague year. Until near the end of his career, when he was living in partial retirement, there are recurrent indications that he still had some access to the customhouse books, to the reports to the commissioners of trade and plantations, and to the letters to the African Company from their governor at Cape Corso.

To the more conservative Tories the landed interest was the main body of the nation, the trading interest a mere extremity if not an excrescence. Defoe was usually willing to admit that some stake in the land was the best qualification for a voter, although he protested that often when land was sold "the purchasers seemed to buy the election with the property." But he declared, "This nation can no more support itself without trade than the Church can without religion." The protection of trade was an issue which really justified war: "Our interest is our trade; and our trade is, next to our liberty and religion, one of our most valuable liberties. If our neighbors pretend to slam the door against our commerce, we must open it; and that by force, if no other means will procure it. To invade our commerce is to invade our property, and we may and must defend it." His passionate attack on Macedonia and Rome for destroying the higher civilizations of Tyre and Carthage concludes thus: "What a loss to the commerce of Europe have these two nations been, which men in those days called glorious; and how have we reason to blast the memory of Alexander the Great and Scipio Africanus with a mark of infamy never to be wiped out, for destroying the only two governments in the world which were qualified to make all the rest of mankind great and happy." Trade seemed to him more important than considerations of diplomacy or military advantage: "No man will say the Pretender is concerned in the affair of the commerce; there are no Jacobites in matters of trade. Neither will they say that we should decline trade with the French because they are Papists, or that the Balance of Power is concerned in this thing. The cant of parties is a mere jargon in trade, and has neither argument or sense in it."[6]

The attempted prohibition of English trade with France in wartime seemed to him as foolish as it was ineffectual. The French were not starved into submission, war munitions got through in spite of the prohibitions, and the profits went to England's less scrupulous allies, the Dutch. He regarded the hostility to reopening trade with France in 1713 as a political subterfuge to strengthen the attack of the Whig junto on the government: "It is most certain the party are fallen into this clamor about trade, not from their zeal for commerce but for a handle, and to raise a party against the Ministry." He remarked that "all the while we have shut our doors against the trade to France, [the Dutch] have had an open trade with them, and have crowded them with those very goods which would otherwise have been sent from hence."[7]

But political management prevailed over national interests, and the "Hanover Tories" were induced to join the Whigs in defeating what a

modern historian has called the "enlightened attempt to develop better relations and what might have been proved a profitable trade with
France." So thoroughly was the policy of reciprocal trade discredited
for a time that—in subsequent writings in which he sought to win a
favorable hearing for Harley from the triumphant Whigs—Defoe was
obliged to allow himself the license of an anonymous pamphleteer to
declare that Harley had only stood passive between Bolingbroke and
the Whigs, and that the Bill of Commerce would have been a disaster
if Parliament had approved it. Defoe did not believe this in 1714 any
more than he did in 1713, and he did not say it in his own person; but
as the anonymous pamphleteer he was not trying to defend the temporarily discredited bill but to save the life of Harley from a vindictive Whig majority. The Whig readers of his defense of Harley
would not have been satisfied with less, and Defoe was writing only
to make an effective appeal to those Whig readers.

In his impatience with the pious fraud of the politicians who condemned trade with France in order to cement their political alliance
with Holland, he exclaimed:

> We are a trading nation, our business is trade, and our end to get money;
> we know no other interest in commerce but gain. No nation, any more than
> any private merchant, ought to trade (if you speak rationally of him) with
> any other nation or merchant any longer than they get by that trade. No
> private circumstances of any nation, no religious interest, no prejudices or
> hatred between one nation and another, has any concern in trade. We trade
> with Turks, Infidels, Idolaters, Gentiles, Heathens, Savages, it matters not
> what gods they serve, so they serve our end, and what can serve our
> interest by trading with them. What if they worship the sun or the moon,
> this idol or that; Vistly-pustly, Teckaoco-man, Mahomet, or Lucifer?
> Getting money is the only idol that trade worships, and it is nothing to the
> merchant who he trades with, if he can make a good return.[8]

In the heat of debate he might sometimes simplify the argument by
a sweeping claim that trade with France had always been beneficial.
But in careful statements he admitted freely that England should re-
strict imports from France by suitable duties and that Scotland had
little to gain by a direct trade with France in 1706 (although he
thought this last had changed by 1713).[9] In the issue of *A General
History of Trade* for September, 1713, he proposed to devote the next
number to a consideration of the ways of making the Bill of Commerce helpful to the English manufacturers by cutting off the wool
which was being smuggled to France and by opening the long-lost
markets of France to English traders. But by October it had become

clear that the Whigs were more concerned in rounding up votes in the House of Commons than in finding foreign markets for English woolen goods, and so the fifth number of *A General History of Trade* was never published.

In the controversy over the proposed trade with France, the Whigs maintained that it would violate the Methuen Treaty, which bound England to a preferential tariff for Portugal. As a defender of the Ministry's Bill of Commerce Defoe might be expected to oppose this view; but the reasons which he gave for his opposition were not party reasons. He held that France and the great inland fairs of the Rhineland (which the Dutch were so eager to reserve for their own traders) offered a far greater market for English goods than Portugal could offer; that the Methuen Treaty gave no rights in Portugal not extended equally to Holland and to France, and so the English paid a high price without securing any special advantage; and that as ambassador extraordinary, Methuen had violated the constitution by limiting the action of future Parliaments, so that "a British Parliament is made a dainty nose of wax, to be turned and twisted, stand this way, and that way, as a plenipotentiary shall please to direct." No such special treaty had ever been needed, because Portugal could not subsist without its trade to England: "The wine, oil, figs, &c. will sell nowhere but here. If we do not take off these productions, what must be the consequence? Truly the vines must be grubbed up, the olive-trees cut down, the figs, oranges, and lemons rot upon the trees, the value of lands must sink, the people want employment; and all the miseries that attend an impoverished nation must follow. Is our trade necessary to them, or is it not?"

His attitude toward Irish trade and manufacture shows the consistent dualism so characteristic of much of his thinking. He admitted freely that England had treated the Irish as a conquered people, and that (although this attitude was morally indefensible) Englishmen of the eighteenth century were not likely to allow their neighbors to develop a manufacture of woolen goods which might soon surpass that of the English. But he declared that it was unjust to prevent the Irish from exporting their wool to the Continent unless England was prepared to buy every pound of wool raised in Ireland.[10]

Throughout his career, perhaps the most controversial trade was that to the East Indies. The unemployment of English weavers was blamed on the importation of printed calicoes, and while the weavers rioted in the streets there was hot debate in Parliament and in the press over whether the advantages of the East India trade overbalanced the loss of the bullion carried out of England.

Defoe held that if the importation of printed calicoes were prohibited, the chief objection would be removed and the company would still have a profitable trade; later he rejected the notion that "interlopers" in an "open trade" would serve the public better than an exclusive company. In 1701 he contended that the controversy between the Old and New East India companies (before their consolidation) should never have been allowed to develop, and that this rivalry was corrupting Parliament. In 1707 he told the Scots that two East India companies had almost ruined England, and that the Union was impossible if the Scots maintained an East India company of their own. In the same year he proposed that calico be manufactured in England to employ the poor. In 1708 he supported the prohibition of the use of manufactured silks from India, China, and Persia. In 1719 he wrote that anyone who preferred calico-printing or the like to the good of his country was "something like the wretched sexton of Cripplegate in the year 1665, who, being employed at the pest-house near Oldstreet, would have had the plague continue, that his fees might not abate, but that he might have people enough to bury." In the next ten years he had much to say of the injury done to England by the fad for goods from the East Indies, and of the vast superiority of undeveloped regions in the South Seas as a foreign market.[11]

From his early years as a merchant in Freeman's Yard Defoe probably had some dealings with Spain and Portugal and with the Spanish and Portuguese colonies in America. He had certainly visited the Continent as a merchant before 1685, but his longest residence may have come soon after the collapse of Monmouth's Rebellion. It is probable that he was in Cadiz representing English merchants when the following report from that city was sent to London (October 14, 1686):

The Galeons which arrived here the 17th of the last Month, under the command of the General *Gonzalo Chacon* brought.
20 Millions in pieces of Eight.
8 Millions of Gold uncoined.
1 Million of Silver uncoined.
1 Million in Doblons or Pistols.
1 Million in Fruits of the Country, *viz.*
200 thousand pounds of the Bark of Trees, called Cascarilla.
150 thousand pounds of Red Wood.
12 thousand pounds of Brazilette wood.

4 Thousand Quintals of Campeche Wood.
12 Thousand Quintals of Cakau of Caracos and Gwakin.
Hides untanned a small quantity.
100 thousand pieces of Eight value in rough Emeralds.
100 thousand pieces of Eight value in different sorts of Pearls.
700 Chests of Indico of *Guatimala*.
200 Chests of *Havana* Sugar for Presents.
Some quantity of Beazar Stones.
12 Thousand Cocos with Balsame.[12]

In a Europe so impoverished by wars and by the stagnation of limited markets, such a list must have suggested to Londoners a new world of infinite treasure; but Defoe was even more struck by the miserable management which forced the Spanish sovereign to anticipate his revenues long before he received them. The news story continued: "Of all this Treasure there is nothing for the King's Accompt in regard his Majesty gave Bills for the satisfaction of those Persons who at Madrid had raised sums of Money for the publick Service; and all the King's Money in the *Indies* came short to discharge the said Bills." This annual deficiency in the revenue could not be met— even with the aid of such a windfall as was reported in the same letter from Cadiz:

There was laden on board the man of War the *Teresa*, which was sent the last year with Quicksilver to New Spain:
5 Millions of pieces of Eight of *Mexico* stampt.
420 Bags of Skins of Couchenille, weighing about 4000 Rooves.
130 Chests of Indico of *Guatimala*.
200 thousands pieces of Eight for accompt of his Majesty.

The increasing poverty of Spain was attributed by Defoe to bad administration of national finances, lack of encouragement of manufactures and industry, and the inability of the Spaniards to carry on their own trade except by foreign agents and with foreign capital. For forty-five years his imagination played over this complex situation, and he continued to look at it from different angles. Sometimes he stressed the fact that Spain's best market was in England, and that Spain could not afford to lose this through war or diplomacy. Sometimes he stressed the importance of the trade from England to Spain and (through the licensed channels in Spain) to the American colonies. Sometimes (especially in his works of fiction) he showed the irregular methods of the English interlopers in the West Indies. His own interest lay in the development of English colonies (especially in Chile and the Argentine) which would provide England with grain and meat and minerals, and which would serve as depots for direct trade with the Spanish colonists.

But always he recognized that the weakness of Spain lay in its national economy. Four years before Cardinal Alberoni became prime minister, Defoe outlined the very policies which that able statesman attempted to put into effect, and he foresaw the difficulties which caused Alberoni's failure:

It is indeed true that, were a politic active prince upon the Spanish throne, that could bring their trade to a new model, encourage manufactures and industry, and set the inhabitants to improve themselves that the immense treasures they possess might not necessar[il]y flow from them to other countries for the manufacture and labor of nations remote to them, that could bring the Spaniards to arts, sciences, industry, and war, they would recover themselves, and be the greatest nation in the world. But this must be the work of time, perhaps of ages, and no prince can expect to bring them to it in his reign.[13]

Defoe held that no part of the world is so barren that it cannot make its special contribution to trade. It is in this flow of goods from place to place that trade is possible. If each community were self-supporting, all trade would be crippled and the carrying trade would stop at once: "These wooden towns we build and people, and then send them abroad freighted with corn, coal, lead, leather, woolen manufactures, &c., and they sell them to the French. The French not only buy those goods, but pay the carriers for bringing them; which payment for the carriage, we may affirm, employs as many families, goes as far to support the public stock, and is as much gain to the kingdom of Great Britain as all the woolen manufactures they carry in them." Lee overstated the case for Defoe as a free trader; but he was far nearer the truth than writers who would represent him as a Whig protectionist who forswore himself to defend the Tory plan to open trade with France in 1713.[14]

Mercantilism stressed foreign trade to the neglect of home trade. Real profit was supposedly made only by trading with foreigners, or in trading with one's colonists as if they were foreigners. One source of the bitter economic struggle with Scotland, the long oppression of Ireland, and the growing rift with the American colonies was England's attempt to secure advantages in trading at their expense. Defoe attacked the English for not making improvements in Scotland after the Union; and he argued for free commerce between the sister nations even before the Union, regardless of the apparent "balance of trade" in favor of Scotland: "'Tis not a subjecting, but communicating of privileges and interests." He pointed out that the repression of Irish agriculture and manufactures drove Irish wool and Irish craftsmen abroad, building up a more formidable competition on the Continent.

His distrust of the mercantilist policy of repression led him into one of his few utterly mistaken prophecies, when he held that the North American colonies would never revolt. Certainly if Defoe's ideal trade relations had been maintained, some of the principal causes of the American Revolution would have been removed. No English writer before Burke was so well informed regarding the American colonies, and no one—not Burke himself—excelled Defoe in the spirit of friendly conciliation: "To fear to make our Colonies too great is as if a father in the educating his child should fear to make him too wise or to give him too much learning, or in feeding him should be afraid of making him too strong or too tall or too beautiful; for the Plantations being our own children, the offspring of the Commonwealth, they cannot, politically speaking, have too much care taken of them or be too much tendered by us."

In his hastier thinking he sometimes accepted the current ideas of his day, as when he assumed that any benefit which one nation gains by trade is balanced by a corresponding loss to the nation with which the trade is carried on, or when he offered to prove that home trade is a mere redistribution of wealth, so that it is as impossible for a nation to grow rich by home trade as for a room full of gamesters to increase their stock by playing among themselves. But in his later and more careful writings he was perhaps the first economist in the world to see the full advantages of an extensive home trade: "The inland trade of England . . . is the foundation of all our wealth and greatness; it is the support of all our foreign trade, and of our manufacturing, and of the tradesmen who carry it on."[15] He gave a vivid picture of the influence of inland trade by enumerating the garments which the poorest countryman wore, indicating the region of England from which each article was brought. But he realized that domestic trade within the British Isles did not offer a sufficiently large market or a sufficiently wide range of goods. These were to be supplied by extending the benefits of home trade to the colonies. He outlined a scheme of empire trade (two centuries in advance of the empire traders) with bounties and preferential duties which he thought would be of equal benefit to England and to the colonies.

As the national debt swelled to undreamed-of proportions, citizens drew into rival camps according to what they considered their special interests. Many regarded land and commerce as mutually hostile and took sides with the landed or the moneyed men. Some were for canceling the national debt entirely; others regarded the high interest rate of 6 per cent as a public obligation not subject to alteration.

Defoe pointed out that land and commerce were inseparable, that commerce depended on the land, and that the value of land rose or fell with the general level of trade. He rejected the extreme Whig notion that national credit depended on any one party or group rather than on the nation's reputation for fair dealing. He rejected the extreme Tory notion that because the debt was owed to individuals within the nation, it could be canceled without national loss.

In one remarkable tract he attempted to cover the main issues of taxation and national debt during the inflation after the first of world wars (the War of the Spanish Succession, 1702–13). He argued that Parliament had no more right to make perpetual debts than it had to make perpetual laws; that the rate of public interest should rise and fall with the rate of private interest; that to continue a rate of 6 per cent interest for ninety-nine years was a bondage to usury; that a lowered rate would make possible the paying-off of the loans, and that lenders who would not accept a lowered rate should have their loans paid off in full; that the landed men had not actually paid more than half of their assessment of five shillings in the pound, whereas a tax on the necessities of life fell heavily on the poor, as in France; that all taxes should be equalized; and that renewed trade and prosperity would follow the reduction of the interest on the public debt.[16]

Retail credit seemed to him to be extended so far as to weaken the fabric of commerce. Much of the difficulty of traders was due to the nobility and gentry, who had been enticed by the luxury of the court (especially under James I and Charles II) to live beyond their means and so to depend on the court.

He was firm against the speculative use of credit, saying that "there are more people ruined in England by over-trading than for want of trade." He pointed out that overproduction depresses any line of trade, and he urged restriction of credit as a means of curtailing it. He painted a vivid picture of the dislocation of trade resulting from temporary overproduction. But he was not impressed by the bogey of general overproduction. He urged that England should manufacture woolen goods for the world. It had the best goods and the best workmen, and should brook no competition.

Although he had a clear perception of the fluctuations in the markets for manufactured goods, perhaps even some notion of business cycles, he laid much of the blame for business failures upon the faults of human nature: "if I am asked why honest tradesmen are ruined, and undesigning men come to destruction in trade, the answer is short; because knaves run away with their money."[17]

He admitted the advantages of regulating commerce when it was necessary for the public interest, but he did not wish to see industry destroyed by the intrusion of government in business. He favored legislation to protect the consumer, such as the law which regulated the price of bread when it was being manipulated by the Company of Bakers; and he attacked the coal monopolists who drove coal up to an unreasonable price in London: "Thus are the poor ground in the dust, in order to fatten a pack of misers who know no mercy. But I hope the government will make 'em honest against their will." His two great books on the Plague Year were published in 1722 partly to support Walpole's unpopular Quarantine Act.

Defoe protested against pauperizing the nation by indiscriminate benevolence. He objected to the mounting cost of poor relief because of the wasteful profusion and the graft in its administration: " 'tis an easy matter to prevent begging in England, and yet to maintain all our impotent poor at far less charge to the parishes than they now are obliged to be at." He took an enlightened attitude in the controversy over charity schools, which some Whigs opposed on two grounds: that the High Church charity schools were breeding Jacobites, and that the education of orphans reduced the number of prospective servants. In several passages he defended the education of the lower classes, and he urged that rightly managed charity schools were beneficial institutions. In *Charity Still a Christian Virtue* (which he either wrote or revised for publication by a High Church clergyman) we find him for the only time in his life supporting Atterbury, the militant Bishop of Rochester.[18]

Defoe held that government subsidies and workhouse labor could be profitably used to introduce new arts and crafts, such as the manufacture of calico or muslin. But if workhouses manufactured woolen goods in competition with the established industry, the market would be glutted and the number of unemployed would be increased.

To him the use of pauper labor, under whatever pretext of workhouses or other public undertakings, was in effect a reduction of wages in general and an unsettling of the security of all employment for laborers. No man, he held, is secure of employment as long as any other man will do the same work for less pay. The use of pauper labor, by lowering the standard of living among the laboring class, would undermine the prosperity of the whole country.[19]

During the depression after Waterloo, the leader of the conservative economists had no remedy for declining profits but to cut wages. Profit, Ricardo held, is the margin above the cost of production. According to Ricardo's "iron law of wages," the "natural wage" will just keep the laborer alive. If wages become too high, laborers increase in number and cut their own wages by competition. If wages become too low, Providence mercifully reduces the number of laborers until scarcity of hands restores wages to the "natural" level.

A century before Ricardo, the world war of 1702–13 had continued so long that the depression had set in before the Peace of Utrecht. England suffered from the early throes of the Industrial Revolution. Her credit sagged under the first great national debt in her history. Her industries were prostrated by the long war and later by the collapse of a speculative market. Yet Defoe advocated high wages—at times to improve the workers' scale of living, at times chiefly as a means of keeping up agricultural prices, an end which mercantilists sought by a protective tariff or by a bounty on exports.

The mercantilists had no definite theory of wages, but they generally held that low wages enabled a nation to undersell competitors abroad. As Defoe dwelt on the subject, he argued that England could not undersell foreign competitors by cutting wages. Rival nations had certain advantages which England could not hope to equal, and the established scale of living among the English was such that English workmen could never compete with foreign labor at an equal wage. He arrived at the modern conception that a high wage scale not only maintains the home market but is economical in assuring a higher grade of work. The quality of English manufactures was due to the quality of English workmen. A reduction of wages would undermine the pre-eminence of English goods. The English must outsell their competitors by quality, not by low prices. He even came to oppose the corollary of low wages, the long working day: "the Englishmen shall do as much business in the fewer hours as the foreigner who sits longer at it."[20]

In his arguments for high wages, Defoe distinguished between real wages and nominal wages, pointing out repeatedly that for the laborers "nothing can do them any service, but what raises the price of their labor or sinks the price of provisions."

His pioneer interest in good roads was partly due to the effect of bad roads upon the cost of living in the cities, as well as to the necessity of highways for the inland trade. But as a lover of highways Defoe was never a mere economist; he was an enthusiastic traveler on horse or foot, and something of a poet and a humorist as well. He loved to picture the scenes of English life which were so dear to his eye:

For the further supplies of the markets of London with poultry, of which these countries [i.e., counties] particularly abound, they have within these few years found it practicable to make the geese travel on foot too, as well as the turkeys; and a prodigious number are brought up to London in droves from the farthest parts of Norfolk; . . . 'tis very frequent now to meet with droves, with a thousand, sometimes two thousand in a drove. They begin to drive them generally in August, by which time the harvest is almost over, and the geese may feed in the stubbles as they go. Thus they hold on to the end of October, when the roads begin to be too stiff and deep for their broad feet and short legs to march in.

Last of all, at heart he was ever the Puritan moralist. He might accept the temporary necessity of high customs duties under Walpole, but his mind lingered on the effect of these duties on the morals of the people: "I must lay it down as a maxim in this case, that clandestine trade, however ruinous, will never cease till we can abate our customs. High duties encourage smuggling, as rich travelers tempt highwaymen."

When Bishop Hoadly, as a party journalist, restated the central mercantilist doctrine, Defoe was shocked by the bad ethics more than by the erroneous economic theory "to hear a divine comment upon trade, and tell us that all trade is carried on to the gain of one side and the loss of another, which is as contrary to the nature of commerce as the poles are opposed to one another."[21]

As early as 1698 Dr. Davenant had rejected as unworthy of serious consideration "the old notion that luxury and some excess may be profitable." In the next generation Bernard Mandeville won fame by his brilliant extension and application of this "old notion," always with the keynote that private vices are public virtues. Defoe was fully aware of the importance of luxury in trade, and he was so fond of paradox that he would have had much to say on this subject even if

Mandeville had never lived. But after making all possible allowances for the ways in which "our vices are so unhappily mingled with our interest in trade," he held a very different ultimate view from that of Mandeville:

> In short, the luxury of the age will be the ruin of the nation, if not prevented. We leave trade to game in stocks; we live above ourselves, and barter our ready money for trifles; tea and wine are all we seem anxious for, and God has given the blessings of life to an ungrateful people, who despise their own productions. Our very plow-fellows drink wine nowadays; our farmers, graziers, and butchers are above malt liquors; and the wholesome breakfast of water-gruel and milk pottage is changed for coffee and tea. This is the reason provisions and corn, &c., are so dear; we all work for the vintners, and raise our prices upon one another to such a degree it will be an impossibility to live, as we shall, of course, become our own devourers.[22]

When Mandeville was dining at the luxurious table of Thomas Parker, Earl of Macclesfield, and was lending his pen to the defense of Macclesfield after his conviction, imprisonment, and fine of £30,-000 for corruption in the high office of Lord Chancellor, Defoe must have recalled the days of 1713 and 1715, when the same Parker had Defoe in his power for writing ironical tracts and a newspaper item against the Jacobites.

According to a proverb current in Staffordshire, that county had produced three of the greatest rogues that ever existed—the robber Jack Sheppard, the thief-taker Jonathan Wild, and Lord Macclesfield. In an anonymous street ballad (which seems to be Defoe's) Jack Sheppard is represented as making the same accusations against "the late Lord Chancellor of England" that Defoe had attributed to Sheppard in his attack on Jonathan Wild three years before:

> Were your virtues and mine to be weighed in a scale,
> I fear, honest Tom, that thine would prevail,
> For you broke through all laws, while I only broke jail,
> > Which nobody can deny.
>
> .　　.　　.　　.　　.　　.　　.　　.　　.　　.
>
> We who rob for a living, if taken, must die;
> Those who plunder poor orphans, pray answer me why
> They deserve not a rope more than Blueskin and I?
> > Which nobody can deny.[23]

Defoe's judgment of trade and of traders was not that of Bishop Hoadly or of Dr. Mandeville. He saw commerce as a noble instrument of civilization, and the tradesman as the means to its employ-ment: "The very name of English tradesman will and does already obtain in the world. And as our soldiers by the late war gained the reputation of being some of the best troops in the world, and as our seamen are at this day, and very justly too, esteemed the best sailors in the world, so the English tradesman may in a few years be allowed to rank with the best gentlemen in Europe; and as the Prophet Isaiah said of the merchants of Tyre, . . . her traffickers were the honorable of the earth."[24]

XXV. FAMILY AND PRIVATE LIFE

...as to those people who look for miracles, I have nothing to say to them.

Review, I, 254

I T W A S N O T U S U A L L Y through any desire for mystery that Defoe kept his family life from the public eye. He sought privacy in his home, and to a large extent he secured it. This was sometimes a matter of caution; his contemporaries might be allowed to guess that he was in Scotland when he was still in England, or in England after he had returned to Scotland. During the first five months of 1703, for a time during the summer of 1715, and again in the last years of his life, he was in actual hiding.

But his personal affairs were largely a secret even from those who might have been supposed to understand them. His son-in-law, Henry Baker, did not know his exact age. When Mrs. Brooke was granted administration of his effects in 1733 to satisfy her claim for alleged debts dating from his second bankruptcy, she should have been precise in her statements. But she put Defoe's death nine months too late; she named Daniel first, as if he were the older son; and she called his wife Susannah instead of Mary—giving rise to the long-held supposition that he was married twice. Charles Leslie, a political opponent who would have given a great deal for a rumor that Benjamin Defoe was illegitimate, admitted his ignorance about whether Defoe had a son. Benjamin was (by the attempt to explain Savage's jest about his inheriting his Billingsgate from an oysterwife) sometimes divided into two different sons of the same name—one legitimate and the other illegitimate. Although the records clearly establish the seniority of Benjamin, he has been represented as the younger brother of Daniel. And the relative ages of the four surviving daughters have been variously stated.

Concerning two of the six daughters, we know almost nothing except the approximate dates of their early deaths. Mary was buried as an infant in St. Michael's, Cornhill, on September 7, 1688. Martha, named in James Foe's will of March 20, 1705, was carried out of Hackney Parish to be buried in 1707.

The four other daughters all outlived their parents. We know their relative ages from the order in which their names appear in the wills of their uncle Samuel Tuffley and of their mother, and from Henry Baker's statement that he courted the youngest of the three sisters then remaining at home.

The oldest of these four, Maria, was married sometime after September 22, 1714, and before 1724. Her husband was named Langley, and he was probably related to the "Henry Langley of Queenhithe Salter" named in Tuffley's will as one of the three men who were to hold his estate in trust for the benefit of his sister, Mary Defoe.

The second daughter, Hannah, as the first assured spinster in the family, was provided for by her father through the purchase of South Sea stock at a deflated price after the Bubble had burst. In 1722 this stock was sold to make possible the purchase of a ninety-nine-year lease on Kingswood Heath, the property of the mayor and commonalty of the borough of Colchester, Essex. (Two years later Defoe made use of a long manuscript account of the siege of Colchester during the Civil War, in the first volume of his *Tour*.) After some confused dealings in which Defoe proposed a factory for making bricks and tiles on Hannah's property, in partnership with a man named Ward, in 1727 he paid off the mortgage which had been necessary to complete the purchase of the Kingswood Heath lease. Through the rapid increase in the value of the estate, Hannah had a secure income until her death in 1759, when she left her property to a nephew, John Boston, the ne'er-do-well son of her sister Henrietta.

When Mrs. Defoe made her will on July 5, 1731, the third daughter, Henrietta, who was then somewhat past thirty, was married to John Boston, of Much-Hadham in Hertfordshire, who moved to Wimborne, Dorset, when he was appointed supervisor of the excise there. Henrietta died on March 5 (or May 5, according to a variant account), 1760; and although she was a Dissenter, like all her immediate family, she was buried in the collegiate church of Wimborne, in the same vault with her husband and her sister Hannah. Her branch of the family came to an end with the death of an only grandson.

Sophia, Defoe's dear "Sophy" or "Sophi," of whose auburn hair and blue eyes Henry Baker wrote in his over-fragrant narrative of his courtship, was baptized at Hackney on December 24, 1701. She was mentioned with her brothers and sisters in three wills and in the legal citation by Mrs. Brooke in 1733; otherwise we know little of her except from the journal of Henry Baker and the letters which resulted from the haggling over her dowry.

Baker was an unpleasant anomaly. He was a sentimentalist who sought every financial advantage for himself, and a scientist who carried to the grave the secret of his method of teaching the deaf and dumb (unless the secret was revealed in the now-lost lessons and exercises listed as Items 21, 22, and 24 in the British Museum's sale catalogue of Dawson Turner's manuscripts [June 6–10, 1859]).

At twenty-two, after his apprenticeship to a bookseller in London, Baker was visiting his relative Mr. Forster, at Enfield, about five miles north of Stoke Newington. It was here that he worked out an ingenious system for teaching Forster's eight-year-old daughter to speak. As his fame grew among the gentry and aristocracy, Baker devoted himself to instructing the deaf and dumb; but he was careful to require a £100 bond from each pupil, guaranteeing that his methods would not be revealed.

Defoe, the amateur of science, invited him to visit at Stoke Newington. In a tract which grew out of the notoriety of the idiot Wild Boy discovered in Hanover, Defoe inserted a poem "On the Deaf and Dumb being taught to Speak"; he argued that "Mr. Baker himself, though he has done more than I believe was ever done before him," could not teach "a dumb fool" to speak; and after raising the question whether the Wild Boy could be taught, he gave Baker a magnificent advertisement: "I am told that nobody can, if he cannot."

On his frequent visits at Stoke Newington, Baker soon fell in love with Defoe's youngest daughter. It was most unfortunate for Sophia that her lover was the son of a chancery clerk, whose closest friend was an eminent attorney. Baker wrote of his prospective marriage with a lawyer's quill, and even in his highest raptures the dry dust of parchment lingered in his veins. For several years the promised marriage of Sophia was delayed while Baker tried to force Defoe to guarantee her dowry by mortgaging property in Essex, by getting a man named Sutton to re-examine the terms of a lease, by mortgaging the family home in Stoke Newington, or by assuring Baker of 5 per cent interest instead of 4 on Sophia's dowry while it remained in Defoe's hands. He also sought some increase in Sophia's dowry through a personal examination of the City Customs. These were, as Mr. F. Bastian has informed me, legally sanctioned traditions which limited the testamentary freedom of citizens of London and gave their children a legal claim on their estates.

For a time Baker won Sophia over to his side, so that she joined in his complaints against her father's mysterious dealings. But to anyone who reads the surviving letters carefully, Defoe comes out of the controversy with high credit. Baker persisted in asking him to pay down more money than he ever promised, to break settlements already made for his other children, and to make financial commitments in his lifetime which Defoe felt he had no right to make until his death.

The bulk of Defoe's property had been assigned to Daniel Jr. as a precaution against having it involved in legal entanglements (for the frivolous and erratic older son Benjamin was no longer mentioned as a member of the family, except in Mrs. Defoe's will in 1732 and in the assignment to Mrs. Brooke in 1733). Baker and Sophia alike came to blame Daniel Jr. as the principal obstruction to their happiness; but it is not clear that Defoe agreed with them. He certainly hoped that Daniel would do his part as a son and brother; but according to his own statements he had power to force a settlement from Daniel, and he did not try to do this. When he was in hiding from the exactions of Mrs. Brooke, so far removed from the usual channels of communication that a letter from Baker took eleven days to reach him, he wrote a reply to Baker in which the following passage occurs (September 12, 1730):

It has been the injustice, unkindness, and I must say, inhuman dealings of my own son which has both ruined my family, and, in a word, has broken my heart; and as I am at this time under a weight of very heavy illness, which I think will be a fever, I take this occasion to vent my grief in the breasts who I know will make a prudent use of it, and tell you, that nothing but this has conquered me or could conquer me. *Et tu! Brute.* I depended upon him, I trusted him, I gave up my two dear unprovided daughters into his hands; but he has no compassion, and suffers them and their poor dying mother to beg their bread at his door, and to crave, as if it were an alms, what he is bound under hand and seal, besides the most sacred promises, to supply them with: himself, at the same time, living in a profusion of plenty. It is too much for me. Excuse my infirmity. I can say no more: my heart is too full. I only ask one thing of you as a dying request. Stand by them when I am gone, and let them not be wronged while he is able to do them right. Stand by them as a brother; and if you have anything within you owing to my memory, who have bestowed on you the best gift I had to give, let them not be injured and trampled on by false pretences and unnatural reflections. I hope they will want no help but that of comfort and council; but that they will indeed want, being too easy to be managed by words and promises.

Defoe was certainly reaching the end of his career. He gave up the editorship of the *Political State of Great-Britain* a few weeks later, and he died in the next spring. At this moment he was being pressed by two urgent claimants: Mrs. Brooke (who professed to hold unsatisfied debts which Defoe had thought of as canceled a generation before) and Baker himself (who, for an ardent young husband, was unconscionably eager to secure every penny of his wife's expected dowry).

Possibly Daniel Jr. was a rapacious son who withheld his father's benevolence; the whole trend of Defoe's portrayal of filial ingratitude in *The Protestant Monastery* (1727) counts in that direction. Possibly he was the accommodating son who acted as his father's silent partner and helped to hold the property together; Defoe's suggestion in 1728 that Baker return a lease to Daniel Jr. supports this view. Perhaps he was not quite either character, but a well-to-do man of early middle age to whom prosperity had come easily, who had profited by his father's bounty, and who proved in a family emergency less blessed in giving than in receiving. Without more evidence we are hardly entitled to bring in a judgment. However, two peculiarities in this passage from the letter to Baker have never been remarked on:

(1) Mrs. Defoe had considerable property in her own name, Hannah was well provided for in her own right, and Henrietta was the only one of the other daughters not already married. Perhaps the "dear unprovided" daughter most likely to be thought of here was Henry Baker's wife.

(2) Although Defoe insisted that the claims against Daniel Jr. were enforceable by law, as "he is bound under hand and seal," he did not appeal to Baker to institute proceedings against his brother-in-law. Perhaps this was meant to avoid giving an opening for Mrs. Brooke, who was seeking to attach the whole estate. But it is clear that he asked Baker to act as a loyal member of the family, protecting the interests of Mrs. Defoe and the girls, rather than to appear as a rival claimant.

Through the series of letters, Defoe remained deeply affectionate toward Sophia (although wounded by her temporary bitterness), and he continued to offer Baker as liberal a settlement as he could honorably make, together with his own friendship and the hand of his favorite daughter. When Baker started the *Universal Spectator and Weekly Journal* in the fall of 1728, Defoe gave him a very able leading article for his opening number.

But Baker was not satisfied with anything Defoe could honorably give him; he was an ambitious young man with a shrewd eye to his own future—one who drove his fiancée almost into a breakdown while he haggled over her dowry. Before his death he had accumulated a fortune of £20,000 and was able to devote his abundant leisure to genteel scientific pursuits, whereas his father-in-law ended a life of intense application to affairs by hiding to avoid arrest for the pretended claims of a greedy creditor.

Even without Baker's constant returning to the dowry, the sentimental tone of his love letters is not altogether pleasing to a modern reader: "Methinks I fold thee in my eager arms, and bask and pant and wanton in thy smiles; and now I hold thee off and gaze upon thy charms with infinite delight, and now all ecstasy I snatch thee to me, and devour thy lips, strain thee with breathless raptures to my bosom, till feeble mortal nature faints, unable to endure bliss so excessive, and sinks with joys celestial." In dealing with a lover of this quality, Defoe must have felt disposed to fall back on his favorite aphorism: "There is no remedy but patience." After the courtship had dragged on more than four years, delayed primarily by the question of the dowry, even Sophia balked when Baker proposed that they take poison and die in each other's arms: "The world telling with wonder our amazing story, pitying our youth [she was twenty-seven and he almost thirty-one] and our too cruel fate. It might be, some brother bard with monumental verse would celebrate our memory and give us down with praise to future times." Still not a word to indicate that he would marry Sophia without her dowry! It is only fair to Baker to recall that he was a poet—a bad one—and that he lived just late enough to be infected with the taint of eighteenth-century sentimentalism.

Henry Baker and Sophia were finally married on April 30, 1729, and—although the dowry remained almost (if not quite) the foremost interest in Baker's mind until Defoe's death two years later—they seem to have lived happily together until her death on January 4, 1772. Baker died in 1774. Of their two sons, David Erskine Baker showed promise as a mathematician, but soon went on the stage and won some distinction as the compiler of a useful stage chronicle called *The Companion to the Play-House* (1764). As the godson of the Earl of Buchan, he naturally received a middle name; biographers have not yet been foolish enough to suggest (as they have often done for his uncle Benjamin) that this middle name proves him illegitimate. Henry, the Bakers' other son, after a brief career as a shabby attorney, died rather young; but it is from him that the English family of Defoe Bakers were descended.

In his heartbroken letter to Sophia about six weeks after the marriage, Defoe upbraided her for ungrateful words used to him and said that ten times as much would not have hurt him if it had been said by "Deb, The *Hasty*, the *Rash*, and So far *Weak*." If Deb was a poor relation or a privileged servant who took part in family discussions, such a comparison would have seemed uncalled for. If she was one of Sophia's sisters, she must have been either Hannah or Henrietta, but called "Deb" as a nickname.

Of the two sons, Benjamin was the elder. His name was mentioned before Daniel's in the wills of his grandfather Foe, his uncle Samuel Tuffley, and his mother. His grandfather left him only a watch and his brother £100 to be used at the age of twenty-one as "Stocking money"—no doubt to help establish Daniel in business, a clear indication that James Foe expected his son to make Benjamin his principal heir. He was entered at Edinburgh University, where Defoe's friend the Rev. William Carstares was the principal, presumably to prepare him to succeed his father in his journalistic enterprises in Scotland. By August 29, 1712, we know that he was in London again, for on that date he was entered at the Inner Temple as the son and heir apparent of Daniel Defoe of Stoke Newington. Three years later another young student of the law, Dudley Ryder (who makes no mention of Daniel Jr.), was a good deal impressed by Benjamin's self-assurance as they frequented Westminster Hall together, attended Hackney Meeting, or walked about discussing public affairs.

Two unpleasant features of Benjamin's character are suggested by Ryder's diary: that he would expect a bottle of wine if Ryder invited him to his home, and that he was a shallow exhibitionist: "He is a talkative sort of young fellow, tells a story tolerably but does not seem to have very good sense, seems to be mighty superficial and talks the notions he has had from his father." Here we see two probable causes of Benjamin's early downfall: a fondness for drink and an itch for dabbling in politics. A third cause is suggested by the will of October 22, 1714, in which Samuel Tuffley left his estate to trustees for his sister, Mary Defoe. Tuffley inserted a remarkable passage urging her not to give one shilling to any child who proved disrespectful or disobedient to either parent, implying that one of the children had already caused difficulty at home.

On September 22, 1718, the graceless and improvident Benjamin was married to Hannah Coates of Norwich, whose mother was a widow. Here again Benjamin was dogging his father's footsteps, for Norwich was a provincial city in which Defoe had strong connections. In the record of the marriage in the church register of St. Helen, Benjamin was listed as a "singleman" of Stoke Newington. On June 6 of the next year the first child of Benjamin and Hannah was baptized in the Octagon Chapel in Norwich. This infant was a second Benjamin (or the third Benjamin in two generations, if we give credence to the attempt to divide Defoe's older son into two different people of the same name).

From 1719 everything seems to have gone wrong with Benjamin. About the end of 1720 or the earlier part of 1721, with a growing family, no capital, and no special aptitude except a facility with his pen, he came back to London and sold his services to the Opposition. The recent collapse of the South Sea Bubble, the unpopularity of Sunderland, and the approaching end of the Septennial Parliament's long term had revived the hopes of the Jacobites and of all other opponents of the Hanoverians and the Ministry. His father was still writing pamphlets and managing the press for the government; but Benjamin put himself under the guidance of the Opposition writer Thomas Gordon and began to contribute to the anti-ministerial paper the *London Journal*. He had the good grace to attempt to drop the name Defoe and to write under the pseudonym Norton; but this offered no real concealment in a London where his father was so well known. It was even rumored, most embarrassingly, that the elder Defoe himself was writing the objectionable articles.

The son escaped punishment by making terms with the government, and from this time on he was variously known as Benjamin Defoe, Benjamin Norton, Norton Defoe, Benjamin Norton Defoe, and B. N. Defoe. No one but Richard Savage (and after him Pope) pretended even in jest to think there was any mystery about his birth. No one supposed that Defoe's older son Benjamin was a different person from Benjamin Norton until later biographers tried to explain two stories which were mutually contradictory. The elder Defoe did not seek to hide their relationship, referring to Benjamin in Applebee's *Journal* for August 26, 1721, not unkindly as "young Defoe," and suggesting that the boy was no dangerous opponent of the Ministry, "but a stalking horse and a tool, to bear the lash and the pillory in their stead for his wages; that he is the author of the most scandalous part, but is only made sham proprietor of the whole, to screen the true proprietors from justice; and we hear their paper sinks upon it every day."

Benjamin's superior on the *London Journal,* the vehement "Patriot" Thomas Gordon, sold out to Walpole and also received a legacy from a freethinker as a reward for his attacks on religion; and so he was able to die wealthy, immensely fat, and somewhat famous as a translator of the classics. Benjamin Defoe also sold out to Walpole; but he lacked Gordon's effrontery or his skill, and he proved too shifty to be trusted by Walpole. His letter to Sir Hans Sloane in 1733 shows him attempting to ingratiate himself with a distinguished stranger by gross flattery:

Sᵣ HANS

As I am a Servant of the Administration's may I be permitted to present to Yourself, as I am by other Noble personages, the Lives of the Princes of The Illustrious House of Orange; One of which has Just now So much, under God, been Indebted to Your Extensive Knowledge for a Recovery from a Dangerous Indisposition: I presume no farther, only to beg leave to assure you Sʳ· that I should Esteem it a peculiar honour to be allowed

Decᵇ: 11ᵗʰ: 1733

Sr Hans
Your Most Obedient
Most Humble Servant
B. N. *Defoe*

The shrewd letter which another Benjamin, the boy Franklin, wrote to Sloane a few years earlier was not only far more manly; it was vastly more successful as well.

At times Benjamin must have broken completely with the Defoes, for his brother was referred to as the only son. But in 1732 his widowed mother bequeathed him one pound to buy a mourning ring, as she did for Daniel Jr. (who was himself on bad terms with his mother and sisters before that time).

In 1737 Benjamin's wife "was brought from Hackney, and buried in Bunhill Fields." Fourteen of his seventeen children were dead, and he was in dire need, when he was writing three letters to the Duke of Newcastle to beg for aid or employment under the government (October 2, 1738; November 11 and 24, 1739). After that time, in the words of Professor Realey, "Benjamin Defoe drops wailing into the limbo of forgotten authors." Except for his notoriety as a writer against his father and the government, and the immortality of a place in *The Dunciad*, his memory was as fleeting as the lives of most of his children.

There have been traditions that he (or possibly his brother Daniel) emigrated to the Carolinas. Through an extensive correspondence with many Defoes still living in the United States, I have repeatedly come near to establishing an unbroken ancestral line; but gaps have always appeared near the middle of the eighteenth century. The most interesting (and apparently the most promising) line leads through Benjamin De Foe of Virginia (whose first child, with the strongly reminiscent name of James, was born on August 16, 1777). This Benjamin was the father of John, whose son Thomas became the father of a family which included Luther M. Defoe, a distinguished professor of mathematics at the University of Missouri while I was an undergraduate there.

In 1705 Daniel Jr. was mentioned in James Foe's will to receive £100 when he came of age. On September 2, 1710, he was referred to in Defoe's letter to Harley as one of his "six children, almost grown up, and perfectly unprovided for." He was not, like his older brother, entered at Edinburgh University or at the Inner Temple, but he was included in his father's assertion that he had educated his children. There are stray indications that both he and Benjamin were sometimes employed by their father as messengers or copyists. On February 10, 1713, the Rev. William Carstares sent his respects to Defoe's lady and the young ladies his daughters, "not forgetting your sons."

By a misinterpretation of the Clerkenwell parish register, it has sometimes been supposed that Daniel Jr. married a girl named Dorothy, and that their son Daniel was baptized on January 1, 1709. Whoever this Daniel Defoe was, he was a considerably older man.

In 1714 Samuel Tuffley's will stipulated that a guinea was to be given Daniel for a mourning ring. From 1719 to 1721 Daniel was interested in the Ram & Colebrook Society (later the London Assurance). As he made himself answerable for £1,000, he must have been fairly well-to-do. At this time, and for some years afterward, he lived in Finch Lane, Cornhill, in St. Michael's—just east of his father's old home in Freeman's Yard and north of the church in which his infant sister Mary had been buried before he was born. On March 20, 1720, he was married by license from the Archbishop of Canterbury in Esq. Aske's Chapel in Hoxton to Mary Webb, of St. Mary, Aldermanbury; and on June 14, 1724, their infant son Daniel was buried at Hackney. Mary Webb was possibly related to Thomas Webb, the Quaker who expressed deep obligation to the elder Defoe for his having "acted a noble and generous part towards me and my poor children" after he had lost his wife in 1725.

In June, 1720, when Defoe was taken up for questioning about his journalistic relations with Nathaniel Mist, young Defoe was one of two men who became his sureties for £100 each (in addition to the £200 for which the elder Defoe was liable). On August 23, 1725, Daniel Defoe, Jr., "of St. Michael, Cornhill, merchant," was named as one of three sureties in the bond for the estate of Samuel Tuffley. In the same year he was listed (with his father) among the subscribers to Charles Lillie's collection of the previously unpublished letters submitted to the *Tatler* and the *Spectator*. On January 21, 1729, he was still living in Finch Lane. On August 12, 1730, he was referred to as the ungrateful son to whom Defoe had intrusted the care of his wife and his unprotected daughters. Like Benjamin, he was named in his mother's will in 1731 to receive a pound for a mourning ring, and he was cited as a member of the family by Mrs. Brooke in 1733.

The unsolved problem about Daniel Jr. is what he did with his father's property, assigned to him as a precaution against having it engulfed by old claims dating from Defoe's bankruptcy. In a bitter letter of August 12, 1730, Defoe wrote that his ungrateful son was "living in a profusion of plenty." In 1736 Daniel Jr., now residing in Hackney, was an unsuccessful candidate for the post of secretary of the Million Bank, receiving one vote. In 1738 he wrote a letter from London to a cousin, Miss Cornwall. Through his descendants the name Defoe was carried down to a great-grandson, after whom his branch of the family survived only in the female line. Unless he suffered financial reverses in his later life, he was far less likely to have emigrated to America than his brother Benjamin.

There is little doubt that Defoe, like Shakespeare and Scott, hoped to establish a family name that would last. He had this in mind when he assumed the title "Gentleman" and when he chose the motto "Laudatur et Alget," which first appeared under the portrait on the frontispiece of his *Jure Divino*. His second home at Stoke Newington was his own equivalent of Shakespeare's house at Stratford or Sir Walter Scott's at Abbotsford. Wright told of a family seal which reproduced the arms inscribed under the *Jure Divino* portrait: "Per chevron engrailed, gules and or, three griffins passant counterchanged." A variant of this coat of arms had been inscribed under his portrait in the 1703 edition of the *True Collection*.

It is not unusual for the family of a great man to die out, or for his scions to show little of the special gifts of their progenitor. Of Defoe's children, only Benjamin became a writer; and of his grandchildren, only Daniel Erskine Baker. The two most striking characteristics shown by his descendants are these: in the Defoe Baker line they tended to become clergymen in the Church of England, and in some of the other lines they often sought for adventurous action. A grandson of Daniel Jr. was hanged as a highwayman; the only grandson of Henrietta was drowned as a sailor; a late descendant near the end of the nineteenth century aroused newspaper curiosity by appearing as a cook on a ship which anchored at New York. Possibly the highwayman, the sailors, and the preachers all represented qualities latent in the ancestral strain. Even more interesting is the fact that the supposed highwayman was probably innocent; according to some contemporary opinions, he was hanged solely because of the panic fear of a wealthy coward who testified against him.

In "Ben Jonson Entertains a Man from Stratford" E. A. Robinson represented an earlier poet as regretting that Shakespeare had wasted his concern on so unworthy an object: "O Lord, that House in Stratford!" But a lover of Scott can hardly regret Abbotsford; and a lover of Defoe realizes that the two homes in Stoke Newington helped him to complete his lifework. There Defoe lived during most of his last twenty-three years. There he saw his six surviving children grow into maturity, and all but two of them leave the family circle during his lifetime for homes of their own. There he built up the collection of books, manuscripts, and maps which made possible so much of his later writing. There he wrote by far the greater part of the works for which he is known today. There he unbent for much of the conversation which meant even more to some of his contemporaries than his writings.

John Bell, the postmaster who served as Harley's agent at Newcastle, had read only part of one of Defoe's books, and he was uncertain whether Defoe had written that; but he had no doubt about Defoe's ability to carry out the mission in Scotland, after he had enjoyed his conversation for two or three days. John Fransham, a linen-draper in Norwich, wrote to Defoe of "the pleasure of your conversation." Henry Baker, before he fell in love with the youngest daughter, "was so pleased with his conversation, that he seldom came to Newington without paying a visit to Mr. D——."

Defoe had the gift of listening as well as of talking. When the High

Fliers of Coventry had exposed themselves by speaking too freely in his presence, he wrote to assure them through his friend Edward Owen that he would never betray their confidence. At times he went in disguise, maintaining whatever character was necessary to hear what others were saying, from Cornwall to northern Scotland. More often he appeared in his own person, and in the company of people who represented the widest possible social range: King William, Queen Mary, and Queen Anne; the Dukes of Queensberry and Gordon; the Earls of Peterborough, Nottingham, Godolphin, Oxford, and Halifax, and almost certainly Lord Somers; Bishop Tillotson and Carstares and other clergymen of all ranks and denominations in England and in Scotland; military men like Lieutenant General Maitland; travelers, merchants, publishers, shipwrights, and projectors; men and women in almost every walk of life, from the great Quaker William Penn down to pickpockets, streetwalkers, highwaymen, and pirates.

They all talked to Defoe, and he preferred the spoken to the written word. Over and over we find him begging Harley for a chance to speak rather than to write to him: "but six words," "I beg a few moments," "but six words." Whenever the discussion did not get out of hand, these conversations were carried on in a spirit of good will. William III smiled, and so did Godolphin, and so—except under extreme provocation from such a man as Nottingham—did Defoe himself.

There was no Boswell to record the talk. Even in Boswell's hands it might have lacked much of the wisdom and humor which come through to us in the conversation of Dr. Johnson. Defoe spoke more often as a projector, a statesman, an economist, or a political reporter, less often as a human being. But he must have been one of the best talkers of his age; and his conversation had one great advantage over Dr. Johnson's—that it was more often shared with sovereigns and church dignitaries and ministers of state, so that it helped to shape the course of public affairs.

Henry Baker has told us that even in Stoke Newington Defoe had to withdraw from the company at times, during attacks of gout or the stone. Sometimes his withdrawals must have been due to the pressure of his many writings. Sometimes they may have been due to the nature of the man, who was even more at home on the desert island than in the familiar haunts of London.

Defoe had a loyal wife, a trusted brother-in-law, and eight children, one of whom was his darling. And yet it was when he was by himself that he expressed his personality most completely. His devoted wife managed many of his affairs, but we see little trace of her in his writings. His brother-in-law Robert Davis traveled with him, shared in several of his projects, and bore some of his confidential messages, but we cannot be certain that Davis knew anything of his deeper thoughts. Of his six children who lived to maturity, Benjamin and Daniel failed him completely in the end, and even Sophia took sides against him when he needed her most.

John Forster's dates were confused by his assumption that Defoe was born a year later than he actually was. But what Forster said of Defoe's disagreement with those Dissenters who welcomed King James's Declaration of Indulgence remains essentially true: "In his twenty-sixth year, he found himself that solitary, restless, independent thinker, which, up to his seventieth year, he remained. . . . He was thus early initiated in the transcendent art of thinking and standing alone."

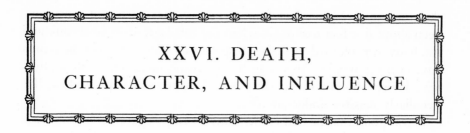

XXVI. DEATH,
CHARACTER, AND INFLUENCE

It was never any part of my character to be afraid of a
man, that shall die, or of the honest cause of Truth, which
shall live.

Review, [IX], 211

On SATURDAY, April 24, 1731, a weary old man passed away in a lodging house in Ropemaker's Alley. According to the parish register of St. Giles, Cripplegate, his ailment was a lethargy, which for a man of Defoe's temperament meant total exhaustion. The springs which had kept mind and body in such active motion had run down at last.

His health had been failing from year to year under his unparalleled exertions. When he lay in hiding from Newgate and the pillory, he could write confidently of volunteering to lead a troop of cavalry in Flanders. By the time he was forty-six, he was urging Harley to preserve his health, citing his own neglect of his iron constitution: "The body is not made for wonders, and when I hint that denying yourself needful and regular hours of rest will disorder the best constitution in the world, I speak by my own immediate experience, who having despised sleep, hours, and rules, have broken in upon a perfectly established health, which no distresses, disasters, jails, or melancholy could ever hurt before." At fifty he was making some use of spectacles.[1] After he was sixty-four, Henry Baker found that gout and the stone sometimes forced him to withdraw from company in his own home. But his hand was able to serve his active brain until almost the very end.

The figure on the bed in the lodging house was not a large one, even for the eighteenth century, when the average human frame was smaller than now. The Earl of Nottingham's informant had called Defoe a middle-sized man. In the nineteenth century, when his coffin was accidentally opened during the erection of a new monument, his skeleton measured five feet four inches—so that his height must have been about five feet five or six when the cartilages were unshrunk and the body was clothed in flesh. He possessed such energy as few men have ever known, but his strength was always moral rather than physical. Those who saw his remains in 1870 were most impressed by "his peculiarly massive under-jaw."[2]

It was good that he had come home to Cripplegate Parish to die. It would not have been safe for him to venture back to the great red brick house in Stoke Newington. And when obliged to remain in London and yet keep hidden from the fury of Mrs. Brooke, he could ask nothing better than the straight and quiet row which ran east and west not far north of the city wall—"*Ropemakers Alley*, pretty broad, with several Garden Houses; which are well built and inhabited." An eighth of a mile to the south lay Fore Street, in or near which he had been born over seventy years before. A quarter of a mile to the north lay Tindall's (later known as Bunhill Fields), where he was to be buried near John Bunyan and so many other Dissenters on Monday, two days later. All through the quiet Sunday which interposed, his body lay at rest.

Sunday had always been observed by Defoe as holy. Of his surviving letters, only four are correctly dated as written (on great emergencies) on that day, although he was often hurried to get letters off to Harley on the Monday post from Edinburgh. He was a Puritan, but no bigot. What he objected to was the abuse of Sunday through idle debauchery: "Not that I am so superciliously strict, to have the Sabbath kept as rigidly here as in Scotland, but then there ought to be a medium between the severity of a fast and the riot of Saturnalia. Instead of a decent and cheerful solemnity, our taverns and public houses have more business on that day than all the week besides."[3]

Defoe had never set up for a saint, but he could defy his detractors to justify any charge of flagrant vice: "I thank God my life, however mixed with misfortune, has not been such that I am ashamed to see it in print." In an age of sensual pleasures, he was an unusually abstemious man. He regarded tobacco as useless except in medicine, and he was free from drunkenness and licentiousness. His greatest fault of character was rooted in the courage which was his greatest virtue; for he fought at least one duel, and he came close to several others. Slow to be aroused (like his own Colonel Jack), when he was really angry he was temporarily beside himself with "the boiling of the blood, the furious agitation of the animal spirits." Far more often, and more characteristically, he kept his temper and smiled at the ruffians who threatened him: "I move about the world unguarded and unarmed. A little stick not strong enough to correct a dog supplies the place of Mr. Observator's great oaken-towel, a sword sometimes for decency, but it is all harmless to a mere nothing; can do no harm anywhere but just at the tip of it called the point—and what's that in the hand of a feeble author?"[4]

A generation earlier a poet whom Defoe admired greatly, John Dryden, had been buried in Westminster Abbey, escorted by a vast train of carriages of the nobility and gentry. Defoe's burial took place so quietly that in eight of the nine contemporary accounts his death was said to have occurred on the day of his funeral. The ignorant person who recorded his burial in the register at Tindall's (Bunhill Fields) misspelled his name as "Mr. Dubow." But the register of St. Giles, Cripplegate, gave him the honor he prized: "Mr. Defoe, gentleman."

On Saturday of the same week a journal which had opposed him in politics paid tribute to his civic character: "A few Days ago dy'd Mr. Defoe, Sen., a Person well known for his numerous and various Writings. He had a great natural Genius; and understood very well the Trade and Interest of this Kingdom. His Knowledge of Men, especially those in High Life (with whom he was formerly very conversant) had weaken'd his Attachment to any Party; but in the main, he was in the Interest of Civil and Religious Liberty, in behalf of which he appeared on several remarkable Occasions."[5] A little later the *Political State of Great-Britain*, which had passed into the hands of his adversaries, referred to him not unkindly in its summary of the news for April: "About the end of this Month died Mr. *Daniel Defoe*, Sen. a Person well known for his numerous and various Writings; by some of which it appears that he had a good natural Genius, and he was generally look'd on as a Man who thorowly understood the Theory of Trade, and the true Interest of this Nation; but he never had the good fortune to be much taken notice of by any Minister of State, so that he got but little by his Knowledge." "Good natural genius," "a man who thoroughly understood the theory of trade, and the true interest of this nation," "he got but little by his knowledge." These are almost the very words in which Defoe would have summed up his own abilities and his career.

On November 13 prospective purchasers were offered a printed catalogue of the library "of the late Ingenious Daniel De Foe, Gent., lately deceas'd. Containing a curious Collection of Books: relating to the History and Antiquities of divers Nations, particularly England, Scotland, and Ireland, . . . N. B. Manuscripts. Also several hundred curious, scarce Tracts on Parliamentary Affairs, Politicks, Husbandry, Trade, Voyages, Natural History, Mines, Minerals, &c." By December 20 of the next year his widow had died and their two unmarried daughters had become executrices of her will. The books which he had used so often were scattered, and no one lived to bear his name except two ungrateful sons and their children.

"But not the Fame!" as Milton had cried out in "Lycidas," his protest against death as the great destroyer of the ordinary satisfactions of life.

One of the most eminent living masters of the art has said that a good biography should encourage people "to believe that man's mind is in truth unconquerable and that character can triumph over the most hostile circumstances, provided only that it remains true to itself."[6]

Defoe's character is in many ways as remarkable as his books. Think of his contemporaries—Steele, crippled by gout in his thirties, and hooted at by street urchins as he rode through the Strand in his sedan chair; Pope in his forties, laced up and coddled with flannels, waited on during winter nights by a servant maid with candles and a brazier of charcoal; Addison in his mid-forties, choking with asthma, and begging his dissolute stepson to see how a Christian could die; Defoe near the end of his fiftieth year, inserting advertisements in the *Review* inviting a companion to join a middle-aged gentleman on a walking tour through western England for pleasure. Only a few months before his death Defoe was writing with his old fire and verve.

His influence lies under much that is best in modern literature, and under much that is best in modern life, as the old bed of the ocean lies under the upper crust of the earth. And sometimes, as in the Grand Canyon of the Colorado, the surface is torn open so that we can see all the way down to the prehistoric bed of the ocean—the grays and yellows and reds and pinks and greens of all human experience. And then we have a masterpiece like *A Journal of the Plague Year*, or like *Robinson Crusoe*—which even so popular a critic as William Lyon Phelps recognized as the greatest book in the world.

In 1750 *Crusoe* gave rise to Paltock's *Peter Wilkins*, which in turn was a primary source for *The Rime of the Ancient Mariner*. In 1762 Rousseau made *Crusoe* the only textbook for the ideal education of his Émile, and some years later a friend who visited Rousseau in Paris found that it was one of the two books in his library. Rousseau's bitter opponent Dr. Johnson was one of *Crusoe*'s warmest admirers, and the same Coleridge who professed to reject Johnson's literary criticism was profoundly impressed by Johnson's beloved *Crusoe*, and Coleridge's severe critic Hazlitt named Defoe as the model of simple English prose. Sir Walter Scott was not only Defoe's first editor, one of his first biographers, and perhaps the greatest collector of Defoe's works in the early nineteenth century; he was profoundly influenced by Defoe's writings. And George Borrow, who stood apart from most of the authors just mentioned, did not lag behind them in his tribute to the man who was—in so many ways—the master of them all. After a magnificent account of his discovery of *Crusoe* at the age of six, "Lavengro" came back again to its praise:

a book which has exerted over the minds of Englishmen an influence certainly greater than any *other* of modern times; which has been in most people's minds, and with the contents of which even those who cannot read are to a certain extent acquainted; a book from which the most luxuriant and fertile of our modern prose writers have drunk inspiration; a book, moreover, to which, from the hardy deeds which it narrates, and the spirit of strange and romantic enterprise which it tends to awaken, England owes many of her astonishing discoveries by sea and land, and no inconsiderable part of her naval glory.

Hail to thee, spirit of DeFoe! What does not my own poor self owe to thee? England has better bards than either Greece or Rome, yet I could spare them easier than Defoe, "unabashed Defoe," as the hunchbacked rhymer called him.

Indeed, no quality of Defoe's writings is more remarkable than their appeal to such different readers, on so many different subjects and in so many different ways. A psychiatrist sends me a reference to a German article on Defoe's theory of treating the insane. A Japanese sends me a study of Defoe's economic ideas. The chairman of the planning commission of a very large city speaks of Defoe's influence on Benjamin Franklin, the most civic-minded of Philadelphians. A businessman of national eminence is interested in Defoe's theories of trade. An honors graduate of Oxford and a member of the Parisian Académie Malagaise, an Englishman born in Madagascar and the author of a remarkable book on that island, writes that when his mission school opened in the interior of the country, one of his first pupils, who had walked hundreds of miles overland through forests and over mountains from his home at the southern tip, seemed to have stepped out of the pages of *Robert Drury's Journal*.

The correspondent of Cotton Mather and the close friend of such eminent clergymen as Carstares and Dr. Williams was the same man who wrote *Moll Flanders*, by the discovery of which in nineteenth-century France a new school of realistic fiction was inspired. The economist and the adviser of statesmen was also the begetter of Thoreau's solitude at Walden and of Stevenson's lifelong quest of islands in the Hebrides or the South Sea.

Of Defoe, perhaps more than of any other English author but Shakespeare, it could be truly said, "There is no land where his voice is not heard." What the clownish Chremes of Roman comedy said in jest, he might have declared in sober earnest: "Whatever concerns mankind is of interest to me." For Defoe, above almost any other, we may recall the words of Sir Francis Bacon: "he is a citizen of the world, and . . . his heart is no island cut off from other lands, but a continent that joins to them."

CHRONOLOGICAL OUTLINE

1660—Daniel Defoe born in London (perhaps in Fore Street, Cripplegate). Son of James and Alice Foe. James a tallow-chandler (later a member of the Butchers' Company and probably, although perhaps not quite certainly, a butcher) from Etton, in Northamptonshire, where his Flemish ancestors had settled in the sixteenth century. Alice's father had owned a country estate; there are some indications of a family connection in Leicestershire. Defoe's sister Mary born November 13, 1657; married Francis Barham (or Bartham), Jr., a shipwright, May 20, 1679. Defoe's sister Elizabeth born June 19, 1659; later married Robert Davis, engineer and builder, Defoe's personal representative in several transactions and his companion on many travels.

1662 (St. Bartholomew's Day, August 24)—The Foes and their pastor, Dr. Samuel Annesley, forced out of the Church of England by the Act of Uniformity. They became Presbyterians.

1665—Lawrence Marsh of Dorking died, leaving funeral rings to Cousin Foe and his wife. Marsh owned extensive property in Essex, in London, and in Dorking.

1665-66—The Great Plague. Perhaps (like the brother in *A Journal of the Plague Year*) James Foe removed his family to the country while Henry resided in London.

1666 (September 2-5)—The Great Fire of London.

About 1668—Death of Defoe's mother. Alice Foe was mentioned in the will of Lawrence Marsh (1665) but not in that of his widow, Elizabeth Marsh (1671).

1668(?)—Defoe's first known trip from London, a winter visit to Harwich and Ipswich, perhaps to stay with relatives during his mother's illness or after her death.

1670(?)—Defoe's first visit to Bath, to drink the water for his health.

Early 1670's—Defoe attended the Rev. James Fisher's school at Dorking, in Surrey, twenty-five miles southwest of London.

1671 (December 15)—James Foe became executor of the estate of Elizabeth Marsh in Dorking. Defoe and some of his classmates played ghost in the untenanted Marsh mansion.

1674(?)-79(?)—Defoe attended the Rev. Charles Morton's academy at Newington Green, just north of London, to prepare for the Presbyterian ministry.

1676 (about October)—Defoe was one of a "young company" employed to recover the fish from the inundated fish pond at Beechworth Castle in Surrey.

1679—Active in London agitations concerning the Popish Plot.

1681 (February 20 to near November)—Attended series of six sermons in London by Rev. John Collins on the call to the ministry, recording his own religious thoughts in manuscript verse. Communicated with Protestants in France; possibly attended their great meeting at Charenton. In or near this year decided against entering the Presbyterian ministry. Unconfirmed reports tell of his serving afterwards as a lay preacher in the suburbs of London, especially at Tooting.

1682—Compiled and prepared for the press a manuscript called *Historical Collections* (now lost). Saw the Duke of Monmouth, in high popular favor, at a horse race near Aylesbury (Buckinghamshire).

In or before 1683—Established as a merchant in a high-rent district, in Freeman's Yard, on the north side of Cornhill and about twenty-five yards east of the Royal Exchange.

About 1683—Captured by Algerian pirates between Harwich and Holland, but soon released.

1683—Published first political tract (now lost), an attack on those Whigs who favored the Turks against the Imperial defenders of Vienna. (December 28)—Marriage license granted.

1684 (January 1)—Married Mary Tuffley, about twenty years old, with a dowry of £3,700. Her father is said to have been a wine-cooper. Her brother Samuel became a staunch supporter of Defoe.

1685 (parts of June and July)—Engaged in Monmouth's Rebellion in Somersetshire.

1685-92—Traveled widely as a merchant in Great Britain and in most countries of western and central continental Europe, including Italy. (Much of this travel cannot be dated exactly, and it may belong in large part to the early 1680's.) Engaged in trade in London as wholesale hosier, importer of wine and tobacco, part-owner and insurer of ships. (At frequent intervals throughout later life dealt in real estate; manufactured pantiles and bricks; traded in wool, oysters, cheese, and salt; engaged in fisheries, in shipbuilding, in the weaving of linen, and in other mercantile undertakings.)

About 1687—Published his second political tract (now lost), a protest against the addresses of thanks to James II for his illegal religious indulgence by royal decree.

1688 (January 12)—Admitted to Butchers' Company by virtue of his father's freedom.

(Probably late summer)—Published his first extant political tract, an exposure of James II's policy of offering illegal religious indulgence.

(September 7)—Burial of the Defoes' infant daughter Mary in St. Michael, Cornhill.

(Evening of December 11)—Saw a London mob destroy "a seminary of Popery"—old Berkeley House near St. John's Street.

(December 12-13)—Rode to Windsor and Slough and Reading

and on to Henley, where he joined the advancing forces of the Prince of Orange (later William III). Shortly afterward visited Gravesend, where James II had been captured in his attempted flight.

1689—In London during the establishment of the reign of William and Mary. (Served both sovereigns in various capacities until Mary's death in 1694 and William's in 1702.)

(April 9)—License granted for the publication of *Reflections upon the Late Great Revolution*, Defoe's first pamphlet in support of the new reign.

(Evening of October 29)—Rode with the volunteer Royal Regiment to attend William and Mary to the Lord Mayor's banquet in the Guildhall.

Late 1689 or early 1690—Attended Queen Mary when she viewed the ground at Nottingham House, which was being remodeled as Kensington Palace.

Sometime between 1689 and the end of 1694—Appeared as a witness before the House of Lords, the House of Commons, and the Privy Council, to testify in favor of opening the trade to France.

1690 (June 4–8)—Accompanied William as far as Chester on his way to Ireland and the Battle of the Boyne. Went on to Liverpool and elsewhere, probably traveling as a merchant.

1690–91—Contributed occasionally to Dunton's *Athenian Mercury* (first connection with a periodical).

1692—Attempted unsuccessfully to raise civet cats for perfume.

(Perhaps in autumn)—Bankrupt for £17,000, primarily through losses from underwriting marine insurance in wartime.

1693(?)—Arranged composition with the majority of creditors.

1693 (February 3)—Joseph Williams sued Defoe and a goldsmith in controversy over a diving machine for salvaging wrecks.

1694 (March 9)—The House of Lords, on the second reading, rejected the Merchants Insurers' Bill, which would have enabled Defoe to settle with all his creditors.

1694 (?)—Declined an offer from English merchants to serve as commission agent at Cadiz.

1695–99—Accountant for commissioners of the new Glass Duty (a tax on windows).

1695 (October)—The prefix "De" first publicly affixed to his name, in the *Post–Boy*'s announcement of a royal lottery.

1695–96—Manager-trustee of royal lotteries (October, 1695, and March, 1696).

1697–1701—Increasingly intimate with William III, and active as his agent in England and Scotland. During the summer of one of these years visited a Jacobite (George, first Duke of Gordon) to sound him out for William; in June of the same year went northward to the farthest extremity of Scotland. Had written occasional tracts in support of William since his accession to the throne; now became his leading pamphleteer and a confidential adviser. Received rewards from William which he invested in his prosperous brick and pantile works near Tilbury, in Essex.

1701 (January)—Published *The True-Born Englishman,* most widely sold poem in English literature up to that time, a satire in defense of William and his Dutch friends.

(May 14)—Appeared at the door of the House of Commons to present his *Legion's Memorial* to the Speaker, Robert Harley. The two men had never met before.

(On or shortly after June 24)—Guest of honor with the newly liberated Kentish Petitioners at a great banquet in Mercers' Chapel, Cheapside.

(December 24)—Baptism of Sophia, Defoe's youngest child, later the family beauty.

1702 (March 8)—Death of William and accession of Anne. End of Defoe's hopes for any considerable political advancement.

(December 1)—Published *The Shortest Way with the Dissenters,* a satire against High Church tyranny. This was not the real cause of Defoe's prosecution; but it gave an excuse for the Earl of Nottingham, Secretary of State for the Southern Department, to attempt to coerce him into betraying the Whig leaders who had supported William's plan for a partition of the Spanish Empire in order to avoid a war with France.

(Near the end of December)—Taken up for questioning about *The Shortest Way,* but escaped from the Queen's messenger.

1703 (January 3)—Nottingham issued warrant for the arrest of Defoe, after Edward Bellamy had betrayed his authorship of *The Shortest Way.*

(January)—During the month, Defoe's wife made several attempts to intercede for him with Nottingham.

(February 24)—Indicted in Justice Hall in the Old Bailey.

(February 25)—The House of Commons ordered *The Shortest Way* to be burned by the common hangman.

(February 27)—Queen Anne's address to both houses of Parliament expressed a wish for further laws restricting pamphlets and libels, with a hope that the existing laws would be strictly enforced "to prevent and punish such pernicious Practices."

(April 17)—First published collection of Defoe's writings (John How's pirated edition of genuine works, two of which Defoe could not well reprint in his own *True Collection* in July).

(Until May 20)—In hiding from the Queen's messengers, planning a permanent removal to Scotland (where he had apparently established some connection). Returned secretly to London with his brother-in-law Robert Davis to sign papers to prevent the confiscation of his estate. Accidentally discovered as the result of a general search in Spittlefields for disaffected persons.

(Early morning of May 21, or possibly on the evening of May 20)—Defoe's second arrest, at the house of Sammen, a French weaver in Spittlefields (Spitalfields). Held in confinement by a Queen's messenger.

(May 22)—Nottingham examined Defoe at his office in Whitehall for the first time, then committed him to Newgate for trial at the next assizes (July 7-9). During the next two months Nottingham re-examined Defoe several times.

(June 5)—Defoe released by Richard Warre on £1,500 bail.

(Late June or early July)—Refused the advice of friends to break bail, accepted Nottingham's promise of favorable treatment, and returned to Newgate.

(July 7)—On the first day of the session of Oyer and Terminer in Justice Hall in the Old Bailey (just south of Newgate Prison) Defoe threw himself on the court's mercy. He was given an exceptionally severe sentence.

(From sometime before July 12 until July 27)—William Penn attempted to intervene for Defoe with Nottingham and Godolphin. Robert Harley's first message to Defoe was delivered to him in Newgate (apparently by Penn). Execution of the sentence to the pillory was deferred while Nottingham and other officials sought to induce Defoe to betray Whig leaders. His brick and pantile works near Tilbury had failed completely as a result of his enforced absence.

(July 11)—William Colepeper carried a petition from Defoe to Nottingham at Windsor. By a question which Colepeper asked which seemed to reflect on Admiral Rooke's absence from duty, he provoked the long feud between Rooke and Defoe.

(July 22)—Publication of the *True Collection*, an authorized edition of twenty-two of Defoe's poems and tracts with the first known portrait of Defoe.

(Between July 23 and July 27)—The Earl of Nottingham and the Duke of Buckinghamshire and Normanby visited Defoe in Newgate, attempting to extract information against the Whig leaders. But on July 27 Nottingham notified the Sheriff of London that Defoe's exposure in the pillory (which had been repeatedly deferred at Nottingham's request) should be executed without further delay.

(July 29, 30, and 31)—Defoe stood in the pillory for one hour on each of three successive days, sometime between noon and two o'clock—first before the Royal Exchange, secondly in Cheapside, last before Temple Bar. His *Hymn to the Pillory* and several other writings were sold in the streets to the sympathetic throng.

(About November 1)—By Harley's carefully delayed intercession with Queen Anne through Godolphin, Defoe was discharged from Newgate and taken into the service of the Ministry just before Parliament convened. The Queen had already paid his fine and given some financial relief to his family. With few intermissions thereafter, Defoe was employed to promote the government's public relations, writing for whatever Ministry was in office until shortly before his death.

(November 24–December 1)–The Great Storm, in recording which Defoe first served as a reporter of public events.

1703–4 (December, 1703, or early 1704)–Defoe rode through much of Kent.

1704–14–Defoe served as reporter, editor, pamphleteer, political agent, and often confidential adviser for the government (under Harley, Godolphin, and later Harley again), traveling from Cornwall to the northern counties of Scotland. Afterward he referred to his dangerous secret service in a foreign country (i.e., Scotland, in 1706–7, to promote the Union). He defended the Treaty of Utrecht, especially the eighth and ninth articles designed to reopen the trade with France.

1704 (February 19)–Began the *Review* (1704–13), second of twenty-six journals with which he had some connection.

(Late spring or early summer)–Considered for secret mission in Holland to report on the "Scotch Plot," an alleged Jacobite conspiracy.

(May or June?)–Wrote of his wife as "mother to seven beautiful and hopeful children" (their sons, Benjamin and Daniel, and five of their six daughters). Mary had been buried as an infant on September 7, 1688; but Martha, who died in 1707, was living. Four daughters (Maria, Hannah, Henrietta, and Sophia) and both sons survived him.

(July 31)–Pardoned by Queen Anne. Soon afterward Defoe was admitted to her presence, kissed her hand, and received confirmation of the appointment Harley had proposed for him as a servant of the crown. The Queen expressed regret for Nottingham's severity.

(August)–According to the *Tour* (Everyman ed.; I, 288–330) Defoe witnessed a storm off Plymouth. Actually Defoe saw this storm in early August of 1705.

(September)–First long trip in Harley's interest, a tour of more than three weeks through the eastern counties.

(October)–Defoe made a hurried return to London to force Robert Stephens, messenger of the press, to admit that he had no warrant for Defoe's arrest.

1705 (February 10 and March 5)–Asked by a select committee of the House of Lords to lay before Prince George his plan for recruiting seamen.

(July 16–November 6–Second long tour for Harley, this time through western, central, northern, and east-central England. Reported on the election and presumably helped to elect Harley's candidates for Parliament.

(September 8)–Apparition of Mrs. Veal supposedly seen in Canterbury. Defoe's account of this widely believed happening (written and published soon after his return to London) was the first and one of the most remarkable of his narratives.

1706 (March 11)–Testified at the bar of the House of Lords in favor of adding a clause to the "Bill to Prevent Frauds, Usually Committed by Bankrupts."

(August 21)–Last attempt to arrange a composition with all his creditors, at a meeting in the chamber of his brother-in-law Robert Davis in the Middle Temple.

(September 13)–Took horse for Scotland to represent Harley and to promote the Union.

1706–8–Edinburgh correspondent for Fonvive's *Post-Man* during his stays in Scotland.

1706 (about December 15)–Death of his father in London.

1707–Death of a daughter, Martha, who was carried out of Hackney parish to be buried.

(Summer)–Offered some post in the Scottish customs, but declined it in order to continue as secret agent for the Ministry.

(September)–Renewed complaint against Defoe by the Swedish ambassador in London on account of reflections on Charles XII in the *Review*.

(December 31)–Arrival in London after longest stay in Scotland.

1708 (February and early March)–Godolphin ousted Harley from the Ministry, and Defoe entered his service. Defoe was introduced to Queen Anne a second time, kissed her hand, and had his appointment renewed.

(March 22)–Godolphin wrote to the Earl of Leven, commander-in-chief of the forces in Scotland, recommending Defoe to his protection "as a person employed for the Queen's service in Scotland for the revenue, etc."

(April 17)–Defoe arrived in Edinburgh.

(Late spring or early summer)–Electioneering trip for Godolphin (probably in Scotland rather than in northern England).

(Mid-November)–Left Edinburgh to return to England.

1709 (summer)–Proposal to Godolphin of a plan for settling refugees from the Palatinate in southern England.

(Late August)–In Scotland again as Godolphin's agent.

(September)–Wrote from northern Scotland, probably from Sutherland, "above 150 miles north of Edinburgh," where he observed the unusually fine crops.

1710 (New Year's Day)—The magistrates of Edinburgh voted him twenty guineas for his services to Scotland (in the *Review* and elsewhere). (Before February 1)—Called back hurriedly from Edinburgh to aid Godolphin's ministry in its controversy with Sacheverell.

(March 8)—Wrote to General Stanhope to suggest that Sacheverell be prosecuted for his bad character and known Jacobitism.

(April 22)—Advertised two places where the *Review* could still be purchased, after all hawkers and all other shops had been coerced into dropping its sale.

(April 25)—*Review* now published by John Baker, after Sacheverellites had frightened the previous publisher, John Matthews. During part of 1710 attempts to silence the *Review* were so violent that Defoe expressed himself most freely in a distant periodical, his *Scots Postman* in Edinburgh.

(August 8)—Godolphin dismissed by Queen Anne. Defoe visited him on the same day and received his permission to serve the new Ministry under Harley.

1710–11—In Scotland for Harley. Arrived in Edinburgh before November 9, after being delayed at Newcastle; arrived in London again before February 13.

1711 (March 3–June 7)—Almost completely out of touch with the Ministry, while Harley recovered from the stab of the French adventurer Guiscard and presented his South Sea scheme. Harley created Earl of Oxford and Earl Mortimer on May 24.

(July)—Active at last in support of Harley's new financial measures.

1712 (September)—Saw the Duke of Marlborough withdraw from the contempt of the crowd at a horse race near Aylesbury (Buckinghamshire).

1712–13 (from September to about January 1)—Visited Derbyshire for his health, on the way to northern England and Scotland for Harley.

1713 (March 23)—Third arrest of Defoe. Political enemies arranged to have him surprised by an "escape warrant" for debt as he was leaving home to visit Harley. Released after an imprisonment of 11 days through Harley's aid and the payment of £150 on a claim of £1,500.

(April 2)—*Review* reflected on Peter the Great, and Defoe was (with or without arrest) required to apologize to the Russian ambassador. (Like most or all such difficulties for Defoe, this attack was probably managed by his political enemies.)

(April 11)—Fourth (perhaps fifth) arrest. Political enemies arranged to have him seized at his home in Stoke Newington on the pretext that his three ironical tracts in staunch support of the Hanoverian succession were treasonable. The arrest was planned for Saturday so that Defoe would be confined in Newgate over the weekend.

(Monday, April 13)—Released on £800 bail.

(April 15)—Lord Chief Justice Parker wrote to Bolingbroke, transmitting the three ironical tracts and the information against Defoe and professing that he assumed that Bolingbroke had not ordered a prosecution only because he had not read the tracts. As Parker could hardly have been stupid enough to misunderstand the tracts so completely, it must be supposed that he (as a staunch party Whig) was abetting the partisan effort to discredit Defoe or to force the Tory Ministry to show its hand by protecting him.

(April 22–May 3)—On Parker's sentence Defoe was confined in the Queen's Bench Prison for protesting (in the *Review*, April 16 and 18) against the unjust treatment he had received.

(May 2)—Released from prison after apologizing to the Court. (Lord Chief Justice Parker, who stood on his dignity toward Defoe, was later the notorious Earl of Macclesfield, who [even under a Whig administration] was fined £30,000 and struck from the list of the Privy Council "for many repeated acts of bribery, extortion, perjury, and oppression." Despite the personal support of George I, Macclesfield was sentenced by the unanimous vote of the ninety-three peers present in the House of Lords.)

(November 30)—Defoe's pardon for the three ironical tracts was signed by Bolingbroke for the Crown.

1714 (August 1)—Death of Queen Anne and accession of George I. Fall of Tory Ministry.

(August 28)—Defoe arrested for editorial revision of a letter in Hurt's *Flying Post* which implied that the Earl of Anglesey (a secret Jacobite, although a regent for George I) was a Jacobite.

1715 (March 31)—*The Family Instructor*, first of Defoe's didactic treatises.

(July 12)—Tried in the King's Court Bench and convicted of libel against Anglesey. Sentence deferred until the next term, when no action was taken. Defoe soon came to terms with the Ministry through Townshend; and he continued to serve as political writer, editor, and government agent under successive Whig ministers until near the end of 1730.

1716 (late March)—Interceded with Townshend for the release of his former publisher Samuel Keimer, without trial at the Old Bailey for sedition. Because of his debts, Keimer left the Gatehouse only to be reimprisoned in the Fleet.

(May 1)—Started *Mercurius Politicus*, first of the Tory journals which Defoe edited on behalf of the Whig Ministry.

(Late summer)—Apologized for mistakes in the July and August issues of *Mercurius Politicus* occasioned "by the Author's Absence."

1717 (July 3)—Harley (now Earl of Oxford) acquitted of high treason after two years' imprisonment in the Tower. Defoe had defended him; now he began to turn against him, perhaps suspecting Harley's secret communication with the Jacobites.

1718 (September 22)—Marriage of Defoe's older son, Benjamin, and Hannah Coates in Norwich. By this time Benjamin seems to have broken with his family completely.

1719 (April 25)—The first part of *Robinson Crusoe*, Defoe's earliest novel.

1720 (June 4)—Mist testified that his *Weekly-Journal* for January 2 (reflecting on the government) had been intrusted to Defoe.

(June 13)—Charles De la Faye, acting for the government, released Defoe on £400 bail to appear in the King's Court Bench on the first day of the next term. The case was dropped, no doubt because it was realized that Defoe served the government in toning down Mist's *Weekly-Journal*.

(Midsummer)—Apparently visited Paris to observe the Mississippi craze.

1721 (August)—Benjamin Defoe, who had been employed to write against his father and the government, arrested for an article in the *London Journal*.

1722—Defoe's last known considerable journey in England (to check doubtful passages for his forthcoming *Tour*).

1724-28—Last long historical work: *A General History of the Pyrates*.

1726—Last life of a criminal: the account of Captain Jeanne in Applebee's *Weekly-Journal* (May 14) and in the pamphlet *Unparallel'd Cruelty* (May 17).

1728 (June 3)—Most extensive statement of Defoe's ideas on commerce and geography, in the letterpress of *Atlas Maritimus & Commercialis*.

1728-29—Legal controversy with Mrs. Mary Brooke, an illiterate widow who claimed payment on bonds presumably canceled a generation before. If Mrs. Brooke was the widow of the wine-importer Brook(e), whom Defoe had supported until after his bankruptcy and his separation from his former partner Hellier, this might imply an old quarrel over commercial claims. Otherwise it seems likely that Mrs. Brooke was, like so many other claimants against Defoe, the unwitting agent of his political enemies.

1729 (April 30)—Marriage of Henry Baker and Sophia Defoe.

(May 24)—Last long fictional narrative: *Madagascar: or, Robert Drury's Journal*.

1729-30—Last connection with a periodical (December, 1729–October, 1730), as editor of the *Political State of Great-Britain* after the death of Abel Boyer.

1730 (December 15)—Last new work published in Defoe's lifetime: *An Effectual Scheme for the immediate Preventing of Street Robberies*.

1731 (January 13)—Last of his books on projects issued in his lifetime—
an expanded edition of *A Plan of the English Commerce*, first
published in 1728.

(April 24)—Died "of a lethargy" in Ropemaker's Alley. (Most
accounts give by mistake the date of his burial, April 26.)

(April 26)—Buried in Tindall's (Bunhill Fields), north of the
London Wall.

(November 15)—Sale of Defoe's library by Olive Payne.

1732 (July 5)—Will of Mary Defoe.

(December 19?)—I have found no confirmation of one biographer's
statement that Mary Defoe died on December 19 and was buried
in Bunhill Fields by her husband's side.

(December 20)—Mary Defoe's will probated. "Hanna De Foe
and Henrietta De Foe" were named as executrices.

NOTES

PREFACE TO THE NOTES

The text is based on so extensive and varied a body of source material (to which Defoe's own writings alone contribute no less than 545 titles) that it has become obligatory to condense and simplify the annotation as far as this can be done with clarity.

The method used is approximately like that made familiar in numerous modern historical writings (such as G. M. Trevelyan's *England under Queen Anne*, where a table of abbreviations used in the notes is followed by clusters of notes arranged according to the chapters to which they have reference). The notes are arranged in sequence corresponding to the passages in the text to which they refer, so that (for instance) the three sentences of the second paragraph of chapter ii are documented by the three successive references under note 2 for that chapter. In general, semicolons are used to bind together notes that document the same statement or idea. Where the same passage in a source is cited repeatedly, the note may omit the later references.

Where no place of publication is given for early eighteenth-century books or tracts, London is usually to be understood. The following abbreviations are used throughout:

Aitken, G. A.
  Aitken (1): "Defoe's Birth and Marriage," *Athenaeum*, No. 3278 (August 23, 1890), p. 257.
  Aitken (2): "Defoe's Wife," *Contemporary Review*, LVII, 232.
  Aitken (3): "Defoe in Trouble, 1703," *Athenaeum*, No. 3505 (December 22, 1894), p. 862.
  Aitken (4): (Ed.), *Romances and Narratives by Daniel Defoe* (London, 1895).
  Aitken (5): "Defoe's Brick-kilns," *Athenaeum*, No. 3207 (April 13, 1889), pp. 472–73.
B.M. Add. MSS: British Museum Additional Manuscripts.
Burton: John Hill Burton, *A History of the Reign of Queen Anne* (Edinburgh and London, 1880), I, 97–98.
Calamy: Edmund Calamy, *An Historical Account of My Own Life*, ed. J. T. Rutt (London, 1829).
Churchill: Winston S. Churchill, *Marlborough, His Life and Times* (New York, 1933–38).
Clarendon: *The Correspondence of Henry Hyde, Earl of Clarendon* (London, 1828).
Clerk: *Memoirs of the Life of Sir John Clerk of Penicuik*, ed. John M. Gay ("Publications of the Scottish Historical Society," Vol. XIII [Edinburgh, 1892]).
Cunningham: Alexander Cunningham, *The History of Great Britain: From the Revolution in 1688, to the Accession of George the First* (London, 1787).
DNB: The Dictionary of National Biography.
Dottin: Paul Dottin, *Daniel De Foe et ses romans* (Paris, 1924).
Drake: James Drake, *The History of the Last Parliament* (1702).
Fea: Allan Fea, *King Monmouth* (New York and London, 1902).
Feiling: Keith Feiling, *A History of the Tory Party 1640–1714* (Oxford, 1924).
Franklin: Benjamin Franklin, *The Autobiography of Benjamin Franklin*, ed. Max Farrand (Berkeley and Los Angeles, 1949).

NOTES

Gordon: Alexander Gordon (ed.), *Freedom after Ejection* (Manchester, 1917).

Healey, George Harris
    Healey (1): (Ed.), *The Meditations of Daniel Defoe* (Cumington, Mass., 1946).
    Healey (2): *Earlier Correspondence of Daniel Defoe (1703–1707)* (Ph.D. dissertation, Cornell University, 1947).
    Healey (3): (Ed.), *The Letters of Daniel Defoe* (Oxford, 1955).

HCJ: Journals of the House of Commons.

HLJ: Journals of the House of Lords.

HL MSS: House of Lords Manuscripts.

H.M.C.: Historical Manuscripts Commission Report.

H.M.C. Bath: Historical Manuscripts Commission, Bath Manuscripts.

H.M.C. Portland: Historical Manuscripts Commission, Portland Manuscripts.

JEGP: Journal of English and Germanic Philology.

Laprade: William T. Laprade, "The Power of the English Press in the Eighteenth Century," *South Atlantic Quarterly*, XXVII (1928), 426–34.

Lee: William Lee, *Daniel Defoe: His Life, and Recently Discovered Writings* (London, 1869).

Leslie, Charles
    Leslie (1): *A View of the Times* (2d ed., 1710).
    Leslie (2): *Cassandra* (1704).
    Leslie (3): *The New Association*, Part II (2d ed., 1705).
    Leslie (4): *The Wolf Stript of His Shepherd's Clothing* (3d ed., 1704).

Loftie: W. J. Loftie, *Round about London* (5th ed.; London, 1887).

Luttrell: Narcissus Luttrell, *A Brief Relation of State Affairs from September 1678 to April 1714* (Oxford, 1857).

Matthews: A. G. Matthews, *Calamy Revised* (Oxford, 1934).

Mist's Miscellany: A Collection of Miscellany Letters (ed. for Nathaniel Mist by Daniel Defoe, 1722–27).

Moore, John Robert
    Moore (1): *Defoe in the Pillory and Other Studies* ("Indiana University Humanities Series," No. 1 [Bloomington, Ind., 1939]).
    Moore (2): "Defoe's 'Lost' Letter to a Dissenter," *Huntington Library Quarterly*, XIX (1951), 299–306.
    Moore (3): "A Riddle by Prior," *Times Literary Supplement*, July 4, 1935, p. 432.
    Moore (4): "Gildon's Attack on Steele and Defoe in *The Battle of the Authors*," *PMLA*, LXVI (1951), 534–38.
    Moore (5): " 'Windsor Forest' and William III," *Modern Language Notes*, LXVI (1951), 451–54.
    Moore (6): Review of *The Meditations of Daniel Defoe*, ed. George Harris Healey, *Journal of English and Germanic Philology*, LXV (1946), 466–68.
    Moore (7): "The Character of Daniel Defoe," *Review of English Studies*, XIV (1938), 69–70.
    Moore (8): "Defoe and the South Sea Company," *Boston Public Library Quarterly*, V (1953), 175–78.
    Moore (9): "A Defoe Allusion in *Gulliver's Travels*," *Notes and Queries*, CLXXVIII (1940), 224–26.
    Moore (10): "Johnson's Falling Houses," *Notes and Queries*, CVC (1950), 342.
    Moore (11): "Defoe's Religious Sect," *Review of English Studies*, XVII (1941), 461–67.
    Moore (12): *Defoe's Sources for "Robert Drury's Journal"* ("Indiana University Humanities Series," No. 9 [Bloomington, Ind., 1943]).
    Moore (13): Introduction to *An Essay on the Regulation of the Press* ("Luttrell Reprints," No. 7 [Oxford, 1948]).

Moore (14): "Defoe, Thoresby, and 'The Storm,' " *Notes and Queries*, CLXXV (1938), p. 223.

Moore (15): "Daniel Defoe: Star Reporter," *Boston Public Library Quarterly*, VI (1954), 195–205.

Moore (16): "Was Jonathan Swift a Moderate?" *South Atlantic Quarterly*, LIII (1954), 260–67.

Moore (17): "Swift as Historian," *Studies in Philology*, XLIX (1952), 583–604.

Moore (18): "Defoe and the Rev. James Hart: A Chapter in High Finance," *Philological Quarterly*, XIX (1940), 404–9.

Moore (19): "Daniel Defoe, Ambidextrous Mercury," *Periodical Post-Boy*, May, 1952, pp. 1–2.

Moore (20): "Dr. Johnson and Roman History," *Huntington Library Quarterly*, XII (1949), 311–14.

Moore (21): *Daniel Defoe and Modern Economic Theory* ("Indiana University Studies," No. 104 [Bloomington, Ind., 1935]).

Moore (22): "Defoe, Steele, and the Demolition of Dunkirk," *Huntington Library Quarterly*, XIII (1950), 279–302.

Moore (23): "Milton among the Augustans: The Infernal Council," *Studies in Philology*, XLVIII (1951), 15–25.

Moore (24): "Defoe's Hand in *A Journal of the Earl of Marr's Proceedings* (1716)," *Huntington Library Quarterly*, XVII (1954), 209–28.

Moore (25): "Defoe's *History of the Pirates*: Its Date," *Notes and Queries*, CLXXIX (1940), 6–7.

Moore (26): "Defoe, Selkirk, and John Atkins," *Notes and Queries*, CLXXIX (1940), 436–38.

Moore (27): "Further Notes on Defoe's Sources for *Robert Drury's Journal*," *Notes and Queries*, CLXXXVIII (1945), 268–71.

Moore (28): "Defoe, Robin and Crusoe," *Notes and Queries*, CLXIV (1933), pp. 26, 249.

Moore (29): "*The Tempest* and *Robinson Crusoe*," *Review of English Studies*, XXI (1945), 52–56.

Moore (30): "Defoe and the Eighteenth-Century Pamphlets on London," *Philological Quarterly*, XX (1941), 38–45.

Moore (31): "Defoe's Workshop," *More Books: The Bulletin of the Boston Public Library*, November, 1948, pp. 1–9.

Moore (32): "Defoe's Project for Lie-Detection," *American Journal of Psychology*, LXVIII (1955), 672.

Moore (33): "Defoe's Use of Personal Experience in *Colonel Jack*," *Modern Language Notes*, LIV (1939), 362–63.

Moore (34): " 'Robin Hog' Stephens: Messenger of the Press," *Papers of the Bibliographical Society of America*, L (1956), 381–87.

Moore (35): "Defoe's Lampoon: *A Speech of a Stone Chimney-Piece*," *Boston Public Library Quarterly*, IX (1957), 137–42.

Morison: Samuel Eliot Morison, *Harvard College in the Seventeenth Century* (Cambridge, Mass., 1936).

N. & Q.: *Notes and Queries*.

Newton, Theodore F. M.

Newton (1): "The Civet-Cats of Newington Green: New Light on Defoe," *Review of English Studies*, XIII (1937), 10–19.

Newton (2): "William Pittis and Queen Anne Journalism," *Modern Philology*, XXXIII (1936), 279–302.

Ogg: David Ogg, *England in the Reign of Charles II* (Oxford, 1934).

Oldmixon: John Oldmixon, *The History of England, During the Reign of King William and Queen Mary, etc.* (London, 1735).

Parker: Irene Parker, *Dissenting Academies in England* (Cambridge, 1914).

PMLA: PMLA: Publications of the Modern Language Association of America.

PQ: Philological Quarterly.

P.R.O.: Public Record Office.

RES: Review of English Studies.

Secord, Arthur Wellesley

Secord (1): "Defoe in Stoke Newington," *PMLA* (1951), 211–25.

Secord (2): *Studies in the Narrative Method of Defoe* ("University of Illinois Studies in Language and Literature," Vol. IX, No. 1 [Urbana, 1924]).

Secord (3): "A September Day in Canterbury: The Veal-Bargrave Story," *Journal of English and Germanic Philology*, LIV (1955), 639–50.

Smith: David Nichol Smith, *John Dryden* (Cambridge, 1950).

Strype: John Strype, *A Survey of the Cities of London and Westminster* (1720).

Sutherland, James

Sutherland (1): *The Life of Daniel Defoe* (London, 1937).

Sutherland (2): "Some Early Troubles of Daniel Defoe," *Review of English Studies*, IX (1933), 275–90.

Sutherland (3): "A Note on the Last Years of Defoe," *Modern Language Review*, XXIX (1934), 137–41.

Thornley: *The Guilds of the City of London and Their Liverymen*, ed. John Charles Thornley and George W. Hastings (London, n.d.).

Tour

Tour (1): Daniel Defoe, *A Tour Thro' England and Wales* (Everyman ed.).

Tour (2): Daniel Defoe, *A Tour Thro' the Whole Island of Great Britain*, ed. G. D. H. Cole (London, 1927).

Tour (3): Daniel Defoe, *A Tour Thro' the Whole Island of Great Britain* (1724–27).

Trent: William P. Trent, *Daniel Defoe: How To Know Him* (Indianapolis, 1916).

Trevelyan, George Macaulay

Trevelyan (1): *England under Queen Anne* (London, 1930–34).

Trevelyan (2): *English Social History* (2d ed.; London, 1946).

Warner: G. F. Warner, "An Unpublished Political Paper by Daniel De Foe," *English Historical Review*, XXII (1907), 132–43.

Wesley, Samuel

Wesley (1): *A Letter from a Country Divine to His Friend in London* (1703).

Wesley (2): *A Defence of a Letter Concerning the Education of Dissenters in Their Private Academies* (1704).

Wilson, Walter

Wilson (1): *Memoirs of the Life and Times of Daniel De Foe* (London, 1830).

Wilson (2): *The History and Antiquities of Dissenting Churches and Meeting Houses* (London, 1808–14).

Wolseley: General Viscount Wolseley, *The Life of John Churchill, Duke of Marlborough* (London, 1894).

Wright, Thomas

Wright (1): *The Life of Daniel Defoe* (London, 1931).

Wright (2): *The Life of Daniel Defoe* (London, 1894).

CHAPTER I

1. *Tour* (1), I, 376. In the frequent controversies over baptism during the Restoration period, the Church of England insisted on the necessity of infant baptism, the Baptists practiced adult baptism, and the Presbyterians usually took an intermediate position. The parish registers of St. Giles, Cripplegate, show that Defoe's sisters Mary and Elizabeth were born (but not christened) on November 13, 1657, and June 19, 1659.

2. Pepys' *Diary*, September 2, 1660.

3. *Captain Singleton* (Tegg ed.), p. 343.

4. Thornley, p. 152.

5. *Review*, [IX], 115; *A Journal of the Plague Year; Commentator*, August 15, 1720; Applebee's *Weekly Journal*, February 2, 1723; September 11, 1725; *Political State of Great-Britain*, XL, 383 (for 333).

6. *Review*, VII, 297; VIII, 614.

7. Applebee's *Journal*, July 16, 1722. See *Review*, I, 96; [IX], 53.

8. *Tour* (1) I, 355–61.

9. *Mercurius Politicus*, December, 1719, p. 766. See Moore (10).

10. *Tour* (1), I, 167–68.

CHAPTER II

1. *Review*, VI, 226. See *A Letter to Mr. Steele* (1714), p. 30; *True Collection* (1705), II, 424.

2. *Tour* (1), II, 85. *Review*, [IX], 176. *Charity Still A Christian Virtue* (1719), p. 10.

3. *A Brief Deduction of the Original . . . of the British Woollen Manufacture* (1727), p. 17. *N. & Q.*, Ser. 11, V (March 30, 1912), 243.

4. Wright (1), chap. i. See also *N. & Q.*, Ser. 11, V (March 30, 1912), 241–43; CLXXIV (February 12 and April 9, 1938), 112–14, 266; CLXXV (July 16, 1938), 44.

5. Sutherland (1), p. 284. Wright (1), p. 4.

6. *Review*, VII, Preface.

7. *H.M.C. Portland*, IV, 373. James Foe lived for a time in Throgmorton Street, and during his last years, at the sign of "The Bell" in Broad Street (Wright [1], p. 147).

8. The St. Giles parish register contains these entries (*N. & Q.*, CLXXV [July 16, 1938], 44): "Mary, daughter of James Foe, tallowchandler and of Alice. Not christened, but born November 13, 1657"; "Elizabeth, daughter of James Fooe tallowchandler, and of Alice. Not christened, but born July 19, 1659." The license for Mary's marriage is entered (May 20, 1679) in *Allegations for Marriage Licenses issued by the Dean and Chapter of Westminster, 1588 to 1699*, ed. Geo. J. Armytage ("Publications of the Harleian Society," Vol. XXIII [1886]), p. 299: "Francis Barham, Jr, of St Mary, Whitechapel, Midx., Shipwright, Bachr, abt 30, and Mrs. Mary Foe, of St Swithin, London, Spr, abt 20; with her father's consent; at St Mary Magdalene, Bermondsey, co. Surrey." However, the name is not Barham but Bartham in James Foe's will (personal letter of May 4, 1951, from Mr. Edward J. Pedley of the Principal Probate Registry, Somerset House, London; confirmed by a photostat of the will now in my possession). For notes on Robert Davis, see Dottin, I, 47, 149.

9. Mary E. Ireland, "The Defoe Family in America," *Scribner's Monthly*, XII (May, 1876), 61–64. The substance of this narrative was used by Miss Ireland in newspaper articles, and it was reprinted with little change in George Johnston's *History of Cecil County, Maryland* (Elkton, Md., 1881), pp. 526–34. The account given by Wright (1) is obviously derived from the same ultimate source, as is the statement given me by

Mrs. Walter W. Ward of Indianapolis (personal letter of November 23, 1948, and subsequent oral communication). For information discrediting the supposed Quaker background of the supposed Elizabeth Maxwell and throwing doubt on the date of the supposed Flemish chair, I am indebted to Professor Frederick B. Tolles of Swarthmore College; to Muriel A. Hicks, assistant librarian of the Friends Historical Society, London (letter addressed to Dr. Tolles on April 10, 1951); and to Marie E. Windell, assistant librarian of the Historical Society of Delaware (personal letter of March 12, 1951).

10. Lee, I, 107. *H.M.C. Portland*, IV, 223.

11. *Tour* (1), I, 219. *A Treatise Concerning the Use and Abuse of the Marriage Bed* (Hazlitt ed.), p. 30. *Whitehall Evening Post*, January 17, 1718/19).

12. *A Defence of the Allies* (1712), p. 7. *Review*, I, 367.

13. Thornley, p. 152.

14. *Review*, VIII, 207; I, 403.

CHAPTER III

1. See Moore (11).

2. Ogg, I, 201.

3. Samuel Pepys, *Diary* (Wheatley ed.), August 17 and 24, 1662.

4. Estimates of ejections on St. Bartholomew's Day have varied. Defoe put the number at 3,000, or about a third of all the beneficed clergy (*A Short View of the Present State of the Protestant Religion in Britain* [Edinburgh, 1707], p. 14); but this was written in the heat of a pamphleteering debate, and it represented the feeling of the Dissenters rather than an accurate statement of fact. Historians have generally adopted Edmund Calamy's list of approximately 2,000. A special student of the problem (Matthews, pp. xii–xiii), attempting to weigh the evidence carefully in spite of his obvious bias against the Dissenters, puts the total number of ejections over the two year period from 1660 to 1662 at 1,760, of which number he has found that 936 fell on St. Bartholomew's Day and 129 at an uncertain date but probably in the same year. The actual number was of far less importance than the character and ability of the Bartholomeans, and the reasons which prompted their exile from the Church.

5. Oliver Heywood's *Diaries*, ed. J. H. Turner (Brighouse, 1882), I, 90.

6. Calamy, I, 55. *The Present State of the Parties in Great Britain* (1712), p. 288.

7. Wilson (2), I, 366.

8. *Original Records of Early Nonconformists under Persecution and Indulgence*, ed. G. Lyon Turner (London and Leipzig, 1911), I, 89. John Stoughton, *History of Religion in England from the Opening of the Long Parliament to 1850* (London, 1901), IV, 53–54. Matthews, p. lix.

9. *Diary of Samuel Sewall*, I ("Collections of the Massachusetts Historical Society," Ser. 5, Vol. V, [Boston, 1878]), 253–54.

10. *A Letter to Dr. Andrew Snape* (1717), pp. 24–26.

CHAPTER IV

1. Pepys' *Diary*, December 19, 1666.

2. Abraham Cowley, *A Proposition for the Advancement of Experimental Philosophy* (1661). *General Heads for the Natural History of a Country, Great or Small; Drawn out for the Use of Travellers and Navigators. Imparted by the late Honourable Robert Boyle, Esq; Fellow of the Royal Society. Ordered to be published in his Life-time, at the Request of*

some Curious Persons. To which is added, other Directions for Navigators, &c. with particular Observations of the most noted Countries in the World: By another Hand (1692).

3. *The Evident Advantages to Great Britain and Its Allies from the Approaching War* (1727), p. 37. *Some Reflections on a Pamphlet Lately Publish'd, Entitl'd, An Argument Shewing that a Standing Army Is Inconsistent with a Free Government* (2d ed.,1697), p. 14.

4. *Commentator*, August 15, 1720. *Review*, [IX], 58.

5. *An Enquiry into the Danger and Consequences of a War with the Dutch* (1712), pp. 34–35.

6. *Political State of Great-Britain*, XL, 222–25. *A Brief Case of the Distillers* (1726), p. 19.

7. *Mist's Miscellany*, IV, 86–87. See *Augusta Triumphans* (Tegg ed.), pp. 31–32. *The Compleat English Tradesman* (1727), II, Part II, 81. *Tour* (1), I, 40; II, 35.

8. Applebee's *Weekly Journal*, May 11, 1723, and September 21, 1723. *Review*, VII, 117.

9. *London Gazette*, May 27–30, 1672. *Tour* (1), I, 351.

10. *The Present State of the Parties in Great Britain* (1712), p. 17. *An Essay upon Projects* (Hazlitt ed.), p. 41. *Tour* (1), I, 257. Mist's *Weekly-Journal*, August 17, 1723 (Lee, III, 172).

11. *Street Robberies, Consider'd* (n.d., but 1728), pp. 55–56. *True Collection* (1703) p. 296. *Tour* (1), II, 190. *An Essay upon Projects* (Hazlitt ed.), p. 41. *Tour* (1), II, 254; II, 143; I, 75–76, 159; II, 14, 78–79, 143, 148, 221. *Review*, VII, 100; [IX], 191. *A Plan of the English Commerce* (Blackwell ed.), p. 105.

12. *Review*, VI, 573. See also *True Collection* (1705), II, 66. *H.M.C. Portland*, II, 338. *Review*, II, 214; V, 182–83; VI, Preface; VI, 285; [IX], 68. Applebee's *Journal*, May 16, 1724 (Lee, III, 264).

13. See Moore (6), p. 467. *The Candidate* (1715). David Erskine Baker, *The Companion to the Play-House* (London, 1764), Vol. I: *The Careless Husband. An Apology for the Army* (1715), pp. 24–25. *Mist's Miscellany*, IV, 306; III, 251–53, 283–87; IV, 104–9.

14. Percy A. Scholes, *The Puritans and Music in England and New England* (Oxford 1934), p. 344. *Tour* (1), I, 332–33.

15. Clerk, p. 15. *Augusta Triumphans* (Tegg ed.), p. 12. *An Essay upon Literature* (1726), p. 36. *Review*, III, 415.

CHAPTER V

1. The conclusions presented in the foregoing paragraphs are largely drawn from the as yet unpublished evidence provided by my friend and collaborator Mr. F. Bastian, of Ashtead, Surrey.

2. *The Whole Works of the Rev. Oliver Heywood* (London and Edinburgh, 1826), V, 590.

3. Moore (4). *Robinson Crusoe* (Tegg ed.), I, 2. Arthur Paul Davis, *Isaac Watts: His Life and Works* (New York, 1943), p. 8.

4. *The History and Reality of Apparitions* (Tegg ed.), pp. 371–73.

5. *Tour* (1), I, 151–54.

6. This was admitted by a hostile critic. See Wesley (1), p. 6. For a very able study of Morton's academy, made subsequently to mine but quite independently, see Professor Lew Girdler's article on "Defoe's Education at Newington Green Academy," *Studies in Philology*, L, 573–91.

7. Wesley (1), p. 9.

8. Wesley (2), p. 44. Gordon, p. 318. *The Present State of the Parties in Great Britain* (1712), pp. 295–96.

9. Morison, I, 238.

10. Parker, p. 59. Wesley (1), p. 7.

11. *The Complete English Tradesman* (Tegg ed.), I, 29.

12. *Review*, VII, 455. *True Collection* (1705), II, 266–67. *Review*, V, 373–75. *Colonel Jack* (Tegg ed.), I, 170–74. *Captain Singleton* (Tegg ed.), pp. 69–70.

13. *The Compleat English Gentleman* (Bülbring ed. [London, 1890;]), pp. 67. 207.

14. *True Collection* (1705), II, 276. Morison, I, 276, 236, 238. For the comparative backwardness in teaching natural science at Yale, see Edmund S. Morgan, "Ezra Stiles: The Education of a Yale Man, 1740–1746," *Huntington Library Quarterly*, XVII, 251–68.

15. *Tour* (1), 247–48, 56–57.

16. *True Collection* (1705), II, 277. *Compendium Physicae* ("Publications of the Colonial Society of Massachusetts," Vol. XXXIII [Boston, 1940]), pp. 98–99. *Tour* (1), II, 41. *Compendium Physicae*, pp. 167, 93. *The History of the Devil* (Hazlitt ed.), p. 60. *The Life and Errors of John Dunton* ("Collections of the Massachusetts Historical Society," Ser. 2, Vol. II [Boston, 1814]), p. 116.

17. *The Compleat English Gentleman*, pp. 199, 218–20.

18. Professor David Nichol Smith, of Merton College, Oxford.

CHAPTER VI

1. *Review*, IV, 358–60. Healey (1).

2. See the chapter on "Puritan Preaching" in Horton Davies' *The Worship of the English Puritans* (Westminster, 1948), especially pp. 182, 184, 186, 188, 202.

3. *N. & Q.*, Ser. 11, I (December 9, 1910), 505. I am indebted to Professor Healey for a transcript of the source of the statement repeated by several biographers. Josiah Thompson, a Baptist clergyman (1724–1806), at some unknown date made the following entry in his account of the Tooting congregation (Dr. Williams' Library, *Thompson MSS, Records of Nonconformity*, X, 295–96): "No. 11. Tooting. The Congregation of Protestant Dissenters at lower Tooting in Surrey, Owes its original to the Celebrated Mr. Dan¹ De Foe, who first endeavoured to form the Dissenters resident in this Neighbourhood into a Regular Society, they met for sometime in a private House, & the first Pastor was Mr (afterwards Dʳ) Joshua Oldfield, Son of Mr. John Oldfield an Ejected Minister of Great Eminence, both for his Piety, & Learning." It will be noted that this statement says nothing about Defoe's serving as lay preacher.

4. Calamy, I, 89. *The Shortest-Way with the Dissenters: . . . With its Author's Brief Explication Consider'd* (1703), pp. 2–3.

5. Wesley (2).

6. *Review*, II, 153. *Little Review*, No. 8, p. 30. *The History of the Principal Discoveries* (1727), p. 218.

7. *The Compleat English Gentleman* (Bülbring ed.; London, 1890), pp. 200–201.

8. Franklin, p. 28. *Serious Reflections of Robinson Crusoe* (Hazlitt ed.), pp. 36, 35.

9. Hester Lynch Piozzi, *Anecdotes of the late Samuel Johnson, LL.D.* (London, 1786), p. 281. Robert Louis Stevenson, "A Gossip on Romance," *Works* (New York and London, 1921–23), XII, 192.

10. *Subjection and Obedience to Principalities, Powers, and Magistrates. A Sermon, Preach'd at Great Grandsen in Huntingdon-shire; on Monday August the First, 1715*, by John Jenings, M.A. (1715).

11. *The Present State of the Parties in Great Britain* (1712), pp. 317, 351–52.

CHAPTER VII

1. Calamy, I, 114–15.

2. *Allegations for Marriage Licences Issued by the Vicar-General of the Archbishop of Canterbury, July 1679 to June 1687*, ed. George J. Armytage ("Publications of the Harleian Society," Vol. XXX [1890]), p. 155. *Reliquiae Baxteriana* (London, 1696), Part III, p. 180. "Richard Hollingsworth," *DNB*. Francis F. Madan, *A New Bibliography of the Eikon Basilike* (Oxford, 1950). Edward Ludlow, *A Letter from General Ludlow to Dr. Hollingsworth* (Amsterdam, 1692).

3. Strype, Book II, p. 16.

4. *Ibid.*, Book II, p. 27. *The History of the Plague Year* (Tegg ed.), pp. 65–69.

5. *Ibid.*, pp. 60–61, 59.

6. *An Appeal to Honour and Justice* (Hazlitt ed.), pp. 14–15.

7. Sutherland (2), p. 286. Secord (1), p. 212 n. 3. Sophia was baptized there in 1701, and Martha was taken from Hackney to be buried in 1707.

8. Secord (1), pp. 215–16. Dottin, I, 285. *Review*, III, 547, 549; II, 292, 296, 300, 308 (No. 76), 308 (No. 77), 324, 328, 336, 344, 352, 356, 360, 364, 368, 372, 376; III, 30; IV, 564. *H.M.C. Portland*, IV, 302. Letter to Henry Baker, August 12, 1730 (Healey [3], pp. 475, 476).

9. *London Post*, May 21–24, 1703; *Post-Man*, May 22–25, 1703; *Daily Courant*, May 24, 1703. See later reference to Defoe's friend Sammen the weaver in *H.M.C. Portland*, IV, 138.

10. *An Appeal to Honour and Justice* (Hazlitt ed.), p. 16. *Some Considerations upon Street-Walkers* (n.d., but 1726), p. 15.

11. *Little Review*, No. 5, p. 18. *Review*, supplement for December, 1704, p. 15; IV, 223. Applebee's *Weekly Journal*, October 6, 1722, and August 22, 1724. *Little Review*, No. 9, p. 34. *Review*, I, 379.

12. *Robinson Crusoe* (Tegg ed.), II, 5, 7.

13. *Review*, IV, 220.

14. *Flying-Post*, September 20, 1711; a hostile account appeared in the *Supplement*, September 14. Will of Samuel Tuffley, dated October 22, 1714; proved August 23, 1725. (Somerset House, P.C.C. Romney, 183).

15. *H.M.C. Portland*, IV, 214, 88.

16. *A Treatise on the Use and Abuse of the Marriage Bed* (Hazlitt ed.), p. 13.

CHAPTER VIII

1. *H.M.C. Portland*, III, 384–85. *Review*, IV, 670; V, 194.

2. Wolseley, I, 273. Fea, p. 225.

3. *Tour* (1), II, 14, 148.

4. Fea, p. 264. *Tour* (1), II, 35.

5. *Ibid.*, 269. *The Consolidator* (1705), pp. 135–36. Fea, p. 293. *London Gazette*, July 6–9, 1685.

6. Sir Edward Parry, *The Bloody Assize* (London, 1929), p. 260. J. G. Muddiman, *The Bloody Assizes* (Edinburgh and London, 1929), Preface.

7. *H.M.C. Portland*, III, 388.

8. *The Present State of the Parties in Great Britain* (1712), p. 319. *Mere Nature Delineated* (1726), p. 122.

9. Lord George Scott, *Lucy Walter: Wife or Mistress* (London, 1947), esp. p. 206. *Jure Divino* (Hazlitt ed.), pp. 64, 11. *An Appeal to Honour and Justice* (Hazlitt ed.),

p. 9. *The Succession . . . Considered* (1701), pp. 18, 10. *An Expostulatory Letter to the B—— of B——* (n.d., but 1717), pp. 8–9.

10. *A Brief Reply to the History of Standing Armies in England* (1698), p. 12. *Review*, [IX], 154, 56. *An Account of the Proceedings against the Rebels* (2d ed., 1716), p. xxv. *The Succession . . . Considered*, pp. 34, 10.

11. *Review*, VII, 598; VIII, 422. Moore (2). *What If the Swedes Should Come?* (1717), pp. 10–11.

12. *The Succession . . . Considered*, pp. 6, 9, 26, 27, 34.

13. *Ibid.*, pp. 22–25, 28. *H.M.C. Portland*, III, 625–42; IV, 3, 7–13. Fea, p. 367. *Animadversions on the Succession to the Crown of England, Considered* (1701).

14. *H.M.C. Portland*, III, 625–42; IV, 7–13. Churchill, II, 231–32. Warner, p. 138. *The Consolidator* (1705), pp. 132–33. *Jure Divino* (Hazlitt ed.), p. 82.

15. Mr. Godfrey Davies of the permanent research staff, Huntington Library.

16. *Some Reflections on a Pamphlet Lately Publish'd* (2d ed., 1697), p. 21. *An Essay upon Projects* (Hazlitt ed.), pp. 39–41. *An Apology for the Army* (1715).

17. *Robinson Crusoe* (Tegg ed.), II, 273. *Memoirs of the Church of Scotland* (1717), pp. 195–97, 198. *The Present State of the Parties in Great Britain* (1712), pp. 41–47. *Tour* (2), II, 800. *The History of the Principal Discoveries* (1727), pp. 229–31.

18. *Memoirs of Dr. Williams* (1718), p. 74. *A View of the Scots Rebellion* (1715), pp. 25–26, 31–40. *Tour* (1), II, 202–3. *Strike While the Iron's Hot* (1715), pp. 43–41 (for 6–7), 41–42 (for 7–8).

19. *Political State of Great-Britain*, XXXVI, 33–62. *The War of the Succession in Spain during the Reign of Queen Anne 1702–1711* (London, 1808). Ballard, *The Great Earl of Peterborough* (London, 1929). J. B., in *N. & Q.*, Ser. 4, XI (July 21, 1873), p. 509. *Mercurius Politicus*, September, 1717, p. 631.

20. Churchill, V, 446–62. *Minutes of the Negotiations of Monsr. Mesnager* (1717), p. 32. Wilson (1), II, 379, n. 2. The *Observator* (December 17 and 20, 1707; January 7, 10, and 17, 1708) discusses the advantages of a sea war with France rather than a land war, blaming William III for preferring a land war because he was interested in the Dutch barrier fortresses. But the editor obviously thinks in terms of the warfare of Edward III and Henry V rather than of Marlborough's time. On January 3, 1707, he cites Major Wildman's advice to William to fight France chiefly at sea, and to invade it from the Channel; but he shows no conception of Defoe's bold flanking project, nor even of a powerful naval diversion in the West Indies, such as Defoe often suggested.

Three projects were proposed by Wildman or the editor of the *Observator*, all of them futile: an isolated invasion of France, a direct attack on the Channel ports, and major engagements at sea. An isolated invasion was quite impractical so long after the time of Henry V; attacks on the Channel ports proved to be bloody failures; and (with the French restricting their naval operations to privateering) major engagements at sea were no longer possible. Defoe's proposal seems to have had a unique priority.

CHAPTER IX

1. Smith, p. 63. *A Short View of the Present State of the Protestant Religion in Britain* (Edinburgh, 1707), p. 16.

2. John Evelyn, *Diary*, April 10, 1687 (Bohn ed.; II, 276). *London Gazette*, May 23–26, 1687. *Review*, VIII, 422. *A Short View of the Present State of the Protestant Religion in Britain*, p. 15.

3. *Ibid.*, p. 38. *Mere Nature Delineated* (1726), p. 85. *A Short View of the Present State of the Protestant Religion in Britain*, p. 36.

4. Thornley, p. 152. See also W. Carew Hazlitt, *The Livery Companies of London*

(London, 1892), p. 403. *A Vindication of the Press* (1718), p. 30. Thornley, p. 154. Arthur Pearce, *The History of the Butchers' Company* (London, 1929), pp. 180–81. *The Lists Of The Liveries Of The Fifty six Companies, In the City of London: . . . With an Account who Poll'd, and who did not at the Late Election of Members of Parliament for the said City of London* (1701). *The Poll Of The Livery-Men Of The City of London, At The Election for Members of Parliament: Begun Munday, October 9th, 1710* (London, 171[0?]; date partly broken off in the British Museum copy).

5. Moore (2). *Review*, VIII, 422. *Registers* ("Publications of the Harleian Society"), VII, 270.

6. *What If the Swedes Should Come?* (1717), pp. 10–11. *Review*, VI, 598.

7. Hugh Speke, *Some Memoirs of the most Remarkable Passages and Transactions On the Late Happy Revolution in 1688* (Dublin, 1709), pp. 38–39. *Tour* (1), I, 298.

8. Clarendon, II, 224–25. *The Compleat English Tradesman* (1727), II, Part I, 250–54.

9. *Review*, II, 318. See also VII, 308. *HCJ*, X, 15. *HLJ*, XIV, 110.

CHAPTER X

1. *London Gazette*, February 7–11, 1688/99. *London Intelligencer*, February 9–12, 1689. Moore (2).

2. *Reflections upon the Late Great Revolution* (1689), p. 68. *The Danger of the Protestant Religion Consider'd* (1701); see Lee, I, 42. *The Compleat English Gentleman* (Bülbring ed.; London, 1890), pp. 102, 226.

3. *An Appeal to Honour and Justice* (Hazlitt ed.), p. 4. Moore (3).

4. Luttrell, I, 501. *A Letter to the Whigs* (1714), p. 40. Luttrell, I, 472. *Mercurius Reformatus: or, The New Observator*, November 6, 1689.

5. Oldmixon, p. 37. White Kennett, *A Complete History of England* (1706), III, 587.

6. *The Weakest Go to the Wall* (1714), p. 25. *The Battle of the Authors Lately Fought in Covent-Garden* (ca. 1720), p. 15; for Gildon's authorship, see Moore (4).

7. H. C. Foxcroft, *The Life and Letters of Sir George Savile, Bart. First Marquis of Halifax, &c.* (London, 1898), II, 222, 224, 226–27, 228, 229, 231, 233, 235, 236, 238, 243, 247, 249.

8. William Minto, *Daniel Defoe* (London, 1879), pp. 15–16.

9. *Tour* (1), 166. *Review*, IV, 423. *The Felonious Treaty* (1711), p. 5.

10. Loftie, p. 16. *Tour* (1), II, 10. Loftie, p. 20.

11. *Tour* (1), II, 15. Luttrell, II, 52. Clarendon, II, 316. *Tour* (1), II, 71. Luttrell, II, 55. *Tour* (1), II, 255–56. Macaulay, *History of England*, IV, 1847–48.

12. *Review*, III, 619. *An Appeal to Honour and Justice* (Hazlitt ed.), p. 4. *Review*, VII, 578.

13. Sutherland (1), p. 48. The British Museum Catalogue lists two tracts on the lotteries written by Dalby Thomas in collaboration with Thomas Neale. *Review*, VIII, 482–83; III, 65; IV, 100.

14. Churchill, II, 277. *Review*, V, 619; VII, 391. *The Felonious Treaty* (1711), pp. 4–5. *Review*, [IX], 140; VIII, 59. *The Succession of Spain Considered* (1711), p. 45.

15. *A Vindication of the Press* (1718), p. 29. *H.M.C. Portland*, IV, 148.

16. *Review*, VII, 511; VIII, 165, 513. *An Essay upon the South Sea Trade* (Hazlitt ed.), p. 13. *Mere Nature Delineated* (1726), pp. 106–7. *The Evident Advantages to Great Britain and the Allies from the Approaching War* (1727), *passim*. *Reasons for a War* (1729), pp. 27–29. *A Plan of the English Commerce* (1730), Appendix. M. Grosley, *A Tour to London*, trans. Thomas Nugent (London, 1772), II, 56. *Marchmont Papers*, I, 43. Walter Sichel, *Bolingbroke and His Times* (London, 1901), p. 318. Hardwicke's

Miscellaneous State Papers (London, 1778), II, 340–41 (letter from Kensington, April 8– March 29, 1698). James Ralph, *The Other Side of the Question* (London, 1742), p. 208.

17. *Review*, VIII, 202. See also Abel Boyer's *Political State* (1711), II, 191. *Review*, V, 128, 198–99. *Ibid.*, II, 78; IV, 354; VI, 38, 367. *Ibid.*, I, 393. *Ibid.*, III, 255. *True Collection* ((1705), II, 73.

18. *Review*, VII, 379. *H.M.C. Portland*, IV, 88. *Review*, VIII, 374. *Hannibal at the Gates* (2d ed., 1714), p. 44.

19. *H.M.C. Portland*, IV, 148. *The Felonious Treaty* (1711), pp. 5–6. *Review*, VIII, 354.

20. *A Reply to a Pamphlet Entitled, The L——d H——'s Vindication*, pp. 8–9. *Review*, IV, 67. See also IV, 574; VI, 341.

21. *Tour* (1), I, 166. *Review*, VIII, 210–11. *Ibid.*, IV, 158–60. *The History of the Union* (Edinburgh, 1709), pp. 35 ff. (for pp. 36 ff., "Of Affairs in Both Kingdoms"); *A Letter to a Merry Young Gentleman* (1715), p. 19.

22. *Review*, II, 382. *An Argument Proving that the Design of Employing and Enobling Foreigners, &c.* (1717), pp. 59–60.

23. *Review*, [IX], 43. See also IV, 173, 443. *True Collection* (1705), II, 477. *Review*, II, 355. *The Weakest Go to the Wall* (1714), pp. 23–25. *Faction in Power* (1717), pp. 11– 14. *Review*, I, 394. *The Compleat English Tradesman* (2d ed., 1727), pp. 241–42. *A Brief Reply to the History of Standing Armies* (1698), pp. 17–18; *Considerations on Seamen* (1728), p. 22. The opposing view was stated by Sir John Dalrymple, *Memoirs of Great Britain and Ireland* (London, 1790), III, 237–38. *Review*, III, 154; IV, 487. *True Collection* (1705), II, 348–49. *Advice to the People of Great Britain* (1711), p. 20. *An Apology for the Army* (1715), p. 34. *A Letter to the Whigs* (1714), pp. 39–40. *Tories and Tory Principles Ruinous to both Prince and People* (1714), pp. 82–83. *The Englishman's Choice*, p. 9. *Jure Divino* (Hazlitt ed.), p. 50. *True Collection* (1705), II, 129. *Review*, I, 191, 193, 195; VII, 514–15. *Ibid.*, I, 93; II, 162; IV, 390; VI, 7; VII, 190. *True Collection* (1705), II, 118–19, 128, 172, 178. *Remarks on the Letter to the Author of the State-Memorial* (1706), p. 16. *An Apology for the Army* (1715), pp. 34–35. *Review*, V, 207.

24. *Minutes of the Negotiations of Monsr. Mesnager at the Court of England* (1717). See all other allusions to the meetings of Louis and Mesnager, especially pp. 4–16. *Review*, VII, 372. *London Gazette*, April 20–23, 1702. *True Collection* (1705), II, 92. *Review*, VIII, 2. See also IV, 557.

CHAPTER XI

1. *Robinson Crusoe* (Tegg ed.), I, 5; II, 230.

2. *Review*, II, 149. Lee, I, 14.

3. *Review*, II, 498.

4. *Ibid.*, VIII, 614; VII, 297; II, 498–99; IV, 530–31. *The Question Fairly Stated* (1717), pp. 11–14.

5. *The Compleat English Tradesman* (1727), II, 118–19.

6. Strype, I, Book II, pp. 150, 149 (material for Strype supplied by Richard Blome).

7. Oldmixon, p. 519. *Observations on the Bankrupts Bill* (1706), p. 35. Giles Jacob, *The Poetical Register* (1723), II, 293. *The True-Born Hugonot: or, Daniel Defoe. A Satyr* (1703), p. 10. *The Monster: or, The World turn'd Topsy Turvy. A Satyr* (1705). *The Shortest Way with the Dissenters: . . . With its Author's Brief Explication Consider'd* (1703), p. 9. Oldmixon, p. 37. Old manuscript note in the Indiana University copy of "A Man with Hebrew Prophet's Name (p. 1, l. 1, in Edward Ward's *In Imitation of Hudibras. The Dissenting Hypocrite, or Occasional Conformist* [1704]). *Gulliver's Travels* (Temple Scott ed.), p. 18.

8. Newton (1). Sutherland (2). *Review*, II, 149. Moore (1).
9. *The Complete English Tradesman* (1726), pp. 14–15. *Review*, [IX], 193. *Tour* (1), I, 341. *An Appeal to Honour and Justice* (Hazlitt ed.), p. 4. *A Reply to a Pamphlet Entituled, The L——d H——'s Vindication of His Speech* (1706), p. 7. *The History and Reality of Apparitions* (Tegg ed.), pp. 167–71. Sutherland (2), pp. 277–80. *Colonel Jack* (Tegg ed.), pp. 164, 167, 189.
10. *Review*, I, 369. *Tour*, I, 303. *Political State of Great-Britain*, XXXIX (June, 1730), 658. *Commentator*, June 17, 1720.
11. *Review*, VIII, 496. Sutherland (2), p. 286. *An Humble Proposal* (Hazlitt ed.), p. 8. *Review*, VII, 154, 212. Lee, I, 362. Wright (1), p. 362. Sutherland (1), p. 263. Sutherland (3), p. 141.
12. *Spectator*, July 9, 1711. *Flying-Post*, July 28, 1711. *Supplement*, March 24, 1711 (1712).
13. *Review*, [IX], 110. *The Compleat English Tradesman* (1727), II, Part II, 13. *The History of the Principal Discoveries* (1727), p. 154. *The Compleat English Tradesman* (1727), II, Part II, 5–6.

CHAPTER XII

1. *A Reply to a Pamphlet Entituled, The L——d H——'s Vindication of his Speech* (1706), p. 7.
2. *Review*, III, 149, 22–23; V, 596; IV, 99. *The Unreasonableness and Ill Consequences of Imprisoning the Body for Debt* (1729). *Review*, III, 103.
3. *Robinson Crusoe* (Tegg ed.), I, 123, 43. *Review*, III, 85.
4. *Ibid.*, V, 454; I, 370, 369. *HL MSS*, New Series, I, 358, 358–59.
5. *HCJ*, XI, 8, 25, 30, 31, 38, 59, 80, 84–85, 87, 102, 110. *HLJ*, XV, 381, 382.
6. *An Essay upon Projects* (Hazlitt ed.), p. 3. *Review*, I, 370. *HCJ*, XI, 563, 573, 592, 765; XII, 149, 242, 320. *Review*, V, 590–91. *H.M.C. Portland*, IV, 301 (letter to Harley, May 6, 1706). *Review*, II, 214, 231–32, 235–36, 377–78; VI, 490–91; VIII, fifth page of Preface.
7. Letter to John Fransham, a linen-draper of Norwich, on May 24, 1706 (*N. & Q.*, Ser. 5, III, 283). *Review*, II, 304.
8. *Ibid.*, III, 131, 119–20, 122–23, 125–27, 132, 134–35, 138–39. *HL MSS*, New Series, VI, 427. *Review*, VIII, 302.
9. *Remarks on the Bill to Prevent Frauds Committed by Bankrupts* (Hazlitt ed.), p. 12. *Review*, III, 130–31, 142. *The Compleat English Tradesman* (1727), II, 192. See also the account of the wife who persuaded her husband to accept bankruptcy (*The Complete English Tradesman* [1726], pp. 165–75). *Review*, III, 135, 135–36, 74–75.
10. *Ibid.*, III, 141, 109–10, 131, 139, 122. See n. 27. *London Gazette*, July 18–22, 1706.
11. *Ibid.*, August 5–8, 1706. Healey (3), p. 125 n. 2, offers evidence to show that the meeting was on August 21. *Review*, III, 575. *Daily Courant*, September 11, 1706. *Mercator*, No. 101.
12. *Review*, I, 421–22. *H.M.C. Portland*, IV, 76. Sutherland (1), 272–74. Sutherland (3).
13. See "Of the Tradesman's Avoiding Law-Suits," *The Compleat English Tradesman* (1727), II, 280–98. In *A General History of the Pirates* (Hayward ed.), p. 216, Defoe suggests that the pirates tried at Cape Corso Castle in 1722 were more likely to have justice because no professional lawyers were engaged. Sutherland (1), pp. 273–74. César de Saussure, *A Foreign View of England in the Reigns of George I. & George II.*,

trans. and ed. Madame van Muyden (2d ed.; London, 1902), pp. 339, 344–46. *Review*, III, 576.

14. *Mercator*, No. 101. Review, III, 399; IV, 115–16, 119, 123. *A Dialogue between a Dissenter and the Observer*, in *A Collection of the Writings of the Author of the True-Born Englishman* (1703), pp. 222–23. *Review*, III, 399; IV, 343–44.

15. *Works* (Tegg ed.), XX, 9.

16. Dottin, I, 67–68. *Remarks on the Bill to Prevent Frauds Committed by Bankrupts* (Hazlitt ed.), p. 11. *Review*, VIII, 765. Lee, III, 190–92. "Sir John Morden," *DNB*. See also *Tour* (1), I, 96. *The Protestant Monastery* (1727).

17. *The Complete English Tradesman* (1726), p. 286. Arthur Paul Davis, *Isaac Watts: His Life and Works* (New York, 1943), pp. 37–38. Doddridge's letter was written in 1741.

18. *The Compleat English Tradesman* (1727), II, 201, 198–99, 183, 184–85.

CHAPTER XIII

1. *The History of the Kentish Petition* (1701), p. 4. Laprade, pp. 430–31. Moore (1), pp. 25, 27, 28, 32, 44, 49. *The History of the Kentish Petition*, Preface, pp. 7, 14. *Legion's New Paper* (1702), p. 4. HCJ dates the prorogation June 24; Defoe says June 23. *The History of the Kentish Petition*, p. 15. Wilson (1), I, 406.

2. Drake, p. 153. *Jure Populi Anglicani* (1701), pp. 35–36. *The Source of our Present Fears Discover'd* (1703), p. 20. HLJ, XVI, 755, 767, 768, 769. Drake, p. 153, and Preface (A₆ verso).

3. *London Gazette*, February 1, 1691/2. *True Collection* (1703), p. 80. Moore (1), chap. i.

4. John Howe, *Some Considerations of a Preface to an Enquiry, Concerning Conformity of Dissenters, &c.* (1701), pp. 25–26, 33. *True Collection* (1703), p. 315. *Review*, VIII, 374.

5. HLJ, XV, 150. *The Present State of the Parties in Great Britain* (1712), p. 14. "Dr. Henry Sacheverell," *DNB*. Feiling, pp. 350, 367.

6. *The Case of Dissenters As Affected by the Late Bill Proposed in Parliament, For Occasional Conformity* (1703), pp. 20–22. H.M.C. Portland, IV, 50, 52.

7. HCJ, XIV, 14, 35, 46, 51. *True Collection* (1703), p. 381.

8. HLJ, XVII, 178. *A Dialogue between Louis le Petite and Harlequin le Grand* (1709). According to *The Second Part of the Mouse Grown a Rat* (1703), p. 29, the Modern Whigs thought they could manage for themselves and brought out *The Shortest Way* without consulting Halifax, who planned to desert them now that they were out of their depth. Sutherland (1), p. 87. *The Present State of the Parties in Great Britain* (1712), p. 24. *True Collection* (1705), II, 274. See also Charles Hornby, *The Fourth and Last Part of a Caveat Against the Whiggs* (1712), p. 38. *The Original Works of William King, LL.D.* (London, 1776), II, 194.

9. Oldmixon, p. 301. *Review*, II, 297. *The Present State of the Parties in Great Britain*, pp. 18–19. *True Collection* (1705), II, 207–8. *The Consolidator* (1705), p. 209. Moore's name is given in the key to a later edition of the *True Collection*. *Remarks on the Author of The Hymn to the Pillory* (1703), pp. 2–3.

10. Leslie (3), p. 6. *The Safest-Way with the Dissenters* (1703), pp. 4–8. Feiling, p. 369. *Bishop Burnet's History of His Own Time* (2d ed.; Oxford, 1833), VI, 223–24. H.M.C. Portland, V, 661.

11. Luttrell, V, 261, 262, 265. HCJ, XIV, 76. H.M.C. Portland, IV, 53.

12. HLJ, XVII, 192, 306. Luttrell, V, 245, 256. John Evelyn, *Diary and Correspondence*, ed. William Bray (London, 1886), II, 383. H.M.C. Portland, IV, 57.

13. *The Present State of the Parties in Great Britain*, p. 20. Leslie (1), II, 146. B.M. Add. MSS, 29,589, f. 400.

14. *Observator*, January 2, 1703. *The Shortest-Way with the Dissenters . . . Consider'd*, p. 22. Henry R. Plomer, *A Dictionary of the Printers and Engravers, Who Were at Work in England, Scotland and Ireland from 1686 to 1725* (Oxford, 1922), p. 87. *H.M.C. Portland*, IV, 34, 207. Luttrell, V, 253.

15. *The Shortest-Way with the Dissenters . . . Consider'd*, p. 22. *Instructions from Rome*, pp. 10–11. Luttrell, II, 103. *True Collection* (1705), II, 14. *Howell's State Trials*, XI, 1346–49. Hugh Speke, *Some Memoirs Of the Most Happy Passages and Transactions On the Late Happy Revolution in 1688* (Dublin, 1709), p. 74. The indictment of Defoe in the City of London Records. *A Dialogue between a Dissenter and the Observator*, in *Collection* (1703), pp. 219–20, 225, 233.

16. Nottingham's Letter Book, P.R.O. 44/353, ff. 103–4. P.R.O. 44/352, ff. 103–4; 44/104, f. 318. *H.M.C. Portland*, IV, 417, 470. See also *London Gazette*, February 21, 1688/89. *The Shortest-Way with the Dissenters . . . Consider'd*, p. 2. *Review*, I, 375. *Little Review*, No. 10, p. 38. *A hue and cry after D. de Foe for destroying the Queen's hereditary right* (1711). In the *Observator*, July 14, 1703, Tutchin professed to believe that Stephens was an agent for the Jacobites and not properly accredited as one of the Queen's messengers. *H.M.C. Portland*, IV, 88.

17. First printed by Aitken (3), p. 862, from S.P. Anne Dom. Bdle. 2, No. 26.

18. *Collection* (1703), pp. 220, 221, 232. *True Collection* (1705), II, 48.

19. Nottingham's Letter Book, P.R.O. 44/352, f. 106. *Calendar of Treasury Papers 1702–1707*, LXXXIV, 41. *The Bishop of Salisbury's and the Bishop of Oxford's Speeches in the House of Lords* (1710), p. 15. *True Collection* (1705), II, 28. *Review*, VIII, 422. *Collection* (1703), pp. 224–25.

20. Luttrell, V, 458. John Evelyn, *Diary and Correspondence*, ed. William Bray (London, 1886), II, 383. *Howell's State Trials*, XIV, 1098.

21. Strype, Book III, p. 39.

22. *HCJ*, XIV, 207. *Calendar of Treasury Books*, XIX, 409 (November 7, 1704). Abel Boyer, *The History of the Life & Reign of Queen Anne* (London, 1722), p. 48. *The Shortest Way with the Dissenters: (Taken from Dr. Sach——ll's Sermon, and Others.) Or, Proposals for the Establishment of the Church* (n.d., but 1703), p. 20.

23. Moore (1), pp. 55–58. *Mr. William Fuller's Letter to Mr. John Tutchin, Author of the Observator* (1703), p. 5. *Howell's State Trials*, XIV, 1118. *Little Review*, No. 5, pp. 18–19. See also the *Daily Courant*, July 22, 1703.

24. See *N. & Q.*, CLXII, 419, 420. Alfred Jackson supposed that (like the *True Collection*, which appeared three months later) this *Collection* contained a warning against a spurious collection. But the *Collection* of April, 1703, is itself the pirated edition. See pp. 27 and [28] of John Tutchin's *England's Happiness Consider'd* (1705), where How's books are advertised. See advertisement of *More Reformation* (1703).

25. *H.M.C. Portland*, IV, 61, 62. *The Reformer Reform'd: or, The Shortest Way with Daniel D'Fooe* (1703), p. 7. See also the *Daily Courant*, May 24, 1703. Luttrell, V, 300–301. Healey (3), pp. 65, 269. *H.M.C. Portland*, IV, 138.

26. *The History and Reality of Apparitions* (Tegg ed.), pp. 220–22.

27. *The Reformer Reform'd*, pp. 7–8. See also the *Post-Man*, May 25, 1703: "On Thursday Daniel de Foe, Author of the Pamphlet entitled the Shortest Way with the Dissenters was taken and after having been examined, he was committed on Saturday to Newgate." See also the warrant to the keeper of Newgate to receive Defoe on May 22, 1703 (Nottingham's Letter Book, P.R.O. 44/352, f. 162). Luttrell placed the arrest on Friday, May 21.

28. *Calendar of Treasury Papers 1702–1707*, LXXXV, 154. P.R.O. 44/352, f. 162. *Diary of Mary Lady Cowper* (London, 1864), p. 30. *Calendar of Treasury Books*, XIX, 409.

29. *Advice to All Parties* (1705), Preface. *H.M.C. Portland*, V, 58. *Review*, VII, 90–91. See also Defoe's letter to William Penn on July 12, 1703 (Healey [3], pp. 7–9).

30. Chamberlayne's *Angliae Notitia* (1704), p. 443. *English Historical Review*, XXII, 137. Written on the calendar at the back of the sessions roll for July 7, 1703. *Review*, [IX], 184.

31. Letter to Nottingham, January 9, 1703. *True Collection* (1703), p. 441. Letter to William Penn on July 12, 1703.

32. *A True State of the Difference Between Sir George Rook, Knt. and William Colepeper, Esq;* (1704), p. 5. *An Appeal to Honour and Justice* (Aitken ed.), p. 176. *Review*, VI, 454. *A Vindication of the Last Parliament, In Four Dialogues between Sir Simon and Sir Peter* (1711), p. 134. *Review*, II, 376. See also *The True-Born Hugonot* (1703), p. 16. *The Examination, Tryal, and Condemnation of Rebellion Ob[servator]* (1703), p. 5. *A Vindication of the Late Parliament*, p. 134.

33. *Calendar of Treasury Books*, XIX, 408 (three entries). Moore (1), pp. 19–32. *Poems on State Affairs* (1702–4), III, 437. See Defoe's references to the severities of a recorder: *Review*, II, 41; *Moll Flanders* (Aitken ed.), II, 110; *Colonel Jacque* (Aitken ed.), I, 11. *Review*, III, 218. Moore (1), pp. 16–32. *Review*, II, 41.

34. Sentence written above Defoe's name on sessions roll for July 7, 1703, in the City of London Records. See also *London Gazette*, August 2, 1703; Lee, I, 71; *Howell's State Trials*, XIV, 1098. Luttrell, V, 303, 308 (June 1 and 15, 1703); V, 317 (July 13, 1703); V, 312, 313 (June 26 and July 1, 1703). *A True State of the Difference*, p. 6.

35. *Review*, VI, 454. Wilson (2), III, 19–37, 41–49, 468–87. *True Collection* (1705), II, 63. Moore (1), pp. 34–35. *True Collection* (1705), II, 42, 85–86. *Review*, IV, 348. *London Gazette*, November 28, 1706. Jonathan Swift, "A Description of the Morning." *Review*, I, Preface.

36. Dottin, I, 114. *Correspondence between William Penn and James Logan*, ed. Edward Armstrong (Philadelphia, 1870), I, 351. See also *ibid.*, I, 208 n. 1, 231, 241, 258, 266–67, 274–80, 281, 305, 315, 318, 320, 322, 337, 341, 343, 349. *H.M.C. Portland*, IV, 316. *Bishop Burnet's History of His Own Time* (2d ed.; Oxford, 1833), III, 140 n. d. *H.M.C. Portland*, IV, 316. *Calendar of State Papers Domestic (1703–1704)*, p. 39.

37. *The Friend* (Philadelphia), LXXVI (1902), 1–2, from a copy of the original letter owned by the Society of Friends, Devonshire House, E.C., London, and communicated by Norman Penny.

38. Letter of April 18, 1704, in possession of the Historical Society of Pennsylvania.

39. Godolphin to Nottingham, July 17, 1703 (B.M. Add. MSS, 29,589, f. 628).

40. Burton, I, 97–98. P.R.O., S.P. Dom. Anne, 34, Bdle. 3, f. 3.

41. *Calendar of Treasury Books*, XVIII, 353 (J. Taylour writing from Windsor to Methuen in place of Godolphin). Luttrell, V, 310, 314, 315, 319–20. Nottingham's Letter Book, P.R.O., S.P. 44/104, f. 316. Burton, 98 (from B.M. Add. MSS, 29,589, f. 44). Nottingham's Letter Book, P.R.O., Entry Book 104, f. 318.

42. Oldmixon, p. 301. *The Consolidator* (1705), p. 212. *The True-Born Hugonot* (1703), pp. 18–19. *Review*, VIII, 147; I, 386. *The Felonious Treaty* (1711), pp. 25–26, 5. *The Interests of the Several Princes and States of Europe* (1698), esp. p. 32. *Review*, I, 390; VIII, 34; [IX], 58. *The Felonious Treaty*, p. 45. *Review*, VIII, 391; [IX], 140. *The Felonious Treaty*, p. 7. *Review*, VIII, 354; [IX], 159–60, 24.

43. *Ibid.*, [IX], 158; VIII, 814; V, 466. *True Collection* (1705), II, 22. See also Moore (1), p. 28. *True Collection* (1705), II, 16–17. *A Hymn to the Pillory* (1703), p. 23. Nottingham's Letter Book, P.R.O., S.P. Entry Book 104, f. 320.

44. *N. & Q.*, New Series, VI, 219, 270–72. *London Gazette*, August 2, 1703. *Daily Courant*, July 30, 1703. *Heraclitus Ridens* (quoted by Newton [2], p. 181). *The True-Born Hugonot*, pp. 4, 10, 20.

45. Leslie (1), II, 90, 146. See also Leslie (4), p. 59. *A Hymn to the Pillory*, p. 1.

46. *Review*, VIII, Preface (A₃ verso). Defoe, so reliable on most matters of fact, is often careless about dates. He says here that the change happened "in less than half a year." No previous confinement in Newgate is known or probable.

47. *A Hymn to the Pillory*, pp. 3, 23–24. *The Present State of the Parties in Great Britain*, p. 21. *The Consolidator*, pp. 68–69. *Heraclitus Ridens* (quoted by Newton [2], p. 151).

48. Luttrell, V, 339. *H.M.C. Portland*, IV, 66–67. *H.M.C.*, 8th Report, Part I, p. 43. Luttrell, V, 330. *H.M.C. Portland*, IV, 65–66, 67, 72–73, 74, 65, 66.

49. *Ibid.*, IV, 65, 74, 75. *H.M.C. Bath*, I, 56. Oldmixon, p. 456. On August 3, 1708, Defoe wrote very urgently to Godolphin regarding the importance of a controlled press. Godolphin employed Defoe much as Harley had done; but he trusted him less and made less effective use of him. See *H.M.C. Bath*, I, 115, 152, 167, 177, 178; *H.M.C.*, 8th Report, Part I, pp. 44–45; *H.M.C. Portland*, IV, 155–56. *The Wentworth Papers 1705–1739* (London, 1883), p. 132. B.M. Add. MSS, 28,055, f. 3.

50. Oldmixon, p. 519. *A Detection of the Sophistries and Falsities of the Pamphlet, Entituled, the Secret History of the White Staff*, Part I (1714), pp. 7–8. *A Dialogue between Louis le Petite, and Harlequin le Grand* (ca. 1709), pp. v, vi. *H.M.C.*, 8th Report, Part I, p. 43.

51. *A Brief Reply to the History of Standing Armies in England* (1698) Preface (A₃ recto). *Considerations on the Present State of Great Britain*, p. 49. *An Appeal to Honour and Justice* (Aitken ed.), pp. 175–76.

52. *H.M.C.*, 8th Report, Part I, p. 43.

53. *H.M.C. Portland*, IV, 68–69, 66, 67, 70–74. Luttrell, V, 347, 349, 350. *Calendar of Treasury Books*, XVIII, 416–17. *An Appeal to Honour and Justice* (Aitken ed.), p. 176. *H.M.C. Bath*, I, 61.

54. *Calendar of State Papers Domestic (1703–1704)*, p. 39. Luttrell, V, 348. Ned Ward, *Hudibras Redivivus*, Part the First (1705), pp. 20–21. *H.M.C. Portland*, IV, 72. *HLJ*, XVII, 331–32.

55. *Poems on State Affairs* (1707), IV, 17. *HCJ*, XIV, 238. *The Case of Dissenters As Affected by the Late Bill Proposed in Parliament For Preventing Occasional Conformity* (1703), p. 6. Advertised in the *Post-Man* on September 18 and in the *Daily Courant* on September 20, 1703. The *Post-Man* advertisement was repeated September 21 and 30, October 2, November 13 and 20.

56. *H.M.C. Portland*, IV, 75–76. Luttrell, IV, 302, 359. *Calendar of State Papers Domestic (1703–1704)*, p. 248. *H.M.C. Portland*, IV, 77. Moore (13). *H.M.C. Portland*, IV, 89. *Review*, I, supplement for November, 1704, p. 25. *H.M.C. Bath*, I, 61.

57. *Calendar of Treasury Books* (January, 1704–March, 1705), pp. 33, 237, 245. Luttrell, V, 533. *A Dialogue between Louis le Petite, and Harlequin le Grand*, p. vi. *H.M.C. Portland*, IV, 75–76, 83, 93, 138.

58. *English Historical Review*, XXII, 132–133, 140, 130. *H.M.C. Portland*, IV, 148. See *Remarks on the Letter to the Author of the State-Memorial* (1706), p. 30; *The Present State of the Parties in Great Britain*, pp. 25–26; *Review*, V, 106, and [IX], 25; *The Secret History of State Intrigues in the Management of the Scepter* (1715), p. 30; *Memoirs of Publick Transactions in the Life and Ministry of . . . the D. of Shrewsbury* (1718), p. 44. Feiling, p. 376, expresses doubt that Harley acted on Defoe's advice; but it was widely believed at the time that Harley had allowed the bill to come before the House of Commons for the express purpose of killing it (exactly as Defoe had suggested). See Godolphin's letter to Harley (*H.M.C. Bath*, I, 64–65), Marlborough's letter to Harley (*ibid.*, I, 65), numerous tracts by High Fliers opposing Harley's attempt at a moderate government, and all Defoe's writings on the subject—including the letters written directly to Harley and pamphlets certainly written with Harley's approval.

59. *True Collection* (1705), II, 167. *Robinson Crusoe* (Tegg ed.), I, 215.

CHAPTER XIV

1. *The Storm* (1704), pp. 32, 25, 9, 25, 31, 32–33, 37–38.

2. *Ibid.*, p. 41. Defoe gives this date by mistake as December 2.

3. *Ibid.*, pp. 37, 39, 35, Preface, and pp. 59, 70, 73–74, 81–82, 31–32, 205, 136, 253, 256, 260, 215, 159, 3.

4. *London Gazette*, December 2–6, 1703. From later references in the *Review* (I, 148, 180) it is clear that this advertisement appeared in other newspapers about the same time.

5. *The Storm*, p. 226. Wilson (1), II, 265–66, n. *Review*, I, 148, 184.

6. *The Storm*, pp. 215, 272, 69; Preface and p. 100. Moore (14).

7. A. Gifford, *A Sermon In Commemoration Of The Great Storm, Commonly called the High Wind, In the Year 1703* (London, 1734), pp. 16–19.

8. *H.M.C. Portland*, IV, 98. *H.M.C. Bath*, I, 61. *H.M.C. Portland*, IV, 89. The reference to "H——" has sometimes been taken to mean Hanover, but see the chapter on Scotland.

9. *H.M.C. Portland*, IV, 98. *English Historical Review*, XXII (1907), 132–43. Warner dates this letter in May or June, but Healey gives good reasons for placing it in July. *H.M.C. Portland*, VIII, 41; IV, 136–38, 269–72, 302, 323. See also Healey (3), 124. *H.M.C. Portland*, IV, 324, 326–28. Moore (15). *H.M.C. Portland*, IV, 334. Healey (3), 132.

10. *H.M.C. Portland*, IV, 331, 335, 336. *H.M.C. Bath*, I, 115.

11. *Review*, I, 35–36, 244; II, 79; VIII, 11; III, 479–80. See also *Mercurius Politicus*, May, 1716, p. 84. *Review*, VIII, 29–30; III, 544. *London Gazette*, October 14, 1706; November 4, 1706; January 23, 1706/7. *Post-Man*, October 31, November 26, December 21 and 28, 1706.

12. E.g., *ibid.*, October 22, November 2 and 23, 1706; August 30, 1707. *Ibid.*, October 31 and December 5, 1706. "An Account of the Proceedings . . . with Observations," *The History of the Union* (Edinburgh, 1709), pp. 95–97. *Post-Man*, February 13, March 20, April 1, 1707. *H.M.C. Portland*, IV, 394. *Tour* (3), III, Part II, 61–62.

13. *Post-Man*, April 10, 1707. *H.M.C. Portland*, IV, 398. *Post-Man*, August 12, October 30, December 13, 1707; November 5, 1706; January 23, 1707.

14. *Ibid.*, June 26, September 4, 1708; February 27, March 1, 1707.

15. *H.M.C. Portland*, IV, 394–95.

16. *Commentator*, January 15, 1720.

17. *London Gazette*, September 18–21, 1682. *Mercurius Politicus*, May, 1716, pp. 79–80; June, 1718, pp. 344–45. *A Letter to the Whigs* (1714), pp. 5–7. See an account of the explosion of a powder mill in *Tour* (1), 113. Mist's *Weekly-Journal*, June 29, 1717. *Mercurius Politicus*, June, 1717, p. 404.

18. *Mercurius Britannicus*, June, 1718, p. 287.

19. *Political State of Great-Britain*, June, 1718, pp. 629–30 (for 637–38). *Mercurius Politicus*, June, 1718, pp. 334–45.

20. *Mercurius Politicus*, June, 1718, p. 345. Mist's *Weekly*, July 19 and 26, 1718. *Political State of Great-Britain*, XVI, 73.

21. Mr. Alfred F. Robbins (*N. & Q.*, Ser. 9, IX, 462) regarded Defoe's note in Mist's *Weekly* as a chaffing reply to the announcement in *Applebee's*. Both appeared on the same day, and both seem to have been based on the same letters from the West Indies. Mist's *Weekly*, August 2, 1718.

22. *Mercurius Politicus*, July, 1718, p. 418. Mist's *Weekly*, July 19, 1718. *Mercurius Britannicus*, July, 1718, pp. 350–51.

23. *H.M.C. Portland*, IV, 271–72. Aitken (4), XV, xvi–xxii. C. H. Firth, "Defoe's *True Relation of the Apparition of Mrs. Veal*," *RES*, VII (1931), 1–6. Dorothy Gardiner, "What Canterbury Knew of Mrs. Veal and Her Friends," *RES*, VII (1931), 188–97.

Arthur H. Scouten, *"The Loyal Post,* a Rare Queen Anne Newspaper, and Daniel Defoe," *Bulletin of the New York Public Library,* LIX (1955), 195–97. Scouten, "An Early Printed Report on the Apparition of Mrs. Veal," *RES,* New Series, VI (1955), 259–63. Rodney M. Baine, "The Apparition of Mrs. Veal: A Neglected Account," *PMLA,* LXIX (1954), 523–41; "Defoe and Mrs. Bargrave's Story," *PQ,* XXIII (1954), 388–95. Secord (3).

24. *The Miscellaneous Works of Sir Walter Scott, Bart.* (Edinburgh, 1870), IV, 266–68. *RES,* VII (1931), 6.

25. *Miscellaneous Works,* IV, 268–69.

26. *Review,* VI, 90. *A Plan of the English Commerce* (Blackwell ed.), pp. 42, 12. *True Collection* (1705), II, 462. *Adventures of Captain John Gow* (Aitken ed.), pp. 281–82. *Review,* I, 305; VI, 243. *Collection* (1703), pp. 257–58. *Lives of Six Notorious Street-Robbers* (Aitken ed.), p. 354.

27. *The Bristol Riot* (1714), pp. 3, 29, 19, 14.

28. *An Essay upon Literature* (1726), p. 108. Clerk, p. 11.

29. *A True State of the Difference Between Sir George Rook, Knt. and William Colepeper, Esq;* (1704), pp. 9, 36.

30. Healey (3), pp. 263, 453 and n. 2.

31. *The Wentworth Papers 1705–1739* (London, 1883), p. 393. Healey (3), pp. 115–18. *Review,* V, 1, 3, 6, 23; VIII, 30; [IX], 35. See also *Review,* IV, 470. Warner, 135–37. *H.M.C. Portland,* IV, 106, 396, 430, 582. *Eleven Opinions Regarding Mr. H——y* (1711), pp. 68–73.

32. *Mercurius Politicus,* February 1719, p. 70. *Review,* V, 393; III, 507. *Mercurius Politicus,* May, 1716, pp. 1–2.

33. *Impeachment, Or No Impeachment* (1714). William Minto, *Daniel Defoe* (London and New York, 1887), p. 169. *Times Literary Supplement,* November 9, 1946, p. 543. The passage quoted was not written as a tribute to Defoe but occurs in an anonymous review of Louis Hagen's *Indian Route March* (London, 1946).

CHAPTER XV

1. *Tour* (2), II, 689, 690. George A. Aitken, *The Life of Richard Steele* (London, 1889), II, 94, 151–55, 248–51, 265–66. *Tour* (2), II, 693. *The History and Reality of Apparitions* (Tegg ed.), pp. 220–22. *H.M.C. Portland,* IV, 335.

2. *Tour* (2), II, 730. Healey (3), p. 181, implies that in this description of field-preaching Defoe was making use of an old report from his agent J. Pierce. However, there are abundant indications that Defoe was personally acquainted with the Cameronians, and it would be unlike him to fail to hear a field-preaching if he had the opportunity to do so.

3. *H.M.C. Portland,* IV, 358. *Tour* (2), II, 729, 828. *Review,* V, 177–80. C. E. Burch, "Defoe and the Edinburgh Society for the Reformation of Manners," *RES,* XVI (1940), 306–12. *H.M.C. Portland,* IV, 394, 586, 358. *Review,* IV, 82. *An Humble Proposal* (Hazlitt ed.), p. 8. *H.M.C. Portland,* IV, 358, 394. C. E. Burch, "Defoe and His Northern Printers," *PMLA,* LX (1945), 121–28.

4. C. E. Burch, "Benjamin Defoe at Edinburgh University 1710–1711," *PQ,* XXIX (1940), 343–48. *H.M.C. Portland,* IV, 458. *Tour* (2), II, 823–29.

5. *Tour* (1), I, 254. *H.M.C. Portland,* IV, 412–13, 402–3, 435, 445; V, 13–14. See also *The Melvilles Earls of Melville and the Leslies Earls of Leven,* ed. Sir William Fraser (Edinburgh, 1890), II, 217. E.g., *General History of Trade* (August, 1713), pp. 38–39; *Mist's Miscellany,* IV, 254–58. *H.M.C. Portland,* IV, 634, 642, 659; V, 90–91. *Memoirs of the Church of Scotland* (1717), Part II, pp. 246–47; Part III, p. 245. *Tour* (2), II, 832.

E.g., *Review*, V, 381–83, 385–87; VIII, 103–4, 106–7. *Caledonia* (London, 1707), p. 44. *H.M.C. Portland*, IV, 378.

6. *The Melvilles Earls*, II, 213–14. *H.M.C. Portland*, IV, 425, 436, 461.

7. *Ibid.*, IV, 89, 94, 96, 97, 104–5, 114–15, 119–20, 140, 155, 156. *The Republican Bullies* (London, 1705), pp. 1, 2, 3, 7. Moore (1), pp. 147–54. Moore (17), p. 602. John Hill Burton, *History of Scotland* (London, 1853), I, 2.

8. *H.M.C. Portland*, IV, 323. Healey (3), pp. 124, 125. *H.M.C. Portland*, VIII, 240–41, 326–28. Healey (3), p. 132 and n. 1.

9. *Correspondence of George Baillie of Jerviswood* (Edinburgh, 1842), p. 27. *Bishop Burnet's History of His Own Time* (2d ed.; Oxford, 1833), VI, 95, n. *y*. *H.M.C. Portland*, V, 663. Lord Oxford's advertisement in *London Gazette*, July 9, 1715.

10. *The Writings of William Paterson*, ed. Saxe Banister (2d ed.; London, 1859), III, 268–69. "Of the Carrying on of the Treaty in Scotland," *The History of the Union of Great Britain* (Edinburgh, 1709), pp. 29–30. *H.M.C. Portland*, IV, 467. *Review*, III, 611, 671.

11. *H.M.C. Portland*, IV, 382, 383, 385, 387, 390, 397, 398, 401, 403, 404, 412–13, 418, 419, 425, 427, 432, 436, 444–45, 449, 450, 453, 458, 461; V, 13–14. *H.M.C. Bath*, I, 152. *H.M.C. Portland*, IV, 444.

12. *Review*, IV, 347. *H.M.C. Portland*, IV, 358, 385, 394, 587–90. *The History of the Union of Great Britain* (Edinburgh, 1709), p. 2.

13. William Law Matthieson, *Scotland and the Union: A History of Scotland from 1695 to 1747* (Glasgow, 1905), p. 146 and n. 1. Clerk, p. 58. *Memoirs of the Life . . . of . . . Daniel Williams, D.D.* (1718), pp. 60–61. *Review*, VIII, 66–68. *Memoirs of the Church of Scotland* (1717), Appendix. *HCJ*, XVIII, 522.

14. *H.M.C. Portland*, IV, 427, 436, 444, 445, 449, 450, 453, 458, 407. Luttrell, V, 122; VI, 64, 164–65, 596, 709. John Chamberlayne, *Magnae Britanniae Notitia* (London, 1708), p. 746. *H.M.C. Portland*, IV, 473. *An Appeal to Honour and Justice* (Hazlitt ed.), p. 6.

15. *The Melvilles Earls*, II, 217. Healey (3), p. 255 and n. 2. Although Prince George died on October 28, 1708, Defoe was too remote from London to mention his death in the *Review* until November 23. *Review*, V, 417, 445, 142. *Memoirs of the Life . . . of . . . Daniel Williams, D.D.* (1718), p. 48.

16. *An Appeal to Honour and Justice* (Hazlitt ed.), pp. 15, 6.

17. "Remarks on some Affairs in Scotland since my going thither, in October, 1709" (Bodleian MS, North a 3).

18. Healey (3), pp. 265–66. *An Appeal to Honour and Justice* (Hazlitt ed.), p.8. *H.M.C. Portland*, IV, 648.

19. *Ibid.*, V, 213, 219, 350–51, 355–56, 359, 375, 461.

20. *Memoirs of the Life . . . of . . . Daniel Williams, D.D.* (1718), pp. 51–52. *Review*, VIII, 101–7, 114–16. *The Journal of Mr. James Hart* (Edinburgh, 1832), p. 64. In Moore (18) I am inclined to regard the £100 as a possible bribe. The evidence does not now seem to point in that direction. *H.M.C. Portland*, X, 289. *The Correspondence of the Rev. Robert Wodrow* (Edinburgh, 1843), II, 542–43. Letter to John Fraser, Westminster, London (undated, but fairly late). William Adam, *A Letter from the Country Containing Some Remarks Concerning the National Covenant and Solemn League* (Edinburgh, 1707), p. 3.

21. *The Advantages of Scotland by An Incorporate Union with England* (1706), p. 25. *H.M.C. Portland*, IV, 360, 385, 389, 395. *A Reproof to Mr. Clark, And a brief Vindication of Mr. De Foe* (Edinburgh, 1710), pp. 7–8.

22. *Caledonia* (London, 1707), p. 23. *H.M.C. Portland*, IV, 404, 458. *Tour* (2), II, 773, 733, 734.

23. *H.M.C. Portland*, IX, Part II, 469. *Tour* (2), II, 691. *Caledonia* (London, 1707), p. 54.

CHAPTER XVI

1. *The Protestant Jesuite Unmasked* (1704), p. 42. Charles Leslie, "Postscript to Legion," *A View of the Times* (2d ed.; London, 1710), VI, 180. *Tatler*, No. 155. *The Conference: or, Gregg's Ghost* (London, 1711), p. 11.

2. *Review*, VIII, 496. *Mere Nature Delineated* (1726), p. 84. Moore (2). *Memoirs of the Life and Writings of Mr. William Whiston* (London, 1749), p. 304.

3. *Review*, VII, Preface, p. 1. *H.M.C. Portland*, III, 465, 655. *Letters and Correspondence . . . of . . . Bolingbroke*, ed. Gilbert Parke (London, 1798), I, 252–53, 339 n. *The Diary of Mary Countess Cowper*, ed. the Hon. Spencer Cowper (2d ed.; London, 1865), p. 84. *A Letter To The Honourable A—— M——re, Com——ner of Trade and Plantations* (London, 1714), p. 27. John Morley, *Walpole* (London, 1896), p. 127.

4. H. N. Fieldhouse, "Bolingbroke's Share in the Jacobite Intrigue of 1710–14," *English Historical Review*, LII (1937), 454, n. 1. R. W. Frantz, *The English Traveler and the Movement of Ideas 1660–1732* ("University Studies," University of Nebraska, Vols. XXXII–XXXIII [Lincoln, 1932–33]), p. 61, n. 163; also pp. 85, 86, 88, 94. *True Collection* (1705), II, 211–12. *H.M.C. Portland*, IV, 148; V, 58–61; IV, 350, 366. *H.M.C. Bath*, I, 115.

5. *The Republican Bullies* (London, 1705), p. 1. A. L. Smith, "English Political Philosophy in the Seventeenth and Eighteenth Centuries," *Cambridge Modern History*, VI, 817. Moore (20).

6. *Street-Robberies, Consider'd* (1728), p. 57. *A Letter to the Dissenters* (1713), p. 33. *The Complete Works of George Savile First Marquess of Halifax*, ed. Walter Raleigh (Oxford, 1912), p. vii. *Review*, [IX], 202. Moore (2). *Rogues on both Sides* (1711), p. 1.

7. *Review*, VIII, 834; II, 382. *A Hymn to the Mob* (1715), pp. 33, 23. *A Letter from Captain Tom to the Mobb, New Rais'd for Dr. Sacheverel* (1710), p. 2.

8. *Tour* (1), I, 236, 261. *Review*, IV, 541–42; V, 69–71, 121–24, 142, 330, 421–23; VIII, 41–42. *Minutes Of The Negotiations of Monsr. Mesnager* (1717), p. 94. *Tour* (1), I, 130. *A Brief Debate upon the Dissolving the Late Parliament* (1722), pp. 5–6, 24, 35. Miss A. E. Levett, "Daniel Defoe," in *The Social & Political Ideas of the Augustan Age 1650–1750*, ed. F. J. C. Hearnshaw (London, 1928), p. 164.

9. Charles Davenant, *Tom Double Returned out of the Country* (London, 1702), p. 460. Moore (22), pp. 292–93. Morley, *Walpole*, p. 83.

10. British Museum Harleian MSS, 7001, f. 269. *H.M.C. Portland*, V, 496. *Political State of Great-Britain*, X, 48–49. P.R.O., S.P. 35-1, Port. I, No. 29. Lee, I, 233–35. Sutherland (1), 205–6.

11. *H.M.C. Stuart*, II, 69–70. *Political State of Great-Britain*, XI, 747–48. Lee, I, x–xi. "A Vision of the Angelick World," appended to *Serious Reflections of Robinson Crusoe* (1720), pp. 48–50.

12. George Chalmers, *The Life of Daniel De Foe* (London, 1790), pp. 49, 50. *Political State of Great-Britain*, XL, 345.

13. Lee, I, xi–xii, 257. Trent, pp. 130–31. Sutherland (1), p. 218. Lord Baden-Powell, *Lessons of a Lifetime* (New York, 1933), pp. 93–126, 109–10.

14. E.g., *An Appeal to Honour and Justice* (Hazlitt ed.), p. 6. Clerk, p. 64. Lee, III, 350. Trent, p. 152. Sutherland (1), pp. 254–55.

15. Moore (19). *Mercurius Politicus*, July, 1717, p. 408. *H.M.C. Portland*, V, 584–87. Lee, II, 163. *Political State of Great-Britain*, XVIII, 459.

16. *The Evident Approach of a War* (1727), p. 21. *Memoirs of the Conduct of Her late Majesty and her last Ministry* (1715). *Review*, IV, 594, 199–200.

CHAPTER XVII

1. Moore (18).
2. Samuel Keimer, *A Brand Pluck'd from the Burning* (London, 1718), pp. 98–99.
3. Moore (1), chap. vi.

CHAPTER XVIII

1. For this quotation I am indebted to Mr. Godrey Davies, who found it in an old notebook of Sir Charles Firth's.

2. Joseph Spence, *Anecdotes* (London, 1820), pp. 258–59. Boswell's *Johnson* (Hill-Powell ed.; Oxford, 1934–1950), III, 268, n. 1. Charles Gildon, *The Life and Strange Surprising Adventures of Mr. D—— De F——, of London, Hosier* (London, 1719), pp. ix–x. *The Diary of a Country Parson*, ed. John Beresford (London, 1924–31), III, 353. The Rev. Mark Noble, *A Biographical History of England* (London, 1806), II, 306.

3. Nathan van Patten, "An Eskimo Translation of Defoe's 'Robinson Crusoe,'" Godthaab, Greenland, 1862–1865," *Papers of the Bibliographical Society of America*, XXXVI (1942), 56–58. *An Historical Account of . . . Sir Walter Raleigh* (1719; actually January, 1720), p. 55.

4. Lee, I, title page and 32. *The History of the Principal Discoveries and Improvements* (1727), p. 32. Moore (28). Moore (29). Moore (11). *Robinson Crusoe* (Tegg ed.), I, 175.

5. *Review*, V, 309–10; VI, 95. *The Family Instructor* (Tegg ed.), I, 304 ff. *Mercurius Politicus*, February, 1718, pp. 134–35. Lee, II, 461 (Applebee's *Weekly Journal*, December 9, 1721). *A System of Magic* (Tegg ed.), p. 376.

6. Wilson (1), III, 444, n. F. W. D. Taylor, review of *Swift and Defoe: A Study in Relationship* by John F. Ross (*RES*, XIX [1943], 90). Louis Rhead, Introduction to *The Life and Strange Surprising Adventures of Robinson Crusoe* (New York, 1900). "In Praise of Robinson Crusoe," *Athenaeum*, April 25, 1909, p. 230.

7. S. T. Coleridge, *The Table Talk and Omniana*, ed. T. Ashe (London, 1884), p. 294. *The Literary Remains of Samuel Taylor Coleridge*, ed. Henry Nelson Coleridge (London, 1836), I, 197. Winston S. Churchill, *The Gathering Storm* (Boston, 1948), p. 79. Kenneth Grahame, *The Winds in the Willows* (New York, 1909), pp. 108–9.

8. Leland Stowe, "The Amazing Crusoes of Lonesome Lake," *Reader's Digest* (February, 1957), p. 86. *Narrative of Travels and Discoveries in Northern and Central Africa, in the Years 1822, 1823, and 1824, by Major Denham, F.R.S., Captain Clipperton, and the Late Doctor Oudney* (2d ed.; London, 1826), I, 285. Pindar, "Fourth Isthmian Ode," trans. Sir John Sandys (*The Odes of Pindar* [Loeb ed.; London and New York, 1919], p. 465).

CHAPTER XIX

1. Sutherland (1), p. 34. *A Vindication of the Press* (1718), p. 29.

2. Moore (6). Franklin, p. 162.

3. *True Collection* (1705), II, 167. *Review*, VIII, 713, 715; VI, 249, 250–52. *The Political History of the Devil* (1726), pp. 36–38.

4. *An Essay upon Projects* (Hazlitt ed.), pp. 35–36. *Review*, I, supplement for September, 1704, p. A₂; supplement for December, p. 10. Reprinted in *A Supplement to the Athenian Oracle* (1710), pp. 6, 17, 8.

5. *The Life and Errors of John Dunton* (1705), pp. 258, 260. *Athenian Oracle* (2d ed.,

1704), I, 198, 237; II, 40–43, 79. See also I, 159–60, 202, 223, 272. Wilson (1), III, 417. Lee, I, 275. Dunton's draft in the Bodleian is Rawlinson MSS Miscell. 72 f. 49b.

6. *Dunton's Whipping-Post* (1706), I, 88–89, 90.

7. Lee, I, 45. *John Bull's Failings. Being selections from Daniel Defoe's "The True-born Englishman,"* ed. Nasarvanji Maneckji Cooper (London and Bombay, 1904). *The English Gentleman Justified. A Poem Written on the Occasion of A Late Scurrilous Satyr, Intituled, The True-Born Englishman* (1701), prefatory note. *Laconics: or, New Maxims of State and Conversation* (1701), Part III, p. 83.

8. *An Account of the Debate in Town about Peace and War* (1701), p. 3. *The English Gentleman Justified*, Preface. See also *The True-Born Englishman: A Satyr, Answer'd, Paragraph by Paragraph* (1701).

9. *The Apostates* (1701), pp. 10–11. *The Wolf Stript of His Shepherd's Clothing* (3d ed., 1704), p. 60. *The True-Born Englishman: A Satyr, Answer'd, Paragraph by Paragraph*, pp. 14, 32. *The Occasional Paper, Wherein the Honour of the English Clergy and Universities Is Endeavor'd to be Vindicated from the Aspersions of a late Pamphlet Called Mrs. Abigail* (1703), p. 18.

10. *A Collection of Several Pieces of Mr. John Toland* (1726), II, 358. *Advertisements from Parnassus* (1704). For a detailed discussion of the collected editions of 1703, 1705, and 1710, see Moore (1), pp. 50–67. *Little Review*, No. 8, p. 30. *Review*, VIII, 442; III, 241.

11. *Ibid.*, III, 360. *Jure Divino* (1706), I, n. (c). *The Proceedings at the Tryal[,] Examination, and Condemnation Of a Certain Scribling, Rhyming, Versifying, Poeteering Hosier* (1705), p. 3.

12. *Jure Divino*, Preface, pp. xxviii, iv, xxv, xvi, xxvii; Book XII, p. 12. The poem was issued July 20, 1706 (see *Review*, III, 344). *Review*, VII, 304–6, 309–10.

13. *The Proceedings at the Tryal*. "Jure Divino toss'd in a Blanket," *Poems on Affairs of State* (1707), IV, 7. *Review*, I, 251. *N. &. Q.*, Ser. 5, III, 261, 262. *Review*, III, 344. *The Proceedings at the Tryal*, p. 3.

14. *Observator*, July 20, 1706. *Review*, III, 347, 360, 372. *The Right Divine of Kings to Govern Wrong* (London, 1821), p. 10.

15. E.g., *The Protestant Jesuite Unmask'd* (1704), pp. 8, 11–12, 24–25. *Review*, I, 251. *Jure Divino*, Preface, p. xxvii. *Review*, I, 412. *Supplement to the Advice from the Scandal. Club* (1705), No. 5, p. 28. Although this is called the supplement for January, it contains one letter dated March 10, 1705. *Review*, III, 11–12.

16. Healey (3), p. 124. *Review*, III, 347, 360, 372. *Jure Divino*, Preface, p. xxvi.

17. E.g., Edmund Blunden, *Votive Tablets* (London, 1931), pp. 87–100, esp. 93–94. *Atlas Maritimus & Commercialis* (1728), p. 237. *Political State of Great-Britain*, XXXIX (1730), 485; XL, 220. *Mist's Miscellany*, II, 276–77. Johnson's *Lives of the Poets*, ed. G. B. Hill (Oxford, 1905), II, 242–43. E.g., Lee, III, 409–12 (from Applebee's *Weekly Journal*, July 31, 1725). References to Pope in *Mist's Miscellany* are more doubtful: Letter xxvii (II, 78) contains a direct personal affront to Pope; but Letter xxiii (II, 64–66) is signed "B. M." (apparently Bezaleel Morris), and there is one highly complimentary reference to Pope (II, 188), which seems to be by Defoe.

18. *H.M.C. Portland*, IV, 385. *Review*, V, 212.

CHAPTER XX

1. *Moll Flanders* (Tegg ed.), pp. 88–89. Applebee's *Weekly Journal*, January 26, 1723 (Lee, III, 95–97). *Ibid.*, July 16, 1720 (Lee, II, 256–58). *An Effectual Scheme for the Immediate Preventing of Street Robberies* (1731, for 1730), p. 62. Mist's *Weekly-Journal*, September 22, 1722 (Lee, III, 52).

2. *Moll Flanders* (Tegg ed.), pp. 5-6. *Roxana* (Tegg ed.), p. 139.

3. *The Memoirs of the Count de Rochefort* (3d ed.; London, 1705), p. 14. This narrative is cited by Defoe in *The Political History of the Devil* (Tegg ed.), p. 347, and elsewhere.

4. *The Compleat English Gentleman* (Bülbring ed.; London, 1890), pp. 206-7.

5. Passage from the *Athenian Gazette* reprinted in the *Athenian Oracle* (2d ed., 1704), I, 198. Applebee's *Journal*, August 22, 1724 (Lee, III, 293-95). *A General History of Trade*, July, 1713, p. 47. Moore (33). *The History and Reality of Apparitions* (Tegg ed.), pp. 220-22.

6. *Colonel Jack* (Tegg ed.), pp. 300-301.

7. Moore (1), pp. 39-49. *The Complete English Tradesman* (London, 1738), p. xi. *Two Accounts of the Escapes of Prince Charles Edward* ("Luttrell Reprints," No. 12 [Oxford, 1951]), pp. 38-39.

8. *Augusta Triumphans* (1728), pp. 8, 38.

9. *London Gazette*, September 11, 1671. *Atlas Maritimus & Commercialis* (1728), p. 252.

10. Walter de la Mare, *Private View* (London, 1953), pp. 57-58. Sir Walter Besant, Introduction to *A Journal of the Plague Year* (New York, 1900), pp. v-vii.

CHAPTER XXI

1. Wilson (1), III, 645, n. z. *True Collection* (1703), p. 368. *H.M.C. Portland*, IV, 385. *Review*, IV (March 29, 1707), 84.

2. *Review*, VIII (April 26, 1712), 688. *A Short Narrative of the Live and Actions of His Grace John, D. of Marlborough* (1711), p. 26. *H.M.C. Portland*, IV, 666, 387-88.

3. *Mercurius Politicus*, January, 1719, p. 14. *Review*, I, Preface; III, 75; IV, 429-30; [IX], 112. *Dyers News Examined as to His Sweddish Memorial against the Review* (Edinburgh, 1707), pp. 1-2. Alexander Cunningham, *The History of Great Britain: From the Revolution in 1688, to the Accession of George the First* (London, 1787), I, 245. *True Collection* (1703), pp. 232-33. Warner, pp. 142-43. *Review*, VI, 237, 263; VIII, 12, 257-58; [IX], 91. *The Justice and Necessity of a War with Holland* (1712), p. 24. *Review*, I, 194. Wolfgang Michael, *England under George I* (London, 1936), pp. 303-4.

4. *Minutes of the Negotiations of Monsr. Mesnager* (1707), pp. 108-9. *The History of the Wars, Of his late Majesty Charles XII* (1720), pp. 249-50.

5. Preface to edition of James Lister (Leeds, n.d.). New edition, with additions, by Edward Jeffery (London, 1792). *Review*, I, 166; III, 477; IV, 255. Winston S. Churchill, *The Gathering Storm* (Boston, 1948), p. iii.

6. Boswell's *Johnson* (Hill-Powell ed.; Oxford, 1934-50), IV, 334. Earl Stanhope, *History of England Comprising the Reign of Queen Anne until the Peace of Utrecht* (London, 1870), p. 551. Lord Mahon, *History of the War of the Succession in Spain* (London, 1832), p. 133. William Stebbing, *Peterborough* (London, 1890), pp. 56, 67, 68, 69, 71, 107, 124, 125. Simon Harcourt-Smith, *Alberoni or the Spanish Conspiracy* (London, 1943), p. 72. Secord (2), pp. 201-3. *The Memoirs of an English Officer* (1728), p. 352.

8. *London Gazette*, February 23-27, 1687/8; June 4-8, 1685. *Commentator*, June 17, 1720. *The Life and Errors of John Dunton* (London, 1818), I, 88-89. *Some Reflections on a Pamphlet* (1697), p. 12.

9. Luttrell, IV, 136-37, 151. Alfred and Guillaume Grandidier, *Collection des ouvrages anciens concernant Madagascar* (Paris, 1903-20), III, 631-38; p. 638 cites as an authority Voltaire, *Histoire de Charles XII*, Book VIII, ed. Pourray (1838), pp. 390-91. *Historical Register*, VIII, 291, 292, 294.

10. *A True Account of the Design, and Advantages of the South-Sea Trade* (1711), pp.

19–23. *H.M.C. Portland*, VII, 293–94. *Review*, IV, 107. See also Archibald Hurd, *The Reign of the Pirates* (New York, 1925), pp. 57–58. *H.M.C. Portland*, IV, 194, 196, 197. *A Plan of the English Commerce* (Blackwell ed.), pp. 234–35.

11. *The Highland Rogue* (London, 1723), pp. vii–viii. For the plagiarism and other methods by which eighteenth-century biographies were padded out, see Moore (30) and Arthur Sherbo, "A Manufactured Anecdote in Goldsmith's *Life of Richard Nash*," *Modern Language Notes*, LXX (1955), 20–22.

12. *Mercurius Politicus*, October, 1719, p. 684. *The History of the Remarkable Life of John Sheppard* (Aitken ed.), p. 197. Moore (25), (1), (12), (25), (26), (27). Mist's *Weekly-Journal*, May 23 and 30, June 13, August 22 and 29, September 5 and 12, 1724. *Mist's Miscellany*, IV, 198.

13. Lee, I, 440. *Street Robberies, Consider'd* (1728), p. 4. *Mist's Miscellany*, IV, 198. Moore (23), pp. 21–25.

14. Charles Sanford Terry, *The Jacobites and the Union: Being a Narrative of the Movements of 1708, 1715, 1719 by Several Contemporary Hands* (Cambridge, 1922), p. xii. Moore (24). T. C. Nicholson and A. S. Turberville, *Charles Talbot Duke of Shrewsbury* (Cambridge, 1930), pp. 25, 27, 57, 76, 153, 168, 179, 180. Donald A. Stauffer, *The Art of Biography in Eighteenth Century England* (Princeton, 1941), p. 213.

15. *A Treatise Concerning the Use and Abuse of the Marriage Bed* (1727), p. 401. *Reasons why a Party among us* (1711), p. 10. *Tour* (1), II, 254. *The Great Law of Subordination Consider'd* (1724), p. 49.

16. *Review*, I, 186. *Mist's Miscellany*, IV, 43. *An Essay upon Literature* (1726), p. 117.

CHAPTER XXII

1. Sale catalogue of Defoe's library (together with that of Philip Farewell) in the British Museum (pressmark C. 57. c. 47). *Tour* (1), I, 303. *Robinson Crusoe* (Tegg ed.), II, 7.

2. "On Poetry: A Rapsody," in Swift's *Poems*, ed. Harold Williams (Oxford, 1937), II, 645–46. *Atlas Geographus & Commercialis* (1728), pp. 252–53.

3. "A Description of Magadoxa," in Defoe's *A General History of the Pyrates* (1724–28), is based directly on the British Museum manuscript, "A Prospect of ye City of Magadoxa" (P. 2854. Slo. 2992).

4. *Tour* (1), I, 305–6. Evelyn's *Diary*, June 16, 1683, and September 6, 1685. George Bickham, Jr., *Deliciae Britannicae* (London, 1742), as quoted by W. H. St. John Hope, *Windsor Castle: An Architectural History* (London, 1913), p. 338. W. H. Pyne, *The History of the Royal Residences* (London, 1819), I, 177–78. Personal letter from the librarian of Windsor Castle, Sir Owen Morshead (April 28, 1951). *Review*, VIII, 127. *Tour* (1), I, 131.

5. *Ibid.*, I, 41; II, 35; I, 159.

6. *Ibid.*, I, 160–61, 103–4.

7. *Review*, III, 383. *Reasons for a Royal Visitation* (1717), p. 39. *True Collection* (1703), p. 377. *Tour* (1), II, 166; I, 195, 305. *Tour* (2), II, 739. *Tour* (1), II, 87. *The History and Reality of Apparitions* (Tegg ed.), p. 182.

8. *Ibid.*, p. 267. *Tour* (1), II, 52, 63, 67. See also *Tour* (1), II, 52, 73.

9. *Mercator*, No. 150. *Tour* (1), I, 165, 168. *Tour* (2), II, 754, 756. *Review*, [IX], 113. Preface to *The True-Born Englishman*.

10. *Review*, VIII, 570. Godfrey Davies, "Daniel Defoe's *A Tour Thro' the Whole Island of Great Britain*," *Modern Philology*, XLVIII, 33.

11. *The History and Reality of Apparitions* (Tegg ed.), pp. 319–20. *Tour* (1), II,

119–20. *Tour* (2), II, 824. In the latter passage Defoe says only that he put his horse's feet into the sea at John o' Groat's House, Scotland. *Tour* (1), I, 254. *Review*, VII, 136, 152.

12. *Ibid.*, VII, 389. *Commentator*, August 1, 1720. *Tour* (1), I, 228. *Memoirs of a Cavalier* (Tegg ed.), pp. xvii–xviii.

13. *Review*, VII, 527, 530; VIII, 175. *The Use and Abuse of the Marriage Bed* (Hazlitt ed.), p. 92. *Street Robberies, Consider'd* (1728), pp. 52–54. *Tour* (3), III, Part II, 3. *Review*, V, 406–7. *The Compleat English Gentleman* (Bülbring ed.; London, 1890), pp. 38–39.

14. *Mist's Miscellany*, IV, 102, 195–96.

15. G. N. Clark, *The Later Stuarts* (Oxford, 1934), pp. 39–40. René Caillié, *Travels Through Central Africa to Timbuctoo* (London, 1830), I, 2.

CHAPTER XXIII

1. Moore (32). *Robinson Crusoe* (Tegg ed.), I, 231. *Portledge Papers*, ed. R. J. Kerr and I. C. Duncan (London, 1928), p. 110. Sutherland (2). *An Essay upon Projects* (Hazlitt ed.), p. 7. *H.M.C. Portland*, V, 351.

2. Newton (1). Moore (7). E. A. J. Johnson, *Predecessors of Adam Smith: The Growth of British Economic Thought* (New York, 1937). Huntington Library copy of Nehemiah Grew's manuscript, *The Meanes of a most Ample Encrease of The Wealth & Strength of England In a few Years* (1706), p. 52. The pressmark of the Huntington copy is HL 1264 [U4Q4]; that of the British Museum copy is BM Lansdowne 691.

3. Sutherland (1), p. 50. Sutherland (2). Aitken (4), I, xvi (Mr. Aitken's reference to *Athenaeum*, May 5, 1894, is erroneous). *The True-Born Hugonot* (1704), p. 14. *Works* (Tegg ed.), XX, 9. Aitken (5). For the date of Defoe's sentence, see Moore (1), p. 10. *H.M.C. Portland*, IV, 88. See also *Review*, II, 34.

4. *Ibid.*, IV, 319. *H.M.C. Portland*, IV, 88. *Tour* (1), I, 102. Dottin, I, 80.

5. *Review*, II, 34. Franklin, p. 16.

6. Wilson (1), I, 227–28, n. According to Saxe Bannister (*The Writings of William Paterson* [2d ed.; London, 1859], I, xxvii), Paterson contributed several of the basic ideas for Dalby Thomas' *An Historical Account of the rise and growth of the West India Colonies*, and Paterson's claims against the government were perseveringly advocated by Sir Robert Davers until they were at length settled, if not satisfied, in 1715. As both Thomas and Davers were friends of Defoe, Bannister's statement (if correct) may suggest an early acquaintance between Defoe and Paterson. See *A Proposal for a General Fishery* (1694); *Propositions for General Land-Banks* (1695); *A Further Account of the Proposals made by T. Neale and D. Thomas, . . . for exchanging the blank tickets* (1695).

7. *London Gazette*, April 19–23, 1694. Luttrell, III, 521 (September 5, 1695). *HLJ*, XVI, 465. Wright (1), p. 45. *An Appeal to Honour and Justice* (Hazlitt ed.), p. 4. *The Complete English Tradesman* (1726), pp. 343–44.

8. Luttrell, V, 339 (September 16, 1703); V, 369 (December 14, 1703). *A Plan of the English Commerce* (Blackwell ed.), p. 252. *Review*, VII, 154, 212; [IX], 79. *A Brief Account of the Present State of the African Trade* (1713); *Mercator*, No. 134; *A General History of the Pirates* (Hayward ed.), pp. 197, xi, 48, 271, 272, 339. *Second Thoughts are Best* (Tegg ed.), p. 14.

9. *Review*, V, 559–60, 622–24; VII, 148, 153–54, 202–3, 567 (for 607); VIII, 71. *The Advantages of Peace and Commerce* (1729). *Review*, VI, 186; VIII, 730. *Robinson Crusoe* (Tegg ed.), I, 257 ff. *Colonel Jack* (Tegg ed.), 139 ff.; *The Family Instructor* (Tegg ed.), II, 303 ff. *True Collection* (1703), p. 77. Wylie Sypher recognizes him as "the

earliest Eighteenth-century writer of importance against Slavery" (*Guinea's Captive Kings* [Chapel Hill, 1947], p. 159). *Atlas Maritimus & Commercialis* (1728), p. 237.

10. *Review*, I, 394. *The Compleat English Tradesman* (1727), I, 241–42. *A Plan of the English Commerce* (Blackwell ed.), p. 128. *Review*, VII, 226. The act was approved by Queen Anne on March 14, 1704–5 (*HLJ*, XVII, 717). Letter to Halifax, April 5, 1705 (Lee, II, 106–7). *Review*, III, 22–23, 149–50. Undated letters to Halifax (Lee, II, 115, 116–18). The order of the letters should be reversed; see Healey (2), p. 185, n. 1. *H.M.C. Portland*, IV, 350.

11. *Strike while the Iron's Hot* (1715), p. 16. *Mercurius Politicus*, July, 1719, pp. 481–82, 513–18. Lee, II, 149–50, 171–73. *The Chimera* (1720); see also Lee, II, 180–81, 189, 210, 215–17, 224–25, 230, 234, 246–50, 255–56, 296. A letter ostensibly dated Paris, June 18, 1720 (*Mist's Miscellany*, I, 262–67), blames Law's rivals and enemies for the run on the bank. *Commentator*, July 19, 1720. Lee, II, 299–301. *The Case of Mr. Law Truly Stated* (1721). Lee, II, 315–16, 339–40, 445–46. *Mere Nature Delineated* (1726), p. 92. Lee, I, 459; II, 189.

12. *The Evident Advantages to Great Britain and the Allies from the Approaching War* (1727), pp. 37–39. M. Grosley, *A Tour to London*, trans. Thomas Nugent (London, 1772), II, 56. *Bishop Burnet's History of His Own Times* (2d ed.; Oxford, 1883), V, 45.

13. *H.M.C. Portland*, V, 51. *An Essay on the South Sea Trade* (Hazlitt ed.), p. 5. *A True Account of the Design, and Advantages of the South-Sea Trade* (1711), pp. 17–18. *HCJ*, XIV, 203–6 (February 16, 17, 19, 1702–3).

14. *H.M.C. Portland*, V, 58–61, 51. *Mercurius Politicus*, August, 1716, pp. 192–93; September, 1719, p. 552. *The Evident Approach of a War* (1727), pp. 41, 59.

15. *The History of the Principal Discoveries* (1727), p. 275. Appendix to the 1730 ed. of *A Plan of the English Commerce*, p. 30. *The History of the Principal Discoveries* (1727), pp. 287, 298. *Mere Nature Delineated* (1726), pp. 106–7. *The Evident Advantages to Great Britain and its Allies from the Approaching War* (1727), p. 16.

16. Moore (8). Lee, I, 364. Viscount Erleigh, *The South Sea Bubble* (London, 1933), p. 166. *A New Voyage Round the World* (Tegg ed.), p. 355. *Reasons for a War* (1729), pp. 28–29.

17. Trevelyan (2), p. 439. Calamy, II, 182. *Tour* (3), III, Part II, pp. 12–13. *Review*, VI, 362, 175, 187–88. *Tour* (3), III, Part II, p. 10. Lady Townshend (quoted by Rosamond Bayne-Powell, *English Country Life in the Eighteenth Century* [London, 1935], p. 69). *Review*, VI, 195.

18. *Tour* (3), III, Part II, 61–62. The American botanist is Professor Ralph E. Cleland (later Dean of the Graduate School), Indiana University. *A General History of Trade*, August, 1713, pp. 34–35. *Review*, IV, 635. *Tour* (1), I, 8.

19. *Review*, IV, 635; [IX], 114; IV, 82. *H.M.C. Portland*, IV, 358. *Mist's Miscellany*, IV, 254–58. *An Humble Proposal* (Hazlitt ed.), p. 8; see also *A General History of the Pirates* (Hayward ed.), pp. 311–12. *An Humble Proposal* (Hazlitt ed.), p. 7.

20. *Tour* (1), I, 8. *A General History of the Pirates* (Hayward ed.), pp. viii, vii. *Some Considerations on . . . Seamen* (1728), pp. 7–8, 6.

21. *An Essay upon Projects* (Hazlitt ed.), pp. 22–23, 45–48. *A General History of the Pirates* (Hayward ed.), pp. vii–viii. *An Humble Proposal* (Hazlitt ed.), pp. 6–7. For Defoe's kindred interest in army enlistments, see *Review*, II, 11, 46–48; III, 54–55. *An Essay upon Projects* (Hazlitt ed.), pp. 45–48. *Some Considerations on . . . Seamen*, pp. 37–38. In *Augusta Triumphans* (Tegg ed., p. 40), Defoe expressed approval of the bill then pending in Parliament for the encouragement of seamen. *HL MSS*, New Series, VI, 116, 223–26.

22. *Tour* (1), II, 184. *Daily Post*, February 8, 1723. See John Guest, *Historic Notice of Rotherham, Ecclesiastical, Collegiate, and Civil* (Worksop, 1879), pp. 538–39. *HCJ*, XX, 705. Guest, *Historic Notice of Rotherham*, p. 539 n.

23. *Review*, II, 54. *Giving Alms No Charity*, in *True Collection* (1705), II, 449, 430. *Review*, IV, 35.

24. *The Medleys for the Year 1711* (1711), p. 228. Trevelyan (1), III, 35–38. *Review*, VI, 153–54, 157–59. *Tour* (1), I, 200–206. *A Plan of the English Commerce* (Blackwell ed.), pp. 15–21. *Tour* (1), 206.

25. *An Essay upon Projects* (Hazlitt ed.), pp. 10, 21. *N. & Q.*, CXCIII, 342. *Mist's Miscellany*, II, 106. Letter and inclosure (August 31, 1935) to Professor R. H. Griffith of the University of Texas from G. C. Hart of the Sun Insurance Office Limited, 63 Threadneedle Street, London, E.C. 2.

CHAPTER XXIV

1. *A Brief Deduction of the Original, Progress, and Immense Greatness of the British Woollen Manufacture* (1727), pp. 8–10. *Review*, V, 574; [IX], 176. *A Plan of the English Commerce* (Blackwell ed.), pp. 36, 94, 114.

2. Joseph Browne, *A Dialogue between Church and No Church; or a Rehearsal of the Review* (London, 1706); cited in Wilson (I), II, 437–38.

3. For much of this chapter see Moore (21). *Review*, VII, 598, 578. Charles Davenant, *Discourses on the Publick Revenues, and on the Trade of England* (London, 1698), Part I, pp. 227, 266.

4. *Review*, [IX], 342.

5. Charles Davenant, *An Essay upon the Probable Methods of Making People Gainers in he Balance of Trade* (London, 1697), p. 17. *Review*, [IX], 210. *The British Merchant* (London, 1721), I, x.

6. *Review*, [IX], 15–16. *Tour* (2), I, 156. *Faction in Power* (1717), p. 25. *The Evident Approach of a War* (1727), p. 32. *The History of the Principal Discoveries* (1727), p. 99. *Mercator*, No. 27.

7. *Review*, I, 337–38, 342–43, 345–46; IV, 216, 218; VII, 577–82, 590–91, 598–601, 566–75 (for 605–14); VIII, 37–38; [IX], 210. "Of Affairs in Both Kingdoms Introductory to A Treaty of Union," *The History of the Union of Great Britain* (Edinburgh, 1709), p. 58. *H.M.C. Portland*, V, 349. *Mercator*, No. 110.

8. Basil Williams, *Stanhope* (Oxford, 1932), p. 193. *Memoirs of Some Transactions during the Late Ministry of Robert E. of Oxford* (1717), pp. 89–90. *Impeachment, or No Impeachment* (1714), pp. 7–8. *A General History of Trade*, August, 1713, pp. 47–46 (for 46–47).

9. *Mercator*, No. 1. *Review*, IV, 218. *A Fifth Essay at Removing National Prejudices* (1707), p. 1. *The Trade of Scotland with France* (Edinburgh, 1713).

10. *Mercator*, Nos. 113 and 121. *Review*, II, 89; VIII, 217. *An Humble Proposal* (1729), pp. 31–36, 40–41.

11. *The Trade to India Critically and Calmly consider'd* (1720), pp. 9, 44–45. *Political State of Great-Britain*, XXXIX, 217, 253–58. *The Free-Holder's Plea against Stock-Jobbing Elections of Parliament Men* (1701). *A Fifth Essay at Removing National Prejudices* (Edinburgh, 1707), pp. 33–34. *Review*, IV, 51, 59. *Reflections on the Prohibition Act* (1708), p. 3. *A Brief State of the Question* (1719), p. 46. *An Humble Proposal* (Hazlitt ed.), p. 14. *A New Voyage Round the World* (Aitken ed.), pp. 155–56.

12. *London Gazette*, October 28–November 1, 1686.

13. *Mercurius Politicus*, December, 1717, p. 905. *The Interests of the several Princes and States of Europe* (1698), pp. 23, 24. *The Succession of Spain Consider'd* (1711), pp. 10–11.

14. *Review*, III, 5–8. *A General History of Trade*, June, 1713, p. 32; July, 1713, p. 32. *Mercator*, No. 5. Lee, I, 214.

15. *Review*, III, 646; II, 85–86; I, 402; IV, 536; I, 365–67; [IX], 78. *The Complete English Tradesman* (1726), p. 387.

16. *Ibid.*, pp. 400–401. *Review*, I, 401–2. *A Plan of the English Commerce* (Blackwell ed.), pp. 264–67. *Review*, VII, 182–83. *Fair Payment no Spunge* (1717).

17. *Review*, III, 33, 26–27, 25. *The Complete English Tradesman* (1726), pp. 429–31. *A Plan of the English Commerce* (Blackwell ed.), pp. 192–93, 199–200. *Review*, II, 26–27, 89–90. *A Plan of the English Commerce*, pp. 113–14, 130. *An Humble Proposal* (Hazlitt ed.), p. 5. *A Plan of the English Commerce*, p. 27. *Review*, II, 66; III, 70–71.

18. *Ibid.*, VII, 63–64, 65–67, 131–32, 135–36. *Second Thoughts are best* (1729), p. 21. *Review*, I, 349; II, 54. Lee, II, 59–61; III, 154–57, 157–59. *Charity Still a Christian Virtue* (1719), p. 72.

19. *Review*, IV, 34–35, 47–48; I, 347; II, 29–30, 37–38, 53–54. *A Plan of the English Commerce* (Blackwell ed.), p. 45.

20. *The Complete English Tradesman* (1726), pp. 386–87. *Review*, II, 81–82, 57–59. *A Plan of the English Commerce* (Blackwell ed.), pp. 44, 31–32. *Review*, II, 89–90, 61–62. *A Plan of the English Commerce*, p. 28.

21. *Review*, II, 81. *Tour* (2), II, 531–32. *Review*, III, 6. *Tour* (2), I, 59. Lee, III, 227, 281.

22. Charles Davenant, *Discourses on the Publick Revenues, and on the Trade of England.* (London, 1698), Part II, p. 74. *A Plan of the English Commerce* (Blackwell ed.), p. 147. *Augusta Triumphans* (Tegg ed.), p. 31.

23. "Thomas Parker, first Earl of Macclesfield," *DNB*. *A Narrative of all the Robberies, Escapes, &c. of John Sheppard* (Aitken ed.), p. 222. *An Epistle from Jack Sheppard to the Late L——d C——ll——r of E——d, who when Sheppard was try'd, sent for him to the Chancery Bar* (London, 1725).

24. *The Complete English Tradesman* (1726), p. 380.

CHAPTER XXV

The statements in this chapter are based on so many scattered fragments of evidence that detailed page references would be prohibitively numerous. I have sought to reconsider every known source of information on Defoe's family and private life, but the following documents or books have been most useful:

The wills of James Foe, Samuel Tuffley, and Mary Defoe (Principal Probate Registry, Somerset House, London).

Benjamin Defoe's letter to Sir Hans Sloane (British Museum Sloane 4053).

Benjamin Defoe's letters to the Duke of Newcastle (B.M. Add. MSS, 32691, ff. 390–91, 409; 32692, ff. 454–55, 480–81).

Sir Hans Sloane's signed copy of the sale catalogue of Defoe's library (*Librorum ex Bibliothecis Philippi Farewell, D.D., et Danielis De Foe, Gen., Catalogus*, British Museum, C. 57, c. 47).

The reports of Charles Delafaye (or De la Faye) on the examination of Mist and on Defoe's recognizance on June 13, 1720 (P.R.O., S.P. 44–79A, pp. 336 and 339).

Henry Baker's manuscript narrative of his courtship (Forster Collection, Victoria and Albert Museum, London).

George Reuben Potter, "Henry Baker, F.R.S. (1698–1774)," *Modern Philology*, XXIX (1932), 308–17.

H.M.C. Portland, Vols. IV and V.

The Diary of Dudley Ryder 1715–1716 (transcribed and edited by William Matthews, London, 1939). I am further indebted to Professor Matthews for a letter (April 1, 1952) explaining his important footnote (p. 39) regarding Benjamin Defoe's entry at the Inner Temple.

Charles Bechtold Realey, *The London Journal and Its Authors* (Lawrence, Kan., 1935).
John Forster, *Daniel De Foe and Charles Churchill* (London, 1855).
Daniel Defoe, *Mere Nature Delineated* (1726), pp. 39–40, 46–53.
Aitken (2).
Secord (1).
N. & Q., Ser. 2, VIII (July 30, 1859), 94; Ser. 5, IV (September 18, 1875), 238; Ser. 7, III (June 4, 1887), 450, and VI (August 11, 1888), 105; CLXCIII (August 7, 1948), 342.
Healey (3).
Lee, I, esp., pp. 362–64.
Sutherland (1) and (3).
Wilson (1), esp. III, 641–50.
Wright (1), esp. pp. 17, 47, 408–11; (2), esp. pp. 397–401.

CHAPTER XXVI

1. Wilson (1), III, 609–10, n. Q. Secord (1), p. 219 and n. 33. *H.M.C. Portland*, IV, 387–88. Healey (3), p. 305.

2. *A Brief Account of the Interesting Ceremony of Unveiling the Monument Erected by the Boys and Girls of England in Memory of Daniel Defoe* (Southampton, 1871), p. 6 (quoting the *Daily News*, September 17, 1870). Aside from a few crude caricatures and one pirated copy of an original, there are only two contemporary portraits, engraved by Van der Gucht for the *True Collection* of 1703 and for *Jure Divino* (1706). The *Jure Divino* portrait is by far the better, with its depth of forehead, width between the eyes, aquiline nose, and firm mouth—the face of an able and alert man who was also a gentleman. But the most vivid description of Defoe was furnished by Nottingham's informant, who told of his brown complexion, dark brown hair (covered by a wig), hooked nose, sharp chin, gray eyes, and a large mole (which the portraits show at the left of his mouth).

3. Strype, II, Book 3, 92. Healey (3), pp. 128, 198, 300, and 405; the letter to Bowrey on p. 254 should be dated on a Monday (March 14, 1709). *Augusta Triumphans* (Tegg ed.), p 30.

4. *Preface to A Fifth Essay at Removing National Prejudices* (Edinburgh, 1707). *Review*, VIII, 740. *A Short View of the Present State of the Protestant Religion in Britain* (Edinburgh, 1707), p. 45. *True Collection* (1705), II, 31. *Collection* (1703), p. 223. *The Englishman's Choice, and True Interest* (1694), p. 21. *An Apology for the Army* (1715), p. 11. *Review*, VII, 451, 454; VIII, 67–68. *Mercator*, No. 101. *Review*, VIII, 68; IV, 78. *The Life of Colonel Jacque* (Aitken ed.), II, 36. *Review*, II, 214.

5. Secord (1), p. 21, n. 33. Wilson (1), III, 610 and n. Q. *Read's Weekly Journal, or British Gazeteer*, Saturday, May 1, 1731 (*N. & Q.*, CLX, 308).

6. *Political State of Great-Britain*, XLI, 429. *N. & Q.*, Ser. 3, IX, 142 n. Sir Harold Nicolson, "The Practice of Biography" (quoted from the *Cornhill Magazine* in *Times Literary Supplement*, August 7, 1953, p. 507).

INDEX

[This is a selective index which lists only names, places, and themes of special significance for Defoe's life and thought.]

Abruzzo, 278
Act of Indemnity, 1
Act of Security, 181
Act of Uniformity, 14, 345
Adam, Rev.William, 193
Addison, Joseph, 49, 68, 197, 233, 274, 342
Adriatic, 275
Africa: Captain Singleton, 251–52, 276; employment by African Company, 309; Governor Dalby Thomas, 142, 244, 289, 311; investment in, 86, 289; pirates, 264–69; trade, 289–90, 308–9; mentioned, 163, 228
"Age's Humble Servant, The," 151, 228
Aitken, G. A., 385
Aix-la-Chapelle, 278
Alberoni, Cardinal, 317
Algerian, Algerine, 86, 265, 267, 346
Allen, Henry, 114–15
Alps, 278–79
Alsatia-men, 102
America, 248, 265, 270, 318
American Revolution, 318
Amsterdam, 278
Anabaptists; see Baptists
Anglesey, Arthur Annesley, fifth Earl of, 108, 146, 206–7, 353
Anglesey, Countess of, 17
Anglesey, first Earl of, 17
Anglicans, 38, 45, 62, 154
Anjou, Duke of (later Philip IV of Spain), 75, 203, 226
Anne, Queen: accession, 56–58, 73, 348; death, 176, 192, 206, 208, 209, 353; Defoe serves her, 145–48, 156, 180, 189–92, 199, 216, 236, 257, 337, 351; Defoe trusts her mercy, 129; favors High Church party, 107–8; gives financial relief, 145, 350; petition to, 4; postpones sentence to pillory, 135–38, 140; reign, 3, 47, 78, 117–19, 127, 181, 214, 255; mentioned, 69, 70, 142, 143, 267, 295, 300, 301, 303, 348
Annesley, Arthur; see Anglesey, Arthur Annesley, fifth Earl of

Annesley, Dr. Samuel, 13, 16, 19, 28, 32, 231, 345
Apoplexy, 215, 257
Applebee, John, 212, 269
Arbuthnot, Dr. John, 8, 287
Archangel, 226
Architecture, 26
Argentine, 280, 295, 296, 299, 317
Argyll, Duke of, 59, 183–84, 191
Ariel, 225
Armstrong, Mr., 126
Army, 21, 265; see also English soldiers
Art, 26
Asiento, 298
Aske, Esq., 334
Assembly, Scottish; see General Assembly
Athenian Gazette, the, 247
Athenian Mercury, 155, 231–32
Athenian Oracle, the, 232
Athenian Society, The, 231–32
Atholl, Duke of, 183–84
Atkins, John, 276
Atkins, Will, 227
Atterbury, Francis (Bishop of Rochester), 207, 248, 320
Attorney-general, 118, 131
Auditor's office, 155
Augustus, King, 197
Austria, 75
Austrian Succession, War of the, 261
Avery, Captain, 252, 265–66, 269
Avignon, 272
Aylesbury, 346, 352
Ayr, 278

B——ge, 268
Bach, Johann Sebastian, 25–26, 273
Bacon, Sir Francis, 281, 344
Baden-Powell, Lord, 211
Bahama Islands, 224
Bail, 11, 128, 335, 349, 353
Baker, Mrs. (Baker's Coffee-House), 87
Baker, David Erskine (grandson), 330
Baker, Henry (grandson), 330–31

INDEX

INDEX

INDEX

INDEX

Gibraltar, 296
Gibson, Bishop Edmund, 29 (The passage attributed to Gibson was actually written by John Evelyn.)
Gifford, A., 154
Gildon, Charles, 30, 71, 232
Girdler, Lew, 362
Glasgow, 159
Glass duty, 74, 280, 288, 308, 347
Glass-houses, 248
Glencoe, 68, 79, 177
Gloucester, Duke of, 58
Gloucester Cathedral, 36
Godolphin, Earl of: accepts Defoe's support, 118, 176, 189–91, 350, 351; allied with Harley, 142–43, 349–51; confers with Defoe in Partition of Spain, 139; Defoe corresponds with, 157, 161, 179, 185, 187, 202, 372; delays Defoe's nomination for office, 188–89; dismissed by Queen Anne, 191, 352; Halifax mentions Defoe to him, 291; hears Defoe's plan for refugees, 303–4, 351; Occasional Conformity Bill, 109, 111–12; promotes Union, 181; prosecution of Defoe, 126–31, 349; recommends Defoe to Leven, 189; urges Nottingham to discover author of *The Shortest Way*, 113; mentioned, 69, 132, 133, 200
Golconda, 87
"Goldsmith, Alexander," 157
Gordon, Duke of, 178–80, 234, 337, 347
Gordon, Thomas, 206, 332–33
Goring, George, Baron, 9
Gout, 270, 339
Government: censorship of newspapers, 201, 207–13; control of Scottish elections, 199; Defoe serves, 155–57, 162, 174, 176, 180, 182–87, 191–92, 206–15, 218, 256–58, 271, 332, 350, 354; fear of Jacobite riots, 171; Harley becomes member of, 147–48; ignorance of conditions in Scotland, 177; indifferent about occasional conformity, 109, 111; interference from clergy, 193–94; needs pamphleteers, 206; promises mercy, 129, 130–31, 134, 140; proposes pardon of Madagascar pirates, 266–67; prosecutes Defoe, 107, 120–24, 128–31, 286; refuses Defoe's services, 131; Whig attack on, 312
Gown-house, 87
Grand Alliance, 295
Grandidiers, 266, 379
Gravesend, 86
Great Mogul, 163, 281
Greece, 48, 203, 343
Greek, 30, 35, 40, 43
Green, Captain Thomas, 181

Greenaway, Henry, 120
Greenland, 223
Greenwich, 21, 48
Greenwich Hospital, 286
Greg, William, 128, 183–84, 267
Grew, Nehemiah, 381
Grey, Lord, 53
Griffith, R. H., 383
Grisons, 279
Grounds and Occasions of the Contempt of the Clergy, The, 36
Groyne, the, 252
Guadaloupe (Guardaloupa), 165
Guiana, 224
Guildhall, 58, 70–71, 120, 347
Guinea, 224, 252, 276, 289, 297
Guiscard, Antoine de. 191, 352
Gulliver, Lemuel, 85, 226
Gulliver's Travels, 222, 226
Gustavus Adolphus, 59, 60, 66, 73, 80, 144, 195, 258, 260–61
Gypsies, 251

Hackney, 47, 49, 326, 331, 334, 351
Hackney coaches, 79
Hairy tribesmen, 163
Halifax (city), 47
Halifax, Charles Montagu, Earl of: association with Defoe, 74, 337; attacked by Tory House of Commons, 106, 110, 112, 117, 119, 130–31; correspondence with Defoe, 202, 382; glorified in *Jure Divino*, 291; message sent through Davis, 11; poet and patron, 230; mentioned, 369
Halifax, Marquis of, 71–72, 203–4
Halley, Edmund, 35
Hamburgh, 278
Hamilton, Duke of, 185, 234
Hampden, Richard, 67
Hampshire, 304
Hampton Court, 47, 81, 291–92
Hannibal, 60
Hanover, Hanoverians, 4, 57–58, 73, 210, 258, 293, 312, 332, 352; *see also* Succession
Hanover Spy, The, 232
Hapsburgs, 75
Harcourt, Sir Simon, 129–31
Harley, Edward, 111
Harley, Sir Edward, 52
Harley, Robert (later Earl of Oxford): accepts Defoe's services, 117; acquaintance with Penn, 133; appeal from Defoe through Paterson, 123–24; awaits trial, 21, 69, 206, 353–54; Carstares and Harley, 176, 193; chosen Speaker, 108; corresponds with Defoe, 50, 76–77, 79, 95, 127–28, 173–74, 248, 286, 334; corresponds

INDEX

INDEX

INDEX